Wandering Peoples

A book in the series
Latin America Otherwise: Languages, Empires, Nations

Series editors:
Walter D. Mignolo, Duke University
Irene Silverblatt, Duke University
Sonia Saldívar-Hull, University of Southern California

Wandering Peoples

Colonialism, Ethnic Spaces, and
Ecological Frontiers in Northwestern Mexico, 1700–1850

Cynthia Radding

Duke University Press   Durham and London   1997

© 1997 Duke University Press

All rights reserved

Printed in the United States of America on acid-free paper ∞

Typeset in Joanna by Tseng Information Systems, Inc.

Library of Congress Cataloging-in-Publication Data appear on the

last printed page of this book.

To Benjamin Irving Radding and Dorothy Lowman Radding

Contents

About the Series

Latin America Otherwise: Languages, Empires, Nations is a critical series. It aims to explore the emergence and consequences of concepts used to define "Latin America" while at the same time exploring the broad interplay of political, economic, and cultural practices that have shaped Latin American worlds. Latin America, at the crossroads of competing imperial designs and local responses, has been construed as a geocultural and geopolitical entity since the nineteenth century. This series provides a starting point to redefine Latin America as a configuration of political, linguistic, cultural, and economic intersections that demands a continuous reappraisal of the role of the Americas in history, and of the ongoing process of globalization and the relocation of people and cultures that have characterized Latin America's experience. *Latin America Otherwise: Languages, Empires, Nations* is a forum that confronts established geocultural constructions, that rethinks area studies and disciplinary boundaries, that assesses convictions of the academy and of public policy, and that, correspondingly, demands that the practices through which we produce knowledge and understanding about and from Latin America be subject to rigorous and critical scrutiny.

Wandering Peoples: Colonialism, Ethnic Spaces, and Ecological Frontiers in Northwestern Mexico, 1700–1850 is an anthropological history of cultural resiliency, colonial relations, and trespassed frontiers. The study takes place in the borderlands of the Spanish Empire in North America during the region's long political transition from a Spanish colony to an independent Republican state. Geographical and political frontiers created spaces of pliant social identities, where boundaries of ethnicity and class intertwined. In this volume, Cynthia Radding offers a new perspective both of the "frontier" and of the "world system" paradigm by rethinking the dichotomy of center and periphery. She views the frontier not as a wall, but as a permeable border where transformations occurred in both the indigenous and Hispanic cultural worlds. Moreover, she suggests that the center and the periphery coexist at the local level, while at the global level the center becomes a distant periphery.

This volume charts processes of emerging borders—those of indige-nous communities and of social class—against the backdrop of human migrations and changing ways of life. Framing this regional history through the lens of social relations governing access to ecological re-sources, Radding demonstrates the cultural intricacies of resistant ac-commodation to dominant political power. Her theoretical approach straddles disciplinary boundaries of anthropology, history, geography, and ecology to bring Sonora's wandering peoples into view.

Walter D. Mignolo
Duke University

Irene Silverblatt
Duke University

Sonia Saldívar-Hull
University of Southern California

List of Illustrations

Figures

Tables

Plates follow page 168

Preface

Wandering Peoples recounts the persistence of indigenous peasant nations in Sonora during the transition from the Spanish Imperium to the Mexican Republic. The principal stories it weaves concern the defense of native polities, ethnic and cultural mixtures, and the material and symbolic foundations of community life. It engages in both narrative and historical analysis and represents a dialogue among different subjects and points of view. This work explores the multilayered meanings of culture, community, and ecology, even as it brings to light the parallel production of colonial and subaltern texts in the course of more than a century of struggles for power and survival.

On one important level *Wandering Peoples* represents a qualitative shift in the historiography of northwestern New Spain. Responding to the call for "a new mission history," it transcends the institutional perspective of the colonial mission associated with Herbert Eugene Bolton and his figure of "the rim of Christendom" and undertakes an ethnohistorical approach centered on the native peoples of Sonora.[1] It views the mission not merely as an instrument of Iberian expansion but as a site of cultural and political confrontation. This alternative vision of the colonial mission underscores the biological consequences of Spanish policies of forced *congregación*, the economic linkages between mission communities and Spanish mercantilist policies, and the cultural and ecological displacements set in motion by the practices of discipline and surveillance established by the religious orders. My purpose is not to demean either the mission or the missionaries; rather, it is to focus centrally on the native subjects of this history, who built and maintained their communities under the duress of Spanish colonialism and articulated an alternative vision of polity to the expansionist project of the early nineteenth-century Mexican nation-state.

By historical convention and geographic location *Wandering Peoples* corresponds to the "borderlands" of territories and populations suspended between Spanish and British America, destined to be divided by the binational border between Mexico and the United States.[2] I contend that this region, commonly seen as marginal to the political cores of both empires, was and is important precisely because of its frontier character. Northwestern Mexico and (what would become) the U.S. Southwest comprised a zone of confluence in which political and imperial boundaries intersected with different ecological and cultural spaces. The physical dimensions of this frontier were not fixed but were historically changing, in both the mental and material worlds.

The interpretive framework I have chosen follows the well-established path of "history from below" first charted for Mesoamerica by Miguel León Portilla, Charles Gibson, James Lockhart, William B. Taylor, and Nancy Farriss; for northwestern Mexico by Edward H. Spicer, Sergio Ortega Noriega, Ignacio del Río, William Merrill, and Susan Deeds; and for the Andean world by Alberto Flores Galindo, Nathan Wachtel, Steve J. Stern, Karen Spalding, Brooke Larson, and Ann Wightman. Without losing sight of the historicity of its subject, my work seeks meaningful comparisons and addresses the wider issues of colonialism, ethnic identities, and ecological and cultural borders that are germaine to Latin America and to the growing field of subaltern and "postcolonial" studies.

Innovative methodological approaches to history, to the social sciences, and to literary criticism—developed from the philosophical currents of postmodernism, poststructuralism, postcolonialism, and subaltern studies—have opened a salutary flow of cross-disciplinary exchanges and have challenged scholars to consider troubling questions concerning the assumed tenets of their academic craft.[3] These labels are not synonymous, nor do they necessarily represent discrete fields of study, nevertheless they exhibit reciprocal influences in their search for new perspectives and in their critical drive to problematize familiar categories and concepts.[4] Emerging from such diverse and, at times, contradictory lines of inquiry, three points of consensus bear on this study: (1) the eschewal of unitary paradigms and linear views of history in favor of heterogeneous theoretical approaches; (2) the dethronement of the "sovereign subject," to be recast in a reflexively constructed dialogue among different historical subjects and cultural traditions; and (3) the power and opacity of language. The rigorous critique of received paradigms and the search for new sources of meaning arise from the moral imperative to reunite the political and intellectual content of scholarly research and to link the author's contemporary world with the historical past.[5] Of the many paths one could follow, I shall comment briefly on four themes that are integral to my work: colonialism, subaltern identities and discourses, symbolic meanings embedded in language, and social ecology.

Colonialism, as relevant to eighteenth-century Sonora, implies political domination by the Spanish Crown over its American territories and peoples, economic exploitation and the transfer of wealth from the colonies to the metropole, cultural dislocation, and diverse responses from colonized indigenous nations and enslaved workers. The concept is not simple, however, nor does it elicit the same meanings in different geographic regions and time periods. Latin American colonialism does not reflect a binary distinction between dominant and subordinate strata, or between colonizer and colonized, owing to the multiracial hybridity of American societies and the complex networks of exploitation, complicity, negotiation, and resistance that developed over three centuries of Iberian rule.[6]

The concept of subaltern has historical and semiotic roots in Gramscian philosophy and political praxis. It refers to subordination according to class, caste, gender, race, or culture and points to the centrality of dominant/dominated relationships.[7] Subaltern peoples may well be directly colonized by a foreign power, or they may encompass those classes and strata which are deprived of wealth and power within a hierarchical society. Following the Gramscian tradition, subaltern status is closely linked to hegemony, understood as a discourse of domination and learned patterns of negotiation. I employ both of these concepts in order to interpret different episodes of conflict, confrontation, and realignment of political forces in Sonora, relating them to the creation of new cultural identities and ethnic spaces.

That language is polysemic, evincing different meanings according to the speakers, translators, and writers of texts and historical documents, is central to the methodological search for a plurality of subjects and authors.[8] Sensitivity to language alerts the scholar to the voice of the subaltern, often muted and distorted in official colonial discourses, and brings out into the open the creative tension of alterity. In writing Wandering Peoples, based largely on standard archival sources, I have had to question what meanings are conveyed by ethnic labels. Who are the subjects behind the documents produced by their colonial interlocutors? When referring to "the Opata villagers," for example, have I merely created an ethnic abstraction? In the changing historical glimpses of the Tegüima, Eudeve, and O'odham nations, viewed through colonial lenses, these Sonoran peoples emerge as subjects who rebuild a fragmented world and articulate a distinctive ethic of territory and community — an oppositional discourse that both mirrors and challenges the colonial project.

Ecology, the dynamic interplay of human and natural environments, informs one of the central arguments of this book. In the Introduction, I define social ecology, a concept that is vitally important to the configuration of ethnic territories and to the interpretation of economic and political conflicts over the land and over the resources for communal survival. Ecological frontiers, underscored by this book's subtitle, refer to the changing landscapes produced by human occupation and to the values that different sets of social actors ascribe to the land. My work draws inspiration from the wells of ecological history and ethnohistory and, to the best of my efforts, contributes to those interdisciplinary fields.[9]

Wandering Peoples has grown out of my own experience in Sonora, where I worked and lived for nearly two decades. My engagement with the peoples and the places described in the book is both professional and deeply personal. During my tenure at the Regional Center of the Instituto Nacional de Antropología e Historia in Hermosillo, I was fortunate to have ample opportunity for archival research and fieldwork. It was in Sonora that I learned to appreciate the fruitful exchange between anthropology and history and to incorporate this academic hybridization into my own work. As a foreigner who adapted to, and was adopted into, Mexican society, I have known both the blessings and the pain of living "in-between" two worlds, of experiencing cultural mestizaje in my own development and in that of my children.

It is my pleasure to acknowledge the assistance I have received from friends, colleagues, and institutions to whom I am indebted far more than words can express. I received financial support from the Instituto Nacional de Antropología e Historia (INAH), the University of Missouri–

St. Louis, and the University of Illinois, Urbana-Champaign, the American Philosophical Society, the American Council of Learned Societies, and the National Endowment for the Humanities, which supported postdoctoral research and time for writing and editing the manuscript. In addition, the staff at Bancroft Library, Newberry Library, Yale Sterling Library, University of Arizona Special Collections, the Archivo General de la Nación and the Biblioteca Nacional (Mexico City), the Biblioteca Pública de Jalisco and Archivo de Instrumentos Públicos (Guadalajara), and the Archivo Histórico del Estado de Sonora, the Archivo de Notarías, and the Archivo de la Mitra (Hermosillo) all greatly facilitated my work.

The friends, colleagues, and family members who have helped me along the way are too numerous to name. I thank especially my co-workers at INAH Centro Sonora: Juan José Gracida, Julio Montané Martí, Elisa Villalpando, Alejandro Figueroa, José Luis Moctezuma, and Manuel Zúñiga. Long and fruitful discussions with Sergio Ortega Noriega, Ignacio del Río, and José Luis Mirafuentes enriched the conceptual framework of my study. I have received advice and encouragement from John Kessell, Bernard Fontana, Thomas Sheridan, Mark Burkholder, James Neal Primm, Kieran McCarty, Charles Polzer, Charles Cutter, José Cuello, Nils Jacobsen, Donna Guy, Robert McCaa and Elizabeth Kuznesof. Susan Deeds, Nicolas Bleser, Roberta Stabel, and Susan Clark Spater have shared with me on numerous occasions their generous hospitality and insights on the past and present of the Sonoran Desert and its peoples. Eric Van Young, friend and mentor, Ann Wightman, Joseph Love, and the anonymous readers for Duke University Press gave me important suggestions for refining the conceptual framework and interpreting the empirical data. I am deeply grateful to Valerie Millholland, whose professional and caring guidance has seen this project to fruition, and to Walter Mignolo and Irene Silverblatt, series editors for Latin American Otherwise, whose cogent observations have improved the manuscript and expanded my own thinking about culture and history. I thank David Pinkard, who assisted me on numerous occasions with computer-related problems; Craig Barton, who took the photographs; Nicanor Domínguez, Pablo Abril, and Jane Domier who drew the maps; and Ariel Yablón who helped prepare the index and glossary.

My extended families in Mexico and the United States have supported my work and enriched my life in innumerable ways: Xicoténcatl Murrieta, Marcelina Saldívar de Murrieta, Joaquín Murrieta, who helped me with the tables and graphs, and Rosa Ofelia Murrieta, who opened her home to me in Mexico City; my sons, Daniel and David Murrieta, who grew with this project and helped bring it to fruition; my parents, Benjamin and Dorothy Radding, who have provided loving support over the years. *A todos, gracias.*

Abbreviations

ACQ AM	Archivo del Colegio de la Santa Cruz de Querétaro (Sonora: Asuntos de Misiones)
AGI	Archivo General de Indias (Seville)
AGN	Archivo General de la Nación (Mexico City)
	AHH Archivo Histórico de Hacienda
	PI Ramo de Provincias Internas
AHGES	Archivo Histórico del Gobierno del Estado de Sonora (Hermosillo)
	TP Títulos Primordiales
AHP	Archivo de Hidalgo de Parral
AIPJ	Archivo de Instrumentos Publicos de Jalisco, Guadalajara
	RTA Ramo de Tierras y Aguas
	LGA Libros de Gobierno de la Audiencia
AMH	Archivo de la Mitra (Hermosillo)
	AD Archivo Diocesano
	AS Archivo de la Parroquia del Sagrario
A NO	Archivo General de Notarías (Hermosillo)
BL	Bancroft Library, University of California–Berkeley
	HHB Hubert Howe Bancroft Collection
BNFF	Biblioteca Nacional Fondo Franciscano (Mexico City)
BPEJ	Biblioteca Pública del Estado de Jalisco, Guadalajara
	ARAG Archivo de la Real Audiencia de Guadalajara
	RC Ramo Civil
DRSW	Documentary Relations of the Southwest (University of Arizona–Tucson)
	UA University of Arizona Microfilm
INAH	Instituto Nacional de Antropología e Historia (Mexico)
UASP	University of Arizona Special Collections (Tucson)
YSMA	Yale Sterling Manuscripts and Archives
	LAMC Latin American Manuscript Collection

Introduction: The Social Ecology of the Sonoran Frontier

We shall see how the history of nature is at the same time social history.

Juan Martínez-Alier, 1991 [1]

Wandering Peoples charts a secular process of both change and continuity in the ecological, cultural, and political relations through which the highland peoples of northwestern Mexico defined their world. It examines the persistence of ethnic polity and peasant economy during the eighteenth and early nineteenth centuries, in order to produce a regional history that addresses some of the core issues of Latin American historiography. [2] As such, this book concerns ethnic divisions and the emergence of social classes, the reconstitution of indigenous communities, and the complexities of cultural adaptation and resistance. The main argument concerns social stratification along ethnic, class, and gender lines during this period of transition between the Bourbon colonial administration and the formative years of the Mexican Republic. While focusing on one province of northern New Spain, this study looks for the linkages which help to explain both the incorporation of this region into the European world economy and the ways in which the responses of indigenous peoples modified Spain's imperial project.

The thematic sequence of *Wandering Peoples* follows multiple strands of conflict in the struggle for control over basic resources in the region, a struggle that points to the ambiguity of the state in a marginal area of the Spanish Empire. Here, metropolitan institutions developed slowly and haltingly, conditioned by local variants in the ecological and cultural bases of colonial society. [3] Research focused on the frontiers of empire alerts us to the historically changing quality of commonly used categories like *peasant* and *Indian*, and helps us to identify different social contenders for power.

The Sonoran Desert and its surrounding upland forests comprised a number of different frontiers in northern New Spain. The provinces of

Sinaloa, Ostimuri, and Sonora constituted an area of geographic, demographic, cultural, and political frontiers marked by fluid and changing
boundaries.[4] The ecological bonds between the physical environment
and the peoples who inhabited it transformed the landscape over time
through changing, destructive, and regenerative processes in nature and
human society. Migrations, conquest, and Spanish mercantilism created
distinct zones of production which, in turn, established changing and
often conflictive borders through countervailing forces of population
dispersal and concentration. The historical quality of these regional formations, derived mainly from the movements of people, created a "Far
North," a distinct territory which nevertheless maintained economic
ties to the central highlands of colonial Mexico.

Sonora was indeed peripheral to the center of viceregal power in
New Spain, and the manner of its inclusion in the empire differed from
that of the "Near North" of New Spain's mining frontiers in Zacatecas,
Durango, Guanajuato, and the Bajío. Following the discovery of rich silver lodes in Zacatecas, the destructive Mixtón and Chichimec wars of
the sixteenth century decimated the native population in the vast territory bounded by Guadalajara, Querétaro, San Luis Potosí, and Zacatecas.
When Spaniards settled the mining provinces and established grain and
cattle haciendas in the Bajío, they brought Indian migrant laborers to
the region as mineworkers and dependent *laboríos*, tenants, and peons.
Tarascan and Otomí warriors, in particular, were subordinate allies of
the Spaniards in their conquest of the nomads, who retreated into the
Sierra Gorda. They settled on colonial estates or in the outskirts of Spanish towns, such as San Miguel, San Felipe, Celaya, and León, and they
formed the bulk of the population at the mission of San Luis de la
Paz. These soldier-farmer-laborers secured the Chichimec frontier for
the Spaniards; however, they did not constitute an autochthonous peasantry, but rather an immigrant work force brought to the area through
conquest.[5]

By way of contrast, the Sinaloan and Sonoran provinces were brought
effectively into the orbit of the Spanish Empire through institutions
of conquest directed to native peasant communities. The *serrano*, or upland, peoples of the western foothills of the Sierra Madre Occidental were a sedentary, farming population that had settled the area for
several millennia before the arrival of the European conquerors. Orga-

nized in rival chieftaincies, native Sonorans had fought among themselves for territory, scarce agricultural resources, and control of trade routes. The relative aridity of their environment meant that foraging as well as horticulture were essential to their survival and, for this reason, cyclical migratory patterns within the region marked their way of life. Nevertheless, Sonoran villagers were settled peoples, whose cultures distinguished them from the bands of nomadic hunters, gatherers, and traders of the North American Great Plains and the central cordilleras of the northern Mexican plateau.[6] *Serrano* peoples traded and fought with the nomads, but their culture and languages placed them in the northern frontier of Mesoamerica. Highland villagers cultivated maize, built homes of adobe and stone, and participated in long-distance trade networks which linked them to Casas Grandes (Chihuahua) and to the Pueblos of New Mexico.[7] If Sonora remained on the periphery of New Spain, and the *serrano* peasants tested the limits of alien dominion, they did so within the confines of the empire, not beyond its borders.

Social ecology is used in this study to explain the nature of the northern frontier and to describe the cultural parameters of Sonoran ethnohistory. *Social ecology* signifies a living and changing complex of relations that developed historically among diverse human populations and with the land they occupied. It refers both to the social structures through which different ethnic communities re-created their cultures and to the political implications of resource allocation in the region. Ecological relations underlay the essential linkages that brought together human and material resources, linkages through which ethnic communities ascribed cultural values to their claims to land and labor. Native horticultural and foraging practices secured access to a wide variety of resources, largely through the complementarity of desert and riverine environments in Sonora.

Under colonial domination, *serrano* peoples fought to maintain access to cropland and water for irrigation and to forests and scrubland for hunting and gathering. Through their struggle for survival, they developed a discourse which juxtaposed their own cultural and ecological standards to the colonial project.[8] This is not to suggest that preconquest Sonorans had achieved a sustained equilibrium with nature that was suddenly and irrevocably shattered following the European invasion of their territory; rather, as we shall see in Chapter 1, *serrano* villagers had

undergone major transformations in their economy and social organization prior to Spanish contact. Nevertheless, this view from the periphery
does underscore basic differences in the mode and intensity of exploitation of human as well as natural resources by Amerindian ethnic polities
and Iberian conquerors. The ecological context of Sonoran responses to
colonialism placed limits on the advance of empire and informed native
modes of political resistance.[9]

In this sense, social ecology provides a unifying framework for the
major themes of this book. Chapter 1 summarizes the anthropological
and historical bases for Spanish-Amerindian relations in northwestern
Mexico, delineating the critical points of change from Jesuit to Bourbon and, later, to Mexican administration. Chapters 2 and 3 contrast
the principles that underlay native subsistence and the colonial economy; Chapters 4 and 5 illustrate the ways in which *serrano* households
and communities reconstituted themselves under the duress of colonial domination; Chapters 6 and 7 analyze opposing systems of land
tenure and point to the political conflicts that arose over the control of
people and resources in this northern province of shifting borderlands.
Finally, Chapters 8 and 9 narrate the Sonoran peoples' responses to conquest and its aftermath, distinguishing between the often contradictory
strategies of accommodation and resistance. The conceptual outline and
the empirical content of this study provide a comparative optical lens
for observing the varied cultural settings in which a peasant class developed as a distinctive social actor. As the opening epigraph of the present
chapter implies, by bringing together the history of nature and the history of society, social ecology addresses basic questions concerning the
persistence of frontier peoples and settled peasantries under alien domination, in different areas of the Ibero-American empire.

The social transformation of Sonora generated conflict that lasted
over two centuries. This study focuses primarily on the mature colony
that coalesced at approximately the mid-eighteenth century and on the
formative years of the Mexican Republic. It concludes prior to the major
political upheavals marked by the U.S. invasion of Mexico, the Revolution of Ayutla, the legislative reforms of the Juárez presidency, and
the French Intervention that led, in turn, to the Porfirian consolidation
of power at the national and the regional levels. Although the opening
and closing dates of 1700 and 1850 serve to limit the temporal span of

the work, several chapters incorporate material pertaining to the pre-conquest and early colonial periods by way of explanatory references. The significant turning points of our story concern the gradual demise of the mission regime following the expulsion of the Jesuits (1767) and the dissolution of the Bourbon administration with the rise of Sonoran *criollo* politics after 1824.

Peasants and Indians on the Sonoran Frontier

The Sonoran peasantry included both sedentary and seminomadic peoples who occupied different ecological zones, distinct one from another in altitude, vegetation, and climate. Piedmont villagers were tillers of the soil, but for them horticulture and gathering were complementary activities, each essential for their survival. This ecological dimension altered the social and political relations obtaining between peasants and the dominant colonial strata of ranchers, miners, and merchants on this northern frontier of the Spanish Empire. The dyad of landlord–peasant so frequently used in European and Latin American rural history is not clearly operable in Sonora, where traditional methods of tribute and tithe collection were not systematically carried out, Spanish settlement was slow to develop until the mid-eighteenth century, and indigenous peoples moved in and out of the colonial domain.

Indian communities of direct producers were the principal source of a peasantry which developed under colonialism, but its social and racial composition changed over time. The ethnic boundaries of this northern peasantry were fluid, comprising a number of Indian groups as well as a mixed population of *vecinos, castas,* and *gente de razón*.[10] Culturally, the demarcation between "Indians" and "non-Indians" was not fixed or immutable, but changing and negotiated over time. At the upper end of the social spectrum, colonial settlers and authorities made substantive demands on native peoples for surplus labor and produce, but their status as a dominant class evolved slowly and unevenly in this frontier province.

Class societies reproduce the conditions for unequal claims or entitlements by different groups to natural resources (land), human resources (labor), technique (instruments, machinery), the products of labor (food, shelter, precious commodities), and symbolic wealth (the

insignia of prestige and leadership). Dominant classes struggle to maintain their control over labor and the surplus product; subordinate classes
find ways to resist, adapt to, and—at times—challenge the prevailing
social order.[11] Two well-traveled paths to the study of class formation
concentrate alternatively on the political mediations of the process and
on the organization of labor. My work develops both of these themes,
as evidenced in the pressures of the Bourbon state on Sonoran peasants
and in the changing labor regimes which indigenous villagers encountered in colonial missions, mines, and haciendas. Its contribution to
the study of ethnic peoples and peasants is directed to the problematic
middle level of abstraction in social theory: that of class formation and
the historical emergence of collective social actors.[12]

Wandering Peoples views this peasant class-in-formation through the cultural, economic, and political dimensions of the social relations of production.[13] I argue that although preconquest serrano polities were not
egalitarian, Spanish colonialism created overlapping spheres of power
and transformed a classless society into a society of classes defined in
terms of property and access to the means of production.[14] My principal
thesis is that social stratification occurred through the internal differentiation of the Indian and the Hispanic segments of Sonoran society, a
process in which the separate lines of class, ethnicity, and gender intersected.

Gender both qualifies the social categories of ethnicity and class and
links them to the internal structures of households and kin groups.
Although the empirical data on gender for this region and time period
are scarce and difficult to systematize, I have analyzed the division of
labor by age and sex, marital practices, family alliances, and native
strategies for reconstituting households in the face of high mortality.
The data summarized in Chapter 4 show that the labor of women and
children was essential to sustain peasant households. Native practices
encouraged racial and spatial exogamy, and spouses were selected from
different villages and ethnic groups as a means of rebuilding households and communities whose numbers were depleted by death and
migration. Gender further helps to clarify the term semiproletarian when
applied to peasant households. It describes the separation of individuals
within the family, or of kin groups from the parent community, because

some are dedicated to cultivation, others to foraging, and still others to wage labor.[15]

Framed in this way, the ethnohistory of analytically marginal groups in northwestern Mexico enriches and broadens the category of *peasants*. These include worker-peasants who combined agriculture and wage labor ("semi-proletarians") as well as seminomadic populations whose livelihood was not restricted to tillage and pastoralism.[16] If we are to use these inclusive terms, it is important to define the upper and lower limits of the peasantry for this frontier region. The lower limit concerns the distinction between tribal units and peasant communities, turning on contrasting degrees of sedentarism and nomadism and on the linkages developed between indigenous groups and the colonial order. Following the conquest and the institution of the mission system, the piedmont villagers of Sonora constituted a peasantry, both in their internal relations of production and in their external relations with colonial settlers and authorities. In contrast, the Cunca'ac (Seri) fishermen, gatherers, and hunters of the arid coastland sustained a nomadic way of life. Although drawn into the missions sporadically, they never became agriculturalists nor did they adopt *serrano* forms of social organization. Similarly, the Athapaskan hunters and raiders who moved through the sierra were organized in bands, rather than villages, and had no long-standing agricultural tradition. Despite the limited success of the Apache peace encampments established in the environs of Spanish presidios during the late eighteenth century and evidence that Apaches bred (as well as stole) herds of livestock, their culture strongly contrasted with that of the settled peoples who farmed the alluvial valleys of Sonora.

The upper limit of the Sonoran peasantry describes primarily the *vecinos*, non-Indian smallholders who had settled in the presidios and formed small communities of farmers, soldiers, and occasional miners (*gambusinos*). Not a few of them were squatters on mission land, gradually claiming de facto possession of cropland and of range for grazing cattle. Presidial soldiers, by virtue of their military service, received small land grants, which became a family patrimony to bequeath, enhance, or sell. Parallel processes of accumulation and fragmentation of these properties over several generations separated a landowning elite, who kept tenant families and hired eventual laborers on their estates, and the far more numerous smallholders, who became increasingly dependent on their wealthy neighbors. As Chapter 7 shows in some detail, poor peasants (Indian and non-Indian alike) faced pauperization, often through indebtedness, while prosperous *rancheros* moved out of the peasant category in the measure that they used a labor force outside their own families through sharecropping, peonage, and tenancy.[17]

In summary, *Wandering Peoples* expands our definition of *peasantry* and sheds new light on the relations of power and interdependency between indigenous peoples, the state, and local elites. This study of the Sonoran highlands confronts the conventional model of peasants and landlords with new empirical evidence and joins the structural analysis of class with the textual analysis of culture.

Peasant Culture and the Reconstitution of Ethnic Space

Scholars frequently use the concepts of culture, ethnicity, and community to connote the stability of "Indian" traditions in Latin America. These very traditions, however, develop through historical processes and are subject to change. Indian communities create new modes of cultural expression through internal pressures and external linkages with the wider society of which they are a part. Culture, then, is immersed in a specific historical context; it conditions and, in turn, is conditioned by the economic, political, and social dimensions of a particular time and place. Following the European conquest, "lo indio" was conditioned by asymmetrical relations of power that subordinated native polities to the colonial state. Ethnic affiliations evolved over time in reference to diverse criteria of race, language, territory, kinship, and lineage; the meaning of these affiliations changed in the course of successive alliances and confrontations that gave expression to distinct cultural values which, in turn, were grounded in the material life of the communities.[18]

The Sonoran peasantry that emerged as an economic class during the eighteenth and nineteenth centuries comprised shifting but discernible ethnic communities. Theirs was an ambivalent ethnicity, reconstituted through the convergence of Amerindian and Hispanic traditions in what some scholars have called *ethnogenesis*, or "ethnic rebirth."[19] To be sure, highland villagers defended tangible values: communal access to land, kinship ties, and traditional modes of leadership. Native Sonorans defended modes of spatial and cultural mobility which forced Spanish authorities and settlers to redefine the territorial and economic ambitions of the colonial project. And they upheld the cultural integrity of their basic social unit: the extended family which brought together consanguine and ceremonial kinfolk. In *serrano* communities authority flowed from internally defined criteria of hierarchy based on the traditional merits of chieftaincy, but fused with the political system introduced by the Spaniards. Indigenous cultures changed over time as peasant cultivators and gatherers selected certain elements of the colonial project, endured others they could not avoid, and resisted still others through negotiation, flight, and revolt.[20]

The political responses of northern peoples to colonialism contrasted with those of the core areas of Mesoamerica. Sonoran modes of resistance reflected both native forms of cultural expression and Spanish methods of domination. Within their own communities, northern village elites used colonial institutions to reconstitute a social hierarchy without recourse to hereditary noble lineages or carefully preserved genealogies. In their place, governing offices created in the mission pueblos and military rankings extended to native warriors in the frontier presidios elevated individuals and their families above the peasant base. In the larger sphere of colonial society, highland villagers who moved between the missions and the mines learned to manipulate the dual columns of Spanish authority represented by military governors and missionaries. Unlike the Nahuatl-speakers of central Mexico, the northern Amerindians were illiterate; for this reason, they did not produce a written record of their preconquest history or elaborate land titles to defend their communal holdings. Furthermore, they had little recourse to litigation, an important contrast with the Mesoamerican and Andean regions, where bulging notarial and tribunal archives bear witness to the Indians' grasp of Spanish legal procedures. Native peoples of northwestern Mexico confronted their overlords orally, and their testimony is preserved in writing only through Spanish interlocutors.

Colonial authorities recognized Sonoran ethnic polities as *naciones*, loose affiliations of communities based on racial, linguistic, and territorial criteria.[21] In their minds, the term connoted the subordination of these communities to imperial rule. Over time, however, serrano villagers assumed the title of *nación* in order to assert their separate identity when dealing with Spanish governors and settlers. Highland peoples used the European concept of "nation" to express their indigenous claims to ethnic space, which encompassed both a geographic territory and a political entity. Thus, the Jesuit Andrés Pérez de Rivas wrote in 1645: "We should understand that what I call 'nations' [in this land] are not nearly so populous as in our Europe, because these barbarous nations have fewer people, but they are greater in number and even more diverse in their languages. . . . [T]hey are continually at war with one another, and recognize separate land divisions and boundaries." [22]

The reconstitution of ethnic territory set the political dimensions of frontier ecology. Sonoran nations defended their claims to vital resources through physical mobility, and regenerated their communities over time in a dynamic process of fragmentation and nucleation. [23] The Opata, Eudeve, and Pima villagers of the Sonoran highlands maintained compact aldeas as well as shifting rancherías, which gave them access to fertile cropland and to mountainous forests for hunting and gathering. Similarly, the O'odham (desert-dwelling Pima) of the western lowlands moved seasonally between their fields (oidag) and wells (wahia) and traveled to different encampments to gather fruit, fibers, and tubers from the desert's bounty. Sonoran tribal peoples worked these patterns of geographic displacement into their modes of social bonding through kinship ties, marital exogamy, and political alliances forged in times of war and at other critical conjunctures. [24]

Ethnic space, then, was centered in the community, and encompassed the resources necessary for its survival. But the nature of this communal life embodied an internal tension between centrifugal and centripetal forces, and its geographic contours changed with historical circumstances. Sonoran pueblos empowered their leaders—religious shamans, war chiefs, and the patrilineal heads of extended kin groups—to secure their material needs and, in a larger sense, to conserve their natural environment and to mediate between the terrestrial and the divine. [25] The serrano concept of ethnic space transcended the political and administrative territory which the colonial order assigned to Indian pueblos. Through the social reproduction of the community and the concrete possession of the lands to which it laid claim, highland villagers united their ethnic territory with the gods' domain over natural features like mountains, rivers, caves, springs, and the sea. [26]

Spanish conquest created a new set of contingencies for conserving the integrity of ethnic polities. *Serrano* peoples vied with the *vecinos* for life-giving resources of land and water, and their leaders confronted a new political entity: the state. By the mid-eighteenth century the Iberian monarchical state had established three essential components of its authority on the Sonoran frontier. The king's representatives claimed a monopoly over the legitimate use of force, asserted the autonomy of the state in legal institutions which affected the very life of ethnic communities, and defined Indians as subject vassals of the royal domain. This notion of vassalage, reworked in the nineteenth century, created the contours of *citizenship*, understood as the normative relation between individuals (Indian and non-Indian) and the Mexican nation-state.[27] Spanish claims to the monopoly of force took concrete form in the military garrisons stationed in the heart of *serrano* territory and in the punitive expeditions launched against the nomads of the Sierra Madre and the coastal deserts. Bourbon administrative reforms dealing with military defense, land tenure, and the internal structure of the pueblos imposed the governing presence of the secular state. Concomitantly, Bourbon economic policies enhanced conditions in the province for the accumulation of wealth and the exercise of power by Sonoran elites.

Traditional historiography has emphasized the patriarchal nature of the Crown's rule over the Amerindian peoples of its overseas empire.[28] To be sure, the impressive body of legislation, tribunals, and administrative posts directed to create policies and resolve disputes concerning Indian pueblos attests to the state's intent to both exploit and ensure the survival of native communities. Furthermore, state and church constituted dual columns of royal authority in the colonies. In central and southern Mesoamerica, the Spanish conquest of densely settled *señoríos* ruled over by noble lineages was accomplished through the institutions of *encomienda* and tribute, which exacted payments in kind and labor obligations from peasant households in established communities. For their part, the religious orders endeavored to teach Christian doctrine, repressed heterodoxy, and demanded personal service as well as the tithe. In northern New Spain, these instruments of colonial dominion proved effective only in the province of New Mexico. Elsewhere, the conquest assumed different forms.

At mid-sixteenth century, Spaniards had failed to implant *encomiendas* or to hold any permanent settlements north of Culiacán. By the close of the century, as the mining frontier spread north from Zacatecas and Durango to Chihuahua, the governor of Nueva Vizcaya appealed to the Society of Jesus to send missionaries to the northwestern frontier. Jesuits called their method *reducción*, whereby the population of numerous small hamlets was concentrated in nuclear towns which controlled sufficient cropland to support a compact community. In the interest of securing dominion over the northern borderlands, the Crown supported the missions financially and provided the legal framework to protect the Indians' land-use rights and shield them from enslavement and the worst abuses of forced labor. For nearly two and a half centuries, first the Jesuit (1591–1767) and then the Franciscan (1768–1842) missions symbolized the colonial pact between the Spanish monarch and his Native American subjects in the frontier provinces.[29] This is not to say that the missionaries' advance through the region did not meet resistance or that the mission enterprise was harmonious; to the contrary, the *reducciones* existed in a climate of tension between the missionaries' objectives and the cultural practices they proposed to change. Nevertheless, that the Indians recognized a colonial pact of reciprocal obligations is revealed by the language of protest they employed during the nineteenth century against Liberal reforms regarding land tenure and village governance. When confronting the nascent Mexican state, *serrano* peoples defended a traditional order that was as much colonial as it was pre-Hispanic and grounded in the economic and political structures established by the missions.

Highland peasants defended their ethnic territory on a number of fronts, even as Spaniards and Indians alike tested the limits of the colonial pact. Spanish officials and miners tried to overrun the missions in order to gain access to land and cheap labor. Sonoran indigenous peoples, for their part, demanded autonomy and respect for their territory in return for their labor and militias to fight the nomads on the margins of Spanish dominion. Sonoran communities defended their ethnic space through the missions, but did so more persistently through their long-standing patterns of mobility which created new *rancherías* outside the confines of the pueblos. The potential for conflict contained within the colonial pact is illustrated particularly by the histories of the Yaqui and Opata nations of Sinaloa and Sonora. While Yaqui history has been extensively researched and published, the Opata experience is less well known.[30] For this reason, *Wandering Peoples* focuses on the Opata, Pima, and Eudeve peoples of the Sonoran highlands.

After Mexican independence a radical renegotiation of the colonial pact occurred between Indian communities and the Sonoran notables who took control of state government. The struggle for territory and power entered a new phase, one that was both decisive and paradoxical. During the first half of the nineteenth century, when the Mexican state was weak at both the national and the provincial level, ethnic polities confronted powerful networks of *criollo* families.[31] These regional oligarchs asserted their strength in order to dissolve the colonial pact and forge new political alignments throughout Mexico. Concomitantly, *serrano* peoples opposed the new Liberal policies by both overt and covert resistance, as will be narrated in detail in Chapter 9. Some *rancherías* chose flight and increased mobility, returning to raid hacendados' granaries and livestock; others retreated further into the desert and mountainous barrancas.

Ethnic leaders petitioned state and national authorities to retain control over village lands; when negotiations failed, they resorted to rebellion. Their defense of communal patrimony concerned not only the material wealth of this productive resource, but also their status as the recognized governors of their people. In each of these stages of conflict, highland leaders developed an alternative discourse to the Liberal ideology of the Mexican state, one that upheld the inviolability of ethnic territory. Was this simply a regional variation of the classical opposition between *Gemeinschaft*, the "folk" or ethnic community, and *Gesellschaft*, the modern nation-state?[32] I will show that *serrano* resistance comprised both a statement of political autonomy and a cultural project that defended a holistic sense of ethnic space.

Ethnic Discourse and the Multiple Voices of Cultural History

More than a decade ago, Eric Wolf challenged historians and anthropologists "to uncover the history of 'the people without history'—the active histories of 'primitives,' peasantries, laborers, immigrants, and besieged minorities."[33] His influential synthesis viewed the emergence of the modern world system through the recorded experience of the subaltern peoples—workers, slaves, subjugated indigenes—whose labor made possible the rise of capitalism. Wolf's central argument cautioned scholars not to reify concepts like *nation, society,* and *culture,* nor to splinter the complex totality of historical processes into isolated units, thereby distorting the interconnected quality of cultural phenomena.[34]

Concomitantly with Wolf, James C. Scott proposed moving beyond the Gramscian notion of hegemony to articulate a theory of public and private "transcripts" spoken by subaltern peoples who practice the arts of covert resistance. Their hidden transcripts, according to Scott, postulate alternative values to those espoused by the hegemonic culture that denies them power and curtails their autonomy.[35] Scott admonished historians and social scientists to read these hidden transcripts; and, like Wolf, he warned that our failure to heed them leads us to partition history and to misunderstand the role of ideology in social conflict.

Parallel methodological and conceptual developments subsumed under the labels of subaltern and postcolonial studies intersect with the premises forwarded by Wolf and Scott and serve to carry the debate forward. Subaltern studies, centered initially in the Indian subcontinent, have inspired new conceptual frameworks and research queries in Latin America, Africa, Asia and the South Pacific, in what Florencia Mallon has dubbed a fruitful South–South debate: "[a] non-hierarchical cross-regional dialogue, where neither of the two cases is taken as the paradigm against which the other is pronounced inadequate."[36] Much of this work focuses on peasant movements and ethnic identities that, in different geographic and political settings, challenged the dominant narrative of the nation-state. Moreover, it leaves behind binary oppositions of "resistance" and "accommodation"—or a simple divide between colonizer and colonized—to relate the complexity of multilayered political struggles that encompassed complicity, protection, advocacy, adaptation, collaboration, individual gain, and collective agency.[37] Numerous authors working on Latin America have shown that the categories of *Indian* and *mestizo* were each historically constructed, often in response to colonial categories and demands for service and tribute.[38]

But, how do we place the indigenous peasants of highland Sonora on center stage as the subjects of this history? How do we hear their voices? Our method begins with the historian's craft; that is, to conjoin theoretical propositions concerning class formation, ethnic persistence, and the emerging quality of relations between state and society with specific historical encounters found in the empirical data. In eighteenth-century Sonora, documented confrontations over concrete issues, such as wages and provisions for Opata and Pima presidial troops, the distribution and sale of food surpluses from the missions, and the exercise of authority in the pueblos, created a cultural lexicon with multiple meanings. These moments of conflict produced historical texts which reveal both syncretic and divergent values in the voices of colonizers and colonized. Their separate discourses developed through repeated encounters and a slow, uneven process of cultural commingling; they are discerned in actions as much as in words.

Texts and discourses may refer to written documents, to pictographic histories (exemplified by the Nahua codices), to mnemonic devices (like the Andean *quipus* or the O'odham prayer sticks), or to oral traditions. Songs, poems, dances, and religious rituals as well as jokes, gossiping, and stories communicate values and constitute different forms of "discourse." Spanish and indigenous symbols mixed and clashed in moments of partial understanding, producing new cultural artifacts in a process that Walter Mignolo has termed *colonial semiosis.* The dialogue expands to include "understanding subjects," the readers who interpret the symbolic codes of this colonial world, bringing to it their psychological, ideological, and cultural frameworks.[39]

Religious practices attest to the convergence of different cultural traditions on the Sonoran frontier, a theme developed in Chapter 8 of the present study. *Serrano* peoples selectively blended Christian ritual and doctrine with their own cults and belief systems. Native Sonorans adapted to their own needs the Spaniards' religious pageantry and symbolism. The artistic and iconographic remains of Sonoran mission life executed by Indians under the direction of Jesuit and Franciscan friars, as well as the religious holidays celebrated by highland villagers, illustrate the mixed quality of cultural values nurtured in the communities. Their significance flows metonymically in the association of diverse symbols which appear and reappear in different forms as used by distinct historical actors.[40] Jesuit narratives, for example, bear witness to nuanced meanings for the cross, the rosary, and baptismal waters, and to the enduring influence of native shamans who cured disease, cast spells, and made hidden burial offerings in caves beyond the missionaries' surveillance.[41]

Concomitantly, Sonoran peoples ascribed particular values to the goods they acquired in the colonial marketplace. In everyday life they found new symbols of prestige which, in different contexts, connoted both accommodation and resistance to the Spanish regime. Canes of office distributed by Spanish magistrates and military commanders to Indian governors and captains bestowed on their holders limited control over their pueblos and auxiliary troops, but underscored their subordinate position to colonial authorities. Bolts of cloth, produced in the *obrajes* of central New Spain or imported from Europe, served as a common mode of payment for native workers in the missions and Spanish enterprises. Although nearly all Sonoran peoples were weavers of cotton *mantas*, the new textiles circulated among them and tied them firmly to the colonial market. Similarly, the gold and silver that *serrano* labor dug out of the Sonoran hillsides represented an entirely new kind of commodity, one that established the monetary value of other trade goods. The Spaniards' insatiable thirst for bullion subjected native mineworkers to arduous labor; however, once these workers learned the purchasing power of gold nuggets and silver bars, they found in mining an alternative to the discipline of mission life. Finally, for villagers and nomads alike, domesticated livestock—especially the horse—brought a new form of wealth and enhanced their freedom of movement. At the same time, the breeding of European quadrupeds severely altered ecological conditions for hunting and gathering in the *monte*.[42]

Sonoran ethnic communities developed an alternative discourse in their use of religious and material symbols that set the boundaries of acceptable claims on their productive energy and common resources. Through "resistant adaptation" they achieved marginal advantages under colonialism.[43] Like nearly all Native Americans, *serrano* peoples opposed initial European conquest in armed combat, but after suffering defeat their ongoing struggle for survival required a dual stance of accommodation and resistance. Highland villagers came to terms with the dominant institutions of colonialism, but they periodically renegotiated the conditions of their subjugation. They accepted mission life, but modified the Jesuit program of concentrated settlements by forming breakaway hamlets. Opata and Pima warriors joined an uneasy alliance with the Spaniards in the ongoing Apache wars. Presidial service brought them wages and a legitimate means of social and political ascendancy based on military rankings. By the same token, Sonoran peasants sought out colonial markets, but balanced their service for hire with subsistence agriculture and foraging.

Sonoran peoples were often not united in their confrontation with the Spaniards. Different ethnicities fought as allies of the Europeans, then turned on each other. Perhaps more telling than tribal differences, social stratification shaped native peoples' options in the colonial economy. Indians who acquired property or, more typically, who accepted permanent status as ranch hands and mineworkers, melted into the racially mixed population of the *gente de razón*. Furthermore, increasing numbers of Indians living under the mission regime opted to leave their ethnic communities by petitioning colonial authorities for the status of *vecino*. Thus, they abandoned communal labor and access to land in the pueblos, and cast their luck in the marketplace.

The ambiguities of ethnicity and class encountered in *Wandering Peoples* underscore the historical and changing quality of these social categories in a frontier setting. The conceptual framework informed by social ecology addresses issues of both political economy and culture. It helps to contextualize the paradigm of *core* and *periphery* and to understand the complexity of the world system. Historical analysis of opposing ethnic groups and social classes in specific areas shows how local confrontations altered the political economy of colonialism. This line of inquiry focuses on peasant subsistence, implying not merely the minimum requisites of physical survival, but rather the complement of resources necessary to ensure both material existence and the social and ceremonial needs of community life. Community connotes, broadly, the ethnic and political relationships that bind individuals to a recognized social unit and a territorial base.

If, indeed, indigenous communities conserve a hidden transcript, how can we discern its existence historically? The search for a culture of resistance is tempered by a sobering reminder of the severe limits placed on subaltern peoples. Recent critiques of this approach assert that methods of domination are so pervasive that they define the limits of autonomous action to which suppressed groups aspire.[44] What are the opposing sets of values concerning work and productivity, equity and the outer limits of exploitation, that emerge from the clash of dominant and subordinate ideologies? Here, we turn to the creative interpretation of language and to sources of information outside the written text. By reading judiciously in archaeology, history, ethnography, and cultural geography, we can infer from recorded actions the cultural values which define the peasants' world and mediate between local polity and alien governance. This study brings together quantitative analysis of demographic and economic data and textual analysis of the claims and counterclaims, petitions, and compromises worked out over a century between Spaniards and Indians, soldiers and missionaries, laborers and proprietors, in a complex web of unequal power relations. My purpose is to tell the story of the highland villagers of Sonora and, in so doing, to increase our understanding of the limits of autonomy for colonized peoples as well as the regenerative quality of their communities.

Part I

Los *Sonoras* and the Iberian Invasion
of Northwestern Mexico

I

Ethnic Frontiers in the Sonoran Desert

The most elderly Indians still alive tell me that the name Sonora comes from a marshy spring about half a league from Guépaca, where a large *ranchería* used to make their houses of reeds and maize husks, which they call *sonot* in their language. When the first Spaniards heard the word, they pronounced it "sonora," and from then on the whole province took this harmonious and pleasing name.

Jesuit document, 1730[1]

The peoples whose history concerns us occupied an area of approximately 225,000 square miles located between 27° and 34° latitude and 108° and 115° longitude in the north-central portion of Sonora (Mexico) and southern Arizona (U.S.A.). The central feature of their territory is the Sonoran Desert, stretching eastward from the Gulf of California to the foothills of the Sierra Madre Occidental. Successive mountain ranges and valleys, running generally from northeast to southwest, constitute the *zona serrana* that rises from the arid coastal plain and culminates in the escarpment of the Sierra Madre. These cordilleras create distinct ecological niches, differing in altitude, temperature, and rainfall. Five principal rivers flow out of the mountains toward the gulf, cutting through the hills and carrying in their courses fertile alluvial deposits. Flanking the eastern edge of the Sonoran Desert, the Río San Miguel and its main tributary, the Río Zanjón, join the Río Sonora just north of Hermosillo (Pitic) and turn westward to drain their waters in the flatlands leading to the sea. Moving eastward, the Moctezuma (Oposura) and Bavispe flow into the Río Yaqui, the largest river system in Sonora, followed by the

Río Mayo which irrigates the southernmost alluvial valley in the state. The main river channels and their innumerable affluents and arroyos nurture human settlement and provide the soils and humidity needed for horticulture.[2]

The colonial provinces of Sonora and Ostimuri extended from the Yaqui Valley, in the south, to the river basins of the Gila and Colorado in the north. They were shared (and disputed) by village agricultural- ists, who settled in the river valleys, and by nomadic gatherers, hunters, and fishermen who camped along the gulf coast and in the rugged terrain of the Sierra Madre. Their sustenance came from the abundant flora and fauna of the desert and from the coastal estuaries; likewise, the low scrub forest of the hills and canyons of the sierras provided shelter, medicine, food, fiber, game, and small plots for cultivation. Nomads wandered in seasonal patterns near the established farming vil- lages with whom they traded. All groups depended on a variety of re- sources in order to ensure subsistence, and climatic variations from year to year altered planting cycles and crop yields. For this reason, as well as the ritual visitations associated with ancient migratory patterns, the movements of different peoples blurred and altered the ethnic bound- aries which crossed and recrossed the Sonoran map (Fig. 1.1). The tribal nomenclature used in reference to agriculturalists and nomads varied widely and changed over time, referring to linguistic and territorial features. The superposition of different criteria, added to shifting resi- dence patterns and the fact that native languages appeared in clusters of dialects, led to some confusion in the documentary record. Colonial observers altered ethnic terminology: the O'odham became Pimas, the Cunca'ac became Seris, the Tegüima became Opatas, and the Yoeme and Yoreme became Yaquis and Mayos.[3]

The O'odham occupied different ecological zones in both the desert and the highlands, and Pima-Tepehuán speakers formed a linguistic chain along the Sierra Madre Occidental extending from Durango and Chihuahua to Sonora and Arizona. Their geographic profusion and the endurance of their languages point to the antiquity of O'odham peoples in northwestern Mexico. The northern Pimas of Sonora proper were further divided among the Hiach-ed or S-ohbmakam (desert nomads), the Tohono O'odham or Papawi Ko'odham (the "bean eaters," whom the Spaniards would call Pápagos), and the Akimel (riverine farmers).[4]

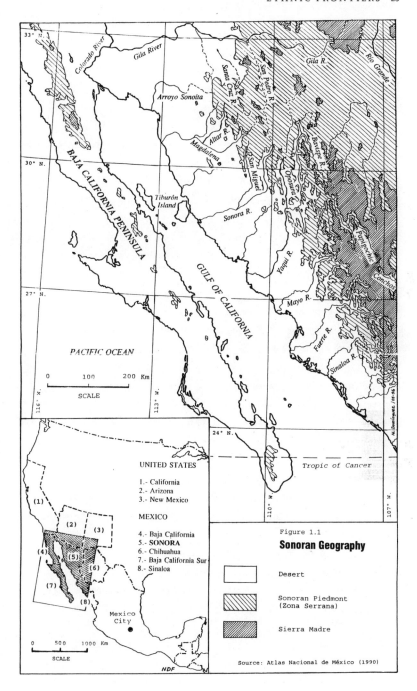

Figure 1.1. Sonoran geography

Jesuit missionaries who first encountered farming peoples in the piedmont region of the middle Yaqui River during the early seventeenth century called them Nebomes, distinguishing between the "upper" and "lower" Nebomes according to their geographic location at different altitudes of the sierra. By the eighteenth century these Nebome villagers were known as Pima Bajo, separated physically from the Pima Alto of northern Sonora by the Opata and Eudeve speakers of the central highlands.[5] Pima agriculturalists formed a number of large communities and many more rancherías along the alluvial floodplains of the lower San Miguel and Sonora valleys. Their territory in the Sierra Madre extended eastward as far as the westernmost Tarahumara villages of Chihuahua.[6] At higher elevations, where rainfall was abundant, Pima villagers planted on terraces and in arroyo beds; at lower elevations, during periods of drought, they carried water to their gardens from natural springs that drew on underground sources and seepage from the surrounding hills. In general, however, all serrano peoples relied on irrigation by gravity, using simple techniques requiring communal labor to channel the water from the riverbed to cleared fields on the adjacent floodplain.

The Opatería comprised various clusters of agrarian communities which, under colonial rule, converged into a nation with common linguistic roots and cultural traditions. They called themselves Heves or Tegüimas, although the name by which they would be known historically—Opatas—derived from the Pima word obagg'ata, meaning "to have an enemy."[7] At the time of European contact, the Opata nation controlled the valleys of Bavispe, Fronteras, Oposura, Sonora, and the middle portion of the San Miguel. They maintained contested boundaries with the Pima and Cáhita peoples to the north, west, and south and, to the east, with the Jobas and other nomadic groups of the Sierra Madre.[8] The Opatas had expanded their ethnic provinces at the expense of the Pimas and Cáhitas, although their "tribal" wars represented ongoing rivalry among groups of villages for control over a valley or hilltop. Eudeves, highland villagers similar to the Opatas in their culture and economy, but distinct in their language, formed two discernible zones located to the southeast and northwest of the Opatería proper.[9]

The profusion of dialects heard among Sonoran peoples conformed to several linguistic families. Nearly all the serrano villagers spoke languages related to the Uto-Aztecan stock and shared certain cultural elements with the Mesoamerican towns of the Mexican altiplano. By way of contrast, the desert Cunca'ac belonged to the Hokan group, which included several agricultural peoples of the lower Colorado Valley—the Yumas, Cocomaricopas, and Halchidomas—who remained largely outside the orbit of Spanish rule.[10] At the time of European contact, the eastern sierra was home to diverse bands of nomadic hunters and gatherers whose languages and territories were never clearly distinguished in Spanish documents. Apache hunters and raiders, Athapaskan speakers who so troubled Spanish defenses in the northern frontier, moved into Sonoran territory during the early seventeenth century as a result of shifting territorial rivalries on the Great Plains following British and French expansion into the North American continent. Their *rancherías* spanned the cordilleras of both Sonora and Nueva Vizcaya. The Spaniards' fear of the Apaches grew after the Pueblo Revolt and the uprisings of Conchos, Sumas, Chinarras, Mansos, Jocomes, and Janos in Nueva Vizcaya.[11] The Apaches, in turn, responded to increased hostilities with important adaptations in their modes of subsistence, warfare, and social organization. They became skilled horsemen who not only stole livestock from Indian pueblos and Spanish settlements but also bred their own herds. They lived mainly by hunting and gathering; although they planted ephemeral crops, their reliance on wild vegetation and game enhanced their movements throughout the sierra.[12]

The ethnolinguistic distribution of native peoples surmised from the historical and archaeological record reflects the chronological depth of human occupation in Sonora, estimated at approximately 30,000 to 15,000 years before the present. Fairly homogeneous cultures of hunter-gatherers depended on the Pleistocene fauna—the American horse, camel, mammoth, and mastodon—which grazed on the lush grasslands produced by a humid, cool climate. The extinction of these great mammals and the evolution of Holocene fauna, such as bears, felines, deer, rodents, and a great variety of fowl, forced changes in the Indians' hunting techniques and led to a greater reliance on gathering plant foods. This transition period occurred approximately from 15,000 to 8,000 years ago, during which Sonoran peoples developed new instruments for grinding fruits and seeds and altered their migratory patterns to accommodate the cyclical maturation of different species of flora. The need to defend specific territories brought about sharper distinctions between kin groups and greater social cohesion within each unit. These "archaic" foragers of the Sonoran piedmont accumulated the knowledge of plant life and created the incipient village structures requisite for the development of agriculture. Native Sonorans began cultivating a part of their food supply at around 3,000 to 2,500 years ago. The "agricultural revolution" came to this region through internal cultural specialization and intermittent contacts with Mesoamerican civilizations in different stages of their development.[13]

Thus, for more than a millennium before Spanish contact, village cultivators acquired the accoutrements of sedentary life. The domestication of animals, although not extensive, included the breeding of dogs, turkeys, and birds valued for their ornamental plumage. *Serrano* villagers produced ceramic ware as well as a variety of utensils woven from vegetable fibers. They created characteristic artwork in their pottery and basketry, and left testimony of their culture in the petroglyphs which abound in the region.[14] Sonoran highlanders exploited a wide range of resources in the agricultural floodplain, the mountainous scrub forest, and the flora and marine life of the gulf coast through trade and seasonal migrations.

Settlement patterns alternated between phases of dispersal and nucleation during approximately eight centuries before the Spanish conquest. Four known cultural traditions with ties to northern Sinaloa, Sonora, and western Chihuahua are summarized in Table 1.1. *Huatabampo* village sites flourished around the lagoons and estuaries of the Mayo and Fuerte rivers from A.D. 700 to 1000. Their inhabitants raised maize and beans to supplement abundant marine resources. They built settlements of noncontiguous dwellings with communal plazas, trash mounds, cemeteries, and offertories. Huatabampo villagers made pottery and shell jewelry and may have traded with diverse groups in Sinaloa and in the area dominated by Casas Grandes. Current research suggests that the Huatabampo tradition had ended before the historical Cáhita peoples occupied northern Sinaloa and southern Sonora.[15] By way of contrast, the Cunca'ac tradition of the Sonoran central coast, extending from Guaymas to Puerto Lobos, exhibited a strong continuity in material culture for more than a thousand years, from as early as A.D. 700 to late historical times. These desert nomads settled in shifting encampments and lived by fishing, hunting, and gathering, moving

Table 1.1 Preconquest Cultural Traditions in Sonora

Dates (A.D.)	Cultures			
	Seri	Huatabampo	Trinchera	Río Sonora
1500		S P A N I S H	C O N T A C T	
1450				4
1400	Continuous	Trade in shell	III 2	
1350	occupation	for turquoise		
1300	and material	and obsidian.		3
1250	culture.	Agriculture,		
1200	Fisher-	Mesoamerican	1	2
1150	gatherer,	influence.	II	
1100	Tiburón		Shell trade,	
1050	plain pottery.		pottery,	
1000			agriculture.	1
950			1 Links to	Agriculture,
900			Hohokam.	trade in cloth
850			2 Cerros de	for copper,
800		I	trincheras.	turquoise.
750				1 Pithouse
700				villages.
				2 Surface
				dwellings.
				3 Towns, Casas
				Grandes
				trade.
				4 Villages.

Summary of Trends:

I   700–1100   Economic consolidation.

II   1100–1300   Consolidation continued in the north, broken in the south.

III   1300–1500   Trinchera and Río Sonora polities decline.

Source: Wilcox and Masse, eds., 1981

beyond their coastal territory to visit and trade with riverine agriculturalists. Their crafts included basketry and remarkably thin-walled pottery
vessels used for storing water.[16]

The Trincheras and Río Sonora cultures relate directly to the *serrano*
peoples who are the subjects of this history. Trincheras village sites
corresponded geographically to the historic Pimería Alta, and their development paralleled that of the Hohokam urban tradition of southern Arizona. These farming peoples built pithouses, produced pottery,
and participated in long-distance trade routes stretching from western
Sonora northward to the Hohokam and eastward to Casas Grandes. During a period of intense rivalry for floodplain land, following the eclipse
of the Hohokam regional system (dated between 1375 and 1450), specific hilltop sites chosen for defense were fortified with rock terraces
called *trincheras*. Population growth and shifting climatic patterns led
to endemic warfare in which different groups fought for control over
the most fertile valleys. The Trincheras culture centered on the Altar-
Magdalena-Concepción drainages and extended to portions of the Río
San Miguel. The historical O'odham probably descended from the Hohokam, but their autonomous village structures contrasted markedly
with the integrated social systems and ranked sites of classic Hohokam
culture.[17]

The term *Río Sonora culture* refers to a broad distribution of village sites
extending from the San Miguel Valley to the Bavispe Valley and along the
upland tributaries of the Yaqui and Mayo rivers.[18] The earliest dwellings,
dated at circa A.D. 1000 on the lower terraces above the floodplains, were
houses-in-pits, semi-subterranean shelters occurring in small hamlets.
In the thirteenth and fourteenth centuries, villages became larger and
more numerous, and combined the house-in-pit with surface structures.
During the following two hundred years, surface buildings had all but
displaced the earlier type, and public ceremonial edifices stood in a few
of the larger towns. House construction combined perishable materials with the art of masonry, using puddled earth and stone, and a few
centers boasted surface structures with foundations aligned in multiple
rows, indicative of an incipient phase of urbanization.[19]

Population growth and external relations impelled the growing cultural complexity of *serrano* peoples. The most important contact for the
eastern Sonoran highlands was Casas Grandes, or Paquimé, the great

trading center of northwestern Chihuahua. From Casas Grandes itself radiated numerous smaller settlements, some of which extended westward into the Sonoran highlands. Elegantly decorated ceramics recovered as far west as the San Miguel Valley indicate the extent of Casas Grandes' commercial and tributary networks. Serrano villagers traded food surpluses, cotton cloth, coral, and slaves in return for turquoise, copper ornaments, and tradeware. The Altar-Concepción villages were an area of craft specialization, where shells gathered on the Gulf Coast were worked into adornments destined for Casas Grandes. Nomadic hunter-gatherers as well as sedentary farming communities participated in long-distance trade as carriers of salt, shells, hides, turquoise, and coral.[20] Casas Grandes began as a cluster of agricultural villages in the eighth century and became an urban center that flourished under Mesoamerican influence from approximately A.D. 1200 to 1490, when the adobe city was burned and partially abandoned. Prior to Spanish contact, it is probable that some Casas Grandes inhabitants migrated to the western slopes of the Sierra Madre, enlarging highland villages and forming new ones; their descendants became the historical Opata.[21]

After the collapse of the Paquimé and Hohokam urban centers, serrano peoples entered a new phase of political division and territorial warfare, as evidenced by the trincheras of northwestern Sonora and by walled towns and signaling sites in the eastern highlands. Upland communities organized around kinship had differential access to the basic resources needed for survival and reproduction. Although these relatively autonomous villages did not conform to a discernible hierarchy, they carried within them the seeds of internal stratification. Their leaders bore the insignia of prestige symbolized by turquoise, shells, and colored plumage which elevated them above the commoners during collective hunts, religious ceremonials, and war. But their authority was not hereditary, nor did they form a noble caste, in contrast to the Mesoamerican city-states of this same era.[22]

When the Spanish explorers of the sixteenth century first confronted the geographic and cultural contrasts of the peoples they called "los sonoras,"[23] they found villagers living in settlements of varying size and complexity who practiced irrigated agriculture, raised food surpluses, and exchanged a variety of goods within local and regional networks. Although the serrano peoples were still avid traders, the cultural norms that structured their economy were substantially different from the mercantilist principles that guided European commerce. As merchant capital advanced toward this remote frontier of the Spanish Empire, it transformed the social relations of production through the growth of a market economy. The conquest brought political and cultural changes as well, which altered the very terms of the struggle for power in the region.

In Search of Cíbola: The Spanish Conquest of Sonora

Within a decade of the fall of Tenochtitlán, pre-Hispanic routes linking western Mesoamerica with the *serrano* and puebloan provinces attracted Spanish explorers in search of slaves, trade goods, and mineral wealth to northwestern Mexico. The first expedition to penetrate this "west coast corridor" moving north from New Galicia was led by Beltrán Nuño de Guzmán, who founded San Miguel de Culiacán in 1530. His kinsman Diego de Guzmán used Culiacán as a base in order to advance as far as Cumuripa (Sonora), leaving a wake of fear and destruction behind him. Repeated slaving expeditions led to the breakdown of the Tahue and Totorame polities, and to massive flight from the Cáhita pueblos. Alvar Núñez Cabeza de Vaca, who traversed the same area in 1536, found it deserted "because the people have fled to the mountains. They do not dare to build houses nor till the land, for fear of the Christians."[24]

The Cabeza de Vaca party, the first to reach Sonora proper, was unarmed and unprepossessing, but augmented by scores of native followers. Three Europeans and an African, the only survivors of the shipwrecked Pánfilo de Narváez expedition off the coast of Florida (1528), traveled westward on foot, in search of "Christians" who had advanced north of the Valley of Mexico. Cabeza de Vaca's early narratives recount episodes of peddling, enslavement, and shamanism as he and his companions endured their eight-year odyssey. They crossed into northwestern Mexico, probably near the confluence of the Río Grande and the Río Conchos (in Chihuahua), and continued southwest through Sonora and Sinaloa until they encountered Spaniards north of Culiacán. An entire Pima *ranchería* followed Cabeza de Vaca to the environs of Culiacán, where they founded the village of Bamoa, motivated perhaps by their fears of rival *serrano* nations and of Spanish slavers.[25] Cabeza de Vaca described abundant agricultural surpluses and received gifts of cotton *mantas*, turquoise, and coral from the "people of permanent houses" along the trail of maize which led through the Sonoran highlands.[26] Both Diego de Guzmán and Cabeza de Vaca encountered Indians with Spanish cloth and pieces of metal armor and tools, indicating that the material signs of contact had preceded the actual arrival of Spaniards in the province.

Cabeza de Vaca's story of wealthy cities north of where he had traveled—the source of turquoise stones and bison hides he had seen in Sonora—created considerable interest in Mexico City. Viceroy Antonio de Mendoza commissioned Fray Marcos de Niza to lead an expedition northward over Cabeza de Vaca's route in search of the elusive seven cities of Cíbola. In 1539, accompanied by Estéban (the black slave from Cabeza de Vaca's party) and Pima Indians from Bamoa, Niza traveled through Sinaloa and Sonora, pursuing his destination as far as the western Zuñi pueblos. On the strength of Niza's report of densely populated and wealthy northern provinces, Francisco Vázquez de Coronado outfitted a large army to conquer Cíbola. His expedition (1540–42) left from Compostela and opened new routes through Sonora. Coronado founded San Gerónimo de Corazones, a settlement in the Sonoran foothills, before moving northeast to the Anasazi towns of the Río Grande. Spanish abuses inflamed the Sonoras and, in 1541, they destroyed Corazones, leaving Coronado without a supply base for the Cíbola expedition. Coronado scored military victories over the Río Grande Pueblos, but at enormous human cost, and he returned to Mexico City basically empty-handed.[27]

Following Coronado's ambivalent conquest and the costly Mixtón War, the imperial frontier advanced slowly. The first silver strikes in Zacatecas (c. 1546) opened Nueva Vizcaya to Spanish settlement. *Reales de minas* (mining centers) at Topia, Nombre de Dios, Sombrerete, Fresnillo, Nieves, Aviño, Chalchihuites, and San Martín gave rise to cattle and grain estates in Zacatecas, Durango, and Chihuahua. The lure of wealth and the demand for laborers brought Spaniards, Indian and black slaves, and free workers (*naborías*) to the *reales*, and inspired new explorations. In 1564, Francisco de Ibarra, the first governor of Nueva Vizcaya, led an expedition westward over the sierra from Guadiana (Durango) to San Miguel de Culiacán. His party explored parts of the Cáhita and *serrano* country and were probably the first Spaniards to see Casas Grandes, then in ruins. Although Ibarra distributed some private *encomiendas*, he failed to create any lasting Spanish towns in Sonora, nor did he reach the coveted riches of Cíbola.[28]

The history of sixteenth-century expeditions in Sonora conditioned the future course of colonization in the area. The western corridor confirmed that the highland provinces of the Sierra Madre Occidental participated in trade networks which marked the furthest extension of Mesoamerican influence. These lines of communication largely determined not only the routes Spanish explorers would follow, but the goals they pursued. Niza and Coronado, believing the exaggerated tales of wealthy cities far to the north, sought "another Mexico," an urban population whose productive capacities could be exploited via tribute and *encomienda*. And therein lay their failure: the Spaniards established no permanent settlements north of Culiacán, nor could they impose the systematic collection of tribute.

Colonization: Missions, Mines, and Presidios

Spanish dominion over Sinaloa and Sonora awaited a new set of institutions and strategies, symbolized by the celebrated formula of the cross and sword. Military force clearly remained an important part of conquest, but not in isolated expeditions. Imperial policies applied the hard lessons of the Chichimec and Mixtón wars to the northwestern provinces, placing permanent garrisons in strategic places along the major routes of communication. The advance of the mining frontier in Nueva Vizcaya, with a growing civilian population in *reales* like Indé, Santa Bárbara (1567), San Bartolomé (1570), and San Juan del Río (1575), and in towns like San Miguel de Culiacán and San Sebastián de Chametla, made it both plausible and imperative that Spanish forces dominate the Cáhita and *serrano* villagers of Sinaloa and Sonora. Presidios were established along the western flank of the Sierra Madre at San Felipe y Santiago de Sinaloa (1585) and El Fuerte de Montesclaros (1610); at the close of the seventeenth century, Santa Rosa de Corodéguachi de Fronteras (1692) became a fixed garrison for the itinerant militias of northern Sonora in the heart of the Opatería.[29]

In order to subdue the *serrano* peoples, the Crown agreed to finance an ambitious missionary project built on the native community itself.

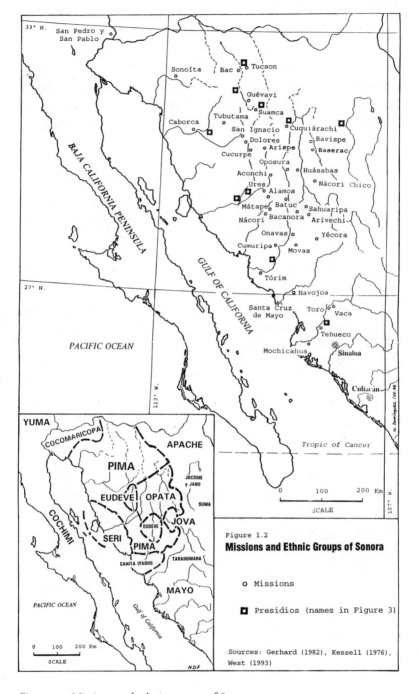

Figure 1.2. Missions and ethnic groups of Sonora

The religious mission had figured prominently in the Spanish domination of the native peoples of Mexico since the conquest of Tenochtitlán, and the Christianization of the Indians became the centerpiece of *patronato real*, a pact between church and state whereby the Crown underwrote the missionary enterprise in the Americas in return for increased royal authority over the ecclesiastical hierarchy.[30] Religious orders—most notably the Franciscans, Dominicans, and Jesuits—surpassed the secular clergy in their outreach to Indian communities in the Mesoamerican heartland and in the outlying provinces. Among the seminomadic peoples of northern New Spain, the missions were to achieve religious evangelization and a new political order, goals which required an agrarian economic base and often the physical relocation of the Indians.

The Crown's interest in establishing new missions quickened as the mining frontier advanced northward. The governor of Nueva Vizcaya, Rodrigo del Río de Loza, appealed to the Society of Jesus to create a new mission field in the western valleys of the Sierra Madre Occidental. In 1591, the Jesuits began their program of *reducciones*, working northward from the Colegio de San Felipe y Santiago de Sinaloa. The Jesuit enterprise unfolded slowly as small groups of missionaries, at times with military escort, at times alone, moved into established communities. In these initial *entradas* the Black Robes baptized and preached the Christian doctrine, often through interpreters.

During the third and fourth decades of the seventeenth century, Jesuit *reducciones* advanced into the middle Yaqui and Sonora drainages; and, by midcentury, they had placed missionaries in the Oposura and Bavispe valleys. From the 1650s to the 1680s, the Jesuits consolidated their gains, bringing outlying *rancherías* into established pueblos of Pima, Opata, Eudeve, and Joba speakers. Then, beginning in 1687, the Crown financed new *entradas* into the Pimería Alta, where further *reducciones* brought the northern O'odham into the riverine villages of the Magdalena, Altar, and Asunción valleys.[31]

The missionaries met both guarded opposition and reluctant acquiescence as they sought to bring the inhabitants of scattered *rancherías* into compact pueblos. Notwithstanding an undercurrent of resistance, the Jesuits' relative success among the peoples of Sonora contrasted with the marked rebelliousness of the Acaxée, Tepehuán, and Tarahumara nations on the eastern flank of the sierra. The missionary project appeared benevolent to highland nations, embroiled in chronic warfare, who recalled earlier, violent encounters with slaving expeditions. Moreover, the missions offered material benefits and new deities in this time of crisis. The traumatic sequel of dislocation, epidemic disease, and forced labor that followed the conquest created a climate of fear which could have made Indians reject the missions or, conversely, accept the *reducciones* as a means of rebuilding their communities. It appears that most *serrano* peoples chose to accept the mission system — owing, in part, to the fact that the Jesuits' advance through Sinaloa and Sonora until midcentury was relatively unencumbered by the demands of civilian colonists. Conversely, in Durango, Topia, and Chihuahua, numerous mining and ranching operations undermined the missionaries' efforts to consolidate native communities.[32]

Civil colonization advanced more slowly on the northwestern flank of the sierra. Following the discovery of rich silver lodes in San José del Parral (Chihuahua) in 1631, prospectors explored westward to try their luck in the highland valleys of Sonora. In that same decade Pedro de Perea, commander of the Presidio de Sinaloa, brought colonists and soldiers from Sinaloa, Chihuahua, and New Mexico to develop mining and ranching in the Sonora and San Miguel valleys. Boasting the title of "Justicia Mayor y Capitán a Guerra de Nueva Andalucía," Perea established his headquarters near the Eudeve village of Tuape. His incursions into the *serrano* communities to bring captive laborers to his ranch and to nearby silver strikes met with stiff resistance; after his death in 1645, the Jesuits began evangelization in the Opata villages of the upper Sonora and Bavispe valleys.[33]

Nueva Andalucía proved to be illusory, but Perea's colony brought Sonora into the mining economy of northern New Spain. *Reales de minas* were established at Nacatóbari (1647), Santiago de los Reyes (1648), and San Pedro de los Reyes (1649). Santiago became the first *alcaldía mayor* of Sonora, although the title passed to the Real de San Juan Bautista in 1657, which became one of the province's foremost silver mines and a center of Spanish settlement. A decade later, mining had expanded to Nacozari, San Miguel Arcángel, and Bacanuche. During the last quarter of the seventeenth century, colonists flocked to several important silver strikes at San Ildefonso de Ostimuri (1673) and Tacupeto (1675) in Pimería Baja.

Ostimuri became the seat of a second *alcaldía mayor*, whose jurisdiction included all the highland territory between the Mayo and Yaqui rivers. Farther south, the Real de los Frailes de los Alamos (1683, Sinaloa) drew on the Cáhita pueblos for laborers and supplies as well as on substantial numbers of immigrant *naborías*, mulatto slaves, and free workers. Continuous silver production at the mines of Promontorios, Quintera, Zambona, and Minas Nuevas maintained processing plants at La Aduana and made Alamos a principal administrative and ecclesiastical center of northwestern Mexico.

The colonial population of Sonora grew steadily with the expansion of mining and stockraising. In 1649, the *alcalde* of Santiago de los Reyes mustered 45 militiamen from the surrounding *reales* and ranches; by 1684, their number had grown to 186, distributed in six localities north of Ostimuri and Alamos.[34] Cart roads and trails linked these nascent colonies to Spanish towns in Nueva Vizcaya and Nueva Galicia. Mule trains hauled silver *planchas* (slabs or plates) and lead ore from Sonora and Ostimuri to Parral, Cusihuiriáchic, and Santa Eulalia in Chihuahua, and brought merchandise to the western mines. From Alamos, communication led south through El Fuerte, Sinaloa, and Culiacán to Guadalajara. Merchants based in Parral supplied credit, in the form of goods, to Sonoran mineowners. They brought tools, luxury goods, craftware and, most important, cloth produced in the *obrajes* of central New Spain. Course woolen sackcloth (*sayal*) and flannel (*bayeta*) became the common form of payment to Indian workers. A Spanish official observed: "Cloth is the money which circulates among the Indians."[35]

The Real de San Juan Bautista had declined considerably in production and population by the early eighteenth century when Motepore (1700) and Aguaje (1717), in Sonora, and Río Chico (1690) and Baroyeca (1701), in Ostimuri, rose to prominence. As centers of mining and commercial exchange, these *reales* attracted growing numbers of colonists from established settlements in Sonora and from outside the province. During the second half of the eighteenth century, gold placer mining became more important than silver extraction in Sonora. Numerous bonanzas large and small attracted growing numbers of merchants, shopkeepers, miners, prospectors, and *gambusinos*—free laborers who panned the arroyo beds and combed mine tailings. Principal *reales* of this period included Aigamé, San Antonio de la Huerta, Trinidad,

Motepori, Saracachi, and San Ildefonso de la Cieneguilla. Of these, San Antonio de la Huerta (1759), located near the Pima villages of Soyopa and Tónichi on the middle Yaqui drainage, became a central commercial nexus between Sonora and Chihuahua, serving missions and mines alike. Cieneguilla, where gold deposits were first discovered in 1770, led to numerous bonanzas in the Altar Desert of northwestern Sonora. The exploitation of San Francisco de Asís, San Perfecto, Quitovac, El Zoni, La Basura, and other sites in O'odham territory continued well into the nineteenth century.[36]

Investments by Spanish mining and mercantile interests in Sonora and Ostimuri were scattered and inconsistent. Prospectors and entrepreneurs moved from bonanza to bonanza without sustaining long-term operations. Extraction and ore-reduction processes were primitive in comparison with the large *reales* of Nueva Vizcaya and central Mexico. Miners relied on shallow open-pit diggings and short, vertical shafts along vein outcrops. Only in large *reales* like San Juan Bautista, San Miguel Arcángel, and Alamos did mineowners dig deep shafts and reinforce horizontal drifts with wooden beams. In order to control flooding — a problem common to all colonial mining — they relied on intensive use of Indian labor rather than installing water lifts (*malacates*) and drainage adits. Likewise, silver refining depended more on smelting in adobe or stone furnaces using lead reagents than on mercury amalgamation. Kilns for making charcoal abounded on the Sonoran hillsides in order to supply fuel for these *hornos castellanos*. Despite such primitive technology, during the period 1670–88, Sonoran output accounted for as much as a third of the silver mined in all of Nueva Vizcaya.[37]

Notwithstanding high short-term production levels, the *reales* of Sonora and Ostimuri rarely achieved longevity. The unsettled character of mining was owing both to fickle investments and an uncertain labor force. Typical of the early stages of conquest were Pedro de Perea's slaving forays into *serrano* communities, but these met with questionable success. Black slaves were brought initially to the *reales* of Pachuca, Zacatecas, and Durango in substantial numbers, but Parral and the Sonoran mines depended principally on Indian labor.[38] *Repartimiento* (paid but forced labor) drafted mineworkers from native villages, and these workers were sent to Spanish estates and mines for stipulated periods of time. From the mid-seventeenth to the early eighteenth century, the burden of *repartimiento* (labor drafts) fell on Opata and Pima Bajo mission pueblos. Spanish *alcaldes* demanded a quota of Indian *tapisques* (recruited workers) from the native governors of villages near mining zones. For example: Onavas supplied workers to Río Chico; Guásabas and Oputo to Nacozari; Arizpe, Chinapa, and Bacoachi to San Juan Bautista and Basochuca; Cucurpe, Tuape, and Opodepe to Bacanuche and Reyes. Missionaries and native governors complained of frequent abuses: employers failed to pay even the minimum statutory wage of two reales a day, demanded *tapisques* in numbers exceeding the legal quota, and took them to mines distant from their home villages.[39]

Repartimiento continued in use in the Northwest longer than in central New Spain. However, by the second half of the eighteenth century, relatively free employment of *naborías* had replaced the forced recruitment of *tapisques* in Sonora, owing principally to the greater number of workers—both Indian and non-Indian—who sought paid labor and residence in the *reales de minas* and haciendas. An important incentive for attracting voluntary laborers to the mines was the *partido*, an amount of ore above the required day's work which the workers could sell on their own account. The *partido* represented a source of income greater than the wage, and it linked Indian workers with local markets developing around the exchange of silver nuggets and maize for merchandise. Even *tapisques* claimed rights to the *partido*, a practice which may have hastened the transition from *repartimiento* to free wage labor.[40]

During the century following the first silver strikes in Santiago de los Reyes, Bacanuche, and San Juan Bautista, Spanish colonization redrew the ecological map of Sonora. Jesuit missions and mining *reales* transformed the economic and social relations which had defined the internal structures of *serrano* communities and their links to external polities. Their natural environment was degraded through deforestation as the excavation and smelting of mineral ores consumed timber for construction and fuel. The felling of woodlands and overgrazing of pastures altered rainfall patterns and stream flow in the Sonoran highlands, affecting native horticulture and foraging.

New trade routes connecting Sonora with Chihuahua and Nueva Galicia increased the movement of people, livestock, and goods, and created avenues of contagion for diseases that decimated the indigenous population of central New Spain. Malaria, typhoid, typhus, dysentery, measles, and smallpox followed the sixteenth-century conquest expeditions up the subtropical coasts of Chametla, Culiacán, and Sinaloa; similar maladies penetrated Ostimuri and Sonora from these southern provinces and from Nueva Vizcaya. Epidemics befell Cáhita, Nebome, and Eudeve villages during the second and third decades of the seventeenth century, within only a few years of the Jesuit *entradas* into their territory. Northern *serrano* pueblos suffered "malicious fevers" and smallpox at midcentury (1645–53), a period when Opatas were clustered into missions and exposed to Spanish colonists in the mining *reales*.[41] These repeated disease episodes disrupted food production and distribution and shattered the internal organization of native communities. As numerous *aldeas* fell below the population levels needed to maintain the ceremonial and civic functions of corporate village life, *serrano* peoples scattered into small *rancherías*. Furthermore, the bacterial conquest which followed the path of Spanish *entradas* sorely tested their religious beliefs. Jesuits reported that the fear of disease caused Sonoras alternatively to flee the missions and to turn to them for help in times of crisis.

Jesuit *reducciones* altered indigenous settlement patterns by consolidating *rancherías* into larger pueblos and, in some cases, by moving whole villages to new sites along the floodplain. The mission system had demographic, economic, and political repercussions for *serrano* communities, evident in the spread of disease, in the distribution of farming plots to individual households, and in leadership ties among different kin and ethnic groups. Civil colonization had an equally lasting impact on highland peoples. The *reales de minas* imposed new forms of coerced labor through the *repartimiento* at the same time that they greatly expanded market relations of production and exchange for free labor and the circulation of native as well as European commodities. Mission districts became key points for local commercial networks: Oposura and Cumpas supplied foodstuffs to Tepache and Nacozari; Ures became a central point for travelers moving through the province; Batuc and Mátape traded with merchants and miners established in San Xavier, Soyopa, and San Antonio de la Huerta.

These combined pressures—disease, dislocation, forced labor, and commercialization of food surpluses—brought a crisis in the colonial order throughout northwestern New Spain during the final decades of the seventeenth century. Spanish settlement had increased appreciably both in Chihuahua, following major silver strikes at Coyachic and Cusi-huiriáchic, and in the mining districts of Alamos, Ostimuri, and Sonora. Repeated abuses of Indian labor—from New Mexico to Durango—and Spanish encroachments on native land led to widespread rebellion. The Pueblo Revolt of 1680 forced colonists to flee New Mexico, retreating south to El Paso del Norte. Although the Río Grande Pueblos were again subjugated in the 1690s, these same years witnessed the combined re-volts of the Conchos and Tarahumaras of northwestern Chihuahua. West of the Sierra Madre the Opatas began to mobilize, aggrieved by miners' slaving expeditions, and northern Pimas who had recently been brought to mission life rose in arms. Sedentary peoples rebelled against Span-ish dominion even as Apache raiding in the sierra presented a serious problem to colonial settlers and presidial commanders.[42] These separate movements were quelled, but taken together they made it clear that the conquest of the northern frontier was contingent upon a negotiated peace with different Indian groups.

Crown, Church, and Colonial Society in Eighteenth-Century Sonora

The northwestern provinces developed in accord with local economic and cultural conditions, but under the shadow of shifts in the balance of power in Europe. After the costly War of the Spanish Succession (1700–13) the Bourbons made good their claim to the Spanish throne and hastened the bureaucratic and military centralization of the Iberian monarchical state. Ever in need of money and wary of rival expansion-ist monarchies in France and England, the Bourbon dynasty pressed its American colonies for fresh sources of bullion and mercantile wealth. Bourbon physiocratic zeal institutionalized the presence of the secular state. Imperial reformers sought nothing less than to close the northern frontier of New Spain by curtailing the independent power of the reli-gious orders and consolidating Spain's military presence in the ancient Chichimeca. Their policies rested on the increased strength and com-plexity of civilian colonization at the same time that they created new pressures on the ethnic polities of Sonora. The Bourbon reforms pro-moted mining and commercial agriculture to satisfy the Crown's con-cern for greater revenues; initiated the secularization of the missions;

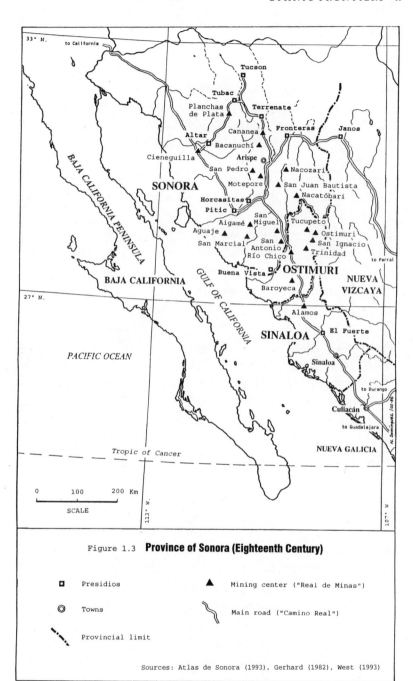

Figure 1.3 **Province of Sonora (Eighteenth Century)**

□ Presidios   ▲ Mining center ("Real de Minas")

◎ Towns   Main road ("Camino Real")

  Provincial limit

Sources: Atlas de Sonora (1993), Gerhard (1982), West (1993)

Figure 1.3. Province of Sonora (eighteenth century)

accelerated the privatization of land, instituting a schedule of fees and payments for land title; relocated numerous Indian pueblos; and established a new line of military defense by shifting military garrisons to new sites and creating additional presidios.

In 1732, the coastal provinces of Sonora, Ostimuri, Sinaloa, Chametla, and Rosario were unified in the Gobierno de Sonora y Sinaloa. The new governorship integrated separate *alcaldías mayores* and their numerous *tenientes de justicia* into a superior secular authority, rivaling the Jesuits' tiered hierarchies that grouped the missions into *partidos* and *rectorados*. This administrative entity, independent of the Reino de Nueva Vizcaya, created a governing body distinct from the missionaries' rule. The governor's civil and military power impinged on the pueblos, especially when requisitioning laborers, auxiliary warriors, and food supplies; yet *serrano* peoples learned to appeal alternatively to religious and secular authorities in order to modify the rigors of mission life or protest certain policies.[43]

One of the most dramatic episodes of this mounting rivalry between secular and religious authorities erupted in 1767, with the expulsion of the Society of Jesus from all Spanish dominions. The sudden departure of the Jesuits radically affected the economic and political life of the Sonoran missions, although *serrano* peoples outlived the Jesuits' departure and re-created the outlines of community under Franciscan tutelage. Conversely, the creation of the Bishopric of Sonora, in 1779, reflected both royal patronage of the secular clergy and the slow maturation of civilian colonization in the province.[44]

In 1750, the royal visitor José Rafael Rodríguez Gallardo defined four main problems and proposed solutions which guided subsequent Bourbon policies in Sonora: population and settlement, commerce, communication, and Indian wars. Rodríguez Gallardo looked askance at the scattered, thinly populated Indian villages—decimated by disease and labor drafts, menaced by the Apaches—and criticized as well the unstable quality of Sonoran mining camps. However, the royal visitor's energetic measures to consolidate dispersed native communities and establish new settlements of *vecinos* had poor results; and his project to import colonies of several hundred artisans never materialized. Seris and Pimas who were settled in the mission of Nuestra Señora del Pópulo rebelled when forced to relinquish their land to the Presidio de San Miguel de Horcasitas, and the removal of Pimas and Opatas from Teuricachi and Mututicachi left northeastern Sonora unshielded from raiding Apaches.[45]

Rodríguez Gallardo observed that regional commerce depended on overland mule trains and suffered from a chronic scarcity of currency. Local systems of barter, whereby merchants bought up surplus grains and supplied imported goods on credit, had a "usurious" effect on the economy. Missions and hacendados alike sold their foodstuffs at reduced prices and paid dearly for merchandise.[46] By the same token, schedules for prices, weights, and measures varied widely from one place to another, creating confusion and inviting abuse. Indian *tapisques* and free laborers were subject to low wages, depreciated even further by the fact that they were paid in goods rather than in silver. Rodríguez Gallardo's recommendations concerning maritime commerce were never implemented; however, the limited liberalization of trade and the establishment of merchant guilds in Veracruz and Guadalajara in 1795, independent of the Consulado de México, legitimated some of the contraband trade which circulated in the Northwest. Over time this north–south orientation between Sonora and Guadalajara acquired greater importance than earlier ties to Parral, and older routes leading across the sierra to Chihuahua declined in use.[47]

Reformist measures proceeded apace during the last third of the eighteenth century. José Bernardo de Gálvez Gallardo, an ambitious bureaucrat in the court of Charles III who would later boast the title of Marqués de Sonora and preside over imperial policy as Minister of the Indies, oversaw the expansion of the colonial state in this frontier area. Appointed visitor-general of New Spain in 1765, with instructions to institute fiscal reforms in the viceroyalty, Gálvez expanded his mandate to include a broad range of military, judicial, and economic policies. He supervised the expulsion of the Jesuits and ordered the violent suppression of popular protests in Guanajuato, San Luis Potosí, and San Luis de la Paz. In Sonora, the exodus of the Black Robes coincided with the arrival of a military expedition led by Domingo Elizondo to subjugate rebellious Pimas and Seris. Gálvez's decree issued from Alamos in 1769 laid the foundation for successive ordinances and instructions concerning land tenure. It defined the standards for measuring, evaluating, and taxing different categories of land according to their use and proximity to Spanish towns and native communities. Gálvez's reforms set an indelible pattern for the future development of the province, intended to increase royal revenues, raise productivity, promote commerce, and exploit the province's mineral resources. To meet these ends, Gálvez established the legal structure which privileged private property over common holdings, opened Indian villages to greater numbers of vecinos, and furthered the separation of Indians from their communities by conferring on them a theoretical equality with the gente de razón as tribute-paying subjects of the king.[48]

These interrelated problems of settlement, production, and commerce were aggravated by a climate of fear generated by the Apache wars. Bourbon policies failed to distinguish between nomadism and "hostility" on the Sonoran frontier and, in most cases, eschewed negotiation for outright suppression of native movements. The pressure of constant warfare waged against this "internal enemy" motivated the Crown to extend the presidial system farther north, founding San Carlos de Buenavista (1742), San Pedro de la Conquista de Pitic (1741), San Felipe de Terrenate (1742), Santa Gertrudis del Altar (1752), and San Ignacio de Tubac (1753). Rodríguez Gallardo ordered the garrison at Pitic moved upstream to San Miguel de Horcasitas in 1749. A quarter of a century later, presidial companies were relocated from Terrenate to the abandoned mission of Suamca (renamed Santa Cruz) and from Tubac to San Agustín de Tucson (1775). Instrumental to these changes were the military inspection of northern New Spain carried out by the Marqués de Rubí (1766–68) and the new regulations issued in 1772.[49]

The Comandancia General de las Provincias Internas, established in 1776, institutionalized the paramount authority of the military across northern New Spain, although nine years later these provinces were again placed under the jurisdiction of the viceroy. A related innovation created the large administrative districts called intendencias, first tried experimentally in Sonora, then applied to all the viceroyalty. The intendants were, in effect, provincial governors named directly by the Court in Madrid. They held wide fiscal and judicial powers and delegated local administration to subdelegados and tenientes de justicia.[50] The Crown intended to centralize political control over the northern provinces through the commandant-general and the intendants, establishing lines of authority emanating from the metropole. In practice, however, the imperial presence on the frontier was mediated through local foci of power. Spanish and *criollo* merchant-landowners used colonial credit systems to their advantage and gained control of presidial captaincies, civil magistracies, and key positions in the intendancy system. Moreover, internal defense depended on the soldier-settlers who manned the presidial garrisons and on Indian warriors who led punitive expeditions against the Apaches.

Independence: From Colony to Republic

The separation of Mexico from the colonial metropolis occurred not so much as a definitive break, but rather as an ongoing process of sociopolitical change in Sonora. Notwithstanding the minimal participation of Sonoran *criollos* and peasants in the independence movement, the crumbling of Spain's empire in America during the turbulent years of 1808–21 had a telling effect in the province. Franciscan missionaries laboring in the Pimería Alta, as in Texas and Alta California, suffered severe interruptions in the delivery of supplies for which they had relied on overland mule trains. Similarly, the presidios and *reales de minas* of Sonora had to make do with irregular shipments of goods coming through Pacific ports and by mule train at inflated prices. The distribution of mercury, essential for processing silver ore, became uncertain during these years. Most important, the wars of independence threatened the (always precarious) defense of the nomadic frontier. As presidial troops were sent south to combat the insurgency, Apaches increased their attacks on Sonoran settlements and roads. Furthermore, the erratic supply of trade goods jeopardized the peace encampments which had induced some bands of Apaches to settle in the environs of presidios like Janos in Chihuahua, and Fronteras, Bacoachi, and Tubac in Sonora.[51]

With the consummation of Mexican independence, Sonora's landed families moved quickly to forge new political institutions favoring the expansion of private property. Legislation promulgated by the state governments of Occidente (1824–30) and Sonora (1831–35) reduced communal property to its minimum expression and called for the distribution of village lands into individual plots. By the second quarter of the century, an active land market developed in Sonora, parallel with the expanding commercial orbits of urban centers like Hermosillo (Pitic) and Guaymas and of inland towns like Ures, Moctezuma (Oposura), and Altar. Nevertheless, some colonial institutions, most notably the mission, lingered until the 1840s, and native communities defended their land well into the nineteenth century.[52]

Mexican independence led to substantive changes in the internal and external relations that linked highland ethnic communities to the newly formed political structures of Sonora. Property rights, production, and village governance became openly contentious issues whose outcome affected not only the material life of the pueblos, but their cultural integrity as *naciones* within the Mexican Republic. The Sonoras defended their polities on several fronts, but the baseline of their strategies for cultural survival was economic subsistence. The following two chapters show the ways in which indigenous and Spanish economies merged and collided in colonial Sonora, revealing the divergent meanings of subsistence, work, and productivity held by Indians and colonists on the northwestern frontier.

2

Amerindian Economy in Sonora

In peasant life . . . family and enterprise are nearly synonymous.

V. Mukhin, [1881] 1987 [1]

In Sonoran native economies the household constituted the basic unit of production and distribution of goods. Consumption, rather than the accumulation of property or the maximization of rent, was the primary goal of indigenous labor. *Serrano* horticulturalists and desert gatherers sought to balance the toil exerted with the benefits of labor that accrued to each domestic unit. Native coercive structures for exacting levels of production beyond the needs of subsistence remained weak in a natural environment of contrasting microclimates and uncertain agricultural yields.[2] Within the area circumscribed by the Sonoran Desert and the escarpment of the Sierra Madre Occidental, Amerind villagers and nomads exchanged foodstuffs, fiber, salt, cloth, hides, shells, turquoise, pearls, and other ceremonial materials among their home communities and between the highlands and coastal plains. Patterns of production and exchange retained this regional character under colonial rule, even in the face of increasing demands for surplus labor and goods.[3] Sonoran highlanders possessed the physical and technological capability for producing agricultural surpluses; after the conquest, some highland communities sought an outlet for this productive energy through the missions and the marketing network that developed around the mining centers and presidios. Opatas from the Oposura Valley, for example, bartered as much as 2,000 fanegas of maize each year with Spanish miners and merchants in exchange for cloth.[4] Nevertheless, subsistence remained their overriding concern, and the colonial sphere increased the tension between subsistence and surplus, toil and reward, which underlay the *serrano* peoples' economy.

This chapter and the following one relate the ecological and cultural dimensions of indigenous subsistence to the problems of survival created by colonial demands on native Sonorans' productive energy. They explore the economic and social ramifications of the problem of *surplus*, meaning the supply of foodstuffs and all essential materials for shelter, clothing, tools, weapons, and the like gathered and stored beyond immediate use. Spanish notions of surplus production as a given quantity of goods and services separable from a baseline of subsistence needs, liable to taxation in one form or another and available for market transactions, contradicted the *serrano* peoples' holistic understanding of livelihood as the combined labor expended to ensure their material existence and satisfy the social and ceremonial needs of community life.

Three Systems of Cultivation

The river creates the *milpas* and destroys them. All we do is plant in them.

Mazocahui peasant, interviewed January 28, 1990

Prior to the coming of the Spaniards, highland and desert dwellers had developed a variety of techniques for growing cultigens in open fields and small garden plots. Experienced horticulturalists, their knowledge of plant selection, soil conservation, and water management enabled them to survive in this semiarid environment. Native agricultural practices established three distinct patterns, each adapted to different ecological zones. The Tohono O'odham planted ephemeral crops at the mouths of arroyos during the summer rainstorms and created 'ak-ciñ fields by diverting water from a number of washes to alluvial flatlands in the desert. Mountainous Pima, such as the Nebome Alto of Onavas, Nuri, Movas, and Yecora, developed swidden agriculture dependent on seasonal rains. Their habitat over a thousand meters above sea level supplied sufficient summer rains for planting on natural terraces, despite the narrow soil deposits along the mountain streams which limited possibilities for irrigation. Floodplain farming, using diversion weirs, living fencerows, and irrigation canals, characterized the Opata and Eudeve territories in the heart of the Sonoran province. Indigenous agricultural techniques in this area, which maximized the flow of water from the arroyos and main river channels to alluvial soils, established the productive base for a durable village economy.

O'odham subsistence based on 'ak-ciñ agriculture maintained a close link between cultivation and gathering, and most of their cultigens were genetically related to wild plants. It has been estimated that the Tohono O'odham obtained only about one-fifth of their total food supply through cultivation. Their livelihood rested mainly on hunting and gathering, supplemented by foodstuffs acquired from the riverine Pima and Yuma in exchange for labor. These nomads found the desert bountiful with the fruit of the saguaro and pitahaya, nopal, cholla buds, mesquite pods, sand roots, tubers, wild greens, and seeds from the ironwood and paloverde trees. Tepary beans and cucurbits illustrate well the blurred lines between farming and gathering in O'odham culture. The "bean-eating" Pápago consumed both the small, gray wild teparies and the slightly larger, white domesticated variety. The O'odham planted pumpkins and squashes as food crops, yet they valued the inedible "coyote gourd"—so bitter to the taste—for its medicinal properties, and they used the scooped-out rinds of wild gourds as containers, cups, and bowls. Tobacco and uña de gato are two more useful plants known to them in both wild and cultivated form.[5]

The desert environment gave rise to different combinations of foraging and planting. The Hiach-ed O'odham, who lived almost entirely by gathering wild foods, had cultivated maize, beans, and squashes on a small scale at Suvuk, southeast of the Tinajas de Pinacate. (Tinajas are natural rock reservoirs filled with water seepage from springs in the hillsides; they are an important source of water for gatherers and part-time cultivators.) The Tohono O'odham irrigated their fields at San Marcelo de Sonoita, a site favored by an arroyo of permanently running water fed by nearby springs. From the late seventeenth through the nineteenth century the O'odham farmed small plots at Quitobac and A'al Waipia—veritable oases formed by fissure springs, although only in Sonoita did the Jesuits attempt to found a permanent mission village.[6]

The seminomadic culture of the Tohono O'odham rested on seasonal movement between two kinds of encampments: the wells (wahia) and the fields (oidag). They hunted and gathered wild foods at wells near permanent sources of water in the foothills during the winter months, then cleared and sowed the fields in the desert flatlands during the brief, intense rainy season following the summer solstice. Their 'ak-ciñ plantings comprised small family plots at the mouths of desert washes. O'odham lands belonged to the tribe; they did not set aside community fields, but families did work the land under reciprocal arrangements. They organized their households and villages under the headship of a patriarchal chief, whose authority extended to overseeing the maintenance of irrigation ditches, the distribution of familial grounds for both gathering and farming, and the conduct of warfare against alien tribes, particularly during the Apache wars of the nineteenth century.[7]

Highland Pimas maintained a similar balance between farming and gathering, although cultigens provided a larger part of their yearly subsistence than they did for the desert O'odham. The agricultural cycle documented for Onavas and surrounding villages combined temporal plantings dependent on rainfall with floodplain farming and garden plots irrigated by hand at the edge of alluvial fields. Soil quality and the width of alluvial deposits varied along the middle course of the Yaqui River. The mission regime introduced the Pimas to the use of oxen and wooden plows, permitting them to expand cultivation into meadows they cleared with metal axes. Yet, these European innovations did not radically alter the indigenous agricultural rhythms of planting and harvesting tied to permanent sources of water. From year to year, following the torrential summer rains, milpas were lost to flooding and shifts in the river's course. The unpredictable supply of alluvial soils from year to year, combined with erratic rainfall, exacerbated the scarcity of arable land.[8]

Pima planting techniques followed the contours of the land. Men cleared their fields of brush and trees with stone axes and, after Spanish contact, with metal implements when they could obtain them. They left the cut vegetation to dry for a season, then set fire to it, and pried out the roots with long stakes fashioned from hardwood. Men, women, and children piled the roots together with any debris left from the first fire. After the roots had dried out for several weeks, they burned these piles in the fields. This rhythm of slash-and-burn cultivation with two firings, requiring at least a full season to prepare the fields for planting, meant that the Pima rotated individual plots and left them to lie fallow.[9] In those portions of the streambed with a poor gradient for channeling river water to the milpas, they dug shallow wells on the margins of the floodplain, similar to the batequis which many serrano villagers scooped out of sandy arroyo beds to find drinking water.[10]

Pima, Opata, and Eudeve agriculturalists who had settled in the San Miguel, Sonora, Oposura, Bavispe, and middle Yaqui valleys carried water to their milpas from different sources. They used diversion weirs to capture rainfall runoff for terrace cultivation and for crops planted in the arroyo beds. During the dry season and in periods of drought, they watered their fields from scattered, permanent springs that flowed from the riverbed. Their economy was rooted in floodplain farming, for which they adapted a simple technology requiring seasonal cooperative labor to harness the downstream current of the river. Communal work parties dug earthen canals to lead water to the milpas they had cleared in the floodplain. In order to raise the water level sufficiently for gravity flow, the Indians built diagonal weirs across the watercourse by driving stakes into the riverbed and weaving branches between the poles, then reinforcing these barriers with mounds of packed earth.

Floodplain farmers improved their fields, drawing on the silt deposited by the swollen river during the summer rains. Just at the edge of the river channel they build living fencerows of cottonwood and willow saplings intertwined with branches and acacia brush, creating a permeable barrier similar to the weirs placed in the stream. The fencerows served to slow the rush of floodwaters and spread fertile alluvium across the milpas. Repeated annual flooding, often requiring the repair of weirs and fences, left accumulated layers of arable soil. Exceptionally heavy floods, however, destroyed the Indians' system of weirs and canals and tore out established milpas. Native cultivators adapted to alternate cycles of degradation and replenishment of floodplain soils by planting serial rows of living fences, placed at angles to one another along the shifting contours of the main channel. Aboriginal farmers drew their livelihood from the river and—like their mestizo descendants to the present day—perceived their technology as dependent on the contrasts of flood and drought that marked the seasonal rhythm of village life.[11]

Highland villagers accustomed to both temporal and floodplain farm-

ing, once exposed to mission life, adapted a rudimentary plow for turning the soil in their cleared *milpas*. They fashioned a rustic, wooden-
tipped device pulled by oxen to make the furrows, plowing the soil only
once for each planting. Native Sonorans rarely fertilized their fields: animal dung was hard to collect since cattle were not kept in stables but
were left to graze freely on open grasslands and desert scrub. In some
areas, the mountain Pima used bat dung to enrich the soil. Crusty German Jesuits like Juan Nentvig, Joseph Och, and Ignaz Pfefferkorn mar-
veled at the fertility of the land in Sonora, considering what they viewed
to be minimal labor in the fields: "Even though it is so poorly cared for,
the soil returns 100 fanegas for each fanega planted of maize; and 30 or
40 fanegas to one of wheat. A good harvest depends only on bringing
sufficient humidity to the soil." [12]

Native Sonorans sowed their fields by hand and tended their crops
with traditional implements: the digging stick (in Pima, *cupiara*) and the
hoe (*quica*, equivalent to the Mesoamerican *coa*). When they worked directly behind the plowmen, they would place the seeds in the furrow
and cover them with their feet. If they seeded the fields a few days after
plowing, then the planters used the digging stick to make the holes in
which to place the seed corn. It was the children's task to scare away
predators with slings and bows and arrows: birds, rodents, and the cun-
ning badger (*tejón* or, in Tegüima, *bapeti*). [13]

Serrano peoples applied these techniques to raise a variety of crops,
drawing upon their own horticultural traditions and adapting new cultigens introduced by the missionaries to their environment. Highland
villagers planted cucurbits, beans, cotton, large squashes (*camote* or, in
Pima, *icobi*), and several varieties of maize. They double-cropped when
winter rains, called *equipatas*, provided enough moisture for sowing in
January. Native garden plots provided food, fiber for weaving, dyes,
medicinal herbs, and ornamental plants. Amaranth, valued for both its
leaves and seeds, chile, tobacco—all native cultigens—grew together
with chickpeas, peas, lima beans, lentils, onions, radishes, parsley, cori-
ander, watermelon, cantaloupe, and sugarcane. Mission orchards produced figs, peaches, apricots, pomegranates, quince, grapes, citrus, and
other fruits of European origin. [14]

Wheat proved to be the most pervasive European field crop, generally planted in the winter and harvested in the late spring. Mission Indians adapted European methods of threshing and winnowing the grain. They placed the harvested wheat in a corral where horses and mules were made to tread on the stalks, trampling the straw and separating the grain from the chaff. Padre Pfefferkorn observed that the animals' "dance," led by Indians brandishing whips, left the straw useless, but enabled them to thresh forty or fifty fanegas of wheat in four or five hours. Pfefferkorn surmised that the Indians had no use for the straw or that, despite its potential utility, they rushed through the job simply in order to finish more quickly. They winnowed piles of grain by throwing it into the air with a kind of pitchfork and then cleaning the fallen wheat of sand and other impurities.[15]

Highland villagers and desert foragers alike processed their food for storage mainly by drying it in the sun. They cut and dried strips of squash called *tasajos de calabazas* and stored gourd squashes and watermelons in the sand for ripening. Native agriculturalists left maize and beans to dry partially on the stalk. They harvested corn either by plucking the dried ears from the plants with a wooden stick (*piscador*) or by pulling the mature plant from the ground and carrying it back to the home village. Native women removed the ears from the plant and spread them on the ground to dry. They piled the stalks into pyramidal shapes and left them to weather in open corrals. These *tasoleras* provided them with thatch for roofing and with fodder for their livestock.[16]

Serrano women ground dried and roasted maize kernels along with seeds gathered from wild plants for a variety of dishes, using aboriginal tools: the *metate* and *mano*. *Pinole*, a basic cornmeal ground from roasted kernels, could be stored for months. It was the preferred food for travelers, hunters, and warriors. They used whole roasted grains (*esquite*) and boiled kernels to make *pozole*, a hearty stew, and *stole*, a thickened pudding. Native women ground boiled maize into a moist dough (*nixtamal*), then fashioned it into tortillas and tamales. The Pima frequently consumed roasted ears of fresh corn (*elote*) in the early stages of the harvest. Their preferred *elote* foods included *chico, elote tatemado, pan de elote, tamales de elote, coricos*, and tortillas; different strains of maize were selected for particular dishes. Sonorans used nearly all parts of the squash and pumpkin plants. The flowers added flavor and nutrition to their soups; squash seeds were roasted, and the gourds were baked or roasted whole. Similarly, different kinds of beans were boiled and eaten whole, combined with *elote* corn, or ground and moistened into a paste.[17]

Usiabagu: A Pima Planting Ceremony

Serrano peoples combined their knowledge of natural resources and cultivation with a repertory of rituals linked to the seasonal cycles of their environment. Native and Catholic traditions merged through the colonial experience, as observed in the fertility rites celebrated at the beginning of the summer rains on June 24, the Fiesta de San Juan. In highland communities built on terraces overlooking alluvial floodplains, all-night drinking and dancing on the eve of the saint's day culminated in a procession carrying his statue to the river. Men and women then bathed in the river to bring on the rains needed for the maize, beans, squashes, and melons planted in this season.

Ritual was an essential part of the indigenous agrarian cycle, accompanying each stage of planting, sprouting, and harvesting of food crops. It helped bring about the natural conditions required for cultivating the earth: the quality of the soil, the seeds selected for planting, and the right combination of sunlight and humidity. A special women's ceremony marked *usiabagu*—the time of planting—in order to ensure sufficient rainfall and make the seeds fertile. The women chosen for each year's rite left the village and spent several days in seclusion. At the appointed time, they returned to the village and danced on a board placed over a large vessel buried in the ground, containing maize, squash, and bean seeds. At the conclusion of their dance, the women ran past a line of men and bathed in the river. When the corn planted in July began to sprout, *tesgüino* (fermented maize) was consumed in copious amounts, while *venado* and *pascola* dancers performed to the music of gourd and cocoon rattles, rasping sticks, and gourd drums.[18]

These farming communities clearly related human sexuality and reproduction with the life-giving fertility of the land. Pre-Hispanic relics recovered by archaeologists include clay figurines of male and female likeness and stone phalluses associated with Sonoran fertility rites.[19] Men and women both participated in the rituals enacted each season, just as they shared the labor of clearing, planting, weeding, and harvesting the milpas. In the O'odham tradition of northwestern Sonora, older men chanted ceremonial songs as they dug holes with a planting stick; the women followed behind, placing the seeds in the ground and covering them. Once the seeds were planted, O'odham farmers "sang up the corn" with different chants for early growth and harvest.[20]

Indigenous villagers conserved their ceremonial practices, albeit in altered form, within the economic and religious structures imposed by mission life. Pimas placed wooden crosses in their milpas and celebrated the onset of the summer rains on prominent feast days in the Catholic calendar, such as the Holy Trinity and the Day of Saint John.[21] Frequent tesqüinadas and borracheras involving ritual drinking, which the missionaries indignantly condemned, were carried out in the relative seclusion of the mountainous scrub forest. Their persistence under the mission regime suggests that native agriculturalists never separated ancient ritual from the ongoing cycle of planting and harvesting. Ceremonialism was intimately connected to the arts of horticulture they had developed over a millennium before the Spanish conquest. Equally important, hunting and food gathering required another set of rites in order to ensure the continued bounty of game and seed plants in the monte.[22]

Foraging, Hunting, and Exchange

Serrano peoples had developed horticultural skills from their accumulated knowledge of seeds and plant germination of the flora of the area. Highland villagers found many species valuable for food, medicine, tools, clothing, soap, and building materials (see Table 2.1). The péchita or mesquite pods ripened in June, the arid month before the summer rains in the agricultural cycle. Temakis, a kind of wild camote, was bitter but edible. Amole, torote prieto, and chayacote provided soap for bathing and washing clothes. Malva leaves were crushed to make shampoo; and Pima women made combs from the thorny fruits of hillside cacti. Sonoran Indians gathered and stored countless root, leaf, bark, and stem herbs which they distinguished for their curative properties and for poisoning arrowheads used against prey and enemy warriors.[23]

Women gathered most of the wild plants but, in the spring, men gathered mescal, the heart of the Agave yaquiana. They roasted it in communal pit ovens and fermented its sweet liquid. Although mescal is best

Table 2.1 Plants and Animals Used by Serrano Peoples

Common Name	Scientific Name
Plants	
Amole	*Agave mayoensis*
Bottle gourd	*Legenaria siceraria*
Buffalo gourd	*Cucurbita foetidissima*
Cholla buds	*Opuntia fulgida*
Cotton	*Gossypium sp.*
Cottonwood	*Populus fremontii*
Coyote gourd	*Cucurbita digitata*
Creosote	*Larrea tridentata*
Devil's claw	*Proboscidea parviflora*
Guegui seeds	*Amaranthus hypochondriacus*
Hecho	*Pachycereus pecten-aboriginum*
Ironwood	*Olneya tesota*
Lechuguilla	*Agave bovicornuta*
Maize	*Zea mays*
Malva (mallow)	*Sida cordifolia*
Mescal	*Agave yaquiana*
Mesquite	*Prosopis velutina*
Nopal	*Opuntia engelmannii*
Palma	*Sabal uresana*
Palmilla	*Nolina matapensis*
Paloverde	*Cercidium praecos*
Pitahaya	*Lemaireocereus thurberi*
Pumpkins	*Cucurbita moschata*
Quelites (pigweed)	*Amaranthus palmeri*
Roots and tubers	*Solanum sp.*
Saguaro	*Carnegia gigantea*
Sotol	*Dasylirion wheeleri*
Squashes	*Cucurbita maxima*
Tepary, cultigen	*Phaseolus acutifolius*
Tepary, wild	*Phaseolus filiformis*
Tobacco	*Nicotiana glauca*
Torote prieto	*Fouquieria macougalii*

Table 2.1 Continued

Common Name	Scientific Name
Tuka	*Amaranthus cruentus*
Willow	*Salix sp.*
Animals	
Berrendo (pronghorn)	*Antilocapra americana*
Deer, mule	*Odocoileus hemionus*
Deer, white-tailed	*Odocoileus virginianus*
Hare	*Lepus californicus*
Opposum	*Didelphis marsupialis*
Porcupine	*Eretheizon dorsatum*
Rabbit	*Sylvilagus audubonii arizonae*
Raccoon	*Procyon lotor*
Squirrel	*Sciurus sp.*

Sources: Campbell W. Pennington, *The Pima Bajo of Central Sonora, Mexico*, vol. 1: *The Material Culture* (Salt Lake City: University of Utah Press, 1980); Flavio Molina Molina, *Diccionario de flora y fauna indígena de Sonora* (Hermosillo: Gobierno del Estado de Sonora, 1989); Gary Nabhan, *Gathering the Desert* (Tucson: University of Arizona Press, 1985).

known today as the raw material for a locally distilled drink—*bacanora*—various species of agave provided *serrano* peoples with food and fiber for weaving. They traded mescal cakes and wove the fibers of the pita agave into cordage. From the *lechuguilla, palma de suelo, sotol,* and *palmilla* the highland Pima prepared fibers of different thicknesses for weaving baskets. Indigenous weavers made watertight vessels used for storage, for winnowing wheat, and even for holding water and for floating provisions across rivers and streams.[24]

Hunting, affirmed Padre Pfefferkorn, constituted the favorite activity of Sonoran men; and wild game was undoubtedly an important source of food for the entire community. In addition, the entire complement of activities associated with hunting—carving wood and stone implements, creating animallike masks, enacting certain rituals and distributing the meat on return to the village—brought together the outward symbols of prestige associated with proven skills in stalking and killing animals and the inner knowledge of spiritualism. Native hunters most frequently sought out rabbit, deer, and antelope. Among the Tohono O'odham only a few well-trained men who bore the title of headbearer could participate in deer hunting. Hunters began their apprenticeship in early childhood, learning the techniques of hunting, the use of special animal disguises, and the songs which lent the chanter magical powers. Headbearers held an honored position in their society, for they controlled the supply of animal skins, sinew, fat, and meat (after supplying the kin group) which was traded throughout the Pimería Alta.[25]

In hunting, as in agriculture, technique and ceremonialism were closely linked in the aboriginal mind. Wi:kita brought together O'odham kinsmen to recite sacred songs, reenact their history in ceremonial dances, cure illness, and ensure an abundance of game for hunting. The desert Pima gathered each year during August in Quitovac (Sonora) and every four years, in November after the harvest, in Gu Achi (Santa Rosa, Arizona) to celebrate wi:kita. Its name comes from wiiki, the soft eagle plumes used to make the praying wand, and indicates the sacred purpose of the festival. Lasting several days, it concerned the hunt, the onset of rains, health and, especially, the communion of families who shared their food. At the heart of the ceremony, male singers recited songs that were both prayers and historical remembrances of the people.[26]

Here I stand,
The wind is coming toward me,
Shaking.
Here I stand,
A cloud is coming toward me,
shaking.

The nawait ceremony confirmed the belief of the Tohono O'odham in the power of sacred chants to create rain-filled clouds. In the intense heat of early summer, women collected the fruit of the saguaro and cooked its juice and pulp, converting them into a sweet syrup. At the conclusion of their work, they carried a part of the syrup to the olas ki:, a round house built of ocotillo branches and desert brush, to be fermented. The singers, dancing around a hearth, entoned their magic poetry with rattles adorned with eagle plumes. The songs fermented the wine (*nawait*) and brought the clouds that would drop their moisture on the parched earth. The O'odham came together on the appointed night to drink the wine, get drunk, and "throw up the clouds" in order to bring rain. Their collective act of drinking, vomiting, and resting followed the rhythm of the songs, affirmed the bonds of community and kinship that united the people, and renewed the annual cycle of rains which nourished their crops and brought desert fruit to maturation.[27]

Ceremonialism, work, and trade were inseparable means of resource procurement, binding individual households into communities. Exchange was an essential part of the Sonoras' economy, and trade took on the apparent simplicity of a gift. The exchange of gifts regulated the Indians' relationship to the environment and strengthened the bonds that held their communities together. Indigenous conventions concerning gift-giving nurtured widely held values of generosity and abundance, defined by their cultural norms of reciprocity. The exchange of gifts played an important role in the redistributive functions of village leaders. Foodstuffs constituted the principal gift item in the trade among kin groups and between tribal areas. For example, the Hiach-ed, who lived mainly by fishing and gathering wild plant foods, journeyed annually to the Yuma and bartered baskets and seashells for maize, teparies, and squashes.[28]

This ethic of reciprocal gift-giving did not necessarily mean the exchange of goods and services of equal value. At times, some trading partners operated under a perceived disadvantage owing to the harshness of their environment or depleted supplies. Reciprocity could embrace different forms of service and even the subordination of one group to another. For instance, the Tohono O'odham traveled long distances to the Gila, San Pedro, and Altar valleys, where they traded candied fruit and beverages made from the fruit of the saguaro and labored in exchange for wheat, maize, beans, mesquite pods, and cotton. In times of hunger the Tohono O'odham would perform a "begging dance" lasting several nights to ask for food in the riverine Pima villages.[29] Likewise, the Joba pastoralists and foragers who lived on the eastern margins of Sonora, in the fastness of the Sierra Madre, traded their woven mats for food and clothing in the missions.[30]

Not wholly separate from these traditional trading networks, the *serrano* villagers' taste for European merchandise grew with increased exposure to the colonial economy through the missions, mining *reales*, and presidial stores. Native craft skills in weaving, carving, and ceramics — developed to provide their households with tools and furnishings — were turned more and more to producing tradeware. Indians living in the missions grew certain kinds of European food as trade items, even though they did not incorporate them into their own diet: "The Sonoras . . . never eat chickens nor eggs, although they cannot explain why. Nevertheless, they raise hens and they like to have them close to their huts. Mission Indians bring chickens and eggs to the Spaniards and the missionaries, and receive in exchange tobacco, knives, needles, and other things."[31]

The "indios conversos," especially Opatas and Eudeves, emulated Spanish modes of dress and actively entered local markets to sell their produce and labor in order to buy the clothing, tools, and other goods they had learned to want. Indigenous peasants of the region gradually transformed their traditional practices into mercantile forms of trade. The contradiction between pre-Hispanic values rooted in the ritualized reciprocal exchange of gifts and the colonial marketplace, where buyers and sellers bartered to gain an advantageous price (even when trading goods for goods) accounted for the Indians' uneven integration into the colonial economy. Native Sonorans seemed often to be "cheated" in the prices they obtained and in the timing of the sale of foodstuffs, particularly when they surrendered their harvests to itinerant peddlers known as *rescatadores* who circulated throughout the pueblos each year. Over time, market transactions based on exchange values weakened the indigenous "economy of abundance" based on use values which had sustained the renewing quality of community life among the Sonoran peoples.[32]

Indigenous Concepts of Work, Time, and Technology

Their favorite occupation is leisure.

Ignaz Pfefferkorn, 1795 [33]

The acquisitiveness that Spanish observers attributed to the Sonoras in order to explain their eagerness to obtain colonial merchandise seemed to contrast with their work patterns. Missionaries and colonial officials alike complained that native villagers left arable land unplanted and suggested that Indian agriculturalists underproduced by European standards. In their view household subsistence needs, reduced to stark simplicity, defined the upward limits of labor expended on resource procurement. In contrast to the discipline that the missionaries tried to instill in their neophytes, *serrano* peoples seemed to be indifferent to the measurement of time and disinclined to intensify their labor. Likewise, they showed little interest in technological advances related to operations they already knew how to perform. Their primitive version of the European plow, used in conjunction with the digging stick, barely turned a shallow layer of earth; and, to the Jesuits' frustration, highland cultivators cared little whether or not their furrows were straight. As for conserving their harvests from season to season, only a minority planted enough to supply their needs for an entire year, and many mission Indians had consumed their stores before the next season's planting. The missionaries usually supplied them with seed and were vigilant, lest they eat the grains they had been given for planting. Pima cultivators at Caborca, along the Concepción drainage on the fringe of the desert, raised little maize and consumed or sold the wheat crop to the *vecinos* shortly after the harvest. "For this reason," wrote Padre Sedelmayr, "each year there is a time of hunger in Caborca." [34]

In contrast to the missionaries' notions of disciplined labor, the Sonorans' proclivity to feast while the harvest was full probably stemmed from the cyclical extremes of bounty and scarcity that marked the seasons of hunting and gathering in their environment. Both physically and culturally, native peoples had learned to consume and share in times of plenty and endure hunger during seasons of drought. Their metabolism could deal with unequal levels of nourishment during the year. Highland and desert dwellers moved periodically to different areas to hunt, fish, and gather seeds and roots, following the natural rhythm of plant maturation and the migratory patterns of local fauna. In times of scarcity or crop failure, when gathering became their mainstay, what the Spaniards interpreted as waste or greed may have been the Sonorans' best defense against starvation: that is, their cultural imperative to distribute all foodstuffs among the kin group. Thus, mission Indians consumed or shared their supplies through networks of gift exchange that extended beyond the fixed community to far-flung *rancherías*. [35]

The missionaries' oft-repeated frustration with the Indians' irregular work habits and consumption patterns reflected distinct cultural values held by both sets of historical actors. The Sonorans' selective use of European innovations and their apparent disregard for technological precision may reflect the greater importance they attributed to ceremonialism for bringing rain and making the land fertile. Conversely, the missionaries' concern with keeping the granaries well stocked was inimical to the *serrano* peoples' ethic of sharing. For them, each season's harvest was a bounty from nature not to be stored against future use, but to be shared among the greatest number of kinsmen possible. They perceived a balance between labor expended and reward obtained in terms that did not conform to the Jesuits' ledgers of "debits" and "credits." The central concept governing native practice rendered work meaningful as labor or service exchanged for food, and included strong components of sociability and play.

Sonoran villagers applied a mix of autochthonous and European technologies to a variety of crafts. Opata and Eudeve women wove garments from cotton and pita, using a simple hand loom, and adapted their weaving technique to wool. Men wove heavier pieces such as blankets and coverlets. *Serrano* weavers produced tightly woven cotton cloth, and their craftmanship was praised for its beauty and utility.[36] They could imitate German embroidery on tablecloths and napkins, and reproduced almost any design that one put before them. Native artisans produced nearly all the linens that graced the missions and private Spanish homes in the province. In addition to weaving cloth, highlanders produced mats, hats, and baskets from natural fibers.

Men and women living in the missions became skilled at tailoring, carpentry, wood carving, and masonry. Furthermore, they made and learned to play European stringed instruments, adding them to their own wind and percussion accompaniments to dances and chants. Opata men had built water-powered flour mills in Arivechi, Pivipa, and Banámichi. Eudeves at Cucurpe fashioned stone containers and implements from the soft *cantera* they cut out of the hills. Padre Nentvig described the Indians' mode of learning in terms of their capacity to imitate what they observed. Once they decided to master a skill, they did not proceed with formal lessons, nor were they guided by the rules of the art. Rather, it was sufficient for them to see it performed once or twice "for it to come out right. Thus, we often say that the Indians have under-standing in their eyes and discourse in their hands." [37]

Sonorans distinguished between "men's" and "women's" work, al-though the sexual division of labor was not rigid. Native agricultural practices required men as well as women to work in the fields, each performing specific tasks. Men cleared the fields, plowed the furrows, and prepared their milpas with the hoe and digging stick, while women planted the seeds and harvested the mature crops. Men dominated the ceremonial skills and hunting techniques, while women gathered most of the wild food plants. Women did all the food processing for storage as well as preparing daily meals; they brought firewood and water to their homes, cared for their children, and carried burdens when traveling. Although men and women both wove cloth and fiber, the art of ceram-ics was reserved for women. The labor discipline established under the mission regime tended to follow indigenous patterns. Men tilled the land assigned to the mission común, while women were occupied in food processing and in the tasks associated with religious services and the upkeep of the chapels. [38]

In summary, native economies had developed a wide spectrum of re-sources for survival in Sonora. Horticulture and gathering provided an impressive variety of cultigens and useful species from the highlands and the desert more than adequate to feed, clothe, and shelter seden-tary and nomadic peoples. Although we lack data on aboriginal agricul-tural yields and the extent of land cultivated, it is reasonable to surmise that seasonal harvests constituted an important part of their subsistence, especially in areas of floodplain farming. Nevertheless, it is probable that time spent in hunting and gathering surpassed that expended for agri-culture. Amerindian techniques for harvesting the desert and farming the floodplain sustained their semiarid environment. Building earthen canals, brush weirs, and living fencerows provided the flow of water for cultivating low terraces just above the river channels, without caus-ing soil degradation through arroyo-cutting or loss of riparian vegeta-tion. They lived with the region's meandering streams, expanding and contracting their cultivated fields in consonance with changing alluvial deposits and shifting rainfall patterns. [39]

Under Spanish domination, work and productivity were a central arena of cultural conflict. For native Sonorans productive and ceremo-

nial labor were integral parts of the internal organization of their households and communities. Equally significant, the division of labor by sex
and age underlay gender relations and kinship networks. Spanish demands for labor, surplus foodstuffs, and crafts taxed native productive
systems and violated the Sonoras' normative values which delineated
different kinds of work and prescribed the rituals necessary for renewing nature's bounty.

Hispanic–Indian relations in other areas of New Spain illustrate a
number of issues concerning the social and cultural dimensions of
work, specifically the distribution of tasks among individuals and communities and the complementarity of ceremonial and productive labor.
In central Mexico, Spanish institutions designed to redirect the flow of
Indian productive energy to colonial enterprises undermined the traditional regulation of communal labor.[40] Maya communities in colonial Yucatán conserved their religious practices through the ceremonial
work carried out by native elites. Likewise, in the Tewa culture of New
Mexico the ceremonial duties of "Made People" linked their ritual calendar to the subsistence cycle of agriculture and hunting. In all these
areas native religious leaders carried out ceremonies and feasts that the
community deemed necessary to maintain the cosmos.[41]

The ceremonial and material components of work were intertwined
with the division of labor across age and gender lines. Agriculture, the
foundation of village peasant life, required the toil of men and women
alike. In Sonora, as we have seen, men and women worked together
in the fields and participated in communal rituals (usiabagu, nawait, and
wi:kita). Similarly, Pueblo societies in colonial New Mexico assigned distinctive roles to men and women and to juniors and seniors. Children
who received ritual gifts from their parents discharged this debt or obligation through obedience and labor. Indeed, age constituted one of
the principal standards of inequality in Anasazi communities. In those
Pueblo towns with matrilineal and matrilocal traditions, women were
heads of household and controlled their families' reserves of food and
planting seed. Although men tended the fields, hunted, traded, and
dominated most of the ceremonial societies, women processed the harvested grain and fed all the members of their extended kindred.[42] Food
processing, particularly grinding maize on stone metates, was a female
task among the sedentary peoples of central Mexico, as in Sonora.

Women assumed a burden that was physically exhausting and enor-
mously time-consuming, but that conferred on them a central role in
the distribution of food within and among households.[43]

The cultural, ecological, and economic dimensions of work, productivity, and livelihood in Sonora underwent profound changes under
colonialism. The following chapter explores the ways in which indigenous systems of exchange and labor collided or blended with the commercial standards emanating from Spanish enterprises. It focuses primarily on the issues of subsistence and surplus in the missions, the
institution that most directly touched native communities, while considering the demands and opportunities that serrano peoples faced in the
mines and haciendas. Chapters 2 and 3 together provide an empirical
foundation for the analysis of ecological and cultural change in the peasant communities of colonial Sonora.

3

Native Livelihood and the
Colonial Economy

It is not enough to sweep the church and keep it clean, rather it must be adorned
with altars, saints, candelabra, crosses, and vestments, so that we all may know
that this is the house of God.

Padre Manuel Aguirre, 1765 [1]

Serrano peoples' holistic sense of livelihood confronted alien standards of
work and surplus production in the colonial order. Individual and familial labor for food, shelter, clothing, and utensils was directed away
from the sustenance of households and communities to the production
and storage of marketable surpluses. The frontier institution that most
directly impinged on the Sonoran pueblos was the mission; its agrarian
structures consolidated native villages and linked them to the wider
colonial economy. Contrary to the image created in much of the Borderlands literature on the missions, they did not comprise isolated, autar-
kic compounds, but participated fully in regional marketing systems. [2]
Jesuit and Franciscan missionaries serving in eighteenth-century Sonora
firmly believed that their commercial ties to the presidios and mines
were essential to maintaining the mission economy. Notwithstanding
their objectives, the flow of foodstuffs and merchandise in and out of
the missions, although it financed church construction and provided
gifts for Indian neophytes, in the end undermined native subsistence.
The missionaries' emphasis on the production of commodities impelled
serrano peasants to seek their livelihood outside the pueblos, weakening

the demographic base of the congregations that Black and Gray Robes had so carefully nurtured.

Mission Economy

Sonoran missionaries, both the sons of Loyola and the Franciscans who carried on their work after 1767, labored to sustain a system of agrarian communities built on the foundations established by indigenous patterns of subsistence. Their objective was to increase native productivity and administer the surplus, passing foodstuffs and cattle from well-established missions to newer pueblos on the frontier. The Jesuits' regular shipment of grains, cattle, and Indian laborers from the prosperous villages of the Yaqui and Mayo valleys to the fledgling missions of Pimería Alta and Baja California during the early eighteenth century exemplified their management of a regional economy grounded in the productive capacities of individual households and communities.[3] The Jesuits' disposal of mission surpluses obeyed a "higher purpose," which was essentially noneconomic in nature: Christian evangelization and the salvation of heathen souls. The missionaries understood their task in religious terms, and they invested a significant part of mission earnings in the construction and adornment of churches. Evolving from simple *ramadas* of forked posts and woven thatch, permanent churches built of adobe, stone, and fired brick symbolized both the Christian sanctuary and the structured town life which the Spaniards strove to impose on native communities.

The organization of labor within the villages reflected the missionaries' economic and political objectives. They worked through Indian officers appointed in each mission district to raise surplus harvests destined for redistribution or sale. Native *gobernadores* and *alcaldes* were charged with the care and cultivation of community lands. They, in turn, assigned tasks for fieldwork and designated shepherds and cowhands to watch over the mission's herds of livestock. In addition to individual *milpas* scattered along the floodplain and worked by native horticulturalists according to their own custom, each village tended communal lands that belonged to the mission. The missionaries compelled the Indians to plant the *común*, supplying them with seeds and tools, and they disposed of these communal harvests in lieu of the tithes and religious

fees collected in secular parishes. During the agricultural cycle of planting, weeding, and harvesting, the missionary fed the Indians assigned
to work in the común "a brimming plate of pozole" three times a day. Communal harvests were distributed among all Indian families who had
performed labor services or held political office in the mission, and surpluses were traded for merchandise. The missionaries purchased cloth
annually to supply the Indians with plain garments as well as tobacco,
medicines not available locally, knives, scissors, needles, and other inci-
dentals.

The missionaries exacted levels of production exceeding immediate
subsistence needs (with varying degrees of success) through a combination of coercion and persuasion. By distributing gifts semiannually and
providing planting seed, cattle, and other amenities, the missionaries
demonstrated their material benevolence for village-dwelling agriculturalists. Furthermore, the creation of elected political offices enhanced
the missionaries' moral authority and established a system of social
rank within the communities whereby the Indians policed one another
concerning work discipline and religious conduct. In addition to the
posts of gobernador, alcalde, fiscal, and mador, the Jesuits employed foremen
(mayordomos), who were either trusted Indians from stable missions or
vecinos, to oversee fieldwork in relatively new reducciones. Underlying these
economic and political controls, the religious content of mission life
supported an ethic of communal labor. Insofar as the Indians accepted
their status as "hijos del pueblo," they may have endowed their "padres"
with some of the patriarchal attributes they had been taught to associate
with God.

Notwithstanding the missionaries' moral arsenal and the undeniable
nucleus of consensus they had achieved, especially in the more settled
villages of Opatas and Eudeves, they confronted daily signs of resistance.
Only a small portion of the land reserved for sustaining the missions
was actually planted each year. Opatas in the upper Bavispe drainage enjoyed high maize yields, but they never sowed more than one fanega for
the mission común. Serrano peasants reduced their labor on behalf of the
mission to a minimum, thereby resisting the Jesuits' attempts to coerce
a greater share of the villagers' productive capacity for their enterprise.
Padre Joseph Roldan complained of the Indians' "superficial" work:

At times, with six Indians on salary the Spaniards accomplish more than the missionary who works with an entire village, even if it has forty or fifty families; first, because all the people never go to work, only a few; second, because the few who do go to labor in the fields go more to eat and visit than to work. Thus, they go late and leave early. How, then, could we pay them with the same formality as [we pay] the salaried Indians [on Spanish estates]?[4]

As Padre Roldan observed, the Indians cultivated communal fields at their rhythm of labor. And when they considered that the burdens of mission life outweighed the benefits, they left the pueblos to forage or work in the mines. The missionaries employed coercion, notably the whipping post, and resorted to intervention by Spanish military commanders when they felt their authority was severely threatened. Generally, however, they reserved corporal punishment and arrest for suspected rebellion and offenses against Catholic codes of conduct, and used other means to force compliance with labor drafts in the pueblos.[5]

There is only fragmentary evidence of the specific tasks assigned to Indian laborers, both men and women, in the missions. Occasionally, second names applied to Indians may indicate a given occupation or skill; for example, carpenter, weaver, shepherd, or cowhand. A death notice of 1766 referred to one Ignacio Hortelano ("gardener") buried in the cemetery at San Miguel de Ures. That same year María Antonia, daughter of Ignacio Texedor ("weaver") petitioned to marry Juan Antonio, a widower.[6] Two years earlier, Padre Andrés Michel hastily wrote a list of names on the back of a letter, referring to rations of corn kernels distributed to families living in Santa Rosalía, the second village under his care in Ures. Because the recipients of maize were women, and Michel noted that each almud "was taken to make pinole," his list may refer to women's work in the missions: roasting and grinding dried maize on their metates. Names indicative of occupations include cantora (singer), labrador (planter or farmer), and carpo (possibly carpintero, or carpenter).[7]

Religious festivals enlivened the daily routine of mission life and reinforced communal discipline. The pageantry of religious processions on Good Friday and Corpus Christi lent dignity to Indian governors dressed in especially elegant clothing. The distribution of ashen crosses at the beginning of Lent and palm leaves on Palm Sunday brought "crowds of people" to the mission churches. Food offerings used to commemorate All Souls' Day and the Day for Remembrance of the Dead marked the completion of the autumnal harvest. And, of course, Christmas brought a new rationing of stored grains in the missions and gifts of cloth, tobacco, and food. Each pueblo had its titular saint's day celebrated with music, feasting, gifts of food and clothing, and visits of Spaniards and Indians from one pueblo to another. Padre Sedelmayr invited his fellow missionaries to the Holy Day of Purification and the Holy Day of the Rosary in Mátape. The Feast of San Ignacio celebrated in Cucurpe lasted three days, its religious content greatly embellished with secular merriment.[8]

Missions and Provincial Markets

These accounts began some time ago, and only God knows when they will end.

Manuel Bernardo Monteagudo to Padre Felipe Segesser, 1754[9]

Religious and economic objectives merged in the close ties of reciprocal dependency that developed between the mission system and Spanish settlements in the province. Under both Jesuit and Franciscan administration, the missions participated in a regional marketing network through the sale of produce and livestock, the purchase of merchandise, and contracts for Indian labor outside the villages. Sonoran missionaries procured their supplies through annual memorias — lists of provisions sent to the order's agents in Mexico City — which they paid for with their personal stipend and the sale of mission produce. In addition to this controlled closed circuit of commercial exchange, the missionaries engaged in frequent transactions with numerous local merchants. Miners and hacendados, too, purchased foodstuffs and woven goods from the missions that, in turn, were used to pay their peones and gañanes.

The mission system, in its entirety, stood at the center of a network of mercantile exchange that extended from Sonora eastward to Chihuahua and southward to Sinaloa. The merchants, miners, and magistrates listed in Table 3.1 belonged to a small, but well-defined provincial elite. Most of them operated out of mining reales, but some resided in mission villages: for example, Miguel de Espinoza y Linares, in Oposura;

Table 3.1   Merchants Who Traded with Sonoran
Missionaries, 1747–67

Name	Place
Phelipe Pérez de la Lastra, *teniente de justicia*	San Francisco de las Llagas (Soyopa)
Manuel Salmon	Antunes
Isidro González, *justicia mayor*	Santísima Trinidad (Ostimuri)
Gerónimo de Chave y Barretia	Río Chico
Buenaventura de Llenes Malla	San Antonio de la Huerta
Joaquín de Cárdenas	San Antonio de la Huerta
Pedro Bringas de Manzaneda	San Antonio de la Huerta
Juan Bautista Feijoo	San Antonio de la Huerta
Josepha Ysidora Feyjoo	San Antonio de la Huerta
Miguel de Yribarren	San Antonio de la Huerta
Juan María Bohorquez	San Antonio de la Huerta
Buenaventura de Vandurruaga	San Antonio de la Huerta
Joseph de los Heros	San Antonio de la Huerta
Matheo de Olivar y Monje	San Antonio de la Huerta
Pedro Antonio Thimeo	San Antonio de la Huerta
Augustín Belderebro	San Antonio de la Huerta
Manuel de Escoto	San Antonio de la Huerta
Vicente Morales, *arriero*	San Antonio de la Huerta
Miguel de Espinoza y Linares	Oposura
Lorenzo de Aguirre	Mátape
Juan Manuel Andrade	Mátape
Joseph de las Caxigas	Santa Rosalía
Joseph María Sembrano	San José de Gracia
Manuel de la Azuela	San Miguel Arcángel
Francisco Messia, *teniente de dragones*	San Miguel de Horcasitas
Murrieta	San Miguel de Horcasitas
Phelipe de Maytorena	San Miguel de Horcasitas
Manuel Bernardo Monteagudo	San Miguel de Horcasitas
	San Pedro de la Conquista de Pitic

Source: AGN *Jesuitas* IV-10, exp. 7, 10, 11, 12, 62, 67, 69, 70, 71, 72, 80, 141, 163, 171, 174, 177, 180, 183, 185, 186, 188, 206, 212, 220, 221, 224, 227, 229.

or Lorenzo de Aguirre and Juan Manuel Andrade, who lived in Mátape. Manuel Bernardo Monteagudo and Francisco Messia, for their part,
came from the presidial companies established in Horcasitas and Pitic.
Provincial traders exchanged goods for goods; however, they set prices
in *reales de plata* in order to establish equivalent values. Typically, in any
one year, the missionaries sent out many shipments of small amounts of
produce—maize, *pinole*, dried chilis, brown sugar, wheat, beans, chickpeas—as the muleteers made their rounds through the pueblos. They
received payment in goods or in uncoined silver.

Although traditional Jesuit practices dictated strong links within the
Order from the viceregal capital to the mission provinces, in the closing
years of their tenure the Jesuits turned to local merchants to supply
their needs. This was owing, in part, to the high cost of freight between Mexico City and the northwestern provinces. In 1766 and 1767,
Pedro Bringas de Manzaneda and Juan Bautista Feijoo of San Antonio
de la Huerta sent detailed lists of merchandise, entitled "Memorias de
géneros," and charged them to the account of Padre Andrés Michel. The
articles purchased, mainly different kinds of cloth, rope, thread, sew-
ing needles, shoes, stockings, ribbons, writing paper, and plowheads,
suggest that Padre Michel's *memoria* included some items destined for redistribution among the *vecinos* living in Ures, Santa Rosalía, and the Real
de San José de Gracia.[10]

Mule trains laden with *pinole*, wheat, brown sugar, lard, soap, and
candle wax as well as with rope, harnesses, cotton *mantas*, rebozos,
woolen *bayeta* and *bretaña*, and even fine silks, trod a well-worn route between the mission pueblos and mining *reales*. San Antonio de la Huerta
constituted a central node in this exchange network.[11] Ranchers and
miners established in the province frequently called on the missionaries
to supply them with needed goods or to tide them over an emergency.
For instance, in 1757, Phelipe Pérez de la Lastra, a miner and *teniente de justicia* in Soyopa, asked Padre Segesser of Ures to supply him with horses,
mares, mules, and jackasses, and with cowboys to ensure their arrival
at the mine, promising payment for the animals and for the herders'
labor sometime in the future. He had already sent to San Ignacio for a
bell-founder to cast some furnaces, "for without them, my operation is
virtually at a standstill."[12]

Civilian *comisarios*, non-Indian administrators in the larger missions, and muleteers (*arrieros*) played an important role in the movement of goods and agricultural produce from the villages to the presidios and *reales de minas*. Some *arrieros* operated as independent agents, veritable small traders who probably owned their teams of mules. More frequently, *arrieros* were in the employ of missionaries, merchants, or provincial governors. Likewise, the *comisarios* oversaw the actual loading of pack trains and kept track of the terms of exchange for produce and merchandise.[13]

The circulation of goods among different kinds of settlements required certain commonly accepted norms of material worth. Missionaries and merchants alike expressed the actual terms of exchange in volume measurements — for example, *fanegas* or *almudes* of grain and *varas* of cloth — although their market value was understood in silver *reales*. Often, the trade of produce for merchandise could not be completed in one transaction because the supplies requested by one or another party were not available. Unfinished trade resulted both from the uncertain delivery of merchandise from Chihuahua or Mexico City and from the vagaries of the agricultural cycle in the province. Thus, indebtedness arising from deferred payment constituted the other face of this regional marketing system. *Libranzas*, mercantile notes used for internal trade in lieu of money or a specified amount of goods, created a chain of "dependencies" between the missions and frontier settlements which, in some cases, linked Sonoran interests to the viceregal capital. These letters of credit were common currency for many kinds of commercial transactions throughout New Spain. A promise to pay constituted an "active dependency," a kind of credit held out against future payment. It was not uncommon for the original beneficiary to sign over the *libranza* in favor of his creditors, in effect turning the document into a form of money which circulated widely. The missionaries owed, and were owed, substantial sums — paid usually in material goods, only rarely in silver coin.[14]

Jesuit correspondence reveals the frequent use of *libranzas* in local trade. In November 1764, Miguel de Yribarren of San Antonio de la Huerta charged Padre Michel's account for the *libranza* which the missionary had extended to Doña Josepha Ysidora Feijoo. Two years later, Juan de la Torre Cossío made casual references to multiple debts of small amounts of grain in the environs of San Miguel de Horcasitas, involving

numerous local traders.[15] The burden of accumulated debts complicated
the mission economy at the close of the Jesuit era and, occasionally,
missionaries and merchants alike would call in outstanding accounts. In
1761, during the general visitation of Padre Ignacio Lizassoaín, the missionary at San Pedro de Aconchi recognized an outstanding debt of 500
pesos against an "active dependency" of more than 800 pesos owed to
the mission, in addition to smaller amounts which he had written off
as virtually irretrievable.[16]

Downstream at San Miguel de Ures, Padre Phelipe Segesser borrowed
substantial amounts of money to be paid with future sales of mission
produce. His successor, Andrés Michel, faced numerous demands for
payment from local *vecinos* and from his fellow Jesuits. In the spring of
1764, Gerónimo de Chave y Barretia, established in Río Chico, demanded
payment of 450 pesos and threatened to take his complaint to the *justicia
mayor* if he did not receive the full amount. Padre Michel had to beg Doña
María Theresa Montes Vidal, of Culiacán, for more time to pay what the
mission owed her. That same year, Joaquín de Cárdenas of San Antonio
de la Huerta acknowledged Padre Michel's shipment of grain in partial
payment of a debt totaling more than 200 pesos. As if these pressures
were not sufficient, the aging Padre Jácobo Sedelmayr of Mátape sent
his confrere in Ures repeated notices concerning a long-standing debt
that he claimed Segesser owed his district. While forestalling his creditors, Michel expended considerable effort to recover sums owed to the
mission. Only a few months before the expulsion of the Jesuit order, he
received promises of payment from Pedro Antonio Thimeo and Agustín
Belderebro of San Antonio de la Huerta. Even when close at hand, *vecinos*
in arrears managed to avoid payment. Manuel Andrade López, *labrador* of
Los Angeles in the San Miguel Valley, demurred at delivering forty fanegas of wheat to the mission of Ures: "If I could pay the full amount I
owe, the benefit would be mine." [17]

At the same time that Jesuits concerned themselves with marketing
surpluses and recording active and passive debts, they dealt with *vecinos*
living in the pueblos. While some squatters maintained a servile stance
toward the missionaries and may have actually made themselves useful,
they repeatedly "borrowed" planting seed, mules, and oxen with little
hope of repayment. Furthermore, non-Indian *mayordomos* and *comisarios*
abused their authority and made liberal use of mission property for their

own benefit. They frequently took unmarked cattle or stock of uncertain brands when the animals ran loose or were taken from one pueblo to another. Cattle theft became so serious a problem that Padre Michel gave powers of attorney to one Urbano Díaz to intercept any unauthorized persons who attempted to take livestock out of the mission fields.[18]

Surplus Production and Mission Wealth

What constituted the measurable wealth of the missions in Sonora? The pueblos under Jesuit tutelage stored grains and kept herds of livestock from which they supplied local mining centers and presidios. This produce, coupled with the land itself, mission buildings, and a modest complement of tools and equipment, made up the común in its fullest sense, the accumulated wealth accrued from the Indians' labor. Formal inventories taken periodically in the Sonoran missions provide a lens for viewing the productive resources that enabled peasant communities to survive and reproduce their economy. These lists help to assess changes in mission wealth over time, although they were incomplete and did not explain how that capital was invested—whether, in fact, it was used to enhance production or to satisfy needs outside the immediate concerns of material subsistence.[19] The following analysis of Jesuit and Franciscan economic practices, based on a variety of sources, shows fluctuations in the production of marketable surpluses and changing priorities for investment over three-quarters of a century.

Table 3.2 gives a baseline overview of mission assets for selected pueblos in the Bavispe and Sonora valleys at mid-eighteenth century, expressed in the monetary value of their marketed surpluses. The source, Padre Juan Antonio Baltasar's visita of 1744, listed the principal villages administered in each mission district, but summarized the population (expressed in number of families), earnings, and expenses by mission. There is a rough correlation between population levels and total volume of trade: the Bacerác and Arizpe districts, with approximately 250 families each showed income and expenses of more than 10,000 pesos, while Guásabas and Ures, with fewer than 150 families each, reported the lowest levels of commercial activity. These tallies reveal substantial deficits in Jesuit accounts, since only three of the missions had a favorable balance. Furthermore, Bacerác, which boasted the highest income

Table 3.2 Overview of Assets for Selected Opata Missions, 1741–44

Mission	Pueblos	No. Families	Income	Expenses	Balance
Valley of Bavispe					
Guásabas	Oputo	70	1,996	1,580	+416
Bacerác	Guachinera	250	14,920	22,806	−7,886
	Bavispe				
	Tamichopa				
Valley of Sonora					
Arizpe	Chinapa	260	12,525	11,121	+1,404
	Bacoachi				
Banámichi	Huépac	120	9,729	11,152	−1,423
	Sinoquipe				
Aconchi	Baviácora	190	9,515	8,210	+1,305
Ures	Sta. Rosalía	125	698	2,014	−1,316
Total	16	1,015	49,383	56,883	−7,500

Source: "Informe del P. Juan Antonio Baltasar sobre la estructura de las misiones de Sonora, 1744," in Ernest J. Burrus and Félix Zubillaga, eds., El noroeste de México. Documentos sobre las misiones jesuíticas, 1600–1769 (Mexico City: Universidad Nacional Autónoma de México, 1986), pp. 171–96. Original in the Beinecke Library of Yale University.

Note: Income, expenses, and balance are expressed in pesos. Total pueblos includes six mission head villages.

of all six missions, carried a debt worth half its earnings. Finally, it is noteworthy that all the amounts listed surpass the missionaries' annual stipend of 350 pesos, dramatically so in the larger missions. More than the Crown's subvention, the commercialization of mission surpluses sustained the entire Jesuit enterprise in Sonora.

Extant Jesuit accounts for the mission district of San Pedro de Aconchi (central Sonora Valley), which comprised two substantial Opata villages surrounded by mining and ranching settlements, illustrate well the dynamic quality of mission interaction with the market. A handwritten ledger kept by successive missionaries of income derived from the sale of cattle and produce, and of expenditures made for provisions, gifts,

Table 3.3   Livestock at Mission of San Pedro de Aconchi,
Sonora, 1749

Pueblo	Horses	Mules	Sheep	Cattle	Total
Aconchi	129	288	939	975	2,331 (58%)
Baviácora	108	362	742	500	1,712 (42%)
Total	237	650	1,681	1,475	4,043 (100%)

Source: AMH AS I, ff. 131–32.

and church adornment, provides a detailed record of the year-to-year
administration from 1720 to 1766. Additional lists of the volume of grain
produced in each of the two pueblos, from 1749 to 1762, afford a comparison with the ledger of sales and expenditures. Combining both these
sources permits us to estimate the relative portions of village production destined for subsistence and for the market. At midcentury, each
pueblo had milpas planted with maize, an orchard, and small plots of
sugarcane and cotton. Livestock was distributed as shown in Table 3.3.[20]

Table 3.4 summarizes the information on grain harvests for 1749–62.
The Jesuits' records show levels of production for each pueblo, but express purchases and sales in terms of the mission district as a whole.
Figures for the sale of foodstuffs represent the annual totals compiled
from various transactions recorded throughout the year. Agricultural
yields varied widely from one season to the next, illustrating the impact
of seasonal variations in rainfall and of fluctuations in the area sown
on the mission economy. Maize harvests suffered adverse drought conditions prevailing from 1750 to 1753. Although maize yields per fanega
of seed sown were higher than those for wheat, the maize crop was
considerably lower throughout the period studied. We may infer that
the missionaries gave priority to the wheat crop, planted in communal
fields with irrigation, while the milpas reserved for maize were dependent on winter and summer rains. Beans, lentils, and chickpeas formed
part of the missions' basic stock of grains planted for both sale and
internal consumption. Only beans are included in this table, however,
because the other grains had production levels that proved too erratic
for making any meaningful comparisons. Frequently, the bean crop was

Table 3.4 Production of Basic Grains by the Mission
of San Pedro de Aconchi, Sonora, 1749–62

	Aconchi			Baviácora			Grain Sold		Portion Not Sold	
	Wheat	Maize	Beans	Wheat	Maize	Beans	Wheat	Maize	Wheat	Maize
1749	345	240	40	406	215	35	260	249	491	206
1750	368	150	112	263	84	34	120	60	511	174
1751	384	151	38	400	150	29	121	25	663	276
1752	320	83	. . .	256	40	. . .	138	95	438	28
1753	252	89	. . .	284	168	. . .	113	110	423	147
1754	542	100	27	528	106	5	150	150	920	56
1755	360	60	12	295	66	. . .	119	31	536	95
1756	372	66	28	310	133	6	22	20	660	178
1757	328	106	35	450	109	15	192	144	586	71
1758	140	126	8	164	70	8	25	24	279	172
1759	410	200	40	518	166	14	20	56	908	310
1760	456	93	. . .	518	203	. . .	175	155	799	141
1761	361	289	. . .	546	160	. . .	318	266	589	183
1762	423	238	. . .	430	200	. . .	80	240	773	198
Total	5,061	1,991	340	5,368	1,870	146	1,853	1,625	8,576	2,235

Source: AMH AS I, ff. 144–46.

Note: Measurements are in fanegas.

lost altogether in years of drought. For this reason the calculations for
the portions of mission crops sold and not sold (in Tables 3.4 and 3.5)
take into account only maize and wheat.

The columns titled "Grain Sold" and "Portion Not Sold" indicate the
proportions of annual harvest destined for sale and for subsistence. The
overriding limitation on a mission's marketing capacity was the volume
of foodstuffs gathered each year—a variable that was itself dependent
on natural conditions. The percentages of crops sold and retained in the
mission raise interesting questions. Wheat harvests were consistently
higher than maize; yet, only one-fifth of the wheat harvest was sold,
while two-fifths of the maize grown on mission lands left the villages
(see Table 3.5 and Figures 3.1 and 3.2). These staples served both sub-

Table 3.5   Production versus Sale of Wheat and Maize by
the Mission of San Pedro de Aconchi, Sonora, 1749–62

	Production	Sales	Difference
Wheat	10,429	1,853	8,576
Maize	3,861	1,625	2,236

Source: See Table 3.4.

Note: These are combined figures for Aconchi and Baviácora. Measurements are in
fanegas. Total wheat sold = 18%; total wheat consumed or stored = 82%. Total maize
sold = 42%; total maize consumed or stored = 58%.

sistence and surplus needs; however, the higher proportion of maize
sold implies a consistent external demand despite uneven levels of production. Indian laborers in the mining camps, dependent on their employers for food, may have demanded maize as part of their payment.
A substantial amount of maize and wheat left the missions as *pinole* and
flour which, having been ground by Indian women on their *metates* and
on stone *tahonas* rotated by animal or human power, brought a higher
price than winnowed grain.[21]

Jesuit correspondence with *arrieros* and merchants provides further
evidence of the external demand for mission harvests of maize. In October 1747, Joaquín Chávez wrote to Padre Phelipe Segesser in Ures concerning 130 fanegas of wheat on order at the mission: "and if you could
change 30 of them to maize, you would do me a great favor, because
no one wants wheat any more." Likewise, in the spring of 1764, Joaquín
de Cárdenas from San Antonio de la Huerta implored of Padre Andrés
Michel, "I would be so grateful if your next shipment [of grain] could
be maize." Two years later, Luis Feliz Díaz reported to Padre Michel from
San Gregorio del Llano Colorado that "maize is scarce in San Antonio
and will fetch a good price."[22]

In addition to surplus grains, the missions sold various kinds of livestock each year. Horses, mules, sheep, yearlings, and beef cattle raised
in the pueblos supplied the presidios and *reales de minas* with meat, pack
animals, oxen and mounts. Missionaries received payment in *géneros* —
cloth, chocolate, sugar, tobacco, wax, soap, wine, and the like — or in

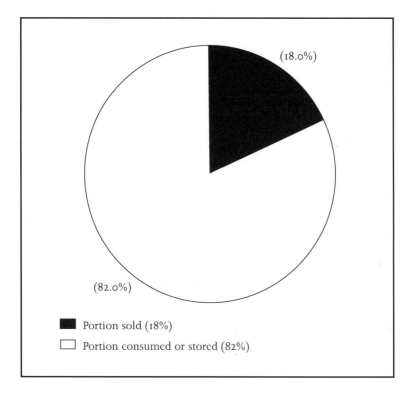

Figure 3.1. Sale and consumption of wheat in the mission district of San Pedro de Aconchi, Sonora, 1749–62

refined, but unminted *marcos* of silver.[23] The Jesuits spent this income in four main areas: productive assets, internal consumption, wages, and the religious life of the mission. Missionaries invested in the agrarian base of their villages: for example, plows, iron tools, planting seed, and livestock to build up the herds. The land itself did not require significant outlays of capital, although occasionally the missionaries paid surveyors' fees for land titles. Consumer goods included cloth and other gifts distributed to the Indians semiannually, as well as food products — sugar, chocolate, and spices — purchased by the missionaries for themselves. Wages covered remuneration in money and in kind to "servants," nonmission Indians who performed services beyond the assigned communal tasks. Although the *hijos del pueblo* labored in the fields and built and repaired mission dwellings in exchange for food, missionaries had

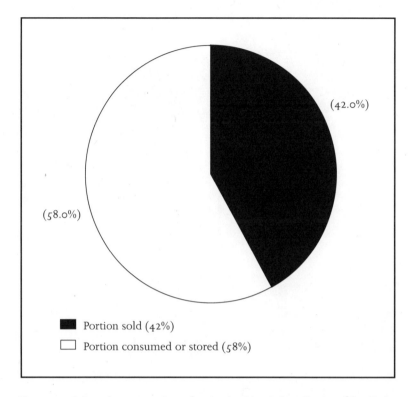

Figure 3.2. Sale and consumption of maize in the mission district of San Pedro de Aconchi, Sonora, 1749–62

occasion to compensate artisans, muleteers, herdsmen, and house servants for their work. Church construction, particularly, called for outside laborers who lived temporarily in the missions and received wages.

The religious cult absorbed considerable community resources. Jesuits adorned mission chapels with saints' images, chalices, organs, and embellished cloth as a means of imparting Christian doctrine to the Indians in their care. The secular administration of the *temporalidades* (with its wearisome bookkeeping) merely provided a foundation for their spiritual labors. That the missionaries considered this their essential task is illustrated by the Jesuit visitor Joseph Xavier de Molina's praise for Padre Juan Echagoyan in 1741: "I join all the visitors who have come before me in thanking the present minister for the use he has made of the fruits of this mission, converting them into exquisite ornaments for the

Table 3.6 Income and Expenses by Category (in Pesos) for the Mission of San Pedro de Aconchi, Sonora, 1720–66

	Income				Expenses			
Total Income	Grain	Cattle	Debts Repaid in Silver	Assets	Goods	Wages	Cult	Total Expenses
89,231	72,826	9,606	6,799	3,730	63,130	2,202	22,969	92,031
(100%)	(81.62%)	(10.77%)	(7.62%)	(4.05%)	(68.60%)	(2.39%)	(24.96%)	(100%)

Source: AMH AS 1

worship of God, and into abundant clothing for the Indians, in whom Padre Juan has nurtured a singular love and respect." [24]

The missionaries' ledgers covering the last five decades of Jesuit administration help to clarify the major sources of mission income and the overall pattern of marketable surpluses. Table 3.6 demonstrates the relative importance of different kinds of revenues and the priorities set for expenditures. More than four-fifths of mission income derived from the sale of agricultural produce, while surplus cattle and direct monetary payments combined accounted for only a small portion of yearly earnings. On the debit side of the ledger, more than two-thirds of material outlays were destined for internal consumption; that is, for clothing and other gifts distributed to the Indians. Nearly one-quarter of the missionaries' purchases were destined to adorn the churches, an amount far greater than their investment in productive assets.

The significance of these figures bears on the logic of Jesuit administration and the way in which the missions participated in the colonial market. If the single most important source of income was the sale of grain, then the mission's capacity to generate surpluses depended heavily on the labor available to plant and harvest communal lands. The decline of harvests and of sales during the closing years of the period studied, as illustrated in Table 3.7 and Figure 3.3, suggests that the pueblos suffered from a lack of manpower to till the fields and, possibly, that the mission's land base was shrinking. Concomitantly, the heavy expenditure in cloth distributed to the Indians each year implies that the mission populace expected these gifts and made them an important part of their negotiations with the priest. Perhaps it was the price of their loyalty, especially in the advancing years of the eighteenth century when the lure of prospecting and wages in the mines drew increasing numbers of Indians away from the pueblos.

The missionaries continued to buy *géneros* for their neophytes even in years of poor harvest. Frequently, purchases exceeded sales of mission produce, although Jesuit superiors who inspected the mission from time to time expressed little concern over this kind of running deficit so long as the missionary did not incur debts by openly borrowing capital or fail to recover money owed to the mission. In 1756, Padre Carlos de Rojas observed that in San Pedro de Aconchi mission earnings fell behind expenditures by more than 1,000 pesos, a debt which had accumulated

Table 3.7   Mean Income and Expenditures, by Five-Year
Averages, for the Mission of San Pedro de Aconchi,
Sonora, 1720–66

	Period	Volume of Grain (Fanegas)	Grain Sales (Pesos)	Consumption (Pesos)
(1)	1720–24	546	1,919	1,538
(2)	1725–29	728	2,941	2,001
(3)	1730–34	727	2,894	1,949
(4)	1735–39	511	2,035	2,080
(5)	1740–44	432	1,651	1,428
(6)	1749–53	259	963	1,860
(7)	1754–58	177	613	583
(8)	1759–66	329	1,106	848

Source: See Table 3.4. AMH AS I, ff. 144–146.

Note: Period numbers (column 1) correspond to period numbers in Figure 3.3.

over several years. In order to offset it, Padre Rojas counted among the
mission's assets a figure of 800 pesos that various persons owed the mission, 1,000 fanegas of stored grain, and the harvest ready to be picked.
Nevertheless, missionaries had to keep expenditures reasonably in line
with their earnings; during the final decade of Jesuit administration,
both income and purchases fell far below former levels.

The balance between earnings and expenses depended not only on
the volume of mission harvests, but also on the price they would bring.
Prices varied widely in different localities and seasons, as well as from
year to year. During the spring and fall of 1749, the Aconchi mission sent
numerous allotments of wheat, maize, and beans to Soyopa and La Ventana, drawing prices from three to four and a half pesos and sometimes
even five pesos a fanega. This increase of more than 60 percent in the
price of basic grains through the harvest season corroborates the missionaries' lament of a poor crop and suggests a scarcity of surplus maize
for sale at the Sonoran mines that year.[25] Typically, the Jesuits sold both
wheat and maize at three pesos a fanega; cargas of wheat flour went for
ten pesos each, although the price could run as high as twelve pesos a

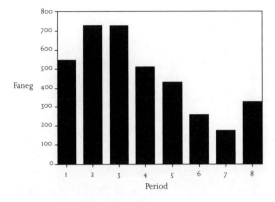

Figure 3.3. Volume of grain, by five-year averages, for the mission district of San Pedro de Aconchi, Sonora, 1720–66

carga. Ground *pinole* usually sold for six pesos a fanega. By the final years of the Jesuit administration, however, prices for wheat and maize had fallen as low as two pesos a fanega, for *pinole* to four pesos a fanega, and for wheat flour to seven pesos a carga. These figures contrast with prices quoted for the late seventeenth century. For example, in 1695, the Mátape mission sold eighty cargas of wheat flour at twenty pesos a carga.[26]

Grain purchases in the province involved mission pueblos, private ranchers and hacendados, and *rescatadores*—itinerant merchants who "gathered" grain from individual producers and delivered it to prospective buyers in mining *reales* like San Antonio de la Huerta, San Nicolás, and Baroyeca. As the Jesuit correspondence cited above illustrates, prices were subject to negotiation among all three agents. Furthermore, the web of indebtedness that bound together producers and merchants set the conditions for delivery of wheat and maize to different consumers. Spanish ranchers were heard to complain that the missionaries undersold them; while the Jesuits typically charged three pesos for one fanega of maize, merchants often doubled the price.[27]

Following the expulsion of the Jesuits, private growers figured more prominently in the provincial grain market. When Pedro de Corbalán summoned the *vecinos* of the Valley of Cumpas and attempted to requisition wheat for the Expedición de Sonora (1768–71), he stirred up vehement protest over prices and the costs of transport. Corbalán demanded wheat at twelve reales a fanega, the going rate at the time of harvest, without taking into account the rescatadores' share. Likewise, he obliged the vecinos to send flour at nine pesos a carga to San Joseph de Pimas in the vicinity of Guaymas, where the expeditionaries had disembarked. Sonoran rancheros argued in vain that they could sell the flour at fourteen pesos a carga in San Antonio de la Huerta, where merchants had, in effect, bought the grain on consignment by advancing goods against each year's harvest. Like the missions, the vecinos were constrained to pay off their debt in wheat flour, "or next year no one will give us so much as a rag to cover us." In their petition to Governor Juan Claudio Pineda, the cumpeños reiterated their willingness to send their wheat to feed the king's army, but they demanded the same price they would get in San Antonio de la Huerta.[28]

The general pattern of prices that characterized Sonoran commerce shows significant contrasts with trends observed for eighteenth-century New Spain as a whole.[29] Colonywide maize prices moved in a severe cyclical pattern, veering from as low as 4 reales to as high as 42 reales a fanega (8 reales = 1 peso). These cycles reflected periodic agricultural crises, in which crop failures and epidemics led to serious food shortages. Richard Garner's comprehensive study has shown that the average maize price for the entire century (1700–1819) was 13.7 reales; however, the average in 1700 was 9.2 reales, and in 1800 it had risen to 19.3 reales. He concludes that a moderately inflationary trend cut through the cyclical movement of prices, with a more pronounced upward turn during the last quarter of the century.[30] Prices for wheat are less well charted than for maize in central Mexico, although it is generally true that with increased urban consumption, the prices for wheat, flour, and bread rose substantially, especially during the last third of the eighteenth century.[31] In Nueva Vizcaya wheat prices varied considerably with transportation costs. Figures compiled for 1791 showed that prices ranged from 24 reales per fanega in the San Buenaventura and Conchos valleys, where wheat was produced, to as high as 88 reales in Batopilas. Wheat sold for 28 reales in Parral, 32 reales in Chihuahua, and 40 reales in Durango.[32]

The prices recorded in the Aconchi mission ledgers diverge from this colonywide pattern of cyclical movements. The average price for maize during the period analyzed here, 1717–66, oscillated between

3 and 4 pesos (24 to 32 reales) a fanega, significantly higher than in central New Spain. By the mid-1760s, Sonoran grain prices had fallen to 16 reales a fanega, while the average for the viceroyalty hovered between 5.8 and 8.4 reales.[33] However, Sonoran prices did not undergo the dramatic cycles that punctuated cereal production in core areas of Mexico. Despite periodic crop failures, which especially affected the maize harvests, Jesuit dealings with buyers and middlemen seem to have been consistent and predictable, and may have been set by previously arranged contracts.[34] Furthermore, wheat and maize prices moved together such that the missionaries frequently recorded their combined sale, in pesos and fanegas, as *bastimentos*. These observations suggest that, in Sonora, wheat as well as maize was commonly consumed by Indians and Spaniards alike. At the same time, the comparatively high price of maize is consonant with the demand noted above in local merchants' correspondence with the Jesuits. In addition, it is probable that these elevated prices included transportation costs.[35]

If we move beyond the numbers themselves, the missionaries' annotations over the years show us how commercial transactions took place between the missions and the colonial sector. *Arrieros* brought the missionaries *marcos* and *granos* of silver and took away small amounts of grain in numerous visits throughout the year, quite possibly under terms of exchange which had been established by previous contracts or even oral agreements. The priest in turn noted the silver as a debit, a kind of deposit against which the *arriero* took produce until the monetary value of the silver was satisfied.

The sale of mission produce inserted the pueblos into this regional marketing network and into the wider sphere of the Jesuit economy. On various occasions, the missionaries of Aconchi sent remittances of silver *reales* to their superiors in Mexico City. For example, at midcentury, Padre Nicolás de Pereza shipped 300 pesos to the *padre provincial* and the Jesuit Colegio de San Pedro y San Pablo, and gave 50 pesos to the Padre Visitador Joseph de Molina. Thus, mission surpluses played a role in the global financial structure of the Society of Jesus, contributing in some measure to the economic support of the order's province of Mexico. Conversely, Jesuit administrative policies for the missions were shaped, in part, by the economic links established between these frontier *reduc-*

ciones and the order's colleges. The missions were not an isolated enclave on the northern fringe of New Spain, but rather an integral part of the Jesuits' involvement with the Spanish Imperium.

Let us turn to the pueblos themselves. The missionaries' ledgers reveal their growing internal complexity. Beginning in the 1740s, in addition to the foodstuffs and gifts distributed to mission Indians, small amounts were noted as wages and remuneration in kind for servants and a resident *mayordomo*, most likely in charge of church building and repair. For example, in 1744, one Padre Duquesnay paid the silversmith Antonio Ballesteros twenty marcos to finish the tabernacle for the high altar in the church at Baviácora. Even in those years for which no wages were recorded, some of the goods purchased were a form of "hidden wage" destined for construction workers. Paid laborers were often Indians from other areas (frequently Yaquis,) and *gente de razón*, who constituted a separate class of residents in the pueblos. In addition, the missionaries bestowed special gifts of fine cloth for religious processions on the *justicias*, the elected officials who formed a select hierarchy in the village.

The contraction of the corporate economy of the missions, coupled with increasing use of wage labor, marked the transition from Jesuit to Franciscan administration. It is unfortunate that accounts for the Aconchi mission following the expulsion of the Jesuits are fragmentary, at best, precluding any systematic comparison with earlier years. A few notes dating from 1779 and 1780 refer only to fanegas of wheat and maize harvested, all of it stored or consumed internally. Moving out of the Sonora Valley and to the Pimería Alta, we find two accounts—for San Ignacio de Cabúrica and Santiago de Cocóspera in 1787–88—which present a simplified version of the Jesuit records analyzed above.

As fray Pedro de Arriquibar explained, mission income for San Ignacio de Cabúrica comprised 520 pesos of the *limosna*, or royal stipend, awarded to each missionary, and 1,959 pesos, 2 reales earned from the sale of mission produce. He acknowledged a deficit of 900 pesos, which he planned to hold over to the following year and balance against the mission's assets of crops and cattle. The mission relied increasingly on paid laborers, owing to the diminishing number of permanent Indian inhabitants in San Ignacio.[36]

In Cocóspera (see Table 3.9), the mission's total income nearly equaled

Table 3.8   Income and Expenses for the Mission of
San Ignacio de Cabúrica, Sonora, 1787–88

Explanation	Income	Expenses
Memoria from Mexico City	2,479p 2r	
Payment on part of the memoria		583p 3r
Shipping charges		456p 1r
Clothing distributed to Indians		809p
Wages for herdsmen on cattle drive		160p
Church and religious cult		470p 6r
Purchase of food, aid to infirm		900p
Total	2,479p 2r	3,379p 2r

Source: BNFF 35/761.

Note: p = pesos; r = reales.

expenses. Crops from the preceding year (1787) had yielded 225 fanegas
of wheat, 40 fanegas of maize, and 3 fanegas of lentils; however, at the
time Fray Juan Santiesteban penned his report, the entire wheat crop
had failed for lack of water. Mission lands, he wrote, were extensive, but
lacked irrigation, and it was necessary each year to search for the most
humid plots in which to sow. The meager maize crop raised in this year
of drought went entirely to preparing pozole for the Indians who planted
and harvested the común. Even in good years, the mission relied on the
sale of surplus produce, the missionary's stipend, and occasional ecclesiastical fees paid by resident vecinos—an innovation since the Jesuit era.

Village population had fallen to seventeen families, joined by three
vecino households. Despite their reduced numbers and a shrinking productive base, Santiesteban praised his neophytes. Pima families worked
in their own fields; they were "decently treated and dressed" and were
"faithful" in the fulfillment of their religious duties. Mission Indians
served as mail carriers and joined military campaigns, supplied with
grain harvested in the pueblo.[37] Notwithstanding Fray Juan's optimistic
tone, his report suggests that the Pimas conserved a community of subsistence, reducing the collective economy of the mission to a minimum.

Table 3.9   Income and Expenses for the Mission of Santiago de Cocóspera, Sonora, 1787–88

Explanation	Income	Expenses
Memoria from sale of last year's crop	1,251p 5r	
Rebate on shipping charges	359p	
Sale of 6 quintales of lead	60p	
Church and religious cult		209p
Clothing for the Indians		713p
Wages for the shepherd		67p 7r
Servant's wages		56p 6r
Gardener's wages		13p 6r
Minister's needs, charity		217p 5r
Livestock purchased		301p
Payments to blacksmith and carpenter		88p
Repairs to the flour mill		10p
Total	1,670p 5r	1,677p

Source: BNFF 35/762.

Note: p = pesos; r = reales.

While they cultivated their own *milpas*, the custody of mission property was increasingly in the hands of paid laborers, and all skilled jobs — carpentry, smelting, and forging — required a wage.

In fact, the missions' corporate assets diminished markedly in the post-Jesuit period. Governor Pedro de Corbalán's *Estado* of 1778 and successive reports submitted by Franciscans and by *alcaldes* or *subdelegados* to the Intendencia de Arizpe, summarized in Tables 3.10 and 3.11, enumerate two basic categories of mission wealth: land and livestock.[38] Arable land, shown in *fanegas* and *suertes*, included fields for sowing grain and garden plots irrigated by hand or by earthen canals. The *fanegas* indicated in 1778 and 1794 refer to land set aside for the *común*, separate from the Indians' family *milpas*, but did not include all the irrigable land claimed by the missions.[39] Some of the cells without data in Tables 3.10 and 3.11 may reflect the failure of local authorities to note the information; likewise, for some of the pueblos in the Sonora and San Miguel

valleys, Corbalán simply wrote, "muchas [fanegas]." Despite these dis-
crepancies, it is worth observing that the 200 to 300 fanegas shown for
Oposura and Cumpas in 1778 do not appear at all in the compilation
of 1794. Converting the figures given to hectares shows a total agricultural base of 3,570 hectares for the mission pueblos in 1778, reduced to
less than 900 hectares for 1794—a loss of nearly 75 percent. It should
be remembered, however, that the figures shown in the tables are probably not exact nor complete. The loss of mission lands, or the failure to
plant arable fields nominally belonging to the común, deprived the communities of their most important resource and called into question the
agrarian foundations of mission economy. During the final quarter of
the eighteenth century, a substantial rise in the Hispanic population increased pressure on the land, and official policies favoring the privatization of rural property eroded the villages' corporate resources. During
this same period, mission herds suffered serious depletion, although
the livestock reported for each community varied widely. The sizable
herds shown for the Oposura mission district in 1778 had virtually dis-
appeared twenty years later, but a few missions, like Mátape, Guásabas
and San Ignacio, for example, increased the number of sheep reported
as mission property. The overall diminution of mission herds resulted
from Apache raids (a universal complaint in Sonora), the missionaries'
practice of selling off livestock to pay their debts, and the theft of feral
cattle by vecinos living in or near the missions.

Conclusions

The economic performance of the missions analyzed in the preceding sections followed the dominant patterns of change in eighteenth-
century Sonora. The most dramatic event of this period, having immediate consequences for native village life, was the expulsion of the
Jesuits in 1767. Civilian comisarios, appointed among the local population
of vecinos to administer the temporalidades, "lost" or otherwise dissipated
communal patrimony. They opened granaries, sold off cattle, and undermined the communal discipline of agricultural labor. Although mission
lands were not officially divided at this time, arable fields found their
way into private hands.[40] The Franciscans who replaced the Jesuits as
spiritual guardians of the pueblos never regained the temporal control

Table 3.10 Inventories of Mission Wealth in Sonora, 1778

	Houses (Adobe)	Land (Fanegas)	Garden (Suertes)	Livestock						
				Horses	Burros (Herds)	Oxen (Pairs)	Cattle	Sheep	Goats	Mules
Sta. Rosalia	1	6	...	...	...	...	...	...	...	...
Ures	18	...	...	131	2	18	445	1,066	112	20
Mátape	16	4	...	59	1	15	147	...	...	43
Yecora	5	3	...	...	...	...	...	...	...	...
Alamos	1	20	...	...	...	...	...	...	...	...
San José Pimas	12	...	...	6	...	5	17	40	80	1
Tecoripa	16	40	...	16	...	9	58	300	400	10
Suaqui	12	...	...	15	...	1	21	...	...	23
Cumuripa	10	...	...	37	...	8	75	240	300	46
Soyopa	15	1	...	27	...	...	300	...	...	10
Nacameri	27	...	1	53	3	14	3,094	50	50	68
Opodepe	5	...	...	8	...	3	121	163	37	...
Oposura	73	200	...	93	...	452	1,998	1,385	95	87
Teonadepa	12	...	...	1	...	72	8	...	...	9
Cumpas	83	300	...	17	...	26	13	...	93	28
Toyverobabi	12	...	...	32	...	22	813	500	50	40
Guásabas	58	20	24	23	10	122	424	...	30	71

Oputo	64	32	··	3	17	56	200	10	··
Guachinera	59	15	··	··	6	··	··	··	··
Bacerác	122	24	12	9	8	86	200	50	5
Bavispe	59	22	··	··	9	··	··	··	13
Cucurpe	110	··	16	··	14	175	660	50	··
Tuape	52	··	3	6	5	··	··	··	1
Arizpe	118	14	58	91	96	6,334	5,915	965	70
Chinapas	132	··	··	··	··	··	··	··	··
Bacuachi	35	··	··	9	··	··	··	··	··
Bacanuche	43	10	··	··	··	··	··	··	··
San Ignacio	34	··	30	8	82	300	300	50	8
Imuris	15	8	3	··	··	··	··	··	··
Cocóspera	29	8	13	4	4	200	200	10	··
Magdalena	18	··	4	··	2	··	··	··	··
Batuco	104	··	113	10	162	129	42	54	23
Tepupa	71	··	56	··	9	113	6	99	11
Bacadéguachi	50	··	252	··	16	160	402	110	63
Nácori	51	··	190	··	16	14	··	··	··
Mochopa	··	··	42	··	··	··	··	··	··
Total	1,542	134	1,319	147	1,213	15,101	11,669	2,645	650

Source: BNFF 34/736.

Note: Total land for 1778 (fanegas + suertes) = 3,570 hectares

Table 3.11 Inventories of Mission Wealth in Sonora, 1788 and 1794

	Land (Fanegas)	Garden (Suertes)	Horses	Burros (Herds)	Oxen (Pairs)	Livestock		Sheep	Goats	Mules	Stored Grain	(Fanegas)	
						Cattle		Sheep	Goats	Mules	Wheat	Maize	Beans
1788													
San Ignacio	...	...	...	...	13	170		900	...	...	230	150	30
Cocóspera	...	...	...	...	...	32		400	...	...	225	40	3
Tecoripa	...	...	6	4	...	46		200	...	2	...	...	...
Cumuripa	...	...	119	...	...	106		443	...	26	...	...	...
1794													
Mátape	...	...	18	...	3	62		406	...	...	22	...	2
Nácori	...	...	...	...	3	...		...	...	...	9	...	...
Alamos	...	...	...	...	3	...		...	...	50	...	...	...
Bacadeguachi	8	2	4	6	8	5		...	...	...	...	6	...
Nácori	4	3	12	1	8	5		...	...	2	5	...	...
Mochopa	1	1	...	...	4	...		...	...	...	...	9	...
Bacerác	11	7	14	...	14	56		...	...	...	...	14	1
Bavispe	...	2	...	...	12	...		...	...	...	10	...	...
Guachinera	...	2	...	...	13	55		298	99	...	25	...	2
Guasabas	21	4	10	...	44	157		1,208	157	14	102	...	...

Oputo	27	3	54	…	24	85	…	…	25	143	1	…
Oposura	…	2	…	…	20	27	…	…	…	8	19	…
Cumpas	…	7	…	…	…	…	…	…	…	15	…	…
Onavas	…	…	75	40[a]	19	352	92	79	15	…	50	6
Tonichi	…	…	142	2	19	591	…	…	3	9	12	2
Movas	…	…	2	…	8	3	30	66	2	…	2	…
Nuri	…	…	105	4	16	126	…	39	16	26	13	3
Arivechi	12	…	63	…	36	378	305	23	13	…	80	…
Pónida	…	…	2	…	19	62	…	…	2	…	…	…
Bacanora	…	…	57	…	37	446	201	10	7	54	60	…
Saguaripa	…	…	29	…	24	65	278	35	…	…	27	…
Taraichi	3	…	24	…	3	19	…	…	…	…	16	…
San José Pimas	6	…	24	…	…	27	300	…	…	…	…	…
Tecoripa	19	…	2	2	15	75	303	…	1	…	…	…
Cuquiarachi	6	…	…	…	…	…	200	400	…	…	…	…
Bacuachi	6	…	…	…	…	25	400	…	…	…	…	…
Cucurpe	8	…	…	…	…	21	…	…	…	…	…	…
Nacameri	18	…	…	…	3	15	…	…	…	…	…	…
Seris de Pitic	6	…	14	…	2	64	…	230	…	…	…	…
Total	156	33	651	53	357	2,721	4,021	1,138	100	478	309	16

Sources: BNFF 35/761/764, 36/797/798/803; AGN PI leg. 5, exp. 13, ff. 375–80.

Note: Total land for 1794 (fanegas + suertes) = 892.5 hectares.

a Single animals.

over the missions that their predecessors had once enjoyed. Friars of the province of Xalisco who took charge of the Opata and Lower Pima pueblos held authority only as religious mentors. Missionaries of the Colegio de Propaganda Fide de la Santa Cruz de Querétaro who were assigned to the Pimería Alta prevailed on the royal visitor José de Gálvez, in 1769, to restore to them the governance of the *temporalidades*. Thus, only in the northernmost frontier of the province of Sonora, where the mission field lay open to the *gentiles* of the Gila and Colorado valleys, was the Jesuit method of economic administration partially conserved under Franciscan auspices.[41]

As telling as these changes proved to be for the survival of mission villages, they flowed from the network of mercantile exchange which the Jesuits themselves had set in place. Overall, they attempted to balance internal consumption with opportunities for marketing the missions' surplus grain. By themselves, however, the figures for mission production are inadequate to measure levels of nutrition as an indication of the upper and lower limits of subsistence, for we lack information on the amount of foodstuffs raised by Indians in their own *milpas* and gathered in the *monte*. In effect, after 1767, *criollo* middlemen (the *comisarios*) who had served as interlocutors in the marketplace gained access to the missions' productive assets. The missionaries' administration of community surpluses, allowing for both internal distribution and sale in the market, proved untenable as overall production levels declined and the loss of land and herds diminished mission patrimony. Even before the expulsion of the Jesuits, Indian villagers eschewed the intensive labor required to produce agricultural surpluses. Although they still received gifts of clothing and foodstuffs from mission supplies, native horticulturalists relied more on their individual efforts as foragers, small producers, and free laborers to sustain their households. Rather than raise harvests of wheat and maize to be stored in mission granaries and marketed by the missionary or his agents, the Indians either retreated into subsistence or tried their own hand at selling their wares and their labor in Spanish settlements. Yaquis, in particular, who sold maize and salt in the *reales de minas* and did not charge freight expenses, undersold Spanish merchants.[42]

As the missionaries' capacity to market produce on behalf of the entire community waned, itinerant *rescatadores* circulated among the pueblos and dealt individually with Indian producers. These grain speculators advanced merchandise to *serrano* peasants against the following season's harvest, committing them to turn over their crops. In 1808, Intendente Alejo García Conde reissued orders drawn up by Comandante Jacobo Ugarte y Loyola two decades earlier, in 1790, in an attempt to regulate the distribution of grain.[43] It had come to his attention that *rescatadores* manipulated prices to the Indians' detriment and hoarded grain in order to sell it at a profit in times of scarcity, "which they, themselves, have caused." Ugarte y Loyola sought to ensure the subsistence of Indian communities by means reminiscent of the Jesuits' rationing of village produce, but working through civilian authorities. He directed that annual lists be drawn up, enumerating the volume of the harvests and the estimated needs of each household. If a surplus indeed existed, then its sale should conform to set priorities: first, to mineowners in order to feed their workers, then to hacendados who had workers in their employ. *Rescatadores* operating in the pueblos should register their presence and be inspected according to the amount of grain they took for resale.

In point of fact, the kind of controlled market that Ugarte y Loyola prescribed seems never to have materialized. Lamentably, detailed yearly censuses of households and harvests attendant upon his orders have not been found. Yet, the tone and content of his directives speak to rural conditions during the waning years of colonial rule. The references to "cuadrillas de peones" in mining camps and haciendas suggest that the number of direct producers in the villages had declined. At the same time, rural laborers, both Indian and *mestizo*, became increasingly dependent on their employers and masters for their basic material needs. Hacendados and mineowners no longer turned to the missions for available surpluses, but purchased foodstuffs from *rescatadores* to distribute — in lieu of salary — to their workers.

As the eighteenth century drew to a close, Bourbon authorities accelerated the secularization of the missions with the dispersal of communal lands. In 1794, Comandante Pedro de Nava ordered the division of what remained of the *común* into family plots, and replaced collective labor in the mission fields with a household tithe of one-half a fanega of maize, or its monetary equivalent, in order to support a resident priest. Two years later, when Bishop Francisco Rouset de Jesús sent a circular to all missionaries and parish priests inquiring into the state of his diocese, friars and curates alike made their complaints heard. *Vecinos* and Indians in Mátape, Cucurpe, Ures, Cocóspera, Oposura, and San José de Pimas paid only a small fraction of the required tithe. Fray Diego Pozo wrote from San José de Pimas, in the desert lowlands, that had he compelled the Indians to contribute the half fanega of maize, he would thereby have threatened their very survival and provoked their flight from the pueblo. When *vecinos* living in the missions paid the tithe or ecclesiastical fees at all, as noted in the 1788 reports for San Ignacio and Cocóspera, such modest emoluments partially replaced the communal harvests of earlier years as a source of mission income.[44]

These scanty tithe collections illustrate, once more, the conflict between the Indians' rationale of livelihood and the Spaniards' logic of mercantilism in the ecological setting of Sonora. Native peoples found the desert abundant in resources for their subsistence needs of food, clothing, tools, and shelter, but the labor required of them to sustain regular levels of marketable surpluses proved taxing over the course of time. Their economic behavior revealed areas of both continuity and contradiction between the mission-as-enterprise and the Indian community. Floodplain farmers had developed strong agricultural traditions which converged with the communal structures reconstituted in the mission pueblos. In the early stages of the *reducción* system, *serrano* peoples entered the missions in order to protect their cultivable land and sustain their agrarian cycle. Over time, however, the Jesuits' use of mission surpluses thrust Sonoran agrarian communities into expanding commercial spheres which redirected their labor to nonsubsistence ends. The measurable decline of surplus production in the late colonial period belied an imbalance between subsistence and market exchange in the missions.[45]

Equally significant were the pressures mounting in the private sector, as *vecinos* occupied arable land and pasturage and created a demand for Indian labor outside the pueblos. As the missions' productive base of land and labor diminished, the Indians turned from agriculture to alternative means of survival. Three economies clashed in the upland communities: (1) the Indians' procurement of a variety of resources for subsistence; (2) the missionaries' husbanding of agricultural surpluses in order to sustain their economic and religious system across an extended territory; and (3) the mercantilist promotion of commercial enterprise to augment Crown revenues and benefit private interests. If, in principle, Jesuit purposes diverged from the colonists' ambitions, in practice the missionaries' commercial involvement aligned them more and more with the colonial sector and weakened the productive base of the communities.

The missions' gradual impoverishment meant that Indians had to choose alternatives via spatial and social mobility. Although a core of native kinsmen remained in the villages, increasing numbers of them migrated to mining camps and private estates in search of a wage. Even though some of these migrants returned periodically to the missions, their insertion into the colonial market as laborers added a new dimension to traditional patterns of seasonal movement related to hunting and gathering. Village-centered peasant agriculture declined and, in its place, wage labor absorbed an increasing portion of the working energy of *serrano* households and communities. Faced with these straitened circumstances, native peoples developed new subsistence strategies to uphold their cultural values beyond the institutional limits of the mission. The Sonoras' responses to the colonial order constitute the central theme of Part Two, concerning family formation, community, and changing ethnic identities.

Part II

The Intimate Sphere of Ethnicity:
Household and Community

4

Sexuality, Marriage, and Family Formation in Sonora

In the early fall of 1800, Father Pedro de Leyva lamented to Bishop Francisco Rouset de Jesús the obstacles that he confronted in ministering to his unruly parishioners of Santísima Trinidad and Guadalupe, two mining towns in marked decline surrounded by numerous ranches and hamlets. The young priest had traversed a mountainous district of more than a hundred square miles in the province of Ostimuri, bounded by the missions of Saguaripa and Yécora and by the newly secularized parish of Onavas.[1] To Leyva fell the task of enforcing Catholic doctrine among an ethnically and culturally mixed population, in the virtual absence of a stable community. Unlike the missions, established in native pueblos and conserved over two centuries by a nucleus of resident agricultural households, the mining *reales* were ephemeral settlements which attracted a floating population. The itinerant laborers, described as "indios volantes y sin pié fijo," who arrived in places like Santísima Trinidad and San Francisco Xavier, coming from across the mountains to the west in Sonora, often formed casual unions and paid little heed to the Catholic vows of matrimony.[2]

On his arrival in Trinidad, Father Leyva was shocked to find "men with six children who had been married for more than twenty years, but who could not even recite the Lord's Prayer or the Creed." Neither he nor any of his predecessors had succeeded in founding a school there. Formal education was a luxury few families could afford; rather, parents sent their children out to scavenge the mining piles for fragments of unrefined ore to bolster their household economy. Leyva had despaired of teaching Christian doctrine to the adults, and even his attempts to catechize the children met with frustration: "The only way I have found to teach the Holy Doctrine is to walk through the *real* on Sunday afternoons, climbing up and down its steep hills, to gather the children together and bring them to church to hear the lesson. But it is never easy. Mothers hide their children, and some of them shout such insults at me that I tolerate it all only for the sake of God."[3]

Father Leyva's overriding concern was to enforce the principles of Christian marriage. Many of his parishioners had left their spouses in other communities and were living with new partners in Trinidad; other couples freely broke the bonds of monogamy. Some women were so brazen as to use their children as messengers and carriers of food for their lovers, instructing them not to let their fathers know of these arrangements. Lacking a *padrón* (official census) of legitimate marriages, Leyva enlisted the aid of the civil authorities and threatened all the wayward with excommunication. Following these measures, 320 adults living in the *real* had complied with the priest's demands and submitted to the formality of Christian marriage.

The Indians living outside Trinidad, however, presented a special problem for the reforming priest. Yaquis and Pimas who came to the mine seeking wage labor had, for the most part, left the disciplined life of the mission villages. Whether they had migrated permanently or only temporarily, the *naborías* lived beyond the effective control of their missionaries and of the curates who served in the mining towns.[4] Some of them brought their families with them, but others formed new households in the vicinity of the *real*. Padre Leyva doubted whether they were formally married and reported scandalous incidents of conjugal infidelity. In order to curtail these "public sins," Leyva set out with the local *teniente de justicia* and his deputies to impose order on the Indians and compile a census of their families. He hoped "to obligate them, first with love, to hear Mass and the word of God." The following night many *naborías* — including men, women, and children — fled the encampment. The families who stayed and those who returned little by little ignored the priest's exhortations to be counted and fulfill the requirements of Christian marriage.

The Indians showed by their actions that they understood as well as Father Leyva the significance of a *padrón*. Not merely a list of names or an impartial summary of the people living in any one place, it was an instrument of social control. Parish priests and missionaries alike took these censuses periodically to distinguish legitimate marriages from casual unions and to identify those adults who had complied with the church's laws concerning the sacraments and nuptiality. As early as 1737, Jesuit authorities had established norms for taking these censuses, and Franciscans and curates of a later period followed the Jesuit model. Ecclesiastical *estados*, or censuses, summarized the number of persons recognized as resident in each parish or mission. The clerics categorized them according to civil status, ethnic group, and progress in Christian indoctrination. The *estados* served to keep a rough count of the souls for whom the priests were held responsible and to demonstrate their diligence in administering the sacraments. In compiling *padrones*, the priests listed the persons living in each household, usually indicating spouses, children, and other dependents. They categorized the families by ethnic group, distinguishing among "indios," "españoles," and "castas," and frequently separated widows and widowers from *casados*, the latter interpreted as patriarchal households headed by a man and his wife.[5]

The bishop's *padrón* of 1796 anticipated the secularization of the missions in Sonora. It would determine which families were eligible to receive the plots of land assigned to individual households out of mission commons and would structure payment of the diocesan tithe.[6] Thus, the church's blessing on marital unions could be understood to legitimate family entitlements to the productive resources of the community. By contrast, the majority of Indians and *vecinos* who had gathered in mining settlements like Trinidad, San Xavier, and Cieneguilla had no prior claim to the land. They lived as common laborers, peddlers, and prospectors, although some may have retained rights to land in their home villages.

The process of family formation in both kinds of communities evolved from indigenous kinship patterns, shaped and molded no less by the material conditions of this colonial frontier. Demographic patterns were rooted in both the political economy of colonialism and in the strategies forged by peasant families to create viable domestic units. Highland Sonorans adapted their shifting communities to long-term ecological constraints and to the labor demands created by Spanish enterprises. Their behavior illustrates the fluid, changing quality of social categories such as family, household, and community. This chapter explores the dynamic relationship between kinship patterns and household economy operative in the *serrano* communities of Sonora by analyzing eighteenth-century *estados* and *padrones*.

Family and Household

Behold, how good and how pleasant it is for brethren to dwell together in unity.

Psalms 133: 1

The terms *family* and *household* connote a constellation of social relations expressive both of affective ties and of the economic functions necessary for the survival of the domestic unit. Family is centered on the bonds of kinship defined by each culture, bonds which tend to establish reciprocal rights and obligations between those persons related to one another through direct descent, marriage, or ritual sponsorship. The household consists of the persons who reside together and who share responsibility for maintaining the relations of production and distribution within their domestic group and within the community to which they belong. Stated more simply, a household includes the people who live and work together and share the same hearth. *Nuclear families*, limited in the strictest sense to the conjugal pair and their surviving children, are single households that may be linked to affinal and fictive kin across more than one generation. *Extended families* frequently contain several households, as new conjugal units are formed; conversely, a large household may include more than one family. Father Leyva's energetic ministry to the "people without religion" in Trinidad confused family and household in his condemnation of "improper unions." Moreover, while seeking to impose marital stability, Leyva failed to comprehend the adaptive process of family formation in the mining camps that made up his parish.

These conflicts between the model of Christian marriage and the reality of conjugal unions in late colonial Sonora stemmed from complex migratory patterns and the exigencies of subsistence. The structure and composition of *serrano* households reflected both the prevailing mode of production and the relations of power involved in apportioning resources and dealing with other domestic units. In societies based on foraging and swidden agriculture, such as the desert O'odham or the mountain Joba, families constituted loosely joined groups of adults and children who banded together to procure the resources they needed. Their levels of production fostered an immediate sharing of the product, without the development of sustained ties of dependency and obligation over time.[7] In contrast, the intensification of agriculture and consolidated settlements of Pima, Opata, and Eudeve villagers underlay familial relations different from those of desert nomads. Increased labor requirements in terms of the time devoted to production and the organization of work, the need to store the surplus product in order to sustain the population over nonproductive periods in the agricultural cycle, and the formalization of individual and collective claims to the land altered the composition of the domestic unit. The family emerged as a cohesive working group, and kinship became an operative ideology invoked to legitimate a hierarchical ranking of relationships, command labor as needed, establish territorial claims, and secure the family's reproduction from one generation to the next. Among these *serrano* peoples, nuclear families belonged to clusters of *rancherías* and pueblos organized for the procurement and distribution of basic resources.[8]

Opata kinship terminology, for example, supported their ethnic identity and provided the basis for governing their communities. Different categories of kinfolk expressed degrees of affinity and distinguished among persons according to gender and age. Tegüima vocabulary connoted distinct sets of relations between parents and children, grandparents and grandchildren, aunts, uncles, nieces, and nephews, siblings and cousins, and the familial alliances created through marriage. These terms varied according to the speaker and to the relatives he or she addressed. Thus, fathers called their sons *noguat* and their daughters *maraguat*, but mothers called their sons *miriguat* and their daughters *aquiguat*. The complexity of their kinship lexicon suggests that the Opatas recognized different levels of authority within households and between families and communities.[9]

Beyond these consanguineal relations, the Opatas strengthened their social bonds through various ceremonies of sponsorship. At birth their children received names during a ritual called *peri*, in which a sponsor formally named the child and assumed a paternal responsibility for him. *Peri* established reciprocal obligations between the sponsor, his kinfolk, and the child's family. Under Jesuit tutelage the Opatas adapted the Iberian tradition of *compadrazgo* and the ritual of baptism to their established custom, conferring godparent terms to their children's sponsors and extended families.[10] Furthermore, Opata villagers formalized friendships among adults through *dagüinemaca,* a public ritual of dancing and gift exchange. Male friends declared their mutual obligations to one another in *noragua;* women strengthened their bonds of confidence and support in *maragua.*[11] Through these ceremonies Opata individuals participated in overlapping kinship networks extending far beyond the nuclear family and strengthened the bonds of reciprocal exchange that held their communities together.

These kinship networks integrated individuals into different segments of the ethnic community and ensured the reproduction of family lines. *Reproduction,* a central concept for the discussion of families and households, comprehends biological, cultural, and economic relations essential for the persistence of discrete societies and ethnicities. Biological reproduction refers directly to the survival of the domestic unit through the continuance of life across generations and the formation of new conjugal households. Yet the term implies not only physiological reproduction, but the re-creation of social patterns and cooperative practices necessary to sustain families and communities. The reproduction of the labor force requires childbearing and the survival of children to adulthood as well as the daily maintenance of the workers, tasks which nearly universally fall to women.[12] Furthermore, families reinforce their cultural values from one generation to the next and renew their bonds across households. Through periodic visits and the exchange of family members, religious ceremonies, and the very language of kinship, domestic communities ensure their persistence, even as they are reconstituted by the cycle of death and birth and by the entry of individuals from alien ethnic groups.

Cultural reproduction of the family entails effective social control over its members by the reputed head of household. In stratified societies, social control of peasant communities through the patriarchal household is closely linked to political control over defined territories. Household size and age composition in different historical moments correspond to the impact of natural phenomena, such as crop failures or epidemics, and to the political pressures of taxation, labor coercion, and other means of extracting surplus resources from peasant households. Thus, in colonial Mexico, the conservation of the patriarchal family was of no small import to the church and the Spanish Imperium. The statistics generated by ecclesiastical and viceregal authorities with the intent of controlling the population under their rule provide abundant materials for studying the history of the family.[13] The following analysis of population data for selected villages illustrates the changing composition of Sonoran families and households over time. This avenue of research builds on the rich ethnohistorical literature for the region; at the same time, it proposes a revisionist critique of conventional interpretations of the demographic patterns observed in this frontier province.

The Population History of Sonora

Population studies for this region are grounded in the tradition of cultural geography developed over half a century and inspired largely by the exemplary work of Carl Sauer, Ralph Beals, and Robert West.[14] These authors and their students combined documentary research with archaeological surveys and extensive fieldwork to build an interpretive framework that related estimates of demographic levels at different points in time to the natural environment. In the absence of systematic tribute or tithe enrollments, and with only fragmentary parish records prior to the second half of the eighteenth century, historical demography has followed the general lines of inquiry established by the institutional and narrative history for northwestern Mexico. These rest principally on Jesuit and Franciscan records, and their main object of study is the mission.

Several studies based on the quantitative analysis of mission censuses during the seventeenth and eighteenth centuries concur in showing a strong, unarrested decline in the indigenous population of Sonora. Their findings rest primarily on the comparison of population counts and mean family size for different ethnic groups and territories, calculated from the missionaries' reports of the souls under their care in different categories of Christian observance: for example, *párvulos, confesantes,* and *comunicantes.* Underscoring the dramatic fall in the number of Indians reportedly living in the missions, some authors have projected the biological extinction of certain ethnic groups. They attribute this demographic collapse to epidemic disease, the breakdown of pre-Hispanic ecosystems and cultural practices, and the usurpation of vital resources—land, water, and labor power—by the Spanish colonists who brought mining and ranching to the province.[15]

Notwithstanding the undeniable impact of these variables on the ethnic survival of Sonora's Indian peoples, the conceptual definitions guiding regional population studies require some revision. Sociodemographic histories concentrate on the resident population in the pueblos and, for that reason, assume the mutual identity of mission and community. Although they recognize the presence of nomads and gentiles— Indian groups living beyond the aegis of the missions—rarely do they explore in depth the ties of kinship and reciprocity between villagers and hunter-gatherers that remained operative under colonial rule. Thus, quantitative analyses of mission population counts show an unmitigated decline of resident neophytes without taking into account the regenerative potential for serrano communities of the economic and cultural ties between sedentary horticulturalists and nomads. In fact, a closer look at the historical evidence for missions and mining reales will show that the difference between sedentary and nomadic was not necessarily hard-and-fast. Rather, native rancherías occupied more than one habitat in accord with the seasons. In addition, individuals separated from their base households to combine different resources from foraging, hunting, and planting.

Cutting across pre-Hispanic traditions of seasonal migration, the colonial economy weighed heavily on indigenous settlement patterns. Undoubtedly, the growth of mining reales and haciendas led to the transfer of material and human resources from native communities to Spanish enterprises. The mercantile interests that underwrote Spanish colonial policies conflicted with the Sonorans' economy of subsistence; nevertheless, village commoners sought out opportunities to sell their produce and labor in the provincial networks of market exchange. Thus, the colonial economy represented both a burden and an opportunity for serrano peoples to buttress and even expand their village economy.

The Indians' physical mobility and participation in the market led to cultural commingling and the blurring of ethnic distinctions. Conventional use of the term acculturation points to the fading of autochthonous patterns and the destabilization of native communities under colonial influence.[16] Without denying at all the violence of conquest and its destructive sequel of mortality, displacement, and loss of autonomy for the Sonoran peoples, the present study questions the tendency to accept an implicit state of social and ecological equilibrium prior to the conquest, now called into question by the archaeological and historical evidence of internal conflict and stratification in pre-Hispanic communities.[17] As colonial society developed over two centuries, new forms of social inequality arose. Conflict occurred at different levels, expressed as ethnic antagonism between Indians and Spaniards, as tribal strife among Indian groups, and as incipient class struggle over the possession of land and the allocation of labor.

Given the mobility of *serrano* peoples, the families resident in the pueblos who appeared in the censuses and *padrones* recorded by the missionaries did not constitute the universe of ethnic population in the province. The Jesuits explained repeatedly that their counts represented only those persons "under their administration" (*de administración*), who obeyed their teachings and participated in the economic and ceremonial life of the missions.[18] The *estados* frequently did not include children younger than seven to ten years, the age at which they became catechumens. Even the house-to-house *padrones* did not necessarily list all the children living in each household. For these reasons, the number of individuals registered in the missions at any given time does not correspond to all the Indians living in and around the villages.[19]

These considerations lead us to alternative interpretations of the population history of colonial Sonora. Despite the downward movement of demographic figures derived from mission records, comparative analysis of summary counts and household enumerations shows both the complexity and the regenerative quality of native family composition. The missionaries' summations of baptisms and burials confirm the biological and social reproduction of Indian as well as *mestizo* households in the pueblos, notwithstanding high levels of mortality. Furthermore, the dichotomy of *Indian* and *non-Indian* should be qualified in order to capture the historical reality behind these ethnic categories.

The language of colonial documents makes it clear that the meaning of commonly used racial nomenclature varied according to time and place. Civil and religious authorities alike employed terms that combined (and confused) different criteria for classifying conquered tribal peoples and the heterogeneous population of *naborías*, freed slaves, and vagabonds who migrated northward to the mining districts. Three main considerations underlay the division of colonial society in this frontier province: the distinction between sedentary and seminomadic peoples; the ethnocultural separation of Spaniards, *castas*, and Indians; and the economic and political differences between *vecinos* and Indians. Those Indians who left their communities definitively, in time became part of the mixed population referred to as *castas* or *gente de razón*.

Within the Indian community itself, the missionaries' distinction between *gentiles* and *hijos de la campana* ("children of the bell") bore on their administration of the pueblos. While *gentiles* visited the missions from time to time, only the *hijos* lived under the missionaries' direct supervision, contributed regularly to communal labor in the pueblos, and had a right to the semiannual distribution of grain from mission harvests. Equally important for the internal life of the missions was the separation between Indians and *vecinos*. The Indians constituted those households which, in principle, belonged to the mission. In exchange for work, they received food, cloth, tools, and seeds for planting their own *milpas*. The *vecinos*, on the other hand, had an ambiguous relationship to the communal economy. Theoretically they should have paid the tithe and other ecclesiastical fees, but the missionaries frequently complained that the *vecinos* contributed little or nothing to the economic life of the missions.[20] Their rising numbers in the pueblos led to a mixed population which, in turn, had important implications for the composition of the domestic unit and the reconstitution of the community. The horizontal mobility of people across mining camps, presidios, and villages accelerated the phenomenon of "passing" from one ethnic category to another, nearly always from Indian to *gente de razón*. This fluid quality of ethnic terms bears on the process of social and demographic differentiation, as shown by the analysis of successive population counts in the missions during the latter decades of colonial rule.[21]

The Quantitative Analysis of Family Formation

The data presented in this section represent only a sampling of the population in Sonora, limited to a large degree by the available documentation and the criteria used by different missionaries to keep track of the people under their care. Thus, it cannot be emphasized too much that the data appearing in the tables and figures below constitute only a portion of the families and individuals — Indian and non-Indian alike — who lived in Sonora during the waning years of colonial rule. Aggregate data compiled from ecclesiastical surveys taken periodically throughout the seventeenth and eighteenth centuries suggest a constant decline in Indians and a gradual rise in the number of *vecinos*, as shown in Table 4.1. These approximate counts represent the resident population of missions and parishes estimated during episcopal visitations and the summaries of mission *estados*.

Table 4.1 shows periods of pronounced demographic fluctuation which correspond to the general direction of colonization. The Opata, Eudeve (subsumed under "Opata" in Table 4.1), and Pima Bajo were in contact with Spaniards continually since the early decades of the seventeenth century in the missions and mines of highland Sonora. In contrast, the Pima Alto (including the Tohono O'odham) of the northern arid plains had only sporadic contacts with Europeans until the end of the century. The Jesuits did not begin their *reducciones* in the Pimería Alta until 1687, and during the first quarter of the eighteenth century they failed to maintain resident missionaries in all their mission districts. Spanish colonists did not enter this zone in significant numbers until the second half of the century.

Ranchers, mining prospectors, and itinerant laborers who traveled the routes leading from Sonora to Nueva Vizcaya and Nueva Galicia spread contagious diseases in their path and altered the ecological and cultural matrices which had sustained *serrano* communities. The Opata, Eudeve, and Pima Bajo suffered dramatic population decline from 1600 to 1678, but showed a slight recovery between 1720 and 1760. The Upper Pimas, however, experienced severe demographic losses during 1678–1720, and their numbers continued to fall throughout the eighteenth century. The northern Pimas whom the missionaries recognized as "hijos de la campana" suffered an uninterrupted decline. Nevertheless, a significant portion of O'odham lived outside the missions. Jesuits and Franciscans recruited fresh neophytes among these *gentiles* who visited the pueblos seasonally, thus replenishing the population in the missions.[22]

All the ethnic groups listed in Table 4.1 suffered another severe demographic decline between 1760 and 1800. This second contraction of the mission population occurred, in part, because of the epidemics which

Table 4.1 Global Population Estimates by Ethnic Group, Province of Sonora, 1600–1800

	1600	1678	% Change 1600–1678	1720	% Change 1678–1720	1760	% Change 1720–1760	1800	% Change 1760–1800
Pima Alto	20,000	16,600	−17	7,600	−56	5,750	−24	1,300	−77
Pima Bajo	10,500	4,000	−62	3,150	−21	3,550	+06	1,800	−49
Opata	50,200	15,200	−70	7,100	−53	8,000	+13	4,450	−44
Total Indians	80,700	35,800	−56	17,850	−50	17,300	−03	7,550	−56
Vecinos	1,400			3,000	+114	7,600	+153	15,000	+97

Source: Peter Gerhard, The North Frontier of New Spain (Princeton: Princeton University Press, 1982), pp. 190, 285.

Note: Eudeve is subsumed under Opata, and O'odham under Pima Alto in this table.

repeatedly swept through the province (see Table 4.2). The drop in the number of persons counted as Indians reflects not only high levels of mortality, but also their geographic and social mobility. A significant portion of the increase in vecinos (difficult to quantify) after 1760 is made up of those Indians who had joined the transient laborers of Sonora's placer mines. Bishop Antonio de los Reyes observed in 1784 that Indians had begun to solicit the status of vecino, thereby accepting implicitly the obligation to pay the parish tithe but evading the obligations of communal labor and political control in the missions.[23]

The data tallied for adult Indians and vecinos living in those highland communities still under mission administration toward the end of the eighteenth century suggest a pattern of change in which Indians as well as vecinos grew in number, but the rate of growth of vecinos outstripped that of Indians. The data summarized in Table 4.3 and Figure 4.1 are derived from tables generated by the Franciscan missionaries in charge of the Pimería Baja in eastern Sonora, Bishop Reyes's report of 1784, and Bishop Rouset's padrón of 1796. Figure 4.1 bears on the hypotheses outlined above concerning alternative explanations of population movement. Although the rising slope of the graph from 1784 to 1799 is no doubt exaggerated owing to the incomplete counts for 1784 and 1796, it appears that the province experienced an undramatic but steady increase in population which mirrors similar trends in other parts of New Spain. Furthermore, the increment in total population parallels the curve for vecinos. Thus, it is probable that the growing non-Indian population with fixed residence in agricultural communities dominated the central tendencies of demographic change during this period. The crossing of the Indian and vecino lines in 1801 suggests a process of differential population growth favoring the castas (mixed groups) rather than any sharp break with earlier demographic patterns.

In order to explain the decline of Indians and the constant growth of vecinos, it is necessary to go beyond the demographic patterns themselves and consider the social, political, and economic structures of the province. Changes in land tenure reduced the agrarian base of serrano villages markedly from the 1780s onward. These same pueblos bore the brunt of military campaigns against Seris and Apaches, further diminishing their core population. It may be that the total increase in village dwellers—Indians and non-Indians—after 1784 corresponded to the reprieve

Table 4.2   Chronology of Major Epidemics in Sinaloa and Sonora

Years	Diseases
1593	Smallpox, measles
1601–2	Measles, typhus, smallpox
1606–7	Measles, smallpox
1612–15	Typhus, smallpox
1616–17	Smallpox, measles
1619–20	Famine and diseases
1623–25	Smallpox, typhus
1636–41	Smallpox and other diseases
1645–47	Malaria
1652–53	Smallpox
1655–57	Famine and diseases
1662	Various diseases
1668–69	Various diseases
1692–93	Smallpox, measles, typhus
1697–98	Smallpox
1709–10	Smallpox
1718	Smallpox
1721	Influenza
1723	Smallpox
1725	Various diseases
1728–32	Measles, dysentery
1737	Various diseases
1742	Various diseases
1744–46	Various diseases
1748–49	Measles, dysentery
1762–64	Smallpox
1766	Various diseases
1768–70	Smallpox, measles
1772–73	Typhus
1781–82	Smallpox
1796–97	Smallpox

Table 4.2 Continued

Years	Diseases
1800–1801	Typhus or typhoid
1805–6	Measles
1808	Smallpox
1816–17	Smallpox
1826–28	Measles
1831	Smallpox
1833–34	Cholera
1838	Smallpox
1843	Smallpox
1851–52	Cholera

Sources: Daniel T. Reff, *Disease, Depopulation and Culture Change in Northwestern New Spain, 1518–1764* (Salt Lake City: University of Utah Press, 1991), pp. 97–179; Robert H. Jackson, *Indian Population Decline. The Missions of Northwestern New Spain, 1687–1840* (Albuquerque: University of New Mexico Press, 1994), p. 167.

Table 4.3 Comparative Population Counts for Selected Missions in Sonora, 1784–1806

Year	Indians	Vecinos	Total
1784	2,407	1,789	4,196
1796	2,516	1,891	4,407
1799	3,466	2,802	6,268
1802	3,366	3,635	7,001
1804	3,139	4,039	7,178
1806	3,077	3,958	7,035

Sources: AMH AD I, AS 22; BNFF 34/759, 36/800, 802, 806.

Note: For ratios of Indians to *vecinos*, see Table 4.4.

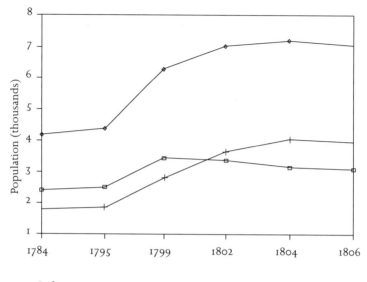

□ Indians
+ Vecinos
◊ Totals

Note: Graph plotted with actual values

Figure 4.1. Comparative population counts for selected missions in Sonora, 1784–1806

obtained in the Apache wars by dint of the heightened vigilance of the Spanish military and the presence of Apache "peace encampments" established near several presidios in the northeastern portion of the province. The divergent tendencies noted for Indians and *gente de razón* are more likely explained by intermixture of ethnic groups and by generally higher levels of mortality (especially infant mortality) for Indians than for vecinos than they are by subsistence crises of epidemic proportions. Different ratios of Indians to *vecinos* calculated from the data summarized in Table 4.3 suggest interesting regional variations in the ethnic division of the population. Regions III and IV (see Table 4.4) constitute the "old" *serrano* areas of missions and mining settlements established during the first half of the seventeenth century, while regions I and II represent the

Table 4.4   Ratios of Indians to *Vecinos* by Region,
1796–1806

Year	I	II	III	IV	V
1796	2.1	.6	2.1		1.3
1799			.7	5.9	1.2
1802			.7	2.8	.9
1806	1.8	.4	.6	1.2	.8

Sources: AMH AD I, AS 22; BNFF 34/759, 36/800, 802, 806.

Note: I = Northwest Pimería Alta; II = Magdalena Valley; III = Arivechi and Sagua-ripa mission districts; IV = Bacerác mission district; V = province of Sonora.

central and western segments of Pimería Alta, the last area of Sonora to come under Spanish dominion.

The global ratios for the province of Sonora (region V in Table 4.4) mirror the general decline in Indians and increase in non-Indians shown in Figure 4.1. Nevertheless, the contrasting ratios obtained within the Pimería Alta and between the Arivechi-Saguaripa and Bacerác mission districts indicate that the decrease in mission Indians and increment in resident *vecinos* did not occur evenly throughout Sonora. The Altar and Santa Cruz valleys in Northwest Pimería Alta retained a substantial num-ber of native villagers despite the flow of Spaniards and *mestizos* to the placer mines at Cieneguilla after 1771. Likewise, the Bacerác and Bacadé-guachi mission pueblos represented the core of what had been a dense pre-Hispanic Opata population with a strong tradition of agriculture and settlement in permanent towns. By contrast, the *vecinos* had virtually displaced the Pima inhabitants of the Magdalena Valley. The Arivechi and Batuc mission districts sustained an important nucleus of native Eudeve population but received increasing numbers of non-Indian settlers.

Basic demographic events, mirrored in the sacramental registers of baptisms, marriages, and burials, determine to a large degree the sta-bility of village population. Table 4.5 summarizes the records supplied by the Franciscans for the missions of the Lower and Upper Pimería at the turn of the nineteenth century. The first set of data for the Pimería

Table 4.5 Sacramental Registers of Life Events

	Pimería Baja					
	Vecinos			Indians		
Date	Bap	Mar	Bur	Bap	Mar	Bur
1798–1802	741	121	225	791	227	608
1804–1806	346	74	143	375	125	385
	Pimería Alta					
	Vecinos			Indians		
Date	Bap	Mar	Bur	Bap	Mar	Bur
1794–1796	49	13	47	93	31	124
1804–1806	185	38	150	217	78	250

Sources: BNFF 36/815, 37/829, 36/802.

Baja (1798–1802) shows that Indians accounted for 52 percent of all baptisms, 63 percent of all marriages, and 73 percent of all burials. Because the missionary gave only aggregate counts of Indians and *gente de razón* for 1804–06, the numbers placed in this row of the table have been calculated, using the percentages for the earlier period. In the Pimería Alta during 1794–96, Indians represented 66 percent of total baptisms, 71 percent of all marriages, and 73 percent of all burials. During the latter two years, Indians accounted for a little over one-half the baptisms, two-thirds of marriages, and about three-fifths of burials. It is difficult to estimate the rates of vital events, because the universe of total population remains an unknown quantity.[24]

At the close of the eighteenth century, then, both the Indian and the non-Indian sector experienced high levels of fertility and mortality. Although Indians represented a declining proportion of the population resident in the pueblos, they accounted for more than half of all births, marriages, and deaths recorded in the missions. Native fertility and nuptiality seems to reflect a constant effort to achieve biological reproduction in the face of high levels of mortality.[25] The most dramatic disparity observed, though, concerns the high percentage of burials attributed to the Indians. An initial reading of the data in Table 4.5 suggests that mortality constituted a formidable ethnic divide between Indians and *vecinos*. Nevertheless, some qualifying factors should be taken into account. It is probable that these figures, taken from mission registers, underrepresent the *gente de razón*, for the communities listed do not include the presidios and mining *reales* where the majority of *vecinos* lived. Furthermore, it should be remembered that these sacramental registers do not record all births, conjugal unions, and deaths—only those legitimated by the church.

The complexity of indigenous mortality, with respect to its causes and the cyclical rhythm of crisis and recovery, poses basic questions about its impact on family and household formation. Native Americans' susceptibility to Eurasian diseases is less well documented (if no less true) for Sonora than for the core areas of New Spain. Research in this area has established an initial periodization of epidemics, but it is not clear when population decline reached its nadir and demographic recovery began (see Table 4.2).[26] The historiography on demographic themes for other regions of colonial Mexico, however, provides valuable guidelines for interpreting the evidence gathered thus far on highland Sonora.[27] As for the causes of high mortality, it is important to distinguish between epidemic and endemic disease and to note that different pathogens targeted specific age groups. Smallpox, which swept across the Mesoamerican population from the earliest days of the conquest, continued to plague indigenous communities and the urban poor of mixed ethnicity throughout the colonial period. Children were particularly susceptible to smallpox and measles, although especially severe epidemics carried off the adults as well. *Matlazáhuatl*, considered to be a combination of certain forms of typhoid and typhus and, in some instances, infectious hepatitis, struck the adult working population. When adults in their reproductive years succumbed to an epidemic, of course, mortality had an immediate effect on fertility. Conversely, when children were the principal victims of disease, the birth rate rose soon after the crisis had passed, but the effects of a "lost generation" would come to bear on nuptiality and fertility several years later.[28] Against this background, an initial reading of late eighteenth-century Sonoran parish registers shows that measles was a common cause of death, particularly for children. It is probable that infant and child mortality accounted for an important part of the overall mortality figures recorded in the missions. Furthermore, stillbirths, miscarriages, and the death of women in pregnancy constitute a "hidden factor" of infant mortality observed indirectly through a declining birthrate in the wake of disease.

Syphilis (*Treponema pallidum*) was a popular explanation among contemporaries for the apparent drop in native population, even as the origins and spread of syphilis have generated debate among scholars from the sixteenth century to the present day.[29] Fray Josef Saenz Pico reported to Bishop Rouset in 1795, from the Presidio de Altar, that "Indian families [in the missions] have declined at an alarming rate, owing as much to the attacks of their enemies, the Apaches, Seris, and Piatos, as to the *morbo gálico* which is so prevalent among them, the contagion passing from parents to children."[30] While syphilis probably was endemic to both the Indian and the non-Indian population, given the movement of laborers and camp followers to and from the mines, it should be remembered that to characterize the native peoples as riddled with the "French disease" was yet another way of denigrating them. The high levels of fertility noted above suggest, to the contrary, that native fecundity was not stained by the *morbo gálico*.

Epidemics did not occur as isolated events, but rather as clusters of disease. They formed part of subsistence crises intensified by crop failures, wars, or dislocations provoked by forced labor drafts. The famines and disease episodes that swept through the native population of Sonora and New Spain at different times were as much the result of social and political factors as of natural causes (flooding and droughts brought on by erratic rainfall patterns).[31] The rigors of *repartimiento*, which removed Indians from the missions to work in the mines, affected early colonial *reducciones* and, by the eighteenth century, Indians were leaving their communities more or less voluntarily to seek wage labor in Spanish haciendas and mining *reales*. Migration, the impact of Apache raiding, and particularly the increasing pressure of non-Indian settlement on agricultural resources, combined to reduce the indigenous population resident in the pueblos and diminish food production for subsistence. All of these pressures affected the Indians' resistance to disease and thus had consequences for the reproduction of native families.

Significantly, the Indians feared disease, as Fray Pico reported for the Altar Valley in 1795: "Each year some *gentiles* come to the missions, and more would stay were it not for their horror of an early death, as they have seen from experience." [32] Earlier, Father Jácobo Sedelmayr had given the Jesuit visitor Juan Antonio Balthasar his impressions of the measles epidemic which had occurred in the same area of the Pimería Alta:

> The scourge of measles which so afflicted the Indians felled half the population of this *cabecera* [head village] of Tubutama, nearly 200 Indians of all ages. During this great contagion there happened what I would never have expected: three desert *rancherías* and one even fifty leagues away, when one should think that they would most likely stay away from the missions, came to be enrolled in my *visita* of Sáric and to receive baptism. *Non est abbreviata manus Domini.* [33]

Indians alternatively avoided and sought out baptism in order to defend themselves from epidemics. Writ large, this same ambivalence characterized their approach to mission life. They incorporated the agricultural cycle of the mission pueblos into their own strategies for survival, but sought sustenance as laborers in Spanish enterprises and as gatherers in the desert. *Vecinos* sustained a parallel movement: they came and went, attracted to the placer mines and living on the margins of the mission economy. Fray Ygnacio Dávalos closed his report on the Pimería Baja in 1806 with the observation that from a total population of 7,293 (Indians and *vecinos*) 808 persons had left the missions during a two-year period. [34]

The native population of Sonora survived, if in markedly diminished numbers, through the biological and social reproduction of their domestic units. The following analysis of the 1796 *padrón* affords a view of how *serrano* peoples reconstituted their households and garnered the labor power necessary for subsistence. This discussion is based on a sample comprising 946 individuals and 239 households distributed through six villages, as shown in Table 4.6. Statistical median values for age of household head, age of women living in male-headed households, and children/woman ratios help to explain different modes of family composition. Thus:

Median Age of Household Head

Men and Women	Men	Women
39	37	50

Table 4.6 Mission Population Sample for Sonora, 1796

	No. Families	No. Persons	Ratio Persons/ Family	Main Ethnic Group
Cocóspera	41	144	3.5	Pima
Batuc	59	236	4.0	Eudeve
San José Pimas	7	35	5.0	*Vecino*
Cobache	56	184	3.3	Pima
San Marcial	4	24	6.0	*Vecino*
Arivechi	72	323	4.5	Opata/*vecino*

Source: AMH AS, caja 22.

The strikingly high age shown for women is owing, in part, to the fact that the missionaries who formulated these censuses considered only widows as female household heads in their own right. The mean age of women appearing as wives in male-headed households hovered at around thirty, regardless of ethnic group. In general, these figures support the impression taken from reading the actual ages listed for adults in the censuses: namely, with the exception of a few relatively young marriages, household heads who remained in the pueblos constituted an aging population. It may be inferred that young adults—men and women—tended to leave the mission villages, as exemplified by the 200 Yaquis and Pimas encamped in the vicinity of Trinidad in 1800 who refused to be counted in Father Leyva's *padrón*, and by the 800 emigrants who left the Pima Baja missions in 1804–6. If this is true, then it follows that the permanent residents of mission pueblos in the late eighteenth century represented precisely that fraction of adult Indians less likely to procreate. Indeed, a substantial number of these households were formed by widows (and occasionally widowers) with unmarried children, grandchildren, nieces, and nephews. Furthermore, the migration of young adults from the pueblos removed an important segment of the native population from mission censuses. Those most likely to contribute to population growth went uncounted in the mission *estados*, a fact which helps to explain the apparent decline of Indians and increase of *vecinos* in the province. Next:

Children/Woman Ratios for Women in Male-Headed Households

Global	Indians	Vecinos
2.7	1.8	2.9

The global ratio is based on total figures of 207 women and 458 children, within the sample of 946 persons. The children/woman ratios for Indians and vecinos correspond only to that portion of the population for which ethnicity was specified:

Women			Children		
Indians	Vecinos	Total	Indians	Vecinos	Total
132	72	204	232	211	443

The ratios shown may be skewed downward, because although nearly all women were categorized by race in the censuses, the priests seldom clarified the ethnic status of the offspring of mixed marriages. The children/woman ratio of 1.8 refers to the product of unions in which both father and mother are identified as Indians. Households headed by Indian men married to non-Indian women were included in the indios section of the padrón, but the children's ethnicity was not specified. Conversely, missionaries included households headed by non-Indian men married to Indian women in the vecino population of their districts. Nevertheless, the priests' standards of classification did not necessarily conform to the serrano peoples' cultural norms. The censuses did not distinguish whether native women who chose Spanish or mestizo mates opted to raise their children as "Indians" or to acculturate them to the dominant society.

The padrones offer qualitative evidence that bears significantly on the issue of household formation. When ages, surnames, and ethnic identity are consistently noted for individuals, certain inferences can be made concerning the linkage of families and the life cycle of households. Second or third marriages after the death of a spouse were common. Young stepmothers frequently cared for their husbands' children from a former marriage; or, conversely, they brought their children and younger siblings to a new conjugal union. Households truncated by

Key to figures 4.2, 4.3, 4.4, 4.5, 4.6, 4.7

△ = man

○ = woman

⬚ = household

∅ △ = deceased

⊓ = parental tie

s = spaniard

y = yaqui

o = opata

e = eudeve

c = coyote

numbers = identification of persons and households in censuses

death replenished their labor power through the exchange of children. These dependent youth were either "shared" among families of the same ethnic group, in the category of orphans, or placed as *criados* (child servants) in the households of *vecinos* or of prominent Indians, such as the village governor. Widows who headed their own households often resided with their adult unmarried children or with nieces, nephews, and grandchildren.

Figure 4.2 expresses visually two examples of convergent family and household structures, taken from the Cocóspera *padrón* of 1796. The Zerda family (Pima) has supplied members to three different households. One surviving daughter (no. 59) from the first marriage of the head of Household 2 has married and formed a separate family (Household 17). Her younger sister (no. 57), only six years of age, lives in a household headed by a single woman together with an adopted adolescent. The Romo and Bustamante households are similarly linked through the movement of children. One son (no. 72) of the Pima governor Cristóbal Bustamente may be living as a *criado*, together with a nonrelated adolescent, in the

Hypothesis concerning Zerda and related households

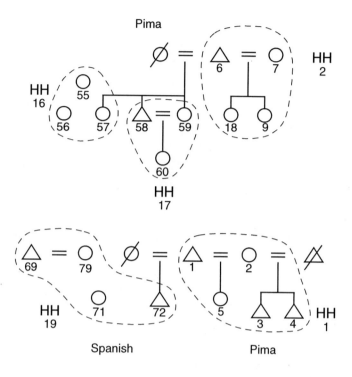

Figure 4.2. Convergent family and household structures in Cocóspera, Sonora, 1796

household of the Spaniard Don Antonio Romo de Vivas. The Romo boys (nos. 3 and 4) who live in the Bustamante household could be the sons of a son (deceased) of Don Antonio and of María Ignacia Vega (no. 2). The exchange of children who are of working age would provide a bond between households—in this case, crossing the ethnic boundary between Pimas and *gente de razón*.[35]

The *serrano* peoples of the Arivechi mission district used similar strategies to maintain their families and to reconstitute domestic units. In 1796, the missionary's *padrón* covered five pueblos and included numerous ethnic categories (see Table 4.6). San Francisco Xavier de Arivechi, the mission's head village, sustained a nucleus of Opata families, while

Table 4.7 Population of Arivechi Mission District, by Key Categories, 1796

Pueblo	No. Families	No. Persons	Ratio Persons/ Family	Ethnicity
Arivechi	72	323	4.5	Opata/vecino
Bacanora	71	332	4.7	Eudeve/vecino
Pónida	50	221	4.4	Joba
Bamuri	35	184	5.3	Vecino
Tacupeto	43	231	5.4	Vecino

| Pueblo | Median Age of Household Head and of Wife | | | |
	Men and Women	Men	Women	Wives
Arivechi	42	40	48	34
Bacanora	40	38	49	35
Pónida	38	37	50	33
Bamuri/Tacupeto	41	39	52	32

Source: AMH, AS caja 22

the indigenous population of San Ignacio de Bacanora was principally Eudeve. A significant number of vecinos, identified variously as Spaniards, coyotes ("mestizos" or racially mixed persons of Spanish, Indian, and Black ancestry), morenos, and mulattoes, had settled in both villages. Jobas, a nomadic tribe from the sierra scattered across numerous rancherías from Bacadéguachi to Arivechi, had requested their own village and missionary at midcentury. Four decades later, more than fifty Joba households remained at Purísima Concepción de Pónida within the mission of Arivechi. Two predominantly Hispanic settlements, Bamuri and Tacupeto, together comprised about eighty families who came under the missionary's care. In all, the padrón listed 271 households and 1,291 persons for the Arivechi district, constituting a defined entity in which to observe the process of family formation among the mixed population of the Sonoran highlands.[36]

The data shown for the five villages of Arivechi in Table 4.7 and the

Table 4.8   Population of Arivechi Mission District,
by Children/Woman Ratios and Sample Size, 1796

Children/Woman Ratios for Women in Male-Headed Households			
Opatas	Eudeves	Jobas	Vecinos[a]
1.7	1.8	1.7	3.0

Sample Size for District					
Women			Children		
Indians	Vecinos	Total	Indians	Vecinos	Total
101	133	234	173	409	582

Source: Table 4.6 (AMH AS, caja 22)

[a] Children/woman ratios for vecinos in pueblo of Arivechi is 2.9; in Bacanora, 2.5; in Bamuri/Tacupeto, 3.4.

ratios calculated in Table 4.8 conform to the general pattern indicated above in reference to the districts of Cocóspera, Batuc, and San José de Pimas. As was to be expected, the persons-to-family ratios are higher for the vecinos than for any of the Indian ethnicities. Moreover, the children/woman ratios for the vecinos are at least a full integer higher than for the Opatas and Jobas (see Table 4.8). The ratios for Eudeves and vecinos living in Bacanora are within a closer range, while the vecinos living in Indian pueblos show a lower mean children/woman ratio than do the gente de razón settled in Bamuri and Tacupeto. The general contrast between Indians and non-Indians may well reflect a better survival rate for the children of Spaniards and mestizos than for indigenous offspring. Nevertheless, the larger family size suggested by the persons/family ratios for the gente de razón probably indicates not only a favorable survival rate for their children, but also the tendency of adolescent and adult children to stay in the paternal household. The relatively high median ages of non-Indian household heads (Table 4.7) is consistent with this hypothesis. When we compare this observation with the evidence cited above on Indian households, it may be argued that Spanish households generally represented extended families, while Indian households tended to be nuclear.

Valle de Tacupeto illustrates the capacity of leading Spanish *vecinos* to support large families and retain their heirs in the same community. Don Juan Ygnacio Trugillo, *teniente de justicia mayor* for the Spanish population in the vicinity of the Real de la Trinidad, headed the census of Tacupeto in 1796.[37] His family accounted for at least eight households in this mining and ranching community. Don Juan and his wife, Doña María Candelaria de Bencomo, lived with one minor, Josef Manuel (age eighteen). However, their adult sons and daughters evidently remained near them, bringing their spouses to Tacupeto. Josef Ygnacio Trugillo and María Valenzuela, as well as María Gertrudes Trugillo and Pasqual Murrieta, had the largest families in the village. Each conjugal pair headed a household with eight dependent minors listed as their children. Josef Antonio Trugillo had married another Valenzuela daughter, while the Trugillo sisters had formed alliances with the Monge, Córdoba, Cota, and González families. Their extended family ties may have formed a local elite in Tacupeto and, to a considerable degree, cemented the social bonds of this highland community.

The household configuration of selected families in Arivechi and Bacanora illustrates the strategies used by Indians and non-Indians alike to maintain viable domestic units in the face of high mortality. Figure 4.3 depicts the probable relationship among five households associated with the Opata governor, Pablo Macasane. The governor himself headed a domestic unit comprising his wife, her child from a former marriage, and their three sons. The missionary labeled Macasane's three daughters as *coyotas* and his son as an Opata. The governor's offspring from an earlier marriage seem to have taken spouses and stayed in their father's village. Conversely, his second wife, María Dolores Quisegua and her daughter (or, perhaps, a sibling or niece) Estefana Quisegua are the only two persons in Arivechi with that surname. They are identified as *coyotas* and may have come to Pablo Macasane's household from another pueblo. The siblings who appear in Households 188 and 231 are each twenty-six years old. This may be an inaccuracy, or one of them could be a niece or nephew, rather than a child, of the elder Macasane. Vicente Macasane, married to María Angelina Badachi and living in Bacanora, is probably a kinsman of the Macasane family of Arivechi. Likewise, the Baduqui and

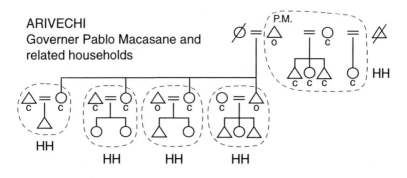

Figure 4.3. Family relations across households and communities in Arivechi and Bacanora, Sonora, 1796

Valencia families sustained several households in both villages. Persons of all three families, living in different communities and identified as Opata, Eudeve, and *coyote*, carried the same surname.

Eight conjugal households represent at least two generations of the Badachi family in Bacanora (Fig. 4.4). Three elder siblings or cousins lived in domestic units with their spouses, surviving single children, grandchildren, or other dependents. Three brothers and two sisters, young adults in their productive years, had each formed their own households. At least two of them (Households 243 and 246) shared their home with a child or relative who was not necessarily their own off-spring. In general, the 1796 *padrón* shows a repeated pattern of household enumerations in which the first "child" appears to be a sibling or child of the wife from her former marriage.

Notwithstanding the prevalence of second and third nuptials, widows frequently headed their own households. Young widows with dependent children appeared in the *padrones* for all the pueblos, although older women stood out among the widowed population. For example, María

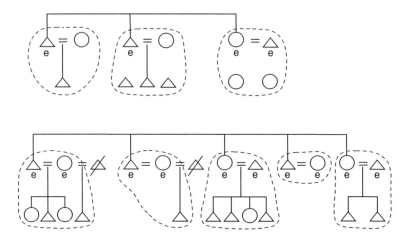

Source: AMH AS Caja 22 Padrón de 1796
Note: Ethnic identity (e=eudeve) is shown for those persons
so designated in the padrón.

Figure 4.4. Different households in Two Generations of Badachi Kinfolk in Bacanora, Sonora, 1796

Eulalia Niguimes, an Eudeve of Bacanora, lived with five minor dependents between the ages of two and ten who were most likely not
her children. Her younger sister had married Juan Lorenzo Guarimea, a
Yaqui. Their household included three surviving children between the
ages of six and sixteen and a baby who may have been a grandchild
of one of the spouses (Fig. 4.5). In Arivechi, Juana María Contreras, an
Opata widow fifty years of age, lived with two adolescent girls and two
young children. The older dependents may have been her daughters and
the younger ones her grandchildren. Her sister, María Contreras, also
identified as Opata, had married Don Manuel Ygnacio Barra y Rivera.
Don Manuel (age sixty) and his wife (age fifty-eight) headed a household comprising María Máxima (*coyota*, age twenty-one) and two small
boys, who could possibly be her children. Just as two and three generations of family members lived under the same roof, the kinship ties
which linked together different households provided a support system
for unmarried women with young children under their care.

Undoubtedly the most complex household enumerated in the 1796

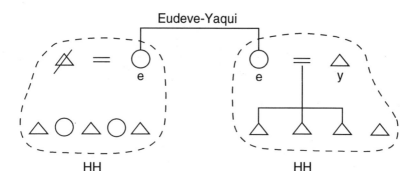

Figure 4.5. A large female-headed household in Bacanora, Sonora, 1796

padrón was that headed by Francisco Carmen Ruiz, a Spaniard who had settled in Bacanora (Fig. 4.6). A total of thirteen dependents lived with Ruiz and his wife, Gertrudes Mendes (*coyota*). The missionary identified six of the children as Francisco's grandchildren, the offspring of his daughter María and her husband, Josef Ramos, both deceased. It is probable that the remaining seven members of the household were children and grandchildren (or other dependents) of the conjugal pair. The three youngest siblings may actually be the children of María Ricarda, twenty-one years of age, although she is identified as "single" (*soltera*) in the census.

The *padrones* offer no direct indication of the physical location of households in the pueblos. However, the fact that different surnames appear in clusters may reflect a residence pattern of family compounds, in which married siblings form separate homes but live in close proximity to each other and to their surviving parents. Figure 4.7 illustrates a probable explanation of the Eudeve-Yaqui households observed in Bacanora. Juan Lorenzo Guarimea may have brought his family from the Yaqui Valley or may have come alone to Bacanora. Sometime after the death of his first wife, he married Juana Micaela Miguimis, a native Eudeve (Household 265). His daughter, María Rosalía Guarimea, offspring of his first marriage, stayed in Bacanora and married Juan Antonio Baduqui (Eudeve). The ages of her children closely parallel those of her half siblings from her father's second marriage. These households follow each other in the *padrón* and may have shared a common house plot.[38]

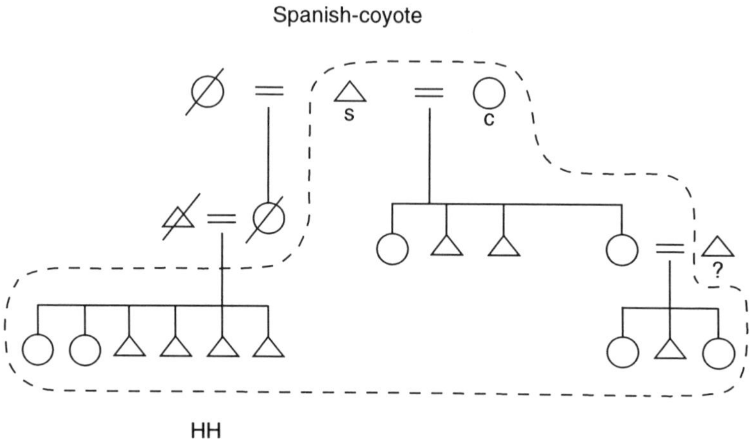

Spanish-coyote

HH

Figure 4.6. A complex, extended household in Bacanora, Sonora, 1796

These individual cases illustrate wider trends of ethnic and geographic mobility in the Arivechi mission district. Only half of the twenty-six conjugal households headed by Opata men in Arivechi pueblo included Opata wives. Eleven Opatas had chosen Spanish or *coyota* spouses, and two had married Joba women. For the remaining five households, headed by Opata widows, the missionary did not specify the ethnicity of the dependent minors who lived with them. By contrast, at first glance, the *gente de razón* living in male-headed households seem to have formed a fairly homogeneous sector in Arivechi, with Spaniards and *mestizos* marrying each other. Only two Opata women had married *mestizos*: María Gertrudes Alday (age fifty) and Ana María Miranda (age thirty), the latter probably a sister or cousin of the numerous Miranda men and women of the same generation spread throughout the Opata households. A closer look at the household composition of Arivechi, however, suggests that some of the "coyota" women married to non-Indians may have been Opata but, for reasons that are not clear, changed their ethnic identity. Stated another way, the priest may have changed their identity to conform to that of their spouses. This seems to be true of the Macasane sisters, daughters of the Opata governor, who chose *mestizo* husbands.

The missionary's count shows a close sexual balance for the *gente*

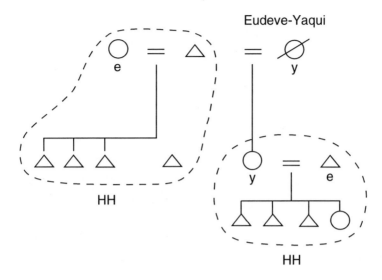

Figure 4.7. Adjoining households in Bacanora, Sonora, 1796

de razón living in Arivechi (100:102), but an apparent deficit of Opata women (66:56). By way of contrast, the *vecinos* living in Bacanora and the predominantly Spanish community of Bamuri showed an appreciable surplus of twenty women in each case. It is probable that some Opata women married out of their communities; for example, Antonia Macasane, an Opata, lived with her Joba husband in the neighboring village of Pónida. The physical mobility of Opata women who married non-Indians and left their home villages seems to have resulted often in changing their ethnic affiliation. The picture that emerges from this brief analysis of Opata–*vecino* relations in Arivechi suggests that ethnic mixtures resulted from spatial exogamy in the Sonoran highlands. The essential question facing adults who sought marriage partners may not have been their "Indian" or "Spanish" status but, rather, the eligibility of a potential mate according to long-standing local custom and the Christian norms of marriage which had to be observed at least formally under the mission regime.

The tighter ethnic endogamy of the Eudeves of Bacanora is more difficult to explain. Of thirty-three conjugal households headed by Eudeve men, six included non-Indian wives. Two Eudeve men had chosen

Yaqui and Joba spouses. The repetition of Eudeve surnames in Bacanora is consistent with an observed tendency to endogamy. Members of the Badachi, Tanori, Sedamur, and Cariaga families are present in two-thirds of the Eudeve conjugal households. The nearest Eudeve-speaking mission villages recorded in the 1796 census was Batuc, no more than ten leagues (twenty-six miles) to the northeast of Bacanora. At least three of the family names characteristic of Bacanora appear in Batuc: Tanori, Sedamur, and Cariaga. It may be that Batuc and Bacanora served as reciprocal pools of marriage partners through which Eudeve households reconstituted themselves from one generation to the next.

In addition to geographic mobility, *serrano* villagers' use of fictive kinship to reinforce and extend their web of reciprocal relations contributed to ethnic mixing. Parish registers captured the designation of spiritual kinsmen through the Catholic formality of naming godparents at religious sacraments, principally that of baptism; however, as we have seen in the context of Opata naming practices, the strength of sponsorship obligations symbolized by *compadrazgo* had deep pre-Hispanic roots. Sonoran peoples used *compadrazgo* both to affirm their cultural identity and to forge ties with Spanish and *mestizo vecinos.*

A preliminary analysis of baptismal records for the Presidio de Pitic, running from 1780 to 1820, illustrates both tendencies among the Pimas and Yaquis who appear most frequently in the presidial registers. They were not village dwellers, for the most part, but tenants and laborers on the haciendas that claimed an increasing share of farmland in the lower San Miguel river valley. Their growing dependence on hacendados for sustenance and on the spiritual bonds of *compadrazgo* reflects deteriorating conditions in their pueblos of origin and an effort to restore the minimal security that earlier generations of their people had found in the missions. Those persons whom the presidial chaplain identified as "Yaquis" more often than not bore indigenous surnames. Usually both parents of the baptized child, as well as the godparents, were Yaquis. Even when one or more of the adults present had Spanish surnames, the priest identified them all as "Yaqui." It appears that Yaqui families removed from their territorial base expanded to include non-Indians through ritual sponsorship. By way of contrast, Pima parents who chose Spanish godparents for their children seemed to underscore their ties of dependency to the landowners for whom they worked. The ritual itself, as well as their tenant status, hastened their passing from the category of Indian to that of *gente de razón*.[39]

Conclusions

The apparent population decline observed in quantitative demographic studies reveals not so much the biological extinction of native peoples as the partial destruction of the community as a fixed entity and its reconstitution in other forms. The foregoing analysis of mission counts, parish registers, and the episcopal census of 1796 substantiates the evolving domestic community of the Sonoran highlands in terms of both the material needs of subsistence and the cultural imperatives of ethnicity. The adaptive quality of *serrano* households revealed through these materials underscores their economic function and the social dimensions of reproduction, even as their internal composition illustrates their capacity for change and belies the simplicity of linear projections for population growth or decline based on aggregate figures.

Household formation comprehended several survival strategies, including spatial mobility, shared labor resources, and extended kinship networks. Geographic mobility explains, in large measure, the composition of Sonoran families who maintained a pattern of short-term migrations within a defined territory. Their principal objective was to gain and defend access to a variety of resources: agricultural produce, wild foods, and the merchandise distributed through the missions and Spanish settlements. Individual members of each household sought temporary wage labor in the mines and hunted and gathered wild fruits in the *monte*. The modus vivendi of these wandering peoples, rooted in the basic features of their land, affected both the configuration of their households and the formation of family lineages over time.[40]

Family ties constituted, in themselves, an important subsistence strategy, reinforcing the bonds of reciprocity among kinsmen. Extended and compound families drew together individuals and households, expanding the domestic unit as circumstances required. The relatively high number of orphans, single adults, widows, and widowers appearing in the *padrones* attests to the severe effects of high levels of mortality on *serrano* households and, moreover, to their ability to absorb solitary individuals and create viable units. Numerous *agregados* appearing in

Indian and mestizo households—children who were not the offspring of the head of household—illustrate further the dynamic quality of family formation. These agregados, like the widows and widowers, were dependent individuals who, when integrated into established households, received a modicum of protection and contributed to the labor power of the entire unit. The Indians' resilience in the face of subsistence crises, although sorely tested, rested on their capacity to reconstitute their households through marital exogamy and the exchange of child labor. That they accomplished this even partially is a tribute to their will to survive.[41]

Sonoran households developed means of support similar to the survival strategies used by peasant societies in other time periods and areas of the world. Labor diversification within households and cooperation among different households contribute significantly to the persistence of small-scale agricultural production in the face of external pressures arising from expanding commercial markets. Nonwage labor and patterns of cooperation among households sustain peasant cultures in precapitalist societies and facilitate their articulation with modern capitalist economies. Conversely, the diversification of tasks demanded of individual household members and the intensification of exchanges among households may accelerate the process of social differentiation between richer and poorer peasants. Thus, the peasant community survives only as it changes.[42]

These same survival strategies propelled Sonoran peasants into migration patterns that were at once traditional and innovative. Serrano peoples alternatively retreated into the monte to live by foraging and escape Spanish surveillance or turned to the Hispanic sector to seek wage labor and tenancy. The Sibubapas, for example, who fled the missions of Onavas, Suaqui, and Nácori in central Sonora, figured in eighteenth-century military reports as renegades and outlaws, while the Pimas, Opatas, and Eudeves of the San Miguel, Sonora, and Oposura valleys became valued laborers and presidial auxiliaries. An important dimension of geographic mobility involved migration at the time of marriage. The marital patterns exhibited in the Arivechi mission district during the 1790s suggest that the movement of women, particularly, from one village to another at the time of marriage crossed ethnic lines and contributed to the growth of mixed races in the province.[43]

Marriage and sexuality constituted a significant cultural divide between Hispanic discourse and local custom. Indigenous conventions treated marriage as an agreement between families rather than a contract between individuals, as it was defined by Catholic Tridentine doctrine.[44] The Sonoran peoples incorporated into the mission system accepted the Christian formalities of marriage and baptism, but continued their own practices of coupling and conjugal residence. While they took care to enter into Christian marriage only once, they permitted the separation of couples at will. Most adults had more than one mate during their lifetime owing to the death of a partner and frequent separations. Native marital traditions tolerated polygyny, which was reserved usually for privileged men in the community and which under colonial rule assumed somewhat covert forms of serial monogamy. The missionaries' insistence on marriage as a sacrament, a vow to be taken between two persons, involved them in "substituting a conjugal for a consanguineal system" and disrupted complex social arrangements.[45]

This disparity between Catholic norms and indigenous values became apparent in divergent interpretations concerning the link between sexuality and family formation. Indians and the majority of *vecinos* who were not of the titled elite accepted premarital sexual relations as commonplace.[46] Frequently, couples lived together for several years and bore children before they sought out the church's blessing for their conjugal life. This social context rendered the distinction between *legitimate* and *illegitimate* offspring ambiguous. The priests who drew up the baptismal records would label any child *hijo natural* who was born outside the sacramental definition of marriage; yet, the term covered a variety of relationships ranging from stable concubinage to casual encounters. For this reason, the *padrones* analyzed above present certain limitations for reconstructing Sonoran marital practices. The missionaries listed conjugal households by naming first the head, followed by the words "y su mujer" to introduce his spouse. It is not clear whether these units represented consensual unions or Christian marriages. In a rare exception, the *padrón* of 1796 for the Seri mission at Pitic set aside a special section for those Indians "married according to their law."[47]

Further evidence for the contradiction between Catholic precepts and customary sexual practices comes from the "hidden" single mothers who appear as daughters in their parents' homes together with very young siblings, who may be their children (as seen in Figure 4.6). Outside the mission villages, the physical mobility of free laborers and the economic instability of most mining camps created a floating population beyond the direct control of parish priests. The Real de la Santísima Trinidad referred to in the opening paragraphs of this chapter typified a society in which casual unions prevailed. The "brazen women" who so confounded Father Leyva's pastoral efforts may have exchanged sexual favors and other services for limited support from several different men, and their children became a subsector of the labor force at an early age. Among the *hijos de pueblo* resident in the missions and the *indios volantes* who lived outside the mining centers, the commitment associated with parenthood and household formation did not necessarily signify a permanent conjugal relationship.

The changing character of highland households reflected the cyclical nature of family composition. Different households assumed the characteristics of nuclear or extended families during successive generational cycles produced by the combined effects of fertility and mortality. Nuclear households truncated by death would re-form through new marriages, bringing dependent minors into an enlarged unit. Conversely, the event of coupling or marriage did not necessarily create a new household, nor were Sonoran residence patterns strictly patrilocal or matrilocal. Rather, these families constituted changing domestic communities that accommodated to the exigencies of their environment and created kinship networks extending outward from households to *rancherías* and villages. Marital exogamy and geographic mobility lent a dynamic quality to rural social structures, integrating long-standing ethnic alliances with survival strategies born of the colonial experience.

The natural growth of a nuclear family in which children reached productive age and eased the burden of labor for their parents (as diagramed by A. V. Chayanov for the Russian peasantry) suffered serious reverses in colonial Sonora. Family size was not merely the result of biological events but was directly related to the economic resources controlled by any one household. The disparity in household size noted above between Indian and non-Indian populations in Arivechi, Bacanora, and Tacupeto suggests the interdependence of demographic variables (e.g., the differential impact of disease) and economic variables (especially individual and communal control over land and labor). Local patriarchs who controlled sufficient land for subsistence and a marketable surplus could retain the labor power of their adult children. Concomitantly, a household with several productive members could conceivably gain access to land or, in the face of a shrinking land base, acquire resources and income through wage labor. Small households with few working members but burdened with dependent persons, such as widows with small children, had limited alternatives for ensuring their reproduction. Relatively small indigenous households no doubt suffered a poor survival rate for their children. In addition, their composition changed as adolescents left home for domestic service or to work in the mines and on the haciendas. These contrasting demographic patterns reflected economic inequalities even as they deepened social and racial differentiation among the *serrano* peasantry.[48]

These differences accruing to the uneven cyclical pattern of household formation did not negate the enduring strength of the domestic unit. As observed in peasant societies elsewhere, the home, or *domus*, stood for the individuals who lived together and shared the products of their labor.[49] This domestic community, formed and reformed over time, was the center of native Sonorans' material and cultural world. Their sense of community stemmed from the household, the basic unit of social organization and the nucleus of their ethnic space. *Serrano* peoples developed kinship alliances as an extension of family, and village polity mirrored the internal structure of power within families. The seminomadic nature of life in the Sonoran highlands, a product of environment, culture, and colonial pressures, left a strong imprint on family formation. Likewise, the nature of community as a geographic and social entity took on special characteristics among these "wandering peoples."

5

"Gypseys" and Villagers: Shifting Communities and Changing Ethnic Identities in Highland Sonora

The present chapter analyzes the meaning of community and explores perceived ethnic differences in light of the changing composition of local settlements. Community implies both a people and a place, and comprehends economic, sociodemographic, and political dimensions. A community is formed by groups of households who possess or use the resources of a given territory; its particular configuration is directly related to the prevailing mode of production, itself a product of the environment and cultural traditions. Kinship plays a central role in defining community membership by establishing bonds of mutual obligation among individuals and households and by legitimating the power structure within a community. Age, gender, and relative position within families skew the distribution of resources and concentrate authority in certain individuals who make decisions that may be binding for the entire group. Ethnicity and kinship, intertwined, largely determine the limits of community, creating a distinction between "we" and "they" and setting the boundaries of reciprocity.[1]

Two types of community characterized the Sonoran highlands, while the actual size of villages varied considerably. Rancherías referred to small clusters of households probably not continuously occupied. Aldeas were larger villages with a substantial nucleus of permanent inhabitants. Just as different members of households hunted, gathered, and labored in separate places, so individuals and even entire families left their communities during certain seasons of the year to look for sustenance. The shifting localities and changing composition of serrano villages illustrates their adaptation to environmental and historical circumstances. Alternating droughts and floods, epidemics, a new mining bonanza, an Apache raid or military campaign were all factors that threatened the on-going life of communities. The pressures of colonialism put into motion an unending sequence of displacements and migrations through which communities perforce split up and formed anew in a different location. Large settlements divided into smaller hamlets and remnant populations of nearly abandoned *rancherías* fused together in new villages, somewhat in the same way that families truncated by death or separation created new domestic units.[2]

The regenerative cycle of families and domestic units explored in the previous chapter impinges directly on the configuration of local settlements. If peasant families do not reproduce themselves from generation to generation in the same village, the community's demographic base, economy, and culture will be seriously affected. By contrast, if the emigration of young adults is not permanent or new domestic units settle in *rancherías* physically separate from the parent village but related to it through trade, reciprocity, and kinship ties, then it can be shown that the community in fact does reproduce itself, *even if not in the same place.* These alternative hypotheses are explored below in reference to the effects of colonial policies on ethnic boundaries and on the formation of highland communities. Native strategies for household reproduction extended to the conservation of village life largely through changing patterns of social and geographic mobility.

Highland Communities under Colonial Rule

Missions were the colonial institution most closely associated with indigenous village organization, and they provided the legal framework through which native communities survived under colonialism. Nevertheless, Jesuit and Franciscan practices frequently collided with prevailing Sonoran patterns of kinship and coresidence. This was particularly notable in the missionaries' policy of *reducción* which concentrated the population of numerous *rancherías* in several large villages. *Reducción* became a central tenet of mission life in order to facilitate the expansion of agricultural production and the missionaries' ideological control over the Indian peoples. This very policy, however, disrupted long-standing settlement patterns. Sonoran pueblos were not fixed entities; rather, they changed over time in accord with the dynamic relationship between the village and the land. Shifting communities, recorded in the colonial documents and observed in archaeological sites, are evidence of the Indians' need to seek out available resources and attest to deeply rooted cultural traditions of seminomadism.[3]

The Opata villages of the Bavispe drainage, centers of dense aboriginal population, illustrate conflicting norms of population dispersal and concentration. When *reducción* began there in 1645 Guásabas, a substantial Opata *aldea*, became the head village (*cabecera*) of the mission district of San Francisco Xavier with its several dependent pueblos and *rancherías*. By mid-eighteenth century, at least three communities of pre-Hispanic origin had been abandoned owing, in part, to hostilities with the Apaches. Tetzicodehuatzi, meaning "where two arroyos meet," and Baibuainoviritzi, "the hill where there is water," were once populous villages. Non-Opata speakers had moved onto Opata lands—"strange people not from here who came on their own to ask for baptism and live under the missionaries' guidance"—and occupied a *ranchería* associated with Guásabas, apparently abandoned by the original inhabitants. The Jesuits founded a new *estancia* for grazing mission livestock, but the Indians had not lived there and, hence, had no name for it.[4]

The Opatas maintained a solid village structure even when obligated to share farming and grazing land with growing enclaves of *vecinos*. The final Jesuit counts for the *hijos de misión* in the Bavispe river drainage, summarized in Table 5.1, show the relative strength of their communities. Jobas and Tarahumaras who had settled in Satechi had learned the Opata language. The *vecinos* listed for Guásabas included forty-two Yaquis settled in the mission, seventeen Spaniards and *mestizos*, and one *negro* (African-American). These population estimates are consonant with the favorable Indian-to-*vecino* ratio of 5.9 shown for this area at the close of the eighteenth century (see Table 4.4 above). Opata pueblos would retain their strong ethnic character until the mid-nineteenth century, following the division of their communal lands.[5]

The Pimas of Tecoripa and Ures in central Sonora followed a similar process. More than a century of Jesuit administration (from 1625 to 1744) had produced an amalgamation of settlements comprising the

Table 5.1   Opata Population under Jesuit Administration, 1765

Mission District	Village	Indians	*Vecinos*	Total
Bavispe	Bavispe	214	0	214
	Tamichopa	70	0	70
Bacadéguatzi	Bacadéguatzi	184	24	208
	Nácori	198	0	198
	Mochopa (Jobas)	92	0	92
	Satechi	45	0	45
Bacerác	Bacerác	478	0	478
	Guatzinera	182	0	182
Guásabas	Guásabas	224	60	284
	Opotu	193	0	193
	Total	1,880	84	1,964

Source: AGN AHH leg. 17, exp. 24.

pueblos of Tecoripa (*cabecera*), Suaqui, and Cumuripa as well as the *rancherías* of San Lorenzo, San Marcial, Buena Vista and San José de Pimas. Native villagers lived by floodplain farming and built their hamlets along several streams that flowed into the Yaqui River. By the 1740s the mission's agrarian base was insufficient to feed its entire population—in part, because of flooding and the loss of irrigable land. Consequently, mission Indians did not reside permanently in their pueblos and migrated to several nearby mining centers in Soyopa, Aigame, and San Xavier. The Jesuit priest assigned to Tecoripa divided his time between the mission and the mining camps of Soyopa, Aguaje, La Ventana, San Miguel, and El Mortero de San José.

A substantial cluster of Pima villages along the lower Sonora River surrounded San Arcángel Miguel de los Ures, enjoying good agricultural land and irrigated fields. Although its population never fell below 400 souls, Ures served several small mining encampments—San Francisco, San José de Gracia, Las Animas, and Gavilán. Its *visita* of Santa Rosalía, twelve leagues distant, exemplified seasonal migratory patterns so prevalent among *serrano* peoples. In the early-spring dry season, a number of Pimas would leave the mission and camp in Pescadero, a place so dry they had to bring in drinking water. During the early eighteenth century, the Jesuit Luis María Marciano persuaded a number of these "Pimas cimarrones" to settle in Santa Rosalía, a site with abundant water for planting. By midcentury some 160 Pimas lived in this village, where they had built houses and a small chapel, but "some had not forgotten their errant ways of living in the monte." [6]

The Indians' strategies for abandoning established villages and forming new hamlets under colonialism responded to numerous constraints. Deforestation and soil erosion, owing to environmental degradation caused by mining and ranching, altered the delicate balance of rainfall and surface drainage necessary for cultivation in this semiarid environment. As the demand for timber to build mining shafts and for firewood and charcoal to stoke the smelters depleted the forests, surface run-off became more difficult to control. During the summer rainy season the "crecientes" often overflowed their banks, destroying the Indians' milpas and carrying away precious topsoil. Cucurpe, an Eudeve village at the headwaters of the San Miguel River, had experienced a noticeable impoverishment of the environment by mid-eighteenth century. Father Nicolás de Acrera observed that the carrying capacity of the land had fallen. The San Miguel stream, laden with silt during the planting months of May, June, and July, could not supply needed moisture to the Indians' fields. Its swollen torrent "robbed" lands from the pueblos of Tuape and Opodepe downstream, resulting some years in insufficient crops. The missions supplied each other in order to provide sufficiently for those villages which had gathered poor harvests. [7]

The conflictive coexistence of Opatas, Eudeves, and Jobas illustrates further the ecological and cultural dimensions of shifting communities in central Sonora. During the early seventeenth century, the Jesuits had expanded their mission frontier to the western slopes of the Sierra Madre Occidental. By midcentury the Rectorado de San Francisco Borja ministered to only a portion of the aboriginal population. Its missions were pueblos-in-formation, separate islands, as it were, through which the conquest penetrated slowly into the dense gentilidad of the sierra. Native converts lived in rancherías scattered along the streams that cut the mountainous slopes into canyons and narrow valleys. In 1678 the Jesuit visitor Juan Ortiz Zapata reported that the Rectorado de San Francisco de Borja comprehended numerous villages and annexes. The missionaries cared for more than 10,000 neophytes of different ethnic groups, gathered into nine *partidos* (districts). Their distribution reflected pre-Hispanic settlement patterns as well as new pressures created by the mining *reales* scattered throughout the sierra. San Francisco Xavier de Aribetzi, inhabited mainly by Ore speakers, became the *cabecera* of the first district. Nine leagues to the west (23.4 miles) the Eudeve-speakers of San Ignacio de Bacanora constituted the principal *visita* of Aribetzi. The Pimas of Santa Rosalía de Onapa lived six leagues (15.6 miles) east of Arivetzi. Their pueblo and associated *rancherías* extended four leagues along the river where the Pimas planted their maize. The entire *partido* included nearly 900 *indios de administración* in addition to a few Spaniards and "other people in their service" who came from the mining camps to the mission to receive the sacraments.[8]

Santa María de los Angeles de Saguaripa, head village of the second *partido*, had a relatively dense Ove population, considered by Zapata to be "*ladinos*, and well treated" in their dealings with Spaniards. Fourteen leagues away, in the eastern mountain range, 100 "Hobas" families (Jobas) had recently gathered into San Joseph de Teopari under the authority of the missionary of Saguaripa. Different groups of *gentiles* visited Teopari from time to time to be baptized and to ask for their own village and a missionary to serve them. The people of San Matheo, yet another hamlet deep in the sierra to the north of Saguaripa, came and went with the seasons. In all, the mission of Saguaripa included several ecological zones and brought together a heterogeneous population of varied dialects and cultural identities. Farther north, the Partido de Santa María Nácori had received a new contingent of Hobas. Oves constituted the majority of its people, living in Nácori and San Luis Gonzaga de Bacabedéguatzi [Bacadéguachi]. The *ranchería* of Santo Tomás de Sereba included the remnants of "an ancient pueblo called Setasun" and a few recently converted families of Hobas. Nácori mission was surrounded by *gentiles*, and mountain trails led from its villages to the Tarahumara settlements of Nueva Vizcaya.

By mid-eighteenth century, Father Joseph Roldán, stationed in the mission of Arivechi, recognized three ethnic groups in the communities under his care: Opatas, Eudeves, and Jobas. His *partido* included three villages: Arivechi (the *cabecera*), Bacanora, and Nátora, formerly a *visita* of the now extinct mission of Teopari. The Opatas and Eudeves constituted a stable core of resident population in Arivechi and Bacanora, but the Jobas continued to stray from village to village. Father Roldán wrote in exasperation to the Jesuit visitor Ignacio Lizassoaín in 1762: "The Jobas are a tribe of gypseys, an untamed and wandering people. Although there are a number of pueblos where they can come and live, most of them migrate like gypseys from canyon to canyon just as they moved about even when Nátora was settled."⁹ In the same vein, Father Manuel Aguirre, the missionary at Bacadéguachi, had bitter memories of his dealings with the Jobas. For fourteen years he had tried unsuccessfully to persuade the families settled in the distant ranchería of Satechi to join other Jobas living in Mochopa, where he could more easily minister to them.

Fathers Aguirre and Thomas Pérez concurred that it would be very difficult to establish a single pueblo for the Jobas, because they did not constitute one nation, but three "branches": that of Mochopa, "an ancient pueblo with a good church, houses, and land for planting"; that of Teopari, the "kidney" or center of the Joba people; and the ranchería of Santa Catarina just outside Bacanora.¹⁰ The crux of the problem, according to Father Aguirre, was to find a place with sufficient arable land and water to support a missionary and neophytes. This experienced Jesuit reminded his superiors that mission economy required irrigated land for producing wheat. The scattered hillside milpas of Joba territory were not adequate to feed a permanently inhabited community. From first-hand knowledge of the terrain, Aguirre outlined the limitations of all the sites considered for founding a new pueblo:

> There is no land for sowing wheat, although some of the seasonal plots belonging to Teopari in a place called Gocopa may yield a wheat crop if the winter rains are good. In Nátora there is sufficient land for melons and maize during the rainy season, but not for wheat. Chamada barely has land suitable for maize. Satechi, the ancient ranchería of Bacadeguatzi, has only a few alluvial deposits along the arroyo; although it is true that north of Satechi, about half a day's journey, there is a small terrace where twelve fanegas of wheat could be sown.¹¹

Father Pérez added that often in Teopari there was not enough water drink. During the dry season, the Indians would dig batequis in the sandy arroyos in order to quench their thirst.

Despite these difficulties, the arguments in favor of setting aside a village for the Jobas emphasized their conflictive relationship with Opatas and Eudeves. Although they all understood one another's languages, they tended to speak only Opata in the missions. The latter group's imposition of their language as a kind of local lingua franca expressed their presumed superior status vis-à-vis the Jobas. Fathers Pérez and Aguirre warned that the Opatas tended to treat the Jobas "as servants," a sign of unequal relations among these ethnic groups. The Opatas and Eudeves, in posession of the best agricultural lands, had the capacity to produce surpluses, store them, and trade with Spanish settlers. By contrast, the Jobas had to make do with scattered milpas on mountain slopes. They depended on seasonal rainfall to gather meager harvests for subsistence. In years of drought they left their highland rancherías and camped outside the mission pueblos, trading their labor for food.

These ecological and cultural considerations help to explain why the Jobas repeatedly asked the Jesuits for a mission of their own, even when they did not stay in the villages provided for them. What did they expect from the missions? Contrary to the Jesuit vision of compact permanent settlements, the Jobas sought a pueblo where they could be independent of the Opatas without necessarily living there all year long. Since the network of mission cabeceras and visitas had confirmed the riverine pueblos in their possession of the most fertile farming land in the Sonoran highlands, the Jobas looked on the mission as a way of gaining access to these valuable lands. Their situation grew more precarious and their need to obtain the resources concentrated in the valleys became more urgent as the Apaches penetrated deeper into the western slopes of the Sierra Madre Occidental. By mid-eighteenth century these Athapaskan hunters and raiders had become "the enemy" of vecinos and Indian villagers alike in Sonora. Their presence in the sierra threatened the Jobas' subsistence, closing off access to areas they had traditionally used for hunting and gathering.

The Jobas presented their last known request for a missionary to the Jesuit visitor Lizassoaín in 1762. Fathers Aguirre, Pérez, and Roldán recommended that Nátora be restored as the Jobas' pueblo. Despite their personal reservations concerning the success of the project, they offered to contribute cattle from each of their missions to provide an economic base for the new reducción. However, the expulsion of the Jesuit order

from New Spain, occurring only five years later, cut short all missionary endeavors. By the close of the eighteenth century, a remnant of the
Jobas of Nátora and Teopari remained in Pónida, a *visita* of Arivechi. At
least fifty families lived there, and only a few individuals had intermarried with Opatas, Eudeves, or *vecinos*.[12] Late colonial documentation has
scant references to the Jobas as a separate ethnic group. It is probable
that the contraction of the mission system following the expulsion of
the Jesuits and the partial secularization of the missions led to the dispersal of wandering tribes like the Jobas. A small minority may have
taken on Opata identity; some may have joined the growing mass of
naborías and *mestizos* who labored in the mines and haciendas; and still
others may have adopted the nomadic life of the Apaches. Their virtual
"disappearance" as a separate tribal entity may be owing to the Bourbon
authorities having confused them with the mounted Athapaskans who
so threatened the Provincias Internas.

The Jobas' contradictory stance toward the missions represents but
one of several cultural responses to the Sonoran environment. Riverine
peoples rooted in the fertile valleys that cut through the western slopes
of the sierra, like the Opatas of Bacerác, Oposura, and Saguaripa or
the Eudeves of Opodepe, Batuc, and Bacanora, were agriculturalists
who built houses of earth and stone and maintained a core population
in stable settlements. By way of contrast, hunter-gatherers of different
tribal designations, who became pastoralists and raiders following the
European introduction of cattle, moved widely through the sierra in
their quest for subsistence. A comparable picture developed in the Pimería Alta. Although the official military and missionary *entradas* did not
reach this region until the 1690s, the northern Pimas had experienced
sporadic contacts with Spaniards during the previous century. Early
Jesuit documents, corroborated by linguistic clues conserved in native
toponyms, recorded numerous *rancherías* scattered through the Magdalena, Altar, and Santa Cruz valleys. During the course of the eighteenth
century, many of these sites were abandoned owing to the devastat-
ing effects of disease and the increasing pressure of the Apaches. From
the 1770s onward, the Franciscans ministered to a core population distributed in eight villages. Even as the permanent resident population of
these missions declined, the Tohono O'odham traveled seasonally between the riverine *aldeas* and their encampments in the desert.[13]

Mission Labor and Geographic Mobility

In addition to the ethnic migrations described above, the demands of mission life spurred *serrano* peoples to short- and long-term movements through the province. Missionaries employed Indian men as muleteers (*arrieros*), mail carriers, and informal messengers. In this capacity the *hijos del pueblo* traveled on foot or with a team of mules from village to village and, frequently, from the missions to the mining centers. They walked over the mountain trails known so well to all the native peoples of the region, carrying letters, mission produce, and merchandise. Mission *arrieros* delivered messages at the same time that they garnered information for themselves concerning Apache raids, troop movements, and new mining bonanzas. Mid-eighteenth-century Jesuit documentation is filled with casual references to the movement of native muleteers among the pueblos. Furthermore, the religious life of the missions led Indians to travel from their *visitas* to the head villages where the priests celebrated Mass. The Indians' movement through numerous villages created a network that carried news and goods across the entire region. For example, in 1764, Father Wenceslao Holvez, stationed in Satevó in the Tarahumara district of Batopilas, wrote to Father Michel of Ures: "My beloved Father Andrés . . . I decided to send you this letter with the *hijos* who return to their pueblo after hearing Mass, because their village is on the way to the other missions where the mail carriers regularly pick up correspondence." [14]

Vecinos called on Indian laborers periodically to work outside the pueblos. Although the formal institution of *repartimiento* had ceased to function by the second half of the eighteenth century, individuals frequently sent requests to the missionaries for small groups of Indians to perform routine tasks associated with fencing, planting, and harvesting. These *tapisques* left their villages for presumably short periods of time, in contrast to the peones who became dependent laborers resident on the haciendas and ranches of the region. Nevertheless, the *tapisques'* labor stints outside the missions reduced available manpower in the villages, affecting individual households and the entire community.

Private settlers contracted laborers from the missions to perform specific jobs on estates and small farms spread throughout the lower Sonora and San Miguel floodplains. Skilled Indians were in high demand: car-

penters, masons, shepherds, muleteers, and *vaqueros*. Rafael Ortiz Galeutes employed several carpenters from Matape and Ures to build some
furniture for the governor of the province. He wrote to Father Michel
in the early fall of 1764 to refute the Indians' complaints that they had
not received full payment for their work. Galeutes claimed that he had
fed the Indians even beyond the stipulated time in which they were to
have finished the job, and that when they finally delivered the cabinets
to the governor (in San Miguel de Horcasitas), he ordered that they be
paid. Galeutes concluded, irately, that he had not received so much as
a bundle of tobacco for his trouble! [15] Little information is available on
the customary wage for *tapisques* and other eventual laborers contracted
from the missions. It is probable that the *vecinos* who hired them converted most of the Indians' payment into mere subsistence—shelter and
the food consumed during the time of their employment.

Spanish military authorities regularly recruited Indian men from the
missions to escort small parties on the trails leading from one village to
another. Not infrequently they expected native escorts to supply their
own mounts and provisions. Indians who traveled between the pueblos
and presidios were exposed to Apache attacks, and their absence was
felt in the community. When the Marqués de Rubí made his extended
tour of inspection through the presidios of Nueva Vizcaya and Sonora
(1766–68), the missions provided Indian auxiliaries, grain, and cattle to
feed and protect the royal visitor and his party. [16]

Periodic campaigns requiring large numbers of Indian auxiliaries created a further burden on the missions, at times virtually removing the
adult male population from the pueblos. Military authorities called on
vecinos and Indians alike to maintain armed militias against the Apaches
and the Seris. Father Juan de Zerquera of Bacerác reported the hardships
suffered by Opata auxiliaries sent to patrol the mountainous country between the Bavispe and Oposura valleys. Although Governor Agustín de
Vildósola had ordered that the Opatas be spared "pointless expeditions"
and that their patrolling be timed in order to allow them to rest and
harvest their crops, the Indian governor of Bacerác and his men were
sorely pressed during the autumn of 1748. The *justicia mayor* of Oposura,
Juan Valdez, had summoned the Opata governor Gerónimo and ordered
him to accompany a small militia to attack a *ranchería* of Apaches. After
a two-month campaign, the Opata warriors returned home in early

December, wounded and sick. Even before their arrival, Valdez had sent another order to Gerónimo to report to duty, but this time the governor protested: "We are all exhausted and many of the men are sick. I have found my own family and all the village stricken with measles. For these reasons, I beg you, in *caridad*, to grant me a few days' rest." [17]

Toward the close of the eighteenth century, the Opatas' military duties took them farther from home. Opata auxiliaries accompanied Captain Juan Bautista de Anza on a long campaign through Chihuahua and New Mexico, with a view to opening new trade routes in 1780–81. They followed presidial troops as far as Nueva Vizcaya and Coahuila, leaving their families and communities for more than a year at a time. Spanish officials praised the Opatas' loyalty and bravery, admonishing colonial authorities to treat them well and conserve their villages so that "such faithful Indians might grow in number." [18]

Reducciones and Displacement

Contrary to the spirit of this advice, Spanish policy repeatedly uprooted established native communities. Military authorities and viceregal visitors ordered the removal of ancient pueblos—often against the pleas of resident missionaries—in order to create new frontier garrisons or to set aside land for private settlements. At midcentury José Rafael Rodríguez Gallardo, armed with the titles of *visitador general* and *juez pesquisidor*, supervised the concentration of Indian villages and the abandonment of numerous *rancherías*. Remnant populations of the first missions founded in the Pimería Alta—Dolores and Remedios—as well as the Pimas of Guachuca were transferred to Santa María Suamca and Santiago de Cocóspera. He enforced similar policies in the environs of the Presidio de Santa Rosa de Corodéguachi (Fronteras). Adducing defensive strategies against the Apaches and the need to plan for the "repopulation" of aboriginal sites because of the numerical decline of Opatas and Pimas, Rodríguez Gallardo justified this new stage of *reducción*. Yet, over the long run, his policies forced settled agriculturalists to leave their land, destroying the cultural and material bases for reproducing their communities. [19]

The Opata and Pima villages in the fertile valleys north of Fronteras illustrate this process. An area of dense aboriginal settlement distrib-

uted in several large *aldeas* and numerous *rancherías*, the mission district of
Nuestra Señora de Guadalupe de Teuricatzi comprised four villages with
more than a thousand souls toward the end of the seventeenth century.
During a quarter-century of patient labor, the Jesuits had formed a stable
nucleus of population in San Ignacio Cuquiáratzi, the mission *cabecera*,
and three *visitas* spread over a distance of eighteen leagues. The Opatas
raised substantial harvests of maize and cotton and gained additional income by working in the mines. By 1749 Rodríguez Gallardo found "three
exhausted pueblos" in the mission of Teuricatzi and ordered the Indians
living at the two remaining *visitas* transferred to Cuquiáratzi.[20]

The northern part of Teuricatzi mission district bordered on the Pima
villages of the upper San Pedro and Santa Cruz drainages. During the
early decades of the eighteenth century, Pima leaders visited the Opata
pueblos of Teuricatzi to ask for missionaries to baptize their children
and establish missions in their own land. In 1730–34, with Crown support, the Jesuits advanced the mission frontier northward with the creation of three new *partidos*, each under the care of a resident priest. The
cabeceras of Santa María de los Pimas (Suamca), Santos Angeles Gabriel y
Rafael de Guebavi, and San Francisco Xavier del Bac represented clusters
of *rancherías*; together they held more than 30,000 inhabitants. Their configuration reflected a history of shifting community sites during nearly
a century of intermittent contact between Spaniards and Indians.[21]

During the ensuing thirty years the eastern Pimas, called Sobaipuris,
suffered a decline in numbers and encroachments on their land. In the
spring of 1762 an estimated 250 Pimas from the San Pedro Valley migrated westward to the missions of Bac, Guebavi, and Suamca. Their
move left the Sobaipuris' homeland dangerously explosed to the sweep
of Apache raids. Moreover, the abandonment of numerous pueblos,
such as San Matheo, Mututicachi, Santa Cruz de Quiburi, San Pablo,
Tres Alamos, and Naidenibacatzi, opened valuable pastures and farmland to the *vecinos*. Jesuit proposals to repopulate these villages with Yaqui
and Pápago families, or with Indians residing on haciendas, were never
carried out.[22]

Prior to the Indians' resettlement, Spanish settlers had cast their eye
on the productive valleys of Santa Cruz, San Pedro, and Cuquiárachi
(formerly the Opata village of Cuquiáratzi). The Romero family claimed
land in the Valley of San Luis, a tributary of the Santa Cruz drainage. In

1750 Nicolás Romero sold the Hacienda de Santa Bárbara, comprising two arable strips along both riverbanks, to Gabriel Antonio de Vildósola, captain and *juez político* at the Presidio de Fronteras. Six years later, Captain Vildósola transferred the property to his wife, María Rosa Bezerra Nieto, in exchange for 250 head of cattle, before several prominent *vecinos*: Joseph Antonio de Vildósola, Juan Bautista de Anza (father), Bernardino de Escalante, Marcial de Sosa, and Juan Pablo Romero. By the close of the colonial era, most of the lands once held in common by Pima and Opata villagers had passed into private hands. Cuchuta, Teuricatzi, and Mututicatzi, former pueblos, comprised substantial haciendas owned by the Escalante and Vildósola families and their associates.[23]

At times the Indians left their *rancherías* voluntarily and settled in the riverine pueblos. Fear of disease, Spanish military pressure, and Apache assaults induced the O'odham and Sobaipuris to seek the relative security of the missions. Not infrequently, however, they resisted colonial policies of *reducción*. During the 1740s Father Jácobo Sedelmayr called on armed *vecinos* led by Miguel de Mendoza y Castellanos to force a group of Tohono O'odham to live in Santa Teresa, a *visita* of Tubutama. The Pimas of the upper Altar Valley petitioned Rodríguez Gallardo to postpone their move to Guebavi until they had harvested all their maize. They pleaded, further, that should they migrate during the winter months, their young children might die on the long journey "through cold country."[24]

Far more dramatic, with lasting consequences, was the resistance mounted by the Seris and Pimas who were forced to surrender their lands to the Presidio de Horcasitas. During the previous century, military pressure combined with missionary persuasion had brought several hundred families of Cunca'ac (Seris) to the agricultural villages of the middle San Miguel river valley, which bordered the desert. Pimas and Eudeves formed the sedentary population of several large pueblos — Cucurpe, Opodepe, and Nacameri — and many *rancherías* along the alluvial terraces overlooking the floodplain. At midcentury most of the Seris who had come to the valley, either captive or free, had settled in Nacameri and its two *visitas*, Pópulo and Los Angeles; the combined mission population of Pimas and Seris numbered 828. In 1748 Rodríguez Gallardo transferred the Presidio de Pitic to Pópulo. He settled the new garrison of San Miguel de Horcasitas with the soldiers of Pitic and the few remaining *vecinos* of the moribund *real de minas* of San Juan Bautista, the first *alcaldía mayor* established in the province. The royal visitor assigned mission lands to the soldier-settlers of Horcasitas, displacing Pima and Seri agriculturalists from Nacameri. When the Indians protested, the Spaniards responded with brutality: they arrested some eighty families and arbitrarily deported the women to Guatemala and other distant provinces of New Spain. Indians who deserted the missions raided *vecino* settlements in the lower San Miguel Valley, prompting a series of punitive campaigns to the desert coast and even to Tiburón Island. Intermittent warfare marked relations between Seris and Spaniards to the end of the colonial period and seriously disrupted traditional community life in the environs of Pitic and Horcasitas.[25]

The outcome of Rodríguez Gallardo's *visita* belied the objectives of *reducción*. Colonial policy sought to secure the defense of this frontier province by "peopling" it with stable farming communities. Spanish officials often railed against the persistent habits of nomadism which seemingly frustrated their ends. Yet, Spanish *reducción* disrupted aboriginal communities more often than it created them. Forced concentration of *serrano* peasants in selected village sites robbed them of the resources for farming, hunting, and gathering that their scattered *rancherías* had afforded them. Over the centuries, native Sonorans had developed strong ties to the alluvial valleys of their territory and persisted in reconstituting their communities, despite the formidable pressures of colonialism. When the ravages of disease halved their numbers, the surviving households consolidated their hamlets or sought refuge in established pueblos. Conversely, when forced to migrate, they formed new *rancherías* outside the missions to which they had been assigned.

Jesuit expulsion precipitated a period of crisis in the *serrano* communities of Sonora. The abrupt exile of Jesuit missionaries from the province in July 1767 removed the principal authority figures the Indians had known for more than a century. Thenceforth, as they were told by royal decree, they should share equal status with the *vecinos* as full owners of mission property. Governor Juan Claudio de Pineda read the *hijos de misión* their rights and obligations: they should receive a wage for their labor and pay taxes (tribute). In reality, during the year that Sonoran missions were without missionaries, Indian *comuneros* did not administer their pueblos' resources. Governor Pineda named lay *comisa-rios reales* to oversee the Indians' work on and off the missions, collect the harvests, and distribute basic staples. The *comisarios*, aided at times by mission Indians and Apaches, depleted communal granaries and live-stock. They sold off mission property or shamelessly divided it among their relatives and *compadres*. By early spring of 1768, hunger and disease ravaged the pueblos. Apache raids intensified throughout the highlands, while the expedition led by Colonel Domingo Elizondo against the Seris in Cerro Prieto concentrated most of the presidial soldiers and Indian auxiliaries in the arid lowlands of the Sonoran Desert.

When Fray Antonio de los Reyes penned his report in 1772 on the Pima missions administered by the Colegio de la Santa Cruz de Que-rétaro, his observations underscored the impact of the Jesuit expulsion and its aftermath on the Indian communities. In pueblo after pueblo Fray Antonio noted the irregular and seemingly careless distribution of houses, mere *jacales* or *ramadas* clinging to the side of a hill or surround-ing the missionary's dwelling. Most of the best lands in the river valleys of Tecoripa, Tónichi, and San José de Pimas, for example, were in the hands of *vecinos*. Writing during the summer planting season, the Quere-taran friar found only a small fraction of communal land sown with crops. The demographic sketch he gave for each mission indicated a de-pleted population with a large number of widows and orphans. Many adult men, as well as entire families, had left the pueblos for the relative safety of nearby presidios or to try their luck in the mining camps. For example, the resident population of Cumuripa, a pueblo with good land on one of the major tributaries of the Yaqui River, had settled "three times" in the Presidio de San Carlos de Buenavista. Similarly, the Opatas and Eudeves of Tónichi were migrating to the new mining bonanzas in the district of Soyopa. The imbalance of persons to families and the high number of orphans in nearly all the villages Reyes visited points to a sociopolitical crisis in the configuration of sedentary communities. The epidemics and small harvests that weakened the demographic structure of the pueblos were themselves consequences of the abrupt change in mission administration, the military campaigns that pitted Pimas and Opatas against Seris and Apaches, and the forced relocation of remnant populations. The events of these years and the decades to follow changed the material conditions of Indians and *vecinos* alike, prompting the passage of rural villagers from one category to the other and reinforcing the fluid quality of community.[26]

Indians and *Vecinos*: An Ambivalent Ethnicity

The terms *indio* and *vecino* covered a variety of social and ethnic meanings. *Naborías*, culturally identified as Indians but removed from their pueblos, formed a mobile pool of laborers in the *reales de minas* and haciendas. In Sonoran villages, where tribute in produce or money was not formally collected, the burden of community for the *hijos del pueblo* centered on forced rotational labor in the mission fields. Not surprisingly, Indians sought to reduce that burden and to supplement village agriculture with alternative means of subsistence. Military service, tenantry, and mining as well as seasonal hunting, fishing, and gathering, constituted viable alternatives for Indians and the lower strata of *vecinos*. Movement in and out of the pueblos affected the structure of *serrano* communities and blurred the differences between Indians and *gente de razón*.

The presidios were clearly a theater for horizontal mobility in this frontier province. By the close of the eighteenth century, ninety soldiers served at the Presidio de Santa Gertrudis del Altar. Sixty families of *vecinos* augmented the total population of Altar, but the chaplain explained that he could not ascertain a fixed residence for them, "because they are close to the missions, and they move back and forth from the pueblos to the presidio." Similarly, the Presidio de Santa Cruz established in the abandoned mission of Santa María Suamca included the military garrison and "the *paysanazgo* or *vecindario* of Spaniards and a few Pimas who live equally as *vecinos*. They stand guard and help when called upon, and live as if they were part of the presidio."[27] The Opata presidios established in San Miguel de Bavispe and Bacoachi and the Pima garrison of San Rafael de Buenavista (located alternatively at San Ignacio and Tubac) drew native soldiers and their families away from the surrounding missions. Military authorities and missionaries alike identified them ethnically as Indians, but their fiscal and sociopolitical status drew them closer to the growing number of *vecinos* in the province.[28]

Geographic and social mobility came together even more dramatically in the mining *reales*. The search for precious metals was the veritable motor of colonization in the Sonoran highlands and northern New Spain. Numerous silver strikes and gold placer mines drew *naborías*, free mulattoes, and laborers recruited from the missions to burgeoning encampments. Although some of these improvised settlements became permanent towns with an established social structure—for example, Baroyeca, San Antonio de la Huerta, Trinidad, and Motepore—by their very nature, the *reales* were shifting communities. Their instability was a result of the playing out of high-grade ores close to the surface, the penchant of miners to avoid long-term investments and move on to new bonanzas, and the seasonal migratory patterns of their workers. Indians and *castas* formed the core of their labor force, passing through different occupations and ethnic identities.

At midcentury, Father Juan Nentvig referred to the population of Santa Ana de Tepache indistinctly as *vecinos* and Opatas. The Valley of Tepache, located between the mission districts of Oposura and Guásabas, was surrounded by silver and lead mines: Arroyo, Nacatovori, Lampazo, Santo Domingo, La Coronilla, Las Guijas, and San José del Alamo. Here, as in many small *reales* scattered throughout the sierra, the same people gathered wild foods and panned for gold nuggets, hoping to turn both into a means of livelihood. Most *gambusinos* who tried their luck at mining traded the grains of precious metals they dug from the earth and scooped from the streams to itinerant merchants for basic provisions: food, clothing, and work implements. These peddlers and *arrieros*, in turn, received supplies from the merchant houses established in the large *reales*, such as San Antonio de la Huerta, Baroyeca, Río Chico, and San José de Gracia. The wealth generated from mining was concentrated in their hands, while the miners in the field remained poor.

Indians migrated to the mines either as independent small-scale prospectors or as laborers recruited in a *cuadrilla*. The latter were servants (*jornaleros* or *operarios*) at the orders of a mineowner or hired overseer. Some Indian miners actually owned mines and small ovens for refining the ore with workers at their command. Colonial law granted special privileges to Indians accredited with discovering mines: they and their descendants were exempt from paying tribute. Whether as *jornaleros* or as prospectors, native mineworkers traveled widely throughout the province. Rodríguez Gallardo called them "newcomers and outsiders, who live in the mines without being registered anywhere else."[29] Their seasonal movements frequently coincided with the agrarian cycle of planting and harvesting. Reports sent from the placer mines of San Ildefonso de la Cieneguilla to the governor of Sonora in 1772–74, for example, estimated the Indian population as oscillating between 1,500 and 2,000; and Governor Antonio Crespo explained to Viceroy Antonio María Bucareli that "the majority of them leave the mines to tend their crops around the end of May and do not return until the beginning of October." [30] During these same years, mineowners in Alamos paid substantial advances on their workers' wages in an effort to keep them at the *real de minas*. Even so, miners complained that their *operarios* tended to leave for two or three days a week and, even worse, abandon the mines during the summer planting season. [31] During the second bonanza of Baroyeca (1792–1807) the number of laborers of mixed ethnic origin varied widely from week to week; their wages were paid in money and in kind. [32]

In addition to the *jornaleros* and *gambusinos* who migrated to the mines, Indians sought their livelihood in Spanish estates. Distinct from the temporary movement of *tapisques* between the missions and haciendas, the migration of entire families created a service tenantry of increasing importance during the late colonial period. Resident families either paid a rent or, more probably, gave their labor to hacienda owners in the peak planting and harvesting seasons. Haciendas and ranches of varying size developed around presidios such as San Miguel de Horcasitas, San Pedro de Pitic, and San Carlos de Buenavista. Indians and *castas* constituted a resident but mobile labor force, serving as fieldworkers, herders, and local militia. In 1803, nine haciendas sustained a total of forty-seven families in the lower San Miguel Valley. Captain Pedro de Villaescusa enumerated six haciendas and ranches within a five-league radius of Buenavista. He noted that, in addition to these estates, "all the *vecinos* of this presidio who have a few head of cattle" followed their herds along the riverbanks, moving from one place to another. Their itinerant herding occupied land, but did not constitute formal ranches. [33]

The Indians' migration from their pueblos weakened the communal economy of the missions, compounding the declining land base with a loss in labor power. In 1784 Bishop Antonio de los Reyes took special notice of the substantial number of *gente de razón* in all the missions and of unplanted fields belonging to the Indians and nominally assigned to maintaining the churches. Opatas of Arivechi and Saguaripa, where the "*vecinos* and Indians who live in the class of *vecinos*" outnumbered the *hijos del pueblo*, had petitioned the *alcalde mayor* to be considered *vecinos*, although it meant paying tribute. Indian *comuneros* of Movas, Cucurpe, and Má-tape had sold or rented much of their land to the *vecinos*. Even in the Opata stronghold of Bacerác and Bavispe the indigenous economy had faltered: "Formerly, these Indians were the most skilled in all the prov-ince of Sonora. They used to grow much cotton and with their textiles, particularly of *manta*, they supplied many pueblos and *reales de minas*. But today, their internal governance and customs show an intolerable excess of presumption, vices, and drunkenness." [34]

Bishop Reyes was given to attributing the decline of the pueblos to the Franciscans' poor administration and to the Indians' abuse of alcohol. Despite such hyperbole, he corroborated evidence from other sources for the same period concerning the atrophy of economic and political structures in the villages. The formality of the Indian *cabildo*, a central tenet of mission life, became meaningless as the *comisarios* and *tenientes de alcalde* who lived in the pueblos arbitrarily appointed and removed native officials to their own advantage. As the declining land base and loss of political autonomy made village life less tenable, Indians sought to live as *vecinos*.

Three currents of population movement transformed the demo-graphic profile of the missions: (1) the Indians' migration to Hispanic settlements and their change of status to that of *vecinos*; (2) the penetra-tion of native villages by the *gente de razón* and their occupation of mis-sion land; and (3) the seasonal migration to and from the villages by the seminomadic *gentiles* who came to barter and help gather in the harvests. Seasonal movement of *serrano* and desert peoples became the mainstay of late eighteenth-century missions. The 1795 census of Tumacácori, for ex-ample, showed 119 adults. Of these only six families were riverine Pimas, who represented the remnant of four villages in the middle Santa Cruz Valley: San Rafael de Guevavi, San Cayetano de Calabazas, San Ygnacio de Sonoita, and San José de Tumacácori. The rest were Tohono O'odham (Pápagos) "who had come in from the *gentilidad*," received baptism, and accepted village life.[35] On the Apache frontier, Fray Santiestéban of Co-cóspera reported that "the *gentiles* who come from time to time only stay long enough to trade their goods and then they leave." O'odham, Seris, and even Apaches exchanged the fruit of the saguaro, wild seeds, salt, shells, herbal medicines, and the like for wheat, maize, cloth, and other merchandise that came to the missions from the presidios and mines. And, occasionally, they stayed to work and learn the rudiments of Christian doctrine.[36]

The *vecinos'* settlement in the pueblos accrued gradually over more than a century. A minority of prominent merchants, hacendados, mine-owners, and presidial officers resided in the presidios and principal *reales de minas*. Provincial notables came from this class: for example, the Urrea, Escalante, Belderrain, Vildósola, Anza, and Elías González de Zayas families.[37] The majority of *vecinos*, however, were common soldiers and prospectors who tried their luck at mining and reverted to subsistence farming. They squatted on mission land, planting crops and grazing small herds. Some of them married into Indian households, others settled in the villages for security and the missionaries' religious services.[38]

Extant baptismal records for the pueblos of Baviácora and Aconchi during the early eighteenth century provide some links between early non-Indian settlers and patronyms that became well known in the Sonora and San Miguel valleys several generations later: Moreno, Zepeda, Bernal, Valencia, Siqueiros, Rodríguez, López, and Espinoza. The same couples stood in for each other as godparents and occasionally baptized Opata or Apache children. Their descendants can be traced on the presidial rolls of San Miguel de Horcasitas and San Pedro de la Conquista de Pitic.[39] These agropastoralists and sometime militiamen drew their livelihood from the mission communities well before the formal establishment of presidial garrisons in the province. After mid-century the growing number of *gente de razón* created a web of relations between the missions, presidios, and mining *reales*. Nicolás Francisco de Bohorquez, Manuel de Monteagudo, Joseph Maldonado, and Santiago Contreras are representative of this stratum of *vecinos* whose influence weighed heavily on native communities during the closing year of Jesuit administration.[40] *Vecinos* and Indians joined together for religious celebrations and special feast days, but poor *vecinos* frequently drew on mission stores against a vague promise of payment in the future. For example, María Josepha de Ochoa wrote to Father Andrés Michel in Ures during the early spring of 1766, begging him to supply her with two fanegas of grain and two almudes of dried beans. She offered to pay in calves "when someone goes to Sonitiate to bring you the price of what I ask for."[41]

More telling were conflicts over arable land and pasturage, having lasting consequences for the entire community. Most of the *vecinos* living in the missions used village land and water, but contributed little or nothing to communal labor nor did they tithe. During the final years of Jesuit administration, Father Rapicani wrote from Batuc:

> It is well known that with the exception of a few Spanish *criollos*, all the rest are mulattoes, *coyotes*, or *lobos*. Because they are not pure Indians, they do not want to belong to the mission, but, oh yes, they do want to live in the pueblo and farm mission land. And they want the padre to serve them, as if he were their priest, even though they have a parish priest at some distance whom they should pay for religious services. They are of no help for the upkeep of the mission churches, and all that work falls on the shoulders of the poor Indians.[42]

After the expulsion of the Jesuits, ecclesiastical and military authorities in the province took opposing views on how to handle the growing number of non-Indians in the pueblos. In 1785 Pedro Galindo Navarro, legal advisor to the commandant-general of the Provincias Internas, angrily protested Bishop Antonio de los Reyes's edict ordering all *castas* to leave the missions. Galindo Navarro argued that the bishop had exceeded his authority and had violated the spirit of the law. He reminded Commander José Antonio Rengel that although Laws 21 to 24 of the *Recopilación* forbade Spaniards, blacks, mulattoes, and *mestizos* from residing in the *reducciones* and native pueblos, the Audiencia de México had resolved not to expel the *gente de razón*, but merely to exhort the missionaries not to consent to their settlement in the villages.

Furthermore, many of the *vecinos* who lived in the pueblos were in fact kinsmen of the Indians and had married into their families:

> As a result of marriage and other arrangements contracted by the Indians, a growing number of mulattoes, *mestizos*, *zambaigos*, and other *castas* are to be found in their villages and missions. [The bishop's order] is contrary to the intent of the law, at least to the extent that it makes an exception of those *mestizos* and *zambaigos* who are the off-

Table 5.2   Population of Sinaloa and Sonora, 1785

	No.	% C/TP	% CP/TP
Total population	87,644		
Castas in the provinces	18,715	21.3	
Castas living in the Indian pueblos	6,238		7.1

Source: AMH AD I

Note: % C/TP = percentage of *castas* to the total population; % CP/TP = percentage of *castas* living in pueblos to the total population.

spring of the Indians, born among them, and who will inherit their houses and farmland, allowing them to live in their pueblos, for it is harsh to separate them from their parents.[43]

Galindo Navarro estimated that approximately one-third of all "people of broken color and *mestizos*" lived in the missions, and he cited the data shown in Table 5.2. Galindo Navarro's definition of *casta* excluded Indians and those *vecinos* who claimed to be Spaniards. Thus, he calculated a mixed stratum comprising slightly more than one-fifth of the total population for the combined provinces of Sinaloa and Sonora, of which less than one-tenth lived in mission pueblos.

Nevertheless, it is significant that despite repeated colonial injunctions against non-Indians residing in native villages, the number of *vecinos* living in the missions increased markedly toward the end of the century. Why did *serrano* pueblos accept them? What were their expectations concerning marriage and settlement of the *gente de razón* in their midst? The Indians' apparent tolerance of the *castas* in their pueblos is consonant with the pattern of marital exogamy (analyzed in Chapter 4 above) that supported the demographic restitution of their households. Moreover, Indians chose *vecinos* as spouses and neighbors in order to expand their web of kinship and create links between their localities and the wider sphere of colonial society.

Native village leaders admitted new members into the community, expecting them to conform to traditional cultural values and to contribute to communal labor, but they suffered disappointments. In 1767, Gover-

nor Juan Claudio de Pineda sharply reprimanded the Pima governor of
Ures for trying to oblige those *mestizo* women married to mission Indians to perform the tasks assigned normally to women in the pueblos:

> "Hijo," governor of the pueblo of Ures: Luis, Cayetano, and Nicolás,
> "hijos" of this pueblo, have informed me that they are married to
> women *de razón*. Because of this, I order you to assign [these three
> men] work loads equal to those of the other mission Indians, without
> obliging them to work harder nor to demand labor of their wives,
> for they are exempt from community service. Concerning the clear-
> ing and planting of farmland and other tasks customarily carried out
> in the missions, you must permit them to sow their land and work
> where it is best for them to support their wives. I trust you to carry
> out my orders and keep the peace in your village, so that I may re-
> ceive no further complaints.[44]

Referring to the assignment of communal tasks and to the distribution
of arable land among households, Pineda sharply curtailed the Pima
governor's authority and, in effect, defined the limits of community autonomy. Indian men who married non-Indian women should not lose
their rights to membership in the community, including access to land
and other village resources. Conversely, the *vecinos* who settled in the
pueblos could not be compelled to contribute to their collective labor
output. Colonial policy protected the *vecinos'* privileges, thereby crippling
both the productive and the reproductive capacity of the community.

Conclusions

The formal community structures of pre-Hispanic *aldeas* and colonial
missions had suffered irreversible decline by the end of the eighteenth
century. Indians who remained in the status of "hijos de la misión" competed in increasingly unfavorable circumstances with the *vecinos* who
came to occupy their pueblos. The flow of *castas* into riverine villages
was swelled by Indians who chose the status of *vecinos*. Faced with the
deterioration of the traditional *común*, *serrano* peoples found new ways of
reproducing community life. The outward signs of indigenous adaptation to their changing environment included geographic mobility, village exogamy, and racial mixture. Native horticulturalists and gatherers

conserved the *ranchería* as the most workable form of community. These clusters of households, expanding and shrinking in demographic cycles, moved from stream to stream as seasonal rainfall permitted short-term plantings. When forced to abandon established fields closer to nucleated settlements, they created new *milpas* out of the alluvial soil carried to the riverbanks in annual floods. Wherever possible, they kept small herds of range cattle and, more frequently, goats and sheep. During droughts, when not even the summer arroyos were running, they resorted to hunting and gathering deeper in the sierra or to occasional labor stints in the mines and haciendas.

Migration was both cause and effect of geographic and social changes owing principally to the pressures of colonialism on aboriginal life. Individuals and families did not move at random, but followed discernible objectives and conformed to regional settlement patterns. The flow of persons from missions to presidios, haciendas, and mines corresponded to perceived needs and opportunities arising from the colonial economy. Migration had a dramatic impact on indigenous communities, leading at different conjunctures to their abandonment and reconstitution in new forms.[45]

The mission regime had created ties of dependency between the "hijos del pueblo" and the institution, personified in the authoritative figure of the missionary. The agricultural village provided the locus for the social reproduction of the community, and colonial law bestowed civic and political status on native peoples in the missions. Furthermore, the religious and ideological components of mission life symbolized the principles of social hierarchy and reaffirmed the villagers' place in the natural order: they were, at once, children of God, subjects of the king, and "sons and daughters of the pueblo." Mission economy oriented native productive capacity to the circulation of agricultural surpluses and drew Indian peasants into a market economy as direct producers and laborers. Conversely, colonial pressures altered the material and cultural dimensions of Sonoran villages. Ecological, economic, and demographic constraints severely weakened the formal structures of highland pueblos and created a disjuncture between the mission and the native community.

The changing proportions of *gente de razón* and native ethnicities in Sonoran mission pueblos arose from a complex series of factors. The increment in *vecinos* at the expense of the Indians corresponded not only to favorable demographic growth and usurpation of village land, but also to marital exogamy, miscegenation, and Indians having elected *vecino* status. In such a mixed and mobile population, ethnicity was not so much an inherited condition as it was a cultural construct. Ethnic identities drawn from the categories imposed on different racial and social groups implied different sets of privileges and obligations: tribute payment, military service, or entitlement to usufruct of communal land. Indians who "passed" into the class of *vecinos* acknowledged that whatever protection the community had offered them as "hijos de misión" was offset by the rewards and risks of laboring in a market economy. Although they may not have physically left the village, the Indians who lived as *vecinos* detached themselves from the collectivity and began to move as individuals in colonial society. As access to land became less a function of community allotments and more a result of sale, rental, or de facto possession, the Indians eschewed an ethnic identity that tied them to the missions and condemned them to deepening levels of poverty. Their change in status initiated them into the ranks of a class-in-formation: the rural peasantry.[46]

Understanding the *serrano* communities' transcient character as a means of survival sheds new light on the structural components of class and ethnicity for this region. Geographic and social mobility brought changes in ascribed status as well as in the material conditions of life. In this context, class and ethnicity are not discrete categories; each comprehends elements of the other, and their historical meaning for Sonora arises from the particular social relations of production generated at the community level.[47] Sonoran villagers took some of the same strategies they had developed for reconstituting their households and applied them to reproducing their communities. Through exogamous marriage, cooperative labor, and geographic mobility the Indians sought to conserve their basic social unit as an essential element in their struggle for subsistence. To that end, they admitted a flexible definition of membership in the ethnic polity and accepted marriage alliances with the *vecinos*.

The colonial Indian communities of Sonora, so closely identified with the institutional mission, were sites of cultural and political conflict. These two chapters, which focus on the intimate spheres of biological reproduction, sexuality, and cultural transmission, illustrate the multivalent and discordant meanings of "community." The colonial town—a supervised polity imposed on the serrano peoples—became, in the course of two centuries, the outward structure of an indigenous community that was neither autochthonous nor Hispanic. Sonoran highland villages endured into the early nineteenth century with a core population of Tegüima, O'odham, and Eudeve kinsfolk, but they were ethnically mixed and geographically mobile. Their marriage practices and settlement patterns in clusters of *rancherías* and *aldeas* were at once practical adaptations to the exigencies of colonial rule and the reiteration of a cultural heterodoxy that challenged the normative assumptions of ecclesiastical census takers.

Figures 2–7 in chapter 4 illustrate hypothetical schemata of household formation based on the families enumerated in the 1796 census of Sonoran missions. My use of patronyms and estimated ages to reconstruct the probable distribution of children and adults across individual households is, in itself, open to question, because it relies on the categories created by the Catholic precepts of monogamy and patriarchy imposed on indigenous parishioners by their priests. Nevertheless, my reading of the census materials looks through these categories to suggest alternative practices that maintained extended families and organized physical space according to flexible principles of kinship and reciprocity.

It seems clear that the reproduction of *serrano* households as well as the demographic and economic sustenance of their communities depended on the exogamous selection of partners. For this very reason, Sonoran strategies for physical and cultural survival fostered racial mixture. The number of "castas" estimated by Bishop Antonio de los Reyes and Pedro Galindo Navarro to be living in putatively Indian villages (see Table 5.2) masked the ambiguity of an ethnic nomenclature that only poorly reflected or even distorted a complex process of social and cultural change. The *serrano* community, intimately related to the bonds of kinship, was sorely tested in the transition from colonial to national rule, when changes in the legal definition of property shattered the foundations of highland pueblos. Their struggle for land and autonomy, in counterpoint with the internal divisions of the Sonoran peasantry, is the guiding theme of Part Three of this history.

View along the Gila: *Cereus giganteus*. George Engelmann, "Cactaceae of the Boundary," in William H. Emory, *Report on the U.S. and Mexican Boundary Survey*, vol. 2, 1, plate facing p. 78 (1857). Courtesy Missouri Botanical Garden Library.

Fronteras, Sonora. John Russell Bartlett, *Personal Narrative*, woodcut, p. 265 (1854).
(Courtesy Missouri Botanical Garden Library)

Arizpe, Sonora. John Russell Bartlett, *Personal Narrative*, woodcut, p. 281 (1854).
(Courtesy Missouri Botanical Garden Library)

Group of Apaches. John Russell Bartlett, *Personal Narrative*, woodcut (1854). (Courtesy Missouri Botanical Garden Library, p. 326)

Eighteenth-Century Church Doorway, San Ignacio. John Russell Bartlett, *Personal Narrative*, woodcut, p. 419 (1854). (Courtesy Missouri Botanical Garden Library)

DOCTRINA
CHRISTIANA,
Y
PLATICAS
DOCTRINALES,
TRADUCIDAS EN LENGUA OPATA
POR EL P. RECTOR MANUEL AGUIRRE
de la Compañia de JESUS.

QUIEN LAS DEDICA
AL ILLmo. SEÑOR DOCTOR
D· PEDRO TAMARON
DEL CONSEJO DE S. M.
DIGNISSIMO OBISPO DE DURANGO.

CON LAS LICENCIAS NECESSARIAS:
Impreſſas en la Imprenta del Real, y mas antiguo Colegio de
San Ildefonſo de Mexico, año de 1765.

Frontispiece to *Doctrina Christiana* (1765) by the Jesuit Manuel Aguirre. (Courtesy of the Edward E. Ayer Collection, The Newberry Library)

Part III

Rival Proprietors and Changing Forms of Land Tenure

6

Land and the Indian Común

Diego, *alcalde* de Xecatacari, Pedro Estudoqui, and all the *hijos* of Xecatacari and
Buena Vista . . . We have our planted fields in Buena Vista, Obiachi and Xecatacari. We had lived and farmed in Buenavista until Captain Ancheta drove his
livestock there and forced us to leave our land. As long as he occupied Buena
Vista we suffered many abuses and injuries against our crops from his cattle and
horse herds and against our persons from Ancheta, who took away our lands.
Two years ago it became abandoned and, for that reason, we implore you to restore Buena Vista to us, the way we had it before it fell into Ancheta's hands, so
that we may found a pueblo there for the good of our souls and the protection
of our lands. . . . We swear by God our Lord and the Holy Cross that this petition is not made in bad faith, but that we do this to come together and to live
in community.

Pedro Berde and Diego Camorlinga, 1716 [1]

Thus, in 1716, Pima commoners of the mission district of San Pedro de
Cumuripa petitioned Thomás de Esquivel, *teniente de justicia mayor* at the
Real de San Miguel Arcángel, to restore their lands and authorize the formation of a new pueblo in Buena Vista "in order to serve both Majesties."
Their testimony revealed the major issues of a prolonged conflict with
one Captain Antonio Ancheta, who had allowed his livestock to destroy
their crops and who used force to remove the Pimas from lands their
ancestors had cleared and cultivated. Ancheta had obliged those few
Indians who stayed in Buena Vista and Obiachi to accept tenant status,
working for him in return for subsistence plots in marginal soils. The in-

digenous peasants of these three villages had scattered, living in mountainous *rancherías*, while Ancheta's livestock roamed over their fields. Two
years before Alcalde Diego brought his petition before Thomás de Esquivel, Captain Ancheta had died, leaving Buena Vista "despoblado." The
Indians' oral presentations (translated from Pima into Spanish) concluded with a census naming male household heads and enumerating
the number of persons in each family. Their language revealed a basic
understanding of Spanish legal norms and practices, which they put to
good use in their stance before colonial authorities. The *teniente* of San
Miguel and the Audiencia de Guadalajara awarded the Pimas their request in recognition of the Indians' longevity as peasant cultivators of
the land, the absence of Spanish settlement there prior to Ancheta's violent occupation of Buena Vista, and the abandonment of the site after his
death, leaving neither cattle nor "servants" in the area. Esquivel argued,
as well, that founding a pueblo in Buena Vista would encourage as yet
un-Christianized Indians from nearby *rancherías* to accept mission life.[2]

Not only did conflicts over land use pit Indians against Spaniards, but
they also divided communities in eighteenth-century Sonora. On July 7,
1723, Juan Baptista Quigue, governor of Cucurpe, presented a formal
complaint against Francisco Montes (alias Pintor) before Captain Juan
Antonio Fernández de la Cabada, the general magistrate appointed for
the province of Sonora. Quigue took legal action "with the voice and
commission" of all the *hijos* in defense of their collective rights to arable
land. Governor Quigue and four Indian officers of Cucurpe signed their
petition in the name of "poor Indians and humble vassals of His Maj-
esty."[3] Fernández commissioned Captain Joaquín de Rivera of the Real
de la Soledad to proceed with the case. Rivera was to receive sworn testimony in Cucurpe from all witnesses who the Indian justices should
bring before him. Fernández charged Rivera especially to take great
pains to investigate "the life and customs" of Montes. Governor Quigue had prepared his case well, presenting sixteen witnesses, including
three *vecinos* who lived in nearby settlements. Of the thirteen Indians who
testified under oath, all but one spoke through interpreters. A young
man himself, Quigue took care to bring before Rivera the elders and all
former officers of his pueblo. Their combined memory provided a con-
vincing history of the conflict which had festered for six years between
the commoners of Cucurpe and the intrusive Pintor.

Los Santos Reyes de Cucurpe, San Miguel de Tuape, and Asunción de Opodepe, three Eudeve communities in the upper San Miguel River between Sonora proper and the Pimería Alta, together had formed an important Jesuit mission since 1647. At the time of their dispute with Pintor, the Indians of Cucurpe claimed floodplain land as far as four leagues north of the pueblo along the Dolores tributary, adjacent to a cattle ranch established by Padre Francisco Eusebio Kino around 1700.[4] As long as the village elders could remember, Cucurpe natives had cultivated that section of the floodplain. The pueblo held the land in common, in accord with "native law," although individual households farmed separate plots by consent of the community.[5] Thus, village justices recognized the legacy of Magdalena, a "daughter of the pueblo," to a small piece of land that her father had cleared and left to her. When she married Francisco Montes, a Pima from Ures, he settled on her inheritance and expanded his holdings to the point that he was planting and irrigating eight milpas located about a league upstream from Cucurpe. In order to secure legal title to the area he had under cultivation, Montes approached Miguel Fernando de Esquer, a land judge commissioned by the governor of Nueva Vizcaya, who came to Sonora in 1717 to measure and legitimate private landholdings. Village leaders protested vigorously at that time, arguing that Montes had no right to register in his name land which belonged to the pueblo and, furthermore, that his extravagant irrigation of these fields deprived native cultivators downstream of the water they needed to grow their crops. The Cucurpeños would have prevailed over Montes's pretensions had not their missionary, Francisco Xavier de Mestanza, intervened on his behalf. Padre Mestanza and Esquer worked out a compromise: Montes could register the land, provided he did not abuse his allotment of water. Should Cucurpe commoners suffer the loss of their crops because the stream flow was inadequate to irrigate their milpas, he would have to give up his property. Village justices went along with the agreement, out of respect for their minister, even though they knew the crafty Pintor would not keep his promise.

Six years later, Governor Quigue and his fellow witnesses brought serious charges against Montes. Numerous commoners had watched their crops fail for lack of water and had suffered Pintor's brazen retort to their repeated complaints: "I will water my fields, and then leave you whatever is left over."[6] Even worse, Montes showed no respect for native justices and dared to flaunt his arrogance before Spanish officials. His public behavior was notoriously uproarious: he drank without inhibition and used "wine" (mescal?) to corrupt two former governors of Cucurpe. Pintor's accusers described his crimes in terms that were bound to excite the interest of colonial officials. Drunkenness, witchcraft, and incitement to rebellion headed the list. Montes was said to have "laid his hands on Padre Luis Xavier Velarde," missionary of Dolores, and indulged in other obscene acts. He had stirred up trouble in the Pimería Alta, arousing fears of an uprising, for which he was imprisoned for several months in Soledad. At the close of the hearings in Cucurpe, Captain Rivera remitted the case to his superior with a strong recommendation in favor of the plaintiff's cause. Fernández de la Cabada reviewed the evidence and sent out an order for Pintor's arrest.

The Indians' defense of village lands in Buena Vista and Cucurpe illustrates the major lines of conflict in eighteenth-century Sonora over competing claims to vital resources and rival standards of authority. Native traditions sustained two separate principles of land tenure: collective ownership and private usufruct. Individual households gained access to arable plots and the water to irrigate them by virtue of their membership in the community. In the case against Montes, village leaders upheld Magdalena's right to her inheritance, but adamantly refused to legitimate her husband's status in the pueblo. Furthermore, the Indians' testimony gives some indication of the upward limits of individual enterprise in their communal setting, even in the absence of specific land measurements. Several witnesses denounced Pintor's "ambition" which led him and his son-in-law to control eight milpas of alluvial soil, an area beyond what was needed to support his family. Land and water rights were inseparable in this environment; for that reason, Montes raised the ire of the Cucurpeños as much by his imprudent use of irrigation water as by his occupation of the land itself. This errant Pima violated the cultural norms of serrano peoples in several important ways. Not content merely to occupy his wife's inheritance, he circumvented native authorities in order to obtain official title to the land. At a time when pressure on village land was mounting because of increased Hispanic settlement in the area, Montes ignored indigenous practices of usufruct and opted for the colonial institution of private property. He openly boasted that he would obey none of the Indian justices and abandoned the posture of deference that all *serrano* villages—leaders and commoners alike—assumed when addressing missionaries and colonial officials. By way of contrast, Governor Quigue approached Spanish magistrates "in all humility," speaking always in the name of the *común* which he represented.

The Pimas of Xecatacari and the Eudeves of Cucurpe asserted the primacy of the *común*, meaning both the kinsmen who occupied a recognized locality and the base of the material resources (land and water) which assured their existence. Their arguments before Spanish authorities integrated the themes of land, culture, and community in the ecological setting of highland Sonora. This chapter documents the gradual formalization of rural property and analyzes the process in terms of colonial legislation and policies, demographic pressures, formal division of mission holdings, and the enclosure of open range. The evidence presented here substantiates the transfer of control over productive resources from peasant villages to private landowners and further clarifies the notion of "ethnic space" that guided indigenous leaders in their defense of communal holdings.[7]

Legal Principles for the Ownership and Usufruct of Land

The procedures for legitimating different forms of land tenure in the Iberian colonies stemmed from the principle of vassalage, applied to Indians and Spaniards. Individual proprietors, whether conquistadores, titled nobility, or common settlers, could claim legal title to land on the strength of their status as loyal subjects of the king. In this vein, royal land grants were frequently bestowed as a reward for military service and outstanding merit. In the course of time, however, these grants evolved from *mercedes de tierra*—essentially, free landholdings awarded by the king—into a privilege obtained through payment of royal taxes and fees. During the seventeenth and eighteenth centuries, *composición* became a legal instrument used widely throughout New Spain to "set things right," that is to legitimate de facto possession of the land. Moreover, *vecinos* obtained grazing land through the *denuncia* and public auction of *realengos* and *baldíos*, untitled and considered part of the public domain. Notwithstanding the impetus toward privatization, abetted by the entrepreneurial cast of imperial conquest, Iberian canon explicitly defended both corporate and common property. Colonial law recognized Indian communities as bona fide landholding units and purported to protect them in the possession of "lands, legacies, and pastures, so that they should never suffer want and have all they need to support their families and households."[8] Just as native pueblos held land in common for the sustenance of member households, so Hispanic colonists who settled in towns and villas enjoyed use rights to arable fields and grazing land as long as they resided in the community, built their homes, tended their herds, and cultivated the land.[9]

Colonial legal traditions combined notions of subsistence need and public service with a recognition of different types of land and their appropriate uses. The value ascribed to individual pieces of property (whether private or communal) corresponded to their expected productivity, often based on available supplies of water, as reflected in the "just price" established as a baseline for public auctions of *realengos*. Arable land fell into several categories: *tierras de pan sembrar* referred to dryland farming; *tierras de pan coger* were dependent on rainfall, but susceptible to irrigation; and *tierras de pan llevar* required irrigation. Pasturage—*tierras de paso* or *tierras de agostadero*—by definition did not include water for irrigation, only watering holes or springs included in a land grant for grazing cattle.[10]

Terms commonly employed to indicate different kinds of land implied, as well, equivalent measurements for related types of property. In practice, both the lexicon and the standards of measurement varied widely from region to region and changed over time. Land grants in eighteenth-century northern New Spain conformed to several basic categories concerning the size and quality of land awarded to corporate and individual proprietors. *Sitio* was grazing land, while *criadero* meant an area for breeding livestock. *Ganado mayor* referred to bovines, oxen, horses, and mules; or, in its more restricted meaning, only to beef and dairy cattle. *Ganado menor* included smaller livestock: sheep, goats, and pigs. *Fundo legal* comprised the minimal allotment to Indian pueblos and Spanish towns as municipal property, conventionally one square league. Part of the *fundo legal* was reserved for common use, but portions of it were awarded to resident *vecinos* in separate grants for house lots, gardens, and irrigated fields. *Solar*, *caballería*, and *suerte* were distinct measurements (usually in *fanegas de sembradura*) of arable land. The *fanega* denoted an

Table 6.1   Categories of Rural Property in Eighteenth-Century Northern New Spain

	Varas	Hectares	Acres
Rangeland			
Sitio de ganado mayor	5,000 × 5,000	1,747	4,316
Sitio de ganado menor	3,333 × 3,333	776	1,918
Criadero, ganado mayor	2,500 × 2,500	437	1,079
Criadero, ganado menor	1,667 × 1,667	194	480
Irrigated land			
Fundo legal	1,200 × 1,200	101	250
Solar	1,000 × 1,000	70	173
Caballería	1,104 × 552	43	105
Suerte	552 × 276	11	26

Source: AGN AHH *Temporalidades*, leg. 1165.

area in which a given volume of seed could be sown; its precise meaning varied in different localities and according to the crop (e.g., wheat or corn). (See Table 6.1.)[11]

Land grants and water rights did not necessarily come together. It could not be assumed that title to property included the faculty to divert flowing water for irrigation. By long-established Iberian tradition, water had to be carefully regulated in the interest of the entire community. Thus, Castilian codes distinguished between public and private use of water: all village residents could take water for drinking and other domestic needs, but water for irrigation or operating grain mills required separate authorization. The only automatic alienation of water with a land grant concerned a spring or stream which originated on that property.[12]

In accord with these principles, various legal instruments came into use for acquiring water rights. The *merced de agua* added water rights to an existing land grant, while the *composición*—as in the case of land occupancy—legitimated previously illegal use of water. Judicial settlement of open disputes resorted to the *repartimiento de aguas*, an enforced sharing of stream flow for irrigation. (The *repartimiento* might have applied to the dispute in Cucurpe, cited above.) Furthermore, town councils sold water allotments for fixed periods of time; in New Mexico, private individuals contracted for secondary rights to *sobras*, the water "left over" from the primary owner's use of a given amount of water. Over time, *sobrante* agreements (frequently unwritten) constituted a form of "rental," illustrating the thin line separating usufruct and outright ownership of riparian resources.[13]

Several bodies of imperial legislation informed these classifications of land and water rights in Spain and America. Castilian law was applied to the sphere of private commercial transactions, inheritance, and similar areas of family law in the colonies. It culled the medieval traditions of the *fuero juzgo* and the *Siete partidas*, the latter molded by Moorish influences with respect to the terms and practices concerning irrigation.[14] *Derecho indiano* was a body of legislation derived from pre-Hispanic antecedents, especially in the core areas of Mesoamerica and the Andean highlands, expanded by the laws written in Spain for the Indies. This burgeoning set of legal prescriptions, at times repetitive and contradictory, formed the basis for the monumental *Recopilación de leyes de los reynos de las Indias* (1680) that remained in force throughout the colonial period.[15]

The *Recopilación* defined the capacity of the state, personified in the king, to grant land titles to persons and corporations such as Spanish towns and Indian pueblos. In practice, the Spanish monarch delegated the power to award land grants to the Council of the Indies, the Audiencia de México, and the viceroy. As the colonial regime matured, provincial governors and magistrates assumed the function of adjudicating land and water rights and of issuing formal title to property. The Bourbon reforms authorized the Crown's intendants to extend land titles and legalize the *composiciones* of land previously occupied without benefit of the royal *merced*. During the final decades of colonial rule in frontier provinces like Sonora, presidial commanders exercised this faculty; and, following the liberal Constitution of Cádiz (passed by the Cortes in 1812 and restored in 1820) town councils began to award land titles.[16]

Decentralization of the power to distribute landed property became apparent as provincial decrees and ordinances acquired the force of law through practical arrangements to legitimate land claims and settle local disputes. In effect, governors, intendants, military commanders, and royal visitors modified the *Recopilación* and created new precedents for future decisions. Furthermore, local custom had considerable weight in the evolution of New Spain's legislative tradition. Magistrates faced with specific conflicts over the allocation of land and water frequently justified their decisions on the basis of prevailing social practice.[17]

Running counter to local tradition, Bourbon political economy imposed significant changes on the Sonoran landscape, proceeding apace with population growth. The royal visitors José Rafael Rodríguez Gallardo (1748–50) and José de Gálvez (1769) turned their attention to the distribution of land and the economic life of the missions. Gálvez set out to raise productivity, promote commerce, and exploit what he believed to be inexhaustible mineral resources in the area. To these ends, he ordered the division of mission lands, traditionally held in common, into *suertes* to be distributed to native households and Spanish settlers living in the pueblos. His decree of 1769 laid the foundation for successive ordinances concerning land tenure and property demarcations. It defined the standards for measuring, evaluating, and taxing different categories of land according to their use and proximity to established communities. Although Gálvez's orders were not carried out with the full rigor he intended, his reforms set an indelible pattern for the future development of the province. They established the legal structure that privileged private property over common holdings and opened Indian villages to greater numbers of *vecinos*. In general, the legislation authored by Gálvez tended to separate the Indians from their communities, conferring on them a theoretical "equality" as taxpaying citizens. José de Gálvez attempted nothing less than to regulate a social process already begun, which turned the "hijos de misión" into subsistence farmers and laborers for Spanish mines and haciendas.[18]

Pedro de Corbalán, first intendant of Sonora, followed the legal principles laid down by Gálvez. In 1772, Corbalán directed the allotment of *suertes* and ordered the construction of a canal for the Seri mission on the southern bank of the Sonora River across from the Presidio de Pitic. He set out to delimit the boundaries of all native communities, distributing family plots to resident Indian families and providing for new colonies of non-Indian settlers. His correspondence gave particular attention to the growth of local markets in the vicinity of mining camps, "where many Indians of several different tribes have gone to sell their grain and other goods made in the pueblos."[19]

During the following two decades, civilian and military authorities repeatedly issued instructions concerning village lands in the spirit of Gálvez's decree. They recommended reserving a minimal area for the común and dividing all the remaining farmland into plots to be distributed according to use rights. These hijuelas could be passed on through inheritance from one generation to another, but not sold or mortgaged. In 1785, Pedro Galindo Navarro defended the vecinos' residence in the pueblos, citing their right to receive houses and farmland in bequest, presumably from their Indian progenitors. Comandante Pedro de Nava pushed privatization a step further in 1794, explicitly ordering the division of mission lands and their distribution to resident families. In theory, his plan would have maintained a balance between the community's control over land, water, and human labor and the private usufruct of those resources. Echoing Gálvez's plan of a generation earlier, Nava ordered that all "caciques, generals, lieutenants, governors, and alcaldes of each pueblo" receive two or three suertes of land and enjoy exemption from communal labor drafts. Eight suertes should be reserved for the común, while the remaining land should be measured and awarded to individual families with a title of possession, but not outright ownership. In effect, Nava proposed to create a reserve of small holdings legitimated by their use value and removed from sale on the open market. As much as Comandante Nava promoted the individualization of production through private landholding, his instructions revealed a lingering concern for subsistence needs and for recognition of householders' property rights derived from membership in the community. Moreover, the need to reiterate orders for distributing mission lands among individual households suggests that Bourbon reformers encountered resistance to the division of communal holdings.[20]

After Mexican independence, fledgling state governments passed legislation that accelerated the division of communal land into private plots and confirmed the role of the state in legitimating the private ownership of property. Sonoran landed notables took control of the governorship and legislature of the states of Occidente and, later, of Sonora and Sinaloa.[21] In the liberal spirit of the Spanish Cortes of Cádiz and the Constitution of 1812, the deputies of Occidente and Sonora passed legislation during the decade of 1825–35 which, in theory, established equality between Indians and vecinos, and defined citizenship in terms of landed property. This new legal framework sought to impose the sovereignty of the state over the pueblos through the institutions of municipal government and the division of communal lands. During this same period, the expulsion of the Spaniards from Mexico, ordered by federal law on December 20, 1827, and applied in Occidente on February 15, 1828, deprived Sonoran pueblos that had remained under mission tutelage— primarily in the Pimería Alta—of their missionaries and left their communal property in the hands of civilian commissioners.

The most important of these laws was Decree no. 89 of 1828, focused on the corporate holdings—*fundo legal*—and all arable lands in the communities. Its significance derived from its radical content and from the persistence with which the governors of Occidente and Sonora applied it in the highland pueblos. The first two articles of the decree called for the restitution of "those lands which have been unfairly taken" from Indian communities or, in default, just compensation, citing the appropriate sections of the colonial *Recopilación* of 1680, and a similar decree issued by the Cortes de Cádiz in 1813. The root purpose of Decree no. 89 concerned the demarcation and division of communal lands; it recognized as legitimate property only those holdings authorized by legal title, thus favoring large landowners and undermining the ancient tradition of the *común*. Concerning ethnic polity, the authors of this law took note of the racially mixed population that characterized many communities and opened their councils and militias to *vecinos* as well as Indians, altering their system of internal governance. In point of fact, contemporary observers criticized the deleterious effects of Spaniards and *castas* who had gained control of political offices in the communities.[22]

The state of Sonora passed a series of laws from 1831 to 1835, based on the tenets of Decree no. 89, that made it easier for private citizens to register "vacant lands" as their own and subordinated Indian pueblos to municipal government. Six different decrees defined the procedures for measuring and auctioning untitled land (*baldíos*). Decree no. 19 of June 11, 1831, concluded the administration of mission properties by civilian commissioners. It restored the missionaries' temporal authority in the pueblos and called for the popular election of Indian governors, to be named "juez económico" and "alguacil." Nevertheless, these native officials exercised only limited authority and were obliged to report to the justices of the peace of their respective municipal touwnships. Decree no. 32, promulgated on September 27, 1831, extended the option of citizenship to the Pimería Alta. Indian "citizens" should theoretically pay taxes and be held accountable to municipal authorities; in return, they were exempted from the political and economic obligations that had traditionally tied them to their pueblos. They would be allotted a plot of land, but would no longer receive a portion of the communal harvests. Decree no. 39 of December 15, 1831, regulated the organization of municipal government in Sonora. Six chapters defined the various offices and duties accruing to district townships and smaller communities. This law expressed unequivocally the intention of state legislators to level all Indian communities to municipal rule, reiterated by Decree no. 84 of September 7, 1835. This ordinance and Decree no. 66, promulgated just three months earlier, removed the final vestige of fiscal autonomy that Indian communities had at one time enjoyed. All income derived from the cultivation or rental of community lands had to be deposited in municipal funds, to be managed by an appointee of the state governor.[23]

That Sonoran governors enforced the new laws to the benefit of local elites is evident in the reports and correspondence that reached the president of Mexico from different sources during these same years. State officials had measured and divided village lands in Arizpe, Bacoachi, Sinoquipe, Banámichi, Huépac, Aconchi, and Baviácora—in Opata territory—and in Saguaripa, Santo Tomás, Pónida, and Arivechi in the Eudeve area of eastern Sonora. These legal innovations placed valuable communal resources in private hands and set in motion two parallel processes, beginning under Bourbon administration and accelerating after independence: the consolidation of a regional landed oligarchy and the division of peasant communities. Their history emerges in a series of confrontations pitting communities against private landowners—a history documented through the *composiciones* and *denuncias* recorded by colonial and national authorities over the course of a century.

Population Growth and Pressure on the Land

Spanish legislation and policy decisions paralleled the social reality of demographic increase and rival claims to the vital resources of land and water. Sonora remained on the frontier of Spanish settlement in Nueva Vizcaya during the early eighteenth century, when private land claims were concentrated in the provinces of Sinaloa and Ostimuri. *Composiciones* filed before colonial magistrates attested to the growing number of miners and ranchers who alienated properties that varied in size from small portions of land measured in *caballerías* to several *sitios*. Furthermore, numerous disputes among these *vecinos* over inheritances and land claims revealed a network of Spanish families that had spread northward from El Fuerte and Alamos to Río Chico, Ostimuri, and Baroyeca over several generations.[24] In the face of these pressures some *serrano* pueblos, guided by their missionaries, took steps to protect their lands, as is illustrated by the Pima villages of Santa María de Mobas and Santa Ana de Nuri. The *composición* awarded to Mobas in 1727 confirmed its possession of those lands which belonged to it "por razón de pueblo" and granted the Pimas seventy additional *cordeladas* for a payment of 14 pesos.[25] Three years later, the mission of Nuri paid 100 pesos and the *medianata* tax for a *composición* which included three *sitios de ganado mayor*, two *potrerillos*, and some "extra lands" (*demasías*), all of which lay outside the pueblo's *fundo legal*. The Indians' claim to the land was conditioned, however, with the proviso that should a Spanish town or hamlet be founded in the additional lands awarded to Nuri, the village would have to cede those lands upon just payment for whatever improvements they had made in livestock, cultivation, or construction.[26]

As the century progressed, land *composiciones* became more common in Sonora, particularly in the Oposura, Sonora, and San Miguel valleys and in the environs of Santa Ana in the Pimería Alta. During the same years (1717–23) that Buena Vista petitioned to form a new pueblo and Cucurpe brought legal suit against Francisco Montes, the governor of Nueva Vizcaya sent commissioned officers to register the *vecinos'* titles to land and cattle brands. Captains Juan Antonio Fernández de la Cabada and Andrés García y Cossío collected the *medianata* from numerous ranchers, miners, and merchants who held landed property near the *reales* of San Juan Bautista, Motepori, and Tetuachi located in the upper Sonora and Oposura river drainages. In the environs of Arizpe, an important Opata village and mission *cabecera* at the headwaters of the Sonora River, six *vecinos* from the *reales* of Bacanuchi, Basochuca, and Santa Rosa de Montegrande registered private holdings.[27] The Jesuit Carlos de Roxas wrote a detailed report of Arizpe in 1744. The three pueblos under his care—Arizpe, Chinapa, and Bacoachi—numbered more than 1,000 native souls. Padre Roxas underscored the administration of communal lands and herds separate from the Indian family milpas, but he made little note of non-Indians living in the villages or occupying mission lands. During these same years, extant baptismal registers show that Spanish residents living in outlying ranches and mining camps like Tetuachi, Basochuca, Guepaverachi, and Chuchuqui came to the mission to receive the sacraments.[28] Three decades later, in 1778, Arizpe's social profile had changed considerably. Some 390 individuals lived in the cabecera of Arizpe, nearly evenly divided between Opatas and "Spaniards of all castas" and distributed among 120 adobe houses scattered over two low mesas on the western bank of the river. The main plaza, graced by the church and the substantial home of Arizpe's one merchant, who served as district magistrate, occupied the northern mesa. The southern portion of the village contained an orchard and a flour mill. The pueblo claimed fourteen fanegas of cropland, while private vecinos had cleared several gardens and fields.[29]

Civilian settlement spread steadily throughout the Sonora Valley, intensifying the competition for available farmland. In 1726, Mission San Pedro de Aconchi, comprising two Opata pueblos, purchased formal title for its lands. Padre Echagoyan paid ninety pesos in royal fees for the land surveyor and sent along two good mules in order to secure the mission's claim to floodplain soil.[30] By the 1740s, San Miguel de los Ures, a pivotal mission for the entire Jesuit system, supported a numerous population of vecinos and Indians. During the following four decades the Spanish population of this mission district gained numerically over the indigenous peasantry. In 1784 the Indian families of Ures and Santa Rosalía numbered nearly 100, while 70 vecino households based in the Real de San Josef de Gracia and surrounding ranches had begun to take over mission lands. Although the Pimas of both villages held title to cropland and range as far as twelve leagues east and seven leagues west of the head village, Bishop Antonio de los Reyes denounced "continual discord" between natives and settlers, as unruly squatters occupied the best floodplain land and allowed their cattle to roam through the Indian milpas. When the Pimas of Ures had appealed to provincial authorities, they were told to fence their fields and gardens; however, the Indians calculated that the fences would cost more than the value of their crops, and many of them abandoned farming altogether.[31]

The Valley of Oposura, across the mountains to the east, saw the gradual settlement of numerous haciendas along its fertile streams (see Figure 6.1). Oposura and Cumpas were two central Opata villages, surrounded by "poblazones" of *gente de razón*. To the north and east lay several Spanish nuclei, most notably the Presidio de Fronteras and the Real de Nacozari.[32] In 1761, the mission of San Miguel de Oposura served the head village and its two *visitas*, Nuestra Señora de la Asunción de Cumpas and San Clemente de Térapa, as well as seven settlements and encampments of Spaniards and *indios laboríos* who had left the missions: Teonadepa, San José de Tamayoa, San Ildefonso de Tocora, Toiserobabi, San Pedro de Pivipa, San Pedro de Tonibabi, and Santa Ana de Tepache—these last two were mining *reales*. The Opatas who lived under Jesuit administration and who were counted in Bishop Tamarón y Romeral's census for that year numbered 378 persons, while the combined population of Spaniards, *castas*, and *indios laboríos* reached 1,466 persons, including 200 who lived in the mission villages. Thus, the *vecinos* and Indians separated from the missionary's direct supervision more than trebled the number of Opatas who remained under the Jesuits' administration. Their relative proportions weighed heavily on the communities' control of their land.[33]

The Hacienda de Jamaica in the Oposura Valley illustrates well the dual pattern of the accumulation and division of landed property in eighteenth-century Sonora. In 1707, officials from Nueva Vizcaya had measured the mission lands of Cumpas and awarded the village its corresponding title. A little over a decade later, Captain Gregorio Alvarez Tuñón y Quiroz had carved out the Hacienda y Real de Jamaica as his private property, adjacent to Cumpas. When Alvarez died in the spring of 1728 (apparently the victim of an epidemic) Alcalde Mayor Gabriel de Prudhom ordered an inventory made of his sizable estate. Although Prudhom's inventory did not provide land measurements, the account books showed considerable amounts owed to the deceased by other military officers and smaller debts accumulated by the parish priest and workers on the hacienda. Don Gregorio's household included four slaves; the house itself was richly furnished and well endowed with religious images. In order to settle accounts, his possessions were sold separately in public auction. Although it is not clear whether Alvarez left heirs, the hacienda did not remain in the family.[34]

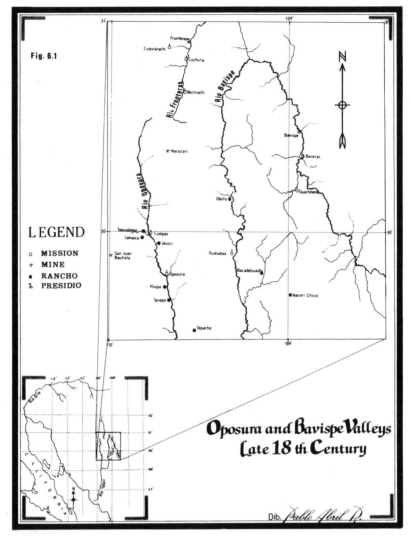

Figure 6.1. Oposura and Bavispe Valleys, late eighteenth century

On the eve of the expulsion of the Jesuits, Don Salvador Julián Moreno owned the Hacienda de Jamaica and let out some of the land to tenant families. Don Salvador and his wife, Doña Beatriz Vázquez, together held property in Tonibabi and Toiserobabi, a ranch in the vicinity of Oposura, in addition to the hacienda—now christened San Joseph de Jamaica. In 1765, Moreno burdened his estate with a *capellanía*—a lien that generated an annual interest payment of 5 percent—to benefit his son Joseph María Buenaventura Moreno, who was studying for the priesthood at the Colegio de San Yldefonso in Mexico City. The principal totaled 4,000 pesos: half that amount came from the legacy (which Don Salvador and Doña Beatriz had matched) of Juan Joseph de Grijalba, a secular priest and family friend. Thirty years later, the *capellanía* remained in place, but the hacienda had deteriorated to the point that the annual payments of 200 pesos had lapsed.[35]

Subsequently the Moreno family lost ownership of Jamaica, and the hacienda was split into several smaller properties. In 1773, Blas Peralta, a long-time resident of Jamaica, registered two contiguous pieces of land measuring approximately six-tenths of a sitio. One portion, named San Antonio de la Platería, he had received in inheritance from his grandfather; the second portion he purchased as grazing land, a *realengo* referred to as "lo de Argüelles." Blas's mother and aunt had sold off sections of their joint inheritance, and Blas wanted to secure this part in which to run his livestock. Peralta's property bordered on Cumpas mission lands to the north; to the east and south it met the private holdings of Juan and Pedro Ballesteros; and to the west it abutted the hacienda. Juan Mazón, *teniente de alcalde mayor y capitán a guerra*, proprietor of the Hacienda de Jécori, approved Peralta's petition and forwarded it to Arizpe. It was not until 1789 that Licenciado Alonso Tresierra y Cano, *teniente letrado y subdelegado*, authorized Peralta's claim in the name of the intendant, avowing that it did not violate the property rights of the pueblo of Cumpas or of any individual Indian families.[36]

Subdelegado Hugo Ortiz Cortés reported to Intendant Enrique Grimarest in 1790 on the mission lands ascribed to Oposura and Cumpas. He asserted that both pueblos had a *labor de comunidad* with more than sufficient land for the Indians to cultivate, although he gave no measurements. Mission herds were woefully depleted, owing to constant Apache raids; thus, each village held title to ranches that were virtually empty of breeding stock. Theoretically, mission Indians could occupy numerous plots of temporal land; however, insufficient rainfall had left such plots unproductive, and even some of the natural springs had dried up. This picture of mission property adjacent to the Hacienda de Jamaica suggests that village commoners were losing control over the best irrigated land in the valley and forced to make do with less productive fields. Half a century later, a remnant population of "hijos" from Térapa and Oposura (renamed Villa de Moctezuma) protested to the Sonoran governor Manuel Escalante y Arvizu that private adjudication of *sitios* contiguous with Térapa threatened to reduce their holdings to the village site itself.[37]

From the 1770s onward, private holdings impinged ever more closely on village commons. In the middle Oposura Valley, place names such as Pivipa, Térapa, Jécori, and Teonadepa, which had once stood for native *rancherías*, now signified Spanish settlements with a mixed population. As for the province as a whole, in 1778 Intendant-Governor Pedro Corbalán compiled a census of rural property in *reales de minas*, haciendas, and ranchos.[38] The number of adobe houses recorded for rural estates indicates that these were congregations of family proprietors and dependent tenants, not merely isolated ranches. Although the *fanegas* of arable land registered for private settlements that year were fewer than for missions, as were the numbers of livestock, the tendency of private holdings to grow in both population and productive resources contrasted with the missions' gradual economic decline over the following two decades. Private accumulation of wealth, together with changes in the social fabric of the communities, hastened the application of Bourbon policies in the Sonoran highlands. These combined pressures weighed heavily on traditional communities, eroding their land base even before the radical division of communal property at the close of the eighteenth century.

The Formal Division of Mission Lands

Prior to Comandante Pedro de Nava's orders of 1794 to assign individual *suertes* to Indian families, provincial authorities surveyed the residual lands belonging to mission communities. Their reports showed that floodplain soil was divided into irregular cultivated fields, with village commons, native household plots, and areas owned or rented by *vecinos* in close proximity to one another. In unison, district officials reported that the missions had no source of municipal income (*propios y arbitrios*) nor ecclesiastical funds other than livestock and the crops raised in the *común*.[39] Comparative information available for Opata villages along the Bavispe River and its tributaries, as well as for Eudeve pueblos in the Valley of Batuc, reveals the limited communal resources available to native peasants at the close of the colonial era.

The Bavispe River formed a series of alluvial valleys that supported numerous agrarian communities in northeastern Sonora. This was the heartland of the Opata nation, where a perceived ethnic identity went hand in hand with communal landowning traditions. Although Opatas intermarried with Spaniards and *mestizos*, they retained control over their highland villages until well into the nineteenth century. In 1777 the Bacerác mission, comprising three pueblos, totaled 1,000 souls, all of whom were considered to be Opatas.[40] In the 1790s, nearly a quarter-century after the expulsion of the Jesuits, Opata family *milpas* and village *labores* were irrigated from the same network of earthen acequias maintained by community labor. These walled adobe villages, situated on terraces overlooking the riverbed, conserved their pre-Hispanic legacy, reinforced by the mission experience.

Santa María Bacerác and San Miguel de Bavispe constituted the core of Opata town life in this area. These two villages, together with Guachinera, had consolidated more than twenty *aldeas* and *rancherías* spread throughout the valley; they first encountered the missionaries' program of *reducción* in 1646.[41] During the late eighteenth century, Bacerác comprised a central plaza enclosed on three sides by the Indians' adobe houses and, on the fourth, by the church and missionary's dwelling. In Bavispe, the church divided the central plaza into two sections occupied by the remnants of the mission village and the Opata military garrison.[42]

Figure 6.2 shows the location of villages and arable fields in the Bavispe Valley. Bacerác and Bavispe each claimed nine separate irrigated fields that varied greatly in size. These *labores* followed one upon the other in long narrow strips along the river bank. Bacerác's farmland began about one-half league north of the pueblo, along the road to Bavispe, where in earlier years a water-powered flour mill ground the mission's wheat. Just beyond the mill, Opatas cultivated two small *labores* each measuring 108 by 54 varas (a total of 11,644 square varas). Farther north, on a terrace called Teharabepa, perhaps an abandoned *aldea*, another field

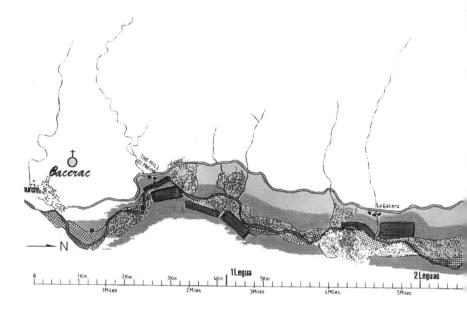

Figure 6.2. Mission *labores* and indian *milpas* in Bacerác and Bavispe, 1790

540 varas long and 133 varas wide (71,820 square varas) was irrigated by
the acequia originally built to power the mill. Two leagues north, the
village maintained two large *labores* separated by an arroyo and an ancient *galera* (a strip of raised land). All of these fields occupied an alluvial
plain extending westward from the river to a low range of hills. On the
eastern bank of the river, opposite the flour mill, the mission had two
labores measuring 218,700 and 171,769 square varas; and, downstream,
the pueblo had recently cleared a larger field of 227,180 square varas.[43]
The larger village *labores* are approximately equivalent to either a *suerte* or
a *caballería*, covering a range of 25 to 100 acres, as shown in Table 6.1.

The village of San Miguel de Bavispe stood on a mesa west of the
river. Across the stream, along the road leading to Fronteras, Bavispe
maintained nine *labores de comunidad*, so closely aligned that they seemed to
blend into one field. They ranged in size from 10,000 to 77,000 square
varas. All these fields were irrigated by the same canal. At the edge of
the community *labores* of both villages, the "hijos del pueblo" had many
small plots of cropland, some under irrigation and others dependent on

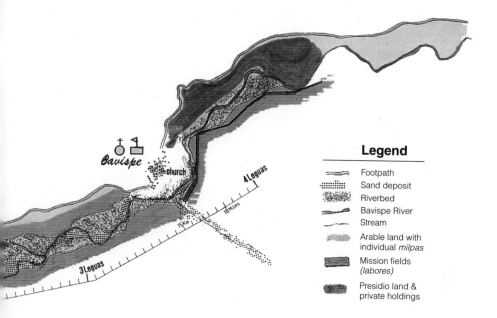

Legend

〰〰	Footpath
⋯⋯⋯	Sand deposit
▒▒▒	Riverbed
▬▬	Bavispe River
‐·‐·‐	Stream
▬▬	Arable land with individual *milpas*
▬▬	Mission fields *(labores)*
▬▬	Presidio land & private holdings

Bavispe
church
4 Leguas
3 Leguas
15 Km
10 Miles

rainfall. Subdelegado Hugo Ortiz Cortés, cited above, stated that along both banks of the river covering the four leagues separating Bacerác and Bavispe, the Indians had more land than they could keep planted in any one season. The best lands with abundant springs, however, had been set aside for the benefit of the Opata presidial company of Bavispe "and *vecinos* who settled near the presidio." Ortiz Cortés named specifically two landowning *vecinos*: his own relative Atanasio Ortiz Cortés and Francisco Ignacio Gil Samaniego, who had registered floodplain land with the authorization of Comandantes Teodoro de Croix and Jácobo de Ugarte y Loyola.[44]

Corresponding reports for the remaining pueblos of Guásabas, Oputo, Batuc, Tepupa, Bacadéguachi, and Nácori showed a similar pattern of separate village *labores* surrounded by individual *milpas*. We may infer from these descriptions that the Jesuits practiced some form of crop rotation, with overlapping sequences of planting and harvesting, while allowing some *labores* to lie fallow. Alternatively, the designation of numerous small fields with access to irrigation canals implies that the missionaries replicated pre-Hispanic land-tenure patterns. The communal fields of ancient *aldeas* became mission *labores*, while the Opatas continued to cultivate household plots using the villages' irrigation systems. The

Sonoran rural landscape of this period reflected the natural conditions of highland terrain, alluvial soil deposits, rainfall, and stream flow as well as the social conventions of household usufruct rights, inheritance, and community boundaries that divided the floodplain into discernible territories. The close association of family *milpas* with pueblo commons which, in turn, were legitimated under Spanish rule through the institution of the mission, linked the *serrano* peasants' sense of property to the community.

These indigenous categories of property collided with Bourbon initiatives to secularize the missions and divide village lands. As we have seen, from Visitor-General Gálvez to Comandante Nava, secularization of the Sonoran missions did not occur as the result of a bureaucrat's stroke of the pen; rather, this was a cumulative process that ran its course for more than half a century, continuing into the early national period. During the closing decades of the eighteenth century, private landholdings expanded appreciably at the expense of village commons. Provincial authorities believed that Indians always had more land than they could plant, the *vecinos* never enough. Their language implies a double standard: for Indians, a subsistence *milpa* should be sufficient; but *vecinos* needed enough land to produce surpluses for sale and to breed ever larger herds of cattle.[45]

The cultural meaning of secularization brings together the separate strands of change associated with demography, land tenure, and political innovation. By the turn of the nineteenth century, *vecinos* outnumbered Indians in Sonora; even the Opata stronghold of the Bavispe and Oposura valleys gave way to an increasingly mixed population. This changing ethnic pattern reflected not so much an alteration in the racial composition of the area's inhabitants as it did the shifting social and economic conditions of ethnicity. Increasing numbers of Indians became *vecinos*—by direct petition in some cases and, more often, by dint of mobility and customary association—because their ethnic status as members of a native community no longer ensured them access to the land. Facing the alienation of soil and water rights, a minority of village commoners retained their smallholdings; the vast majority, however, turned to wage labor or sought minimal security as tenants or sharecroppers on private estates.

The appropriation of land took different forms over this century of transition. *Vecinos* acquired private holdings through *mercedes* (royal grants), *composición* of land occupied without benefit of title, and *denuncia* of *baldíos* and *demasías*—supposedly unclaimed land or extra footage outside formal property demarcations. This last procedure carried over from colonial to national rule and became the predominant legal instrument for establishing private estates in Sonora.

Cattle and Enclosure of the *Realengos*

Public auction of grazing lands in the mountainous areas of Sonora, a common procedure in the late colonial period, involved the community in the privatization of land. *Realengos*, public domain held in the name of the king, referred mainly to the *agostadero* of scrub forest that covered the foothills and low ranges beyond the river valleys. Some cattle *estancias* were established in proximity to the streams that flowed out of the sierra; in general, though, territory outside the alluvial floodplains remained largely unclaimed because of its marginal value for agriculture. By the waning years of colonial rule, the increasing importance of stockraising and the ever expanding herds of *ganado criollo*—locally bred cattle—led Sonoran agropastoralists to turn to the grasslands of the arid cordilleras, dominated by mesquite and white oak, for natural forage.[46]

The *denuncias* of *sitios* in the *agostadero* that proliferated during the early years of the nineteenth century reveal both the ecological constraints of land use and the social conventions of landholding in the province. Public auction (*remate*) of *realengos* began when one or more *vecinos* brought a formal petition before the local authority—presidial captain, *juez político*, or *alcalde*—to claim a given piece of land. Townsmen from the same community measured the site in the presence of all adjoining landowners. At least four officials sworn to carry out the job in good faith walked the site, calling out the measurements "to the four winds" and noting all natural features: hills, canyons, springs, and ephemeral streams. They evaluated the land according to its size and the availability of water. This method of surveying respected the customary rights of neighboring farmers and stockmen. Having determined the proportions and minimum bidding price of the land, the property thus defined was "announced" by the town crier (*pregonero*) for thirty consecutive days. During that time, private citizens or corporate landholders, as in the case of Indian villages, could either protest the *denuncia*, showing previous title to the land, or raise the bid. Following the *pregones*, three witnesses chosen from the same locality testified as to the claimant's capacity to occupy the land by estimating the size of his herds and referring to other properties in his name. The final bidding occurred in the provincial capital of Arizpe. Three public auctions—*almonedas públicas*—announced by the town crier on successive days gave the final opportunity for rival claimants to appear and state their case. The successful bidder (nearly always the original *denunciante*) paid the value of the land and the taxes required to cover the costs of measuring and registering the land. It did not officially become his property until viceregal authorities in Mexico City had reviewed the entire process and given their approval.

The whole procedure could, and did, take years. Each step toward establishing private ownership in open range had to be carefully documented. Aspiring landholders needed authorization from officials at the local, provincial, and viceregal level. This laborious path to proprietorship reflects not so much the famed legalism of Spanish tradition, but rather the concept of property itself. Privatization of *realengos* took place only with the open knowledge of the community and when sanctioned by colonial authorities, made effective by the thirty *pregones* and three *almonedas públicas*. The state, represented in this case by the intendant-governor in Arizpe, made its presence felt in the acquisition of property. The fiscal officer (*promotor fiscal*) carefully reviewed previous stages of the *denuncia* and set the minimum price for auctioning the land. A *real cédula* of 1805 set the value of range land at sixty pesos per sitio for those areas with permanent running water, at thirty pesos per sitio where water could be obtained only by digging a well, and at ten pesos per sitio in arid lands with no source of water.[47] This scale of values reflects the fact that landownership was conditioned by its use—thus the significance of calling witnesses to testify to the claimant's ability to populate the range with cattle. In effect, these *remates* channeled modest payments to the royal treasury and legitimated the de facto possession of rustic property. The cases recorded for the province of Sonora show that *vecinos* rarely bid competitively for portions of the *agostadero* and that the claimant usually had been grazing his cattle on the land for some time before filing for legal title. Furthermore, the amounts paid to the royal treasury in Arizpe represented fees owed to the Crown, not purchase prices for the land. Nevertheless, the increasingly frequent use of the *denuncia* as the nineteenth century advanced created the contours of a regional land market, as the following examples will show.[48]

On the eve of Mexican independence, in 1811, provincial authorities recognized parallel land claims forwarded by the Indian pueblo of Mátape and the "vecindario" who lived in the same community. When Josef Ygnacio Mendoza and his brothers Jácobo and Melchor, joined by the Andrade and Lauterig families, "denounced" Las Animas as *realengo* grazing land, Subdelegado Rafael Ortiz de la Torre took pains to advise all neighboring landowners who might be affected by this new claim. Las Animas lay to the north of an adjoining ranch known as "él de Rodríguez," owned by Alonso Tresierra y Cano (who, as we have seen, held office in the intendancy and resided in Arizpe), and west of the lands belonging to the village of Mátape. With the concurrence of two Indian officers of Mátape, José Vicente Ybarra and Juan José Mendoza, and of Tresierra's *mayordomo* Juan José López, Ortiz de la Torre himself supervised the measurement of an area comprising 1.5 sitios and 1 caballería. Since Las Animas included a few plots of *tierra de pan llevar* and natural pasture for cattle, local residents evaluated it at the rate of thirty pesos per sitio, for a total value of forty-seven pesos, four reales. Three more *vecinos* of Mátape—Juan Antonio Valdez, Mariano and José Ygnacio de la Cruz —testified that the Mendoza brothers had several hundred head of cattle and that their associates each had several smaller herds. Final bidding on the property occurred in Arizpe two years later, without any rival claimants, and Mendoza and his confederates took possession of their land.[49]

The alienation of Las Animas took place within the social bounds of Mátape and her sister villages of Nácori and Alamos. The representatives of both the Indian and the non-Indian parties claimed to represent the *común* of local residents. In effect, the *vecinos* who registered this *realengo* came from several extended families headed by brothers: the Mendoza, Lauterig, and Andrade clans. The Indian governor (who also bore the surname Mendoza) signed "for me and all the *común* of the pueblo," echoing the expression used by the *alcalde* of Xecatacari a century earlier in his petition to found a pueblo in Buena Vista. In this case, it is probable that both "Indians" and "vecinos" descended from the same Eudeve stock and sought their livelihood as agropastoralists. The difference in their status derived from the disparity in their access to land. While the

Indians of Mátape held title to common land through the legacy of the mission and by virtue of their membership in the community, the *vecinos* who resided in the same area resorted to the *denuncia* in order to acquire a tract of pasture land.

Two decades later, Indian commoners of Mátape and Nácori again clashed with private landowners. In 1831, Doña Rosalía Sánchez and her son-in-law Jesús López filed a claim to three *sitios* in Adivino, along the road linking Nácori and Soyopa. Adivino lay within the vicinity of Las Animas, and both properties bordered on the private ranch of Rodrí-guez. Sánchez argued that the natives of Mátape could not document their title to the land and, in any event, had not kept the land "pro-tected and cultivated." The Indians, for their part, were represented by José María Elías and Vicente Ybarra who protested Doña Rosalía's *denun-cia*, citing state legislation that defended their pueblo's right to the land and that expressly forbade measuring private property adjacent to Indian communities. Elías and Ybarra appealed their case at the state level, where the priority of their claim to the land was upheld. State Treasurer José María Mendoza opined that, even in the absence of formal docu-mentation, the Indians' effective occupation of the site was sufficient to establish their property rights to Adivino. He canceled Sánchez's peti-tion to measure the land as a *baldío* and admitted the community's claim under the rubric of *composición*.[50]

Batuc and Tepupa, Eudeve villages east of Mátape with a long-standing tradition of communal landholding, illustrate well the dimensions of social and ethnic differentiation stemming from distinct claims to the land. In 1790 these two pueblos retained a substantial nucleus of mis-sion land as well as numerous household plots worked by Indian fami-lies. At this time, the village of Batuc held 59 households and a total population of 236 individuals.[51] Half a century later, a remnant of Batuc *comuneros* defended their land under the rubric of *fundo legal* against several private claims filed by *vecinos*. As in neighboring Mátape, these villages were composed of two communities of *vecinos* and Indians who occu-pied the same area. In 1808, Juan Antonio Orabuena petitioned for title to a *sitio* called Teguamatari, located two leagues north of Batuc, but he never finished the procedure. Citing this precedent, José María Velarde filed a claim to the same land in the spring of 1833. The state govern-ment forestalled measuring this site, however, until the boundaries of

Table 6.2 Household Heads in the Pueblo of Batuc, Sonora, 1834

José Ysidro López, governor	Luis Vadachi
Cruz Quigui, captain	Juan Vasaca
Marcos Quijada	Antonio Vasaca
Juan José Quijada	Ricardo Sicoco
Pablo Quijada	Albino Sicoco
José Demara	Espíritu Badase
Narciso Dorame	Juan Toruga
Domingo Dorame	Antolino Badero
Lázaro Dorame	Anselmo Yécoro
Nicolás Dorame	Gabriel Para
Cruz Yaqui	Pedro Camu
Francisco Yaqui	Lorenzo Tánori
Pedro Vagela	Juan González

Source: AHGES TP leg. 7, exp. 87.

the pueblo's *fundo legal* should be established. To that end, the following year, the Indian governor José Ysidro López and "all the *hijos naturales*" of Batuc gave power of attorney to Thomas Yvarola, a *vecino* of the same pueblo, to represent them in the formal proceedings. The Indian governor named twenty-six heads of household representing several extended families (see Table 6.2). His census, intended to prove the existence of a viable community entitled to a *fundo legal*, mirrored the count of male heads of household taken in Buena Vista more than a century earlier, in the case cited at the beginning of this chapter.[52] The land was duly measured and the community was assessed the statutory just price and state tax for title to the *fundo legal* of both pueblos. Governor López paid eighty-seven pesos and four reales, in money and horses, for legal title to the land thus secured for Batuc. However, in 1839, the Indians of Tepupa requested a *título de merced* to an area defined by different measurements; this second case remained unresolved.

These conflictive claims to village property resulted from the mixed allotments of private and communal land awarded to Indians and *vecinos* during the previous decades. When Licenciado Alonso Tresierra y Cano visited Batuc to carry out the first assignment of household plots ordered under the auspices of the intendancy in 1789, Juan Francisco Noriega approached him to claim a small piece of cropland that he had planted for several years without legal title. Noriega alleged that he was too poor to pay the official tax, but promised to honor his debt to the king once his fortunes had mended. Tresierra took him at his word, testifying that this modest portion of 14,884 square varas lay outside the land assigned to the Indians. In 1847, José Noriega made good his father's claim. With the authorization of Viviano Ochoa, governor of Batuc, Noriega paid ten pesos in order to secure title to the land. Furthermore, José obtained the signatures of his siblings in order to register his exclusive inheritance of this plot of *tierra de labrantío* which, in fact, he had kept cultivated over the years.[53]

Together with José Noriega, Ramón Molina y Mazón filed an identical claim to cropland measuring 24,300 square varas, which he said did not impinge on the pueblo's *fundo legal*. Like his neighbor, he held this *huerta* (garden or orchard) as a legacy from his grandfather, Pedro Molina. The land in question was bounded by Noriega's *labor* on the north and, on the south, by a private plot owned by the Indian Juan Sami; its eastern and western limits were defined by two acequias. Sixto Castillo filed a companion *denuncia*, naming two Indian smallholders whose property bordered on his claim: Anastacio Olibas and María Ana Carretas. Three witnesses over seventy years of age testified that they remembered Tresierra's measurement of the *fundo legal*, but were uncertain whether private *hijuelas* had been awarded at that time. Two Indian governors gave contradictory opinions, although both of them claimed not to be in conflict with Molina. Viviano Ochoa recalled that when Batuc received formal title to its land in 1833, any private claimants were to come forward at that time to register their property. Since this was not done, Ochoa argued, the area Molina now possessed fell within the boundaries of the pueblo. By contrast, Anselmo Sicoco testified only that he knew Molina and his associates—José Noriega, Sixto Castillo, and José Antonio Silvas—and recognized that the labor Molina now registered had always been considered Molina's. In the end, Molina prevailed and obtained his title at a cost of forty pesos.[54]

That same year, the pueblo of Soyopa paid 111 pesos to secure 1.25

sitios of watered land for the community. The native governor Seráfico Cadagüi cosigned the denuncia with Francisco Moreno and Loreto Encinas, claiming title to Campanaria (or Saporoa) a stretch of floodplain land bounded on two sides by private ranches. Soyopa natives prevailed over a rival claim registered by Francisco Duarte, owner of Rancho Pilitas del Apache. The two parties came to an agreement when Cadagüi and his associates ceded a small piece of land adjacent to Duarte's property. In this case, the community acted like a group of private citizens, purchasing an area of cropland in competition with neighboring vecinos.[55]

In summary, the establishment of fixed legal boundaries for property held in the name of individuals or communities overturned traditional notions of land tenure. The milpa, or indigenous household plot, constituted a shifting portion of floodplain land whose exact dimensions changed with the ebb and flow of meandering streams.[56] Formal land measurements that assigned exclusive title to ownership and inheritance of a given piece of land contradicted the Indian practice of variable use rights to arable land held in common by the entire community. Vecino smallholders, too, placed considerable weight on customary use rights in order to legitimate their claims to property. In Mátape, the Mendoza brothers claimed a sitio of grazing land on the basis of need and apparently met little resistance from village commoners. Yet, the community as a whole opposed the pretensions of two outsiders—Rosalía Sánchez and Jesús López—to register Adivino as a realengo. Likewise, in Batuc, Noriega and Molina called on local residents to confirm their customary rights to small plots of cropland by virtue of their occupation of the land for more than one generation.

Farther north, the range between the main headwater streams flowing into the Sonora and Oposura drainages had attracted Spanish settlers since mid-seventeenth century. Ranchers and miners based in Bacanuche encroached on the lands of Opata and Pima villagers who cultivated the alluvial valleys and hunted in the sierra. As Apache raids intensified through the eighteenth century, carrying off livestock and grain supplies, Opatas, Pimas, and Spaniards fell into a necessary alliance. Bacoachi, one of the principal Opata villages along the eastern tributary of the Sonora River and, after 1784, a presidio manned entirely by Opata troops, had become a mixed settlement of ninety Opata soldiers and a growing number of vecinos by the second decade of the nineteenth century. Together they maintained a bulwark against the Apaches, but the *vecinos* increasingly demanded title to land for grazing and farming.[57]

In 1818, Julián Salazar, *vecino* of Bacoachi, petitioned for title to 1.5 sitios in the Tierra Prieta de San Juan Bautista. The site he picked lay north of San Pedro, a ranch owned by his kinsman Matías Salazar, east of the Hacienda de Bacanuche, west of the presidial lands of Bacoachi, and south of the Valley of Mututicachi. José Manuel de Vildósola, deputy of mining and resident in Arizpe, received the commission to direct the survey of San Juan Bautista. The site comprised hilly, broken country and offered no permanent running streams. Nevertheless, it had good grassland and springs that could be tapped by wells. Local appraisers gave this assessment and set the price at thirty pesos per sitio. Salazar's *denuncia* went uncontested; the Junta de Almonedas met in Arizpe that same year and awarded him title to the land.[58]

José Santiago García of Arizpe and Carlos Palomino of Bacoachi together registered a claim to *tierra realenga* in the "abandoned site of Mututicachi" three leagues north of the presidio. Manuel de Escalante, *vecino* of Arizpe, surveyed and appraised the site. He took care to advise his relative José Escalante, who held the title of "Protector of the Indians of Bacoachi," to be present when the land was measured because its southern boundary adjoined the *sitios* belonging to the Opatas living at the presidio. Escalante's assessment of Mututicachi was favorable to García and Palomino: he recommended that, owing to the locality's exposed situation on the Apache frontier, forty-five pesos per sitio constituted a just price. In the intendancy, however, the *promotor fiscal* (Joseph Pérez) reassessed the land at sixty pesos per sitio, considering that the claimants could count on the protection of "that valient nation of Opatas" in Bacoachi as well as the presidial troops of San Bernardino de Fronteras, and that the property was well watered with stretches of arable land. García and Palomino accepted the higher price and became the owners of Mututicachi.[59]

Across the eastern cordillera, Martín de Zubiría, an Arizpe merchant, laid claim to a *sitio* in the Valley of Teuricachi in the political jurisdiction of the Presidio de Santa Rosa de Corodéhuachi de Fronteras. He chose a site one league south of the Hacienda de Cuchuta, the property of Francisco Escalante, *teniente de vecinos* in Fronteras. Don Francisco, who knew the place well, directed the measurement and appraisal of Teuricachi. At

Zubiría's request, the center chosen for his *sitio* lay "in the plaza found in the ruins of ancient houses." The northern boundary adjoining Cuchuta marked a small pond which provided a natural reservoir for the cattle; to the east, south, and west the property ended in abrupt ravines. The land, abundant in grasses, could support seasonal planting. Assessed at sixty pesos, Teuricachi was first auctioned in Fronteras. On the third day of the *almoneda pública* in Arizpe, Thomas Escalante, merchant and *vecino* of the provincial capital, raised the bid to eighty pesos. Zubiría's representative failed to match the new price, and Escalante received title to the fertile lands of Teuricachi.[60]

Francisco Escalante had first registered the Hacienda de Cuchuta in 1801, paying less than 80 pesos in two different occasions for four sitios. His property included natural pastures, springs, forests, and portions of arable cropland. He had never completed the procedures for gaining legal title, but in 1819 his son Manuel Escalante and two associates, Eduardo Badel and Francisco Sosa, paid to have the land measured and evaluated. They doubled their claim to eight sitios of land and accepted the substantially higher price of 300 pesos. Thus, the second generation of Escalantes expanded the family's holdings over much of the territory bounded by the presidios of Bacoachi, Fronteras, and San Bernardino.[61]

Closer to Arizpe, José Desiderio de Vildósola petitioned for land in Santa Rosa, a site between the provincial capital and Chinapa. Thomás Escalante led the surveying team that measured 2.25 sitios bordering on private ranches to the north and south and enclosed by mountain ranges to the east and west. Santa Rosa had good grassland, but no permanent streams. Vildósola designated the center of his property an abandoned tower ("un torreón viejo"). The eastern boundary ended in the Cerro del Barrigán, where Escalante observed a small natural reservoir for watering cattle "close to the foundations and walls of ancient dwellings."[62]

The ruins of stone and adobe structures observed at Teuricachi, Mututicachi, and Santa Rosa at the time these lands were declared *tierras realengas* indicate that they had not always been abandoned. In effect, this hilly terrain cut by ephemeral streams had supported pre-Hispanic villages and mission pueblos. As we saw in Chapter 5, the Jesuits nearly a century earlier had founded three settlements in order to concentrate the population from numerous *rancherías* scattered along the tributaries of the San Pedro, Santa Cruz, and Fronteras rivers into three pueblos: Suamca,

Guebavi, and Bac. Rodríguez Gallardo's relocation of several villages at midcentury, followed by the expulsion of the Jesuits and the gradual secularization of the missions, forced a contraction of the communal economy. On the eve of independence, both the Apache frontier and the expansion of mining and stockraising led to the dispersal of these ancient villages and the conversion of their lands into forage.[63] A half-century later John Russell Bartlett described the ruins of San Bernardino, a presidio that he thought was an abandoned hacienda, and of Cuquiá-rachi. The village was deserted, but its orchards were in full bloom.[64]

The *vecinos'* claim that this area was a *despoblado,* belonging to no one, underscored a basic contradiction between Spanish and Indian concepts of property. To enclose common woodlands and advance individual claims to marginal land threatened the livelihood of *serrano* agricultural-ists and foragers. Unlimited grazing accelerated the erosion of the soil and stripped away the vegetation cover—reducing, in turn, the flow of intermittent streams. Even without fences, the sheer growth of cattle herds afforded less access to the range for hunting and gathering. The lands stockbreeders called "empty" (*baldíos*) provided campesinos with a precious store of food, fuel, and building material. Although they did not live permanently in the *monte,* they needed its resources in order to survive. For ranchers, these marginal lands acquired value because of their commercial potential.[65]

The public auction of grazing lands carved out private holdings that, in north-central Sonora, typically measured from one to four sitios dur-ing the period 1780–1840. Most of the *remates* recorded were under three sitios, or less than half the area generally defined as a hacienda. Ranches of this size hardly constituted latifundia, even when annexed to previ-ous holdings.[66] Nevertheless, their owners constituted a class of property holders distinct from the peasantry. These were basically family enter-prises developed through the combined efforts of kinsmen like the Es-calantes and the Vildósolas to breed bovines, horses, and mules for sale. Wells (*norias*) to tap underground water were frequently mentioned in the appraisals of *realengos* put up for auction, indicating that enclosure led to the increased exploitation of these properties. Access to well water made new stretches of land susceptible to irrigation, either for market-able production or for the sustenance of resident laborers, and allowed ranchers to pasture ever larger herds of cattle. By the third and fourth decades of the nineteenth century, the number of *sitios* claimed in each *denuncia* as well as the price paid at the final auction tended to rise. For example, two sons of the powerful Elías González clan, Juan Rafael and Ignacio, expanded their family's holdings with four contiguous properties totaling 18 sitios and 12.5 caballerías. They paid nearly 450 pesos for this extension of grassland containing at least one natural spring.[67]

The Escalante and Elías González families accumulated wealth through a combination of mercantile connections and political office, a path followed by many colonial notables. Both families had their roots in the presidial companies of Bacoachi and Fronteras; several generations of their leading men held prominent civilian and military posts in the late-colonial intendancy and in the transition governments of the states of Occidente and Sonora. Their landed wealth was both a product and an instrument of their enhanced family patrimony. This means of social ascendancy overshadowed a complex process of class differentiation closely linked to the formal demarcation of property boundaries within rural communities. Beneath the stratum of an emerging landed oligarchy, the separation of private smallholders and dispossessed *vecinos* changed the social structure of highland pueblos.

Conclusions

Over a century and a half, beginning with Buenavista vs. Ancheta (1717) and Cucurpe vs. El Pintor (1723) and closing with the Batuc *común* and resident *vecinos* in 1848, private and communal landholding coexisted in an uneasy tension fraught with conflicting claims to the vital resources of land and water. Notwithstanding the overriding secular pattern in favor of the growth of private property, the social and cultural reality of the community persisted. But it is equally certain that Sonoran communities changed over this period in significant ways, witnessing internal divisions and the increased commercialization of their economy.

The cases narrated here illustrate two patterns of change in Sonoran land tenure, contrasting the northeastern region of the province — bounded by Arizpe, the capital of the intendancy, and the presidios of Fronteras, Bacoachi, and San Bernardino — with the mission districts of central Sonora. The ethnic corporate communities of Mátape and Batuc became racially mixed villages of peasant smallholders. In north-

eastern Sonora, however, *serrano* communities of Pimas and Opatas (to
wit: Cuchuta, Teuricachi, and Mututicachi) gave way to private ranches.
Their memory lingered only in the adobe "ruins of ancient houses" and
herds of wild cattle. Both patterns of change began during the Bourbon
administration, but their ramifications for *serrano* communities became
clear following Mexican independence.

These findings concerning highland Sonora resonate with the richly
detailed historical literature on land and society in New Spain. Three
themes provide an integrated leitmotif for numerous regional studies
dealing with rural social structures: (1) the relationship of particular
communities to their environment; (2) the diverse characteristics of
private landholding with respect to size, mode of exploitation, market
orientation, and internal labor relations; and (3) the evolving composition of rural communities. Nearly all histories dealing with land tenure
and the use of natural resources in New Spain bring the ecological dimension into their argument.[68] The present analysis of rural property in
Sonora builds on that historiographic tradition, looking with particular care at changes in land use relating to the economy and the locus of
power in this regional society.

A good many scholars working on Mesoamerica underscore the links
between ecology, economy, and land tenure.[69] Their research emphasizes the limitations that the agrarian cycle placed on productivity in
central-highland haciendas. Pointing both to the limited matrix of marketing in New Spain—reduced to the intraregional exchange of food
products—and to relatively fixed levels of technology used on the grain
haciendas of the altiplano and the Bajío, Arij Ouweneel and Richard
Garner, for example, contend that the agrarian economy itself had little
room for expansion. While population growth and rising prices during
the late eighteenth century might have induced hacendados to increase
production, this, in fact, rarely happened—precisely because of the
constraints of climate and technology.[70] Indigenous communities saw
their resources reduced to a minimum, owing to the alienation of cropland by private estates, even as falling real wages and food shortages
worsened living standards for the peasantry and the urban poor alike.
The natural rhythms of planting and harvesting, threatened by the twin
scourges of frost and drought in central Mexico, forced some peasants
who had not joined the dependent work force of the haciendas to turn

to protoindustry, exploiting the labor of women and children in order to survive.[71]

Numerous regional studies of Mexican agrarian structures provide different assessments of labor tenancy and community freeholding. Charles Gibson's classic work on the Valley of Mexico asserted that Spanish haciendas provided a modicum of security for Indians who found the burdens of community life intolerable in the face of a diminished land base. Eric Van Young has shown that population growth in eighteenth-century Guadalajara stimulated increased production in the grain haciendas of Jalisco, and David Brading has argued that the expanding urban centers of León and Guanajuato raised the demand for foodstuffs and provided a ready market for commercially oriented ranches carved out of larger haciendas by enterprising *arrendatarios*. John Tutino followed this same line of research to show that estate tenants forged a tolerable subsistence balance until the early nineteenth century, when hacendados withdrew customary payments in kind and demanded greater labor exactions. Scholars working on colonial Oaxaca point to the resilience of Indian corporate communities, which retained a significant portion of their land base and created syncretic religious and political expressions of their cultural identity.[72]

How do these views of central and southern Mexico compare with the history of land tenure in Sonora? Notwithstanding the limitations on food production imposed by the natural environment and by a relatively primitive technology, it appears that modest increments in productivity were gained through the organization of labor above the household level, whether in the missions or on private estates. Furthermore, hunting and foraging as well as seasonal wage labor supplemented agriculture. The *monte* may have appeared barren to Europeans, but it supplied native peoples with both food and shelter. In northwestern Mexico the possibilities for survival beyond fixed residence either in villages or haciendas mitigated the effects of the contraction of communal lands and conserved the open quality of ecological and social relations.

Here, as in other parts of the viceroyalty, livestock constituted the driving force for Hispanic land occupation, encroaching on indigenous cultivation. While the dichotomy between grazing and horticulture is hardly new, it is worth underscoring its importance for northwestern Mexico.[73] The *estancias* of the Sonoran piedmont were neither seigneurial estates—as François Chevalier once postulated for northern New Spain—nor protocapitalist operations comparable to those described for other regions of the Ibero-American world.[74] They were relatively modest holdings that supported the expansion of family patrimony through stockbreeding and revealed a clear orientation to commercial production. Most of the properties registered in the Sonoran highlands were acquired as *realengos* to the end of the colonial era. The sale and resale of rural properties documented for Guanajuato and Guadalajara during the eighteenth century did not become apparent in Sonora until the second half of the nineteenth century. This time lag in the development of a land market reflects the enduring frontier character of Sonora and the slow maturation of civilian society in the province.[75]

The concentration of landholdings required different means of procuring a labor force. Early colonial estates in Mesoamerica relied on *encomienda* and *repartimiento* to draw workers seasonally from subject Indian communities. By mid-seventeenth century, these regulated systems of forced labor gave way to private contracts or servitude, although the longevity of coercive labor systems in Nueva Vizcaya, Nuevo León, and Coahuila is striking.[76] A growing body of studies points to the importance of theoretically voluntary, but dependent, labor for the stability of the hacienda and to various regional patterns with respect to the source of labor, the terms of contract, and the workers' degree of mobility.[77]

Lacking account books or similar documentation for Sonoran colonial haciendas, it is difficult to ascertain their internal labor relations. While an informal system of *repartimiento* sent some Indian *tapisques* from the missions to nearby haciendas, such arrangements were hardly comparable to the numerous labor drafts reported for Nueva Vizcaya. Nevertheless, the accumulation of land by leading *vecinos* deprived increasing numbers of peasant smallholders of the means of survival, forcing them into dependent status as resident laborers and sharecroppers (or squatters) on estates such as those described above in the San Miguel, Sonora, and Oposura valleys. Landholding was not merely a sign of social status; more important than that, it was an instrument of social control.[78]

Sonoran haciendas and ranchos were clustered in areas of dense indigenous population and close to mining *reales*. Provincial markets remained small and basically local in scope, shifting with different mining bonanzas. The slow and uneven growth of marketing networks in

Sonora, in contrast with Nueva Vizcaya and Nueva Galicia where urban centers developed more steadily, retarded the advance of private land-holding. As villages and haciendas vied for land, water, and labor, what stands out is the resilience of *serrano* communities in the face of ever increasing pressures for privatization of the commons. The following chapter analyzes the social and economic formation of *vecino* small-holders in the context of class differentiation and political conflict.

7

Peasants, Hacendados, and Merchants: The Cultural Differentiation of Sonoran Society

This will be the beginning of discord in the pueblos and unending rivalry among families.

José Miguel Arvizu, 1841 [1]

On March 2, 1817, at the close of High Mass, Captain José Estévan summoned all the landed citizens of the Villa y Presidio de Pitic to a public meeting in the main plaza. As presidial commander, Captain Estévan held both military and political authority in the town of Pitic and its rural environs. The day before, he had instructed the *alcaldes de barrio* to alert all the *vecinos* who held title to either a house lot or a farm to gather at his home after Sunday Mass. Estévan found himself in the center of a brewing controversy over successive allotments of house sites and arable land in Pitic. Some families resident in the presidio had taken matters into their own hands. Tired of awaiting official approval, they had built houses in the middle of streets or invaded their neighbors' property. When Captain Estévan ordered them to halt construction or demolish what they had built, a few irate persons had accused him of acting out of animosity and political favoritism, even of harboring "other depraved intentions." [2]

Estévan realized that the situation was too fractious for him to handle alone and, for that reason, he called the townspeople to a meeting that spring Sabbath morning to choose three of their most prominent citizens for service on a select council called the Junta de Propios. The junta would review all petitions for house and farm plots, evaluating them on the basis of available land and water. The captain instructed them to carry out on-site inspections in order to determine that new land grants would not diminish the resources available to the community at large. Above all, Estévan underscored the importance of rationing water for irrigation, especially during the months of April, May, and June when drought and high temperature could wither the crops if the fields were not adequately watered. In addition, he authorized the junta to serve as a de facto court of first instance to hear and resolve conflicts over land and water. The presidial captain himself acted as the local judge (juez político). By empowering the junta to resolve land disputes, he was calling on them to share the burden of this thorny issue.

The persons elected to the Junta de Propios and the individuals who signed the empowering document represented those families linked to the Pitic garrison who had received the first land grants, issued in 1785, as well as the commercial interests who were gaining ascendancy in the economic and political life of the town. Although Pitic had no formal cabildo (town council), the merchants and landowners who held posts in the local militia wielded considerable influence there. The names appearing on the official account of that meeting in March 1817, shown in Table 7.1, occur frequently in the notarial records of Pitic as executors of wills, guarantors of debts and mortgages, and purchasers of property. The election of the Junta de Propios illustrates the limits of citizenship in this increasingly stratified community. The three vocales elected to the junta received a total of twenty votes, while the sixteen persons who signed the document (including the six elected to the Junta) were those household heads present at the meeting who knew how to read and write. Only property holders were vecinos in the full sense of the word; that is to say, members of the polity entitled to vote and make themselves heard in town meetings. Some women held property in their own right, but there is scant evidence of their participation in public life.

A month later, the prominent citizens of Pitic again convened before the presidial commander. Speaking for themselves and all their neighbors who did not attend the meeting, twenty-six vecinos expressed their concern over the lapsed payment of the parochial tithe. They recalled that approximately twenty years earlier the stockmen who grazed their cattle on presidio land had agreed to donate to the upkeep of the church all the unmarked yearlings gathered each year for branding, to be con-

Table 7.1 Junta de Propios de la Villa de Pitic, 1817

Elected Members	Alternates
Ignacio Buelna	Ignacio Noriega
Xavier Romo	Manuel Rodríguez
Diego Vidal	José Buelna

Signatories	
José Estévan, captain of cavalry and presidial commander	
Manuel Rodríguez, captain of the militia and of commerce	
José María García de Noriega, lieutenant of the militia and *síndico* (land registrar)	
Francisco Monteverde, lieutenant of justice	
Manuel Ramírez	Felipe Noriega
Rafael Díaz	Bernardo Figueroa
Francisco Javier Díaz	
José Antonio García de Noriega	

Source: A NO doc. 44.

sidered common property.[3] Their herds had prospered and multiplied, so that "wherever one looked, there were cattle to be seen, too many even to be counted." In 1813, some Pitiqueños had prevailed upon the majority to discontinue the tithe, calling on the provincial governor to issue a decree to that effect. Divine wrath had punished them with a four-year drought, "turning the verdant fields once covered with grazing animals into graveyards scattered with bones." Now repentant, the cattlemen of Pitic swore to commit themselves and their descendants — without exception — to renew the annual tithe of all unmarked stock at the time the herds were rounded up, separated, and branded. They specified that the funds obtained through their donation should be used for the maintenance, adornment, and enlargement of the presidial chapel, as the growing population of Pitic would soon require a more spacious place of worship, and they elected one of their number, Juan José de Buelna, to be *mayordomo depositario* of the tithe.[4]

The following Sunday at the close of morning Mass, the *vecinos* gathered to the beat of a military drum in the street outside the commander's quarters to hear the public pronouncement of the stockmen's tithe. Anyone who objected to the donation set at the previous meeting should personally register his protest within three days before Captain Estévan himself, Magistrate José María Noriega, or Buelna. Perhaps not surprisingly, no one openly refused to pay the tithe. These three officials had made a private donation publicly binding, declaring solemnly that "the citizenry so desires this gracious contribution to take effect now and forever."

Taken together, these events illustrate the common values and recurring conflicts that structured the daily lives of Pitic residents. The religious and political dimensions of town life ran in close parallel for the soldier-settlers who farmed on the floodplain and ran their cattle on unfenced rangeland. Indeed, presidio, parish, and commmunity were scarcely distinguishable one from the other. The rhythm of weekly Mass set the timing for public gatherings, even as the beat of martial drums summoned the people to meet in the plaza. Issues which affected the entire community, such as land distribution and the tithe, were aired verbally in open assemblies. Decisions became binding, however, when recorded in notarial acts signed by the presidial commander; and only a small minority of the townspeople could read and write.

Equally significant, the election of the Junta de Propios and the renewal of the tithe suggest an overlapping set of principles that guided the demarcation of property rights in Pitic. Legal and social precedent dictated that presidial soldiers and their families should receive farmland and a town site; once distributed, these plots were treated as private property.[5] As we have seen, *vecinos* with prior claims to land were loath to treat newcomers generously. Cattle were owned privately, but herd management followed the conventions of public domain. Settlers of northwestern New Spain bred their bovines (*ganado mayor*), but during a good portion of the year Sonoran herds grazed on desert scrub unattended. Once marked and branded, the animals became private property, a form of wealth highly valued in this agropastoral society. *Criadores* traded cattle for land and sold off some of their animals to pay their debts. They divided their "goods" to provide a dowry for their daughters and an inheritance for all their children. Nevertheless, no one household could manage their herds alone. The seasonal *corridas* or *recogidas* required the labor of all the *vecinos* to drive the cattle off the range and into central corrals for branding. At this time, the newly born calves were considered "common to all" and were thus appropriately assessed by the community through the tithe.[6]

Social conventions concerning property corresponded to the material conditions of livelihood in the environs of Pitic. Captain Estévan's warning against unlimited distribution of farmland reflected the common wisdom that arable land and water were scarce resources in this semi-arid region. While the proponents of the tithe surely exaggerated the scourge which had decimated their herds, in fact a prolonged drought that could destroy crops and waste away cattle was (and is) a constant danger in the area. Thus, the political and economic structures of peasant society in Pitic rested on the ecological constraints for human settlement in this colonial outpost.

A Presidio in the Desert

San Pedro de la Conquista de Pitic, a military garrison established at the confluence of the Sonora and San Miguel rivers in 1741, extended permanent Spanish settlement to the eastern margins of the Sonoran Desert. During unrecorded centuries before the arrival of the Spaniards, the O'odham (Pimas) had built shifting villages in the alluvial valley created between the two rivers. They farmed in the floodplain and hunted and gathered in the mountainous terrain that extended to the north and east. From the west, the desert-dwelling Cunca'ac (Seris) came periodically to Pitiquín to trade, visit, and occasionally skirmish with the O'odham.

Spanish dominion intensified the exploitation of natural and human resources in Pitic. Captain Agustín de Vildósola used captive Indian labor to build adobe walls, dig earthen canals (acequias), and plant vineyards, orchards, and cane fields. Vildósola's ambitions extended to refining silver and extracting the wealth of pearl beds in the estuaries of the Gulf of California, despite the Seris' determined resistance. In 1749, José Rafael Rodríguez Gallardo, judge and viceregal inspector, ordered the garrison moved thirty miles upstream to the Valley of Pópulo and rechristened it San Miguel de Horcasitas. The displacement of O'odham and Cunca'ac families from the mission of Nuestra Señora del Pópulo and the transferral of their land to the presidio unleashed hostilities which turned the region into an armed frontier for more than half a century. Nevertheless, the Spaniards never entirely abandoned Pitic—a few laborers remained to tend the orchards and vineyards—and the fortified town of Horcasitas became a center of political and military operations for the province of Sonora. The missions held customary rights to floodplain land in the San Miguel Valley north of Horcasitas, where Pima and Eudeve cultivators clustered around the villages of Nacameri, Opodepe, Meresichic, and Cucurpe. Private settlers extended their holdings south of the presidio to Codórachi and the wide alluvial valley farther downstream.[7]

In 1780, a full generation later, the presidio returned to its original site on the northern bank of the river across from the Seri mission of Nuestra Señora de Guadalupe. Despite a smallpox epidemic in 1781 and continued skirmishes, Cunca'ac, O'odham, and Spaniards maintained an uneasy coexistence in Pitic until the end of the century, when the Cunca'ac abandoned their mission and returned to their traditional subsistence along the desert coastland and islands of the Gulf of California. In 1783 the settlement received the title of villa, and the residents began construction of a stone and mortar aqueduct. At mid-decade, military officials measured and distributed shares of farmland to Seris, Pimas, and Spanish vecinos who had settled in the valley. Household heads, who received plots of varying size, constituted the core of what would become the civilian population of Pitic.[8]

The census of 1796 showed a combined population of slightly over 1,000 persons settled in the presidio, villa, and mission, as shown in Table 7.2.[9] The soldiers and their families made up less than a third (27.4%) of the total population and were outnumbered by the civilian residents in the villa. Spanish garrison residents and vecinos reached 689 individuals, more than double the 290 Seri, Pima, and Guayma Indians reportedly living in Pitic. Five Spanish families lived on the lands assigned to the Seris. The latter, although registered in the mission, were wont to come and go, fleeing the confinement of village life for the coastal desert they knew so well.[10] The 36 Indian families listed in the presidial census included some Pima soldiers who served in the garrison. Accorded the status of vecinos, they were bound by military regulations, protected by the fuero, and entitled to an allotment of farmland.[11]

Table 7.2 Population of Pitic, Sonora, 1796

	No. Families	No. Persons
Presidio and *villa*		
Soldiers and their families	$(72)^a$	277
Vecinos in Villa de Pitic	156	412
Pima and Guayma Indians	36	86
Total		775
Population of the New Seri Mission		
Families	31	
"Married according to their law"	3	
Widows and widowers	20	
Unmarried youth	14	
Unbaptized (*gentiles*)	3	
Seris living in the mission	204	
Spaniards living in the mission	30	

Source: AMH: Fray Juan Felipe Martínez, *Padrón y inventario de la nueva misión de los seris* (1796).

[a] *Plazas* "soldiers".

Land and Social Division in Pitic

The non-Indian population of Pitic grew considerably after the eighteenth century, comprising a mixed community of garrison residents, farmers, and merchants. The official distribution of land in 1785 assigned unequal lots to eighteen heads of household, as shown in Table 7.3, according to need, family size and, no doubt, the prestige of military office.[12] Subsequent generations sold, rented, and mortgaged portions of their farms, thus fragmenting the original land grants. Notarial records reveal frequent transferrals of property, through which a few households increased their patrimony at the expense of their neighbors. Nine land sales recorded in Pitic from 1793 to 1820 are not a sufficient number to show a pattern. Their content, however, shows the outlines of an incipient land market in this agrarian community. Only one case specifies the size of the property sold. María Rita Mesa, the widow of

Table 7.3   Land Grants for the Presidio and Villa of Pitic, Sonora, 1785

	No. Suertes
Propios for the Villa de Pitic	8
Each suerte 400 × 200 varas	
Land for the Seri mission	27
27 suertes on southern bank of the river	
(5 for the community, 22 for individual farming plots)	
Land for the Pimas in Pitic	25
5 suertes for the community, 20 for	
individual households	
Individual grants for the *vecinos*	
José Moreno	2.25
Francisco Acuña	1.00
Juan Antonio Estrada	2.00
Joaquín Buelna	2.25
Salvador Marciano Quintana	2.25
José Antonio Sánchez	.25
José Tadeo Sánchez	1.00
Juan Pedro Lujan	1.00
Juan Estévan Vidal	.75
Juan Diego Vidal	.75
José María Vidal	2.00
Juan José Valencia	8.00
Juan Puyod	5.00
Manuel de Monteagudo	8.00
Manuel del Valle	1.00
Joaquín de Leon	.75
Jose María Castro	.50
Juan López Aro	3.00

Source: BNFF 32/659.

Note: 1 vara = .83 meter, or 2.7 feet; 1 suerte = 10.5 hectares, or 26.3 acres.

Captain Joseph de Tona, sold one-quarter of a suerte for 200 pesos to José María Noriega, a merchant and leading notable present at the election of the Junta de Propios, as seen above.[13] In general, purchasers and sellers showed greater interest in the productive assets that came with the land—sugar presses (trapiches), equipment for distilling brandy (alambiques), orchards and vineyards, irrigation canals, and buildings—than they showed in the exact size of the plot. The means of exchange varied widely, from five cows to 5,000 pesos. One can infer from the description of each transaction and the discrepancy in prices that real estate values were not fixed but were subject to negotiation.

The widows and children of the 1785 recipients frequently sold portions of their land in later decades. María Rita was one of four women who sold sections of the farms they had inherited from their fathers or deceased husbands. Three of these women could not read or write and relied on relatives or trusted friends to sign for them. Only one of the soldier-settlers named in the repartimiento, Salvador Quintana, exchanged his house and a plot of land for five cows in 1793.[14] By contrast, the purchasers included no women. Typically the landowners who increased their holdings were merchants or farmers and stockmen with a commercial bent: José María Noriega, Antonio Ferrari, Francisco Monteverde, Fermín Méndez, José María Díaz, and Ignacio Araiza.

The language of these notarial transactions reveals the social relations that underlay the value of property in Pitic. House lots and gardens formed irregular squares crisscrossed by the acequias that carried water for irrigation and domestic use and by bridges that connected their separate properties. The vecinos identified their lots according to adjacent properties and common rights-of-way or by the fruit trees planted on them. For example, in the spring of 1819, the merchant Fermín Méndez paid 550 pesos in two installments for José María Ramírez's house and garden adjoining his property to the west, "with a large lemon tree standing in it." The calle real bounded it on the south; to the north ran the common acequia, and to the east the Ramírez lot met the property of Antonio Andrade.[15] Not infrequently, the community continued to name a piece of land by its deceased owner.

The small number of land sales officially recorded during this period leaves open the possibility that people could obtain access to land through informal transactions not requiring a notary's signature. Share-

cropping, rental, "sharing," and "lending" pasture and cropland undoubtedly created bonds among households in Pitic. Nevertheless, the
1817 town meetings show that alongside a nucleus of landholding *vecinos*—the *propios*—lived a growing number of landless residents. Population growth, coupled with the prevailing custom of partible inheritance, led to two parallel processes of fragmentation and accumulation
of property that accelerated the unequal distribution of wealth among
the Hispanized peasantry. Merchant and landowning families, such as
the Noriega, Monteverde, Díaz, and Velasco households, amassed appreciable holdings through the purchase of numerous scattered plots linked
by *canales* to the source of water which rendered them fertile. Furthermore, land sales specified that the property came with rights of access
and with service canals joined to the main acequias. The distribution of
land in the lower Sonora river valley changed in accordance with the
growing complexity of the area's agropastoral economy.

Peasant Economy: Farmers, Peddlers, and Merchants

In the late summer of 1804, Captain Josef Fernández de Loredo, commander and magistrate at the presidio, penned a report to Intendant-
Governor Alejo García Conde on the economy of Pitic and its rural environs; the report was destined for the Consulado de Veracruz.[16] Loredo
listed the annual crop yield for maize and wheat only, and estimated the
size of herds and the market value for different kinds of cattle. Farmers
in the lower San Miguel and Sonora river valleys produced three times as
much wheat as corn. They grew vegetables in small quantities, probably
for household consumption. Although Captain Loredo gave no information on cotton, sugar, or tobacco, we know from other sources that
local producers grew sugarcane, pressed the stalks, and boiled the sweet
syrup into hard brown loaves (*piloncillo*) which they traded among each
other and sold throughout the region. Stockraising was clearly important to rural livelihood in Pitic (see Table 7.4). A mule was worth almost
three times as much as a horse and over four times as much as a cow.
Its relatively high value reflects the not inconsiderable costs of breeding
mules and their high demand in mining and commerce.

According to Loredo, if we discount the salt deposits (*salinas*) along
the coastal estuaries, the district had no mines. Pitic lacked roads and

Table 7.4 Livestock in the Partido de Pitic, Sonora, 1804

	No. Head	Value per Head
Bovines	5,000	5p
Sheep	3,422	1p
Goats	435	4r
Horses	2,138	8p
Mules	367	22p 4r

Source: BNFF 36/819.

Note: p = pesos; r = reales.

bridges (perhaps the commander had little respect for the earthen constructions in the *villa*). The *vecinos* did not pay *alcabalas* or tribute; nor
had they established *estancos*, monopolies for the sale and taxation of tobacco, gold, silver, and playing cards.[17] Merchandise from Castile, Asia,
and China was unknown, nor were local products shipped to the major
ports of Veracruz, Acapulco, and San Blas. Pitic boasted no tanneries
nor cotton, silk, woolen, porcelain, or glass manufactories. Pitiqueños
did produce brandy (*aguardiente de castilla*), though—as much as 12,000
cuartillos each year.[18] In short, Captain Loredo depicted Pitic as a self-
contained, agropastoral community living basically on the grains, vineyards, and cattle produced in the locality. In truth, Pitiqueños produced
few of the items listed in the questionnaire issued by the Consulado de
Veracruz. In contrast to this picture, however, the wills, mortgages, and
letters of credit recorded by acting notaries reveal a diversified economy
oriented increasingly toward the market.

The detailed lists of household possessions included in wills provide
a key to understanding peasant livelihood. Descriptions of property,
tools, clothing, and personal effects bring into focus the means of production and draw us closer to the quality of life in this frontier society.
The language used in the documents indicates that neighbors and kinsmen recognized one another's private rights of possession and usufruct
through local custom and common knowledge of the terrain.

When Luis Valencia dictated his last will and testament in the spring
of 1790, he had amassed a sizable patrimony and gained the stature of

a landowner. He owned the Hacienda de Codórachi in the San Miguel Valley, holding legitimate title to that property as part of the military company of Horcasitas. Valencia hired peones to help work the land and defend his property against the Apaches. The hacienda included several irrigated fields and a water-powered mill; in addition to Codórachi, Don Luis claimed a piece of arable land of undetermined size in Torreón, downstream from the Presidio de Pitic. The community recognized this *labor* as his according to the rights of possession established by the first owner, Juan José Valencia, who had received eight suertes in 1785 (Table 7.3), even in the absence of any formal title save a document registered some years earlier in the magistrate's office. More important to the Valencias than the land measurements were the fruit trees they had planted on it. Don Luis carefully enumerated the number of saplings in fruit, which represented the results of his work and the productive assets he had brought to the land. Valencia had enhanced his property with a sugar press, a small loom, and metal basins used, perhaps, for making *piloncillo*. He had nearly 200 head of livestock in goats, horses, and steers, including 30 mules with the necessary gear for hauling cargo.[19] A middling hacendado with roots in presidial service, Don Luis left his heirs two farms with orchards and grainfields, cattle, and his own mule train for carrying produce to market.

Nearly twenty years later, María Juana Espinoza Bernal described a smaller legacy derived from the military allotment of land to presidial households in 1785. María Juana was the widow of José María Vidal, a recipient of two suertes of farmland. In 1809 she declared two small separated plots of irrigated land: "one in the place called Chanate, between two lots understood to belong to Pedro Valencia, and the other in Torreón suitable for an orchard." Her house was typical of rural dwellings in the province. She lived in three rooms built of thick adobe walls; her kitchen, partially out-of-doors, was enclosed by woven mats reinforced with a mixture of mud and dung.[20]

José Antonio Bernal, born in the mining *real* of San José de Gracia in the Sonora Valley, lived as a soldier and pastoralist in Pitic. The possessions he declared in 1808 suggest a modest estate based principally on stockraising. He owned a house and two small farming plots in the presidio. Yet the legacy he considered most important was his cattle: oxen, burros, mules, and horses. Bernal could not give an exact count of his animals, but trusted that his heirs would recognize his brand. Among his personal effects Bernal listed a statue of San José, a pair of rider's breeches, an old serape, a saddle, and his firearms.[21]

Ignacio Encinas hailed from the village of Batuc in the eastern sierra of Sonora. He owned no land in the *villa*, and made his living as a stockman, muleteer, and miner. He recognized a debt of 110 pesos to the merchant Javier Díaz of Pitic for merchandise he had taken to Batuc. Encinas's property included small herds of cattle and the equipment for making and repairing tools used in tanning leather, refining silver, and making firearms.[22]

Similarly, José Thomás Rico from Papigochic, Chihuahua, rode the mule trails from Pitic to the sierra. He occupied a small room in Pitic and owned a house in Mulatos, a village in the mountain fastness between Sonora and Chihuahua. Although he held no land, he declared as his property seventy-four mules equipped for carrying cargo, a herd of mares, and a stallion for breeding. Upon his death in 1817, the presidial captain José Estévan and Judge Ignacio Monrroy drew up a detailed list of Rico's personal possessions in Pitic, consisting principally of clothing, firearms, and all the accoutrements for traveling by horseback.[23]

These brief portraits of Pitic *vecinos* show different sources of livelihood and forms of property, and the web of daily transactions recorded in the *villa* reveals the social relations that underlay the local economy. Written and oral contracts created bonds of reciprocity and dependency within and among different households. Sonoran families established conjugal property, distributed legacies and dowries, sold or rented land, and shared resources, thereby creating links from one generation to the next. These arrangements were often conflictive, but they rested on a common set of values and norms that structured their world.

José María Vidal, cited above, gave his daughter María Josefa a small piece of a *suerte* when she married José María Fernández. The Vidal family treated her dowry as a form of inheritance-in-life. The land that María Josefa and her husband came to own included a vineyard already in fruit and an adobe house.[24] In a similar manner, Luis Valencia gave his daughter Josepha a portion of his *labor* in Torreón when she married Ignacio Rivera. Valencia's son-in-law had himself planted a substantial vineyard and orchard and had built a house "with his own labor." When the elder Valencia died in 1790, the family recognized this "donation" as permanent, ceding ownership of the house and farm to Josepha and her husband.[25]

Miguel Atienta y Palacios, a migrant from Puebla who had established residency in Pitic, noted in his will that his wife Manuela de Arce y Rosales brought to the household a few milking cows and two pieces of silver which he had "used" (sold or otherwise disposed of) during the course of their marriage. In order to restore her property, Don Miguel stipulated that his house with its furnishings and a small amount of silver be reserved for her, separate from the goods to be divided among his children. Palacios was a working landowner; his legacy bespoke a life dedicated to soldiery, animal husbandry, and tilling the soil. He left twelve mules and an undetermined number of branded cattle, a variety of iron tools, a digging stick (*coa*) and a full complement of firearms appropriate for a mounted militiaman. Palacios had prospered and found acceptance in the community. Ignacio Noriega, from one of the prominent merchant families named above, figured as part owner in Don Miguel's Rancho de la Puente and married his daughter María del Carmel.[26]

The Palacios–Noriega alliance illustrates the ties of interdependency forged among Pitic households and sealed, at times, through marriage and the dowry. Households generally treated dowries as an asset the wife had brought to the marriage, one that she could recover in some form of equivalency and pass on to her children should she outlive her husband. The use of the dowry in Sonora during the early nineteenth century contrasts with the core areas of New Spain, where it was beginning to fall into disuse in favor of direct forms of paternal inheritance.[27]

Sonoran society practiced partible inheritance as established by Iberian legal traditions. Nearly uniformly, testators named surviving spouses and children as their only legitimate heris. Of the property and goods remaining after paying outstanding debts, funeral services, and religious vows, the widow (or widower) received half and the children received shares of the other half. Inheritance practices rested on the value of labor inputs which justified an individual's claim or entitlement to household resources, but partible inheritance did not lead to an egalitarian distribution of wealth. In principle, all legitimate offspring inherited equally, but testators could favor one heir with as much as one-fifth or one-third of the estate. Furthermore, once the property had been divided, it was not uncommon for joint heirs to sell out their shares and

leave landed property to one among them.[28] The choice of an executor (*albacea*) and the way in which property was managed explained the
differential treatment of household members as well as the long-term
trend toward consolidation or fragmentation of the family's patrimony.

Luis Valencia, cited above, named three of his sons as *albaceas* of his
estate, but he placed full power of decision in his second son, Ignacio.
At the time Don Luis dictated his will, Ignacio managed and virtually
owned the Hacienda de Codórachi, and intended to retain title to that
portion of his father's property. In addition, the younger Valencia reserved for himself one-fifth of the estate, promising to share the rest
equally with his siblings and his mother after paying all debts and religious obligations. Ignacio confirmed his sister's possession of the land
she had received in dowry and, after some discussion, recognized as a
debt against the estate the capital his mother Josepha Robles had brought
to the household at the time of her marriage: twelve steers, two jackasses, and a horse. ("The enemy," probably Apaches, had taken these
animals years ago and, for that reason, the heirs questioned whether her
dowry constituted a viable asset.) One may speculate from the negotiations that occurred just prior to and following the elder Valencia's death
that Luis Valencia did not intend to favor any of his children over the
others. Rather, he may have hoped that despite the formality of individual inheritance, Ignacio would manage his combined properties as a
family patrimony.[29]

Household economy rested on the joint property of husband and
wife. Women frequently owned land and cattle and, with or without
the formality of a dowry, they could claim a share of the total patrimony belonging to the household. The few women of Pitic who dictated a will left expressive testimony of the relationship they perceived
between *property* and *family*.[30]

Juana Games de Lorenzana drew up her will in 1820, after forty years
of marriage with Ignacio Díaz, lieutenant of cavalry in the presidial
company of Altar. At the time she gave her testament, her husband was
"far away," serving with the royalist troops engaged in battling the insurgency. Juana declared that when she and Ignacio were married in San
Miguel de Horcasitas, "my husband was a soldier and neither he nor I
had any property other than the horses and gear corresponding to his
military service. Today, by the grace of God, we own our house and an

orchard planted with vineyards in the *ejidos* surrounding the presidio."[31] Juana Games claimed the furniture and belongings in her house as her own. She had raised seven children; in her husband's absence, she named her eldest son, Rafael, and two of her sons-in-law, Guillermo Games and Matheo de Uruchurtu, a prominent Pitic merchant, as executors of her estate. She trusted that without any need to go to court, the three *albaceas* would inventory, appraise, and divide her possessions in equal parts, conserving "peace and harmony among all the brothers and sisters, as I can hope for nothing more so that God may conserve them in his holy grace."[32] Juana Games's choice of *albaceas* within the family contrasts with the following case.

María Josefa Nicolasa Borjórquez, widow of the presidial soldier Juan María Nicanor Araiza, drew up her will in the spring of 1817. She declared that ten years earlier, when her husband died, he had left her only a small vineyard (seven *tablas de viña*), and noted that "all I possess today is thanks to my effort and husbandry." Although María Josefa did not describe her property, she seemed to be a woman of some means. She left a donation of fifty pesos to the parish and an equal amount to pay for the Masses to be sung for her after her death. María Josefa had kept a record of the persons who owed her money and had taken the precaution to have the presidial commander sign it. She ordered that two *peones* (*labor* tenants or field hands) who worked for her be forgiven their debts, "in recompense for their loyal service." Perhaps because her three children were young, María Josefa chose three local merchants as *albaceas*: Manuel Rodríguez, Ambrosio Noriega, and José María Noriega. She expressed special confidence in Manuel Rodríguez, naming him to be her children's guardian.[33]

Josefa Iñigo Ruiz, daughter of a wealthy landowning family in the San Miguel Valley, ceded to her husband Manuel Rodríguez the power to testate her estate. Her first marriage to José Belas de Escalante, captain of the Presidio de Fronteras, had left her a widow with four young children. During her second marriage Josefa had given birth to three sons. She entrusted Rodríguez to care for all her children, to pay her debts, and to use his judgment in distributing her possessions among the heirs.[34]

When Juan José Díaz dictated his will in 1817, his only heirs were his wife, María Ygnacia Escalante, and his young daughter María Dolores. Neither Juan José nor María Ygnacia had any property when they married, but during the course of their life together they had accumulated a secure patrimony. Díaz's resources included an irrigated plot of land with all the equipment needed for farming and 6 yoke of oxen, 200 head of cattle, and 50 mules outfitted for loading cargo. He named Manuel Rodríguez executor of his estate and tutor of both his wife and daughter, directing them to entrust Don Manuel with all decisions concerning their welfare. Díaz, a farmer, stockman, and trader, ceded the management and usufruct of his property to Rodríguez, a Pitic merchant. Two years later, Manuel Rodríguez brought suit against the Valencia family for payment of more than 200 pesos he claimed José Valencia owed the estate of María Dolores Díaz.[35] When testators had recourse to *albaceas* outside the family, effective control over the property passed, in time, from the heirs to the administrators. Management of small proprietors' estates was an important way in which merchant-landowners gained control over productive resources they did not formally own. The fact that women did not enjoy full control over the property they held in their own name may have contributed to the subdivision of small-holdings and enhanced the accumulation of land in the upper strata of society.[36]

The only case of legal adoption recorded during this period carried this kind of tutorial relationship one step further and gave poignant expression to the ties of dependency established between unequal households. Juan Albarracín and María Julia de los Ríos, advancing in years, signed with a cross the document that transferred all paternal rights over their adolescent daughter Juana to Francisco Velasco and his wife, María de Jesús Artiaga. Juana served in the Velasco household, and her parents acceded to the adoption, confident that Don Francisco and Doña María would feed and clothe her, teach her Christian morality, and train her in the tasks appropriate for a woman.[37]

The following cases of land sales and rentals illustrate the economic and social dimensions of reciprocity and dependency. Ignacio Valencia used the Hacienda de Codórachi as a base of operations to rent additional land and thereby increase his commercial production. In 1790, Fernando Iñigo Ruíz agreed to lease him for ten years the Hacienda de San Benito del Torreón, a property he had acquired from his father-in-law, Manuel de Monteagudo, one of the original recipients of farmland in the Presidio de Pitic.[38] In return for 10 cargas of *piloncillo* (31.5 bushels) each year, Valencia acquired use rights to a substantial hacienda complete with houses, an orchard, and five sugar presses. He pledged to pay the stipulated rent or its equivalent in money at twenty-five pesos per carga; should he forfeit, he mortgaged his team of mules and herds of livestock. Both parties formalized the agreement. Should Iñigo die before the lease expired, his heirs could demand payment of the rent but could not rescind Valencia's rental of the hacienda.[39]

Some years earlier the same Monteagudo had entered into a sharecropping arrangement with Antonio Estrada, a *vecino* of Pitic. They planted wheat "a medias"—sharing costs and dividing the harvest by halves—in a field measuring about 1 suerte (26.3 acres). When Manuel de Monteagudo died, the two *labradores* had a crop sown in the field. Estrada drew up his own will, stipulating that the harvest of 10 fanegas (15 bushels) of wheat should be given to Monteagudo's heirs, while the land itself should go to his younger son Ramón, "who had served him faithfully."[40]

As these examples show, landowners accepted rental payments in the marketable products of their farms, such as wheat and sugar. Even when contracts stipulated payment in money, often they allowed for extending amortization over time. Ignacio Villaseñor purchased a flour mill ("on the other side of the river" from Pitic) which had belonged to the deceased José Basols. He agreed to pay Basols's estate a total of 500 pesos in various installments over three years. Villaseñor signed the agreement in 1803; the price having been satisfied, but without any payment of interest, the mill became his property in 1805.[41]

Quotidian practices in Pitic concerning the use of property and the disposition of inheritances and dowries supported a mixed economy of market as well as nonmarket forms of exchange. Although we have little infomation on actual procedures for buying and selling, the prices set for basic grains, sugar, brandy, and different kinds of cattle allow us to infer that a market did, in fact, exist. Beyond a doubt, itinerant traders (*arrieros*) played an important role in the movement of goods within the region and from one province to another. Mule trains constituted the principal means of transport in colonial Sonora, carrying maize, wheat flour, cloth, *piloncillo*, brandy, hides, tools, firearms, and ammunition from the lower river valleys to the mining camps in the eastern sierra and the placer mines in the desert to the northwest. *Recuas de mulas* formed the capital of itinerant merchants whose trade, in turn, fueled the provincial economy. The data are not sufficient to characterize this regional trading network according to a given model, but we can visualize it as a web with various points of exchange.[42] Population grew in nuclei like Pitic, Altar, and Horcasitas after 1800, but no one town dominated the flow or reception of goods. Rather, the Sonora and San Miguel valleys comprised numerous, closely related communities of producers who traded with each other.

Nonmarket forms of exchange included the sharing and borrowing of resources accounted for in the wills of Pitic residents. Households kept track of the goods, and property passed back and forth in this way more often in kind than according to their monetary value. Farmers lent one another a given number of *fanegas* of wheat or maize for planting from one season to the next, and *criadores* sent livestock from one corral to another. They used their neighbors' bulls, stallions, and mares for breeding, or they borrowed calves, colts, plowing oxen, and pack animals when needed. In this same vein, farmers, shopkeepers, and *arrieros* often left accounts pending. Wheat flour delivered, but not yet paid for; a load of merchandise sent on consignment from Pitic to a mountain village; tanned hides stacked in a corral to be traded for sugar, brandy, or flour: all these exemplify the close proximity between trade and reciprocity.[43]

This rhythm of exchange helped to sustain a network of indebtedness that touched every household in Pitic and its environs. All the wills from this period contain a long list of petty debts, specified in kind or in monetary value, and nearly all testators were both debtors and creditors. The goods they owed one another may represent unfinished transactions concerning shared resources or delayed payment for produce or for services rendered. Sonoran smallholders carried these debts from one year to the next without too much concern, until death became imminent. *Albaceas* performed a practical function by collecting outstanding debts and paying the amounts owed, thereby closing the accounts of the deceased.

The testament of Juan García de Noriega, dictated in 1816, illustrates this communitywide web of indebtedness. A scion of the powerful Noriega clan, Don Juan imbued his will with a spirit of generosity born of his own prosperity and of the strands of dependency which linked him to other households. He named his wife and his brother José

Antonio as the executors of his estate, instructing them to distribute 100 pesos to the poor, to give a horse or burro to his housekeeper, to forgive the debts of his peón Juan María, to make several gifts of money and brandy to relatives and friends, and (blessed with a sense of humor) to give a small jug of brandy "to each of the *beatas*" in Pitic.[44] Noriega's list of debts covered the full spectrum of local society. He owed 170 pesos to Manuel Rodríguez and smaller amounts to his brother José María and to his brother-in-law. A total of thirty-four persons owed him over 1,000 pesos, expressed in small amounts of money, *fanegas* of wheat, and barrels for fermenting wine. His debtors included María Bojórquez (whose will was cited above), Mendibal "del yaqui," "la china" Gertrudis, the *arriero*, and "el coyote" Juan. Notwithstanding Don Juan's generosity, his executors took his bookkeeping seriously. A year after his death, José Preciado held power of attorney to collect the amounts owed Noriega by "many persons living in different parts of this province."[45]

Perhaps because none of his children survived him, Juan García de Noriega bequeathed his property in the following way:

> Of all my property, land, houses, orchards, and other possessions recognized as mine, half should be separated and given to my wife, as their legitimate owner, for her to use as she sees fit; of the other half, the part remaining after paying all debts and charities should be divided into three parts. The first part shall be given to my wife in addition to what I have already said, the second part shall go to my brother and *compadre* José Antonio Noriega, and the third part shall be divided among my remaining brothers and sisters.[46]

Noriega did not divide his patrimony equally; nevertheless, he remembered everyone and tried to ensure that all members of his family would receive some part of his wealth. He favored his wife and closest brother, while distributing small charities among his servants and other persons who had depended on him in some way during his lifetime. Don Juan's testament confirmed the basic values that ordered Sonoran colonial society.

Of a very different nature was the indebtedness local *vecinos* incurred with merchants. Beginning around 1814, professional merchant-creditors (*mercaderes viandantes*), based in Guaymas, Tepic, San Blas, and Guadalajara, extended power of attorney to local hacendados and traders in order to collect outstanding debts in Pitic. Not only were the amounts considerably higher than the debts regularly noted in wills, but the terms of payment were more stringent. Creditors demanded specific periods of tolerance of six months or a year, and debtors were obliged to mortgage their property as a guarantee against default. José Francisco Velasco, Seferino Gaitán, Ignacio Noriega, and Francisco Monteverde headed the list of *apoderados* vested with power to collect payment—the very same persons who so frequently managed the estates of their deceased neighbors. These local entrepreneurs provided the link between merchant capital and the peasant economy of the Sonoran province.[47]

At times, local custom tempered the harshness of debt collection. In 1801, Francisco Luis de Retes, from the mining town of Aigame southwest of Pitic, brought legal action against Ignacio Araiza, agropastoralist, trader, and blacksmith in the *villa*. Araiza owed Retes 1,251 pesos; they worked out the following terms of payment. Araiza should pay Retes that same year 100 pesos "from the fruit of his vineyard and other resources at his command." Araiza agreed to pay Retes 300 pesos each year thereafter, until he satisfied the full amount, and to cover court costs that Retes had incurred in San Francisco Xavier, Aigame, and Pitic. In order to ensure payment, Araiza pledged his house (with an animal corral and vineyard) as well as a small amount of livestock.[48]

Ignacio Araiza appeared several times in the presidial court as creditor, debtor, and *apoderado*. In 1816, he owed more than 5,000 pesos to Juan Francisco Pérez, a Tepic merchant who operated in the *villa*. Pérez demanded payment in twenty days "in local coin or in silver or gold at the prices current in the province." The following year, Araiza was forced to sell his vineyard and orchard in order to repay a substantial debt to Manuel Rodríguez. Francisco Monteverde purchased his property, including the land "enclosed by a fence and wooden stakes" in the northern section of the *ejidos* surrounding the presidio, thirty barrels and distilling equipment, plows, iron tools, and a house. Monteverde assumed Araiza's debt, paying two installments to Rodríguez, and paid Araiza half the value of his hacienda in coin.[49]

On various occasions parents assumed payment of their children's debts at considerable hardship. Manuela Cervantes, illiterate and widowed, mortgaged her house in the *villa* in order to guarantee payment of the debt her son-in-law, Iginio Robles, owed Matheo de Uruchurtu.

Don Matheo gave Cervantes and Robles four months to pay 138 pesos "in merchandise or in coin" or forfeit the property.[50] That same year, Manuel Rodríguez sued Tomás Valencia for nearly 400 pesos, the amount his son José owed Rodríguez directly and to the estate of María Dolores Díaz. Having issued José an oral threat of imprisonment, Rodríguez gave Don Tomás six years in which to pay the debt. The elder Valencia morgaged his *labor* in Torreón, measuring about 1.7 suertes (45 acres) in order to guarantee payment.[51]

The foregoing analysis of property and of the customs governing inheritance, dowry, and indebtedness reveals varying means of livelihood that were neither primitive nor fully capitalist. This diversified economy of simple commodity production rested on the daily transactions between merchant-landowners and peasants. These *labradores* and *criadores, arrieros*, sometime soldiers, and occasional miners (*gambusinos*) alternately worked the land and sold their labor. Their work created wealth, unevenly distributed among households, that led to modest levels of accumulation within the community. Hispanized peasants generated surpluses with commercial value that extended beyond the locality to the eastern sierra and, by the second quarter of the nineteenth century, to the port of Guaymas. Merchant capital expanded its network of credit into the upper reaches of this peasant society, capturing an important part of the wealth generated in Sonoran agropastoral communities. Quotidian transactions disclosed in wills, sharecropping contracts, and liens, as well as political conflicts over town lots and the tithe, underscore a dual process of social and cultural differentiation. Means of production such as land, animals, orchards, vineyards, dwellings, plows, tools, and weapons comprehended material goods and social values. Their importance as economic assets is difficult to separate from their meaning as cultural artifacts. These very things, the tangible rewards of labor, objectified the bonds created among households and thus converted places like Pitic and San Miguel de Horcasitas into communities.[52]

Patterns of Land Tenure in the Valley of Horcasitas

At the turn of the nineteenth century the middle valley of San Miguel de Horcasitas comprised distinct concurrent patterns of land tenure, as shown in Figure 7.1. In the lower portion of the alluvial valley, where the

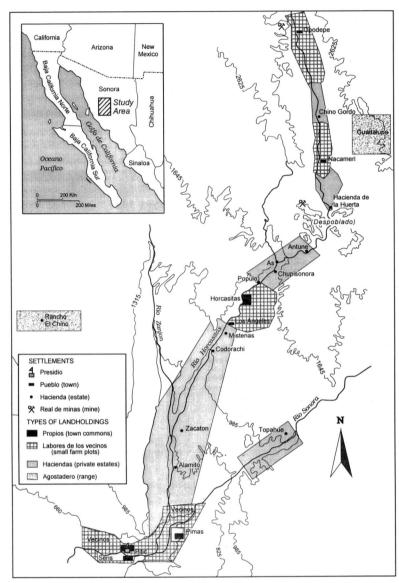

Figure 7.1. Patterns of land tenure in Pitic and the Valley of Horcasitas, 1785–1820

Zanjón, San Miguel, and Sonora rivers converged on the shallow floodplain, the military allotment for the Villa de Pitic had assigned common
lands to the Pimas and Seris living outside the presidio (see Tables 7.2
and 7.3). The 1785 measurement had reserved approximately one-fifth of
the land measured for each of the ethnic communities, to be destined
for communal use, and the rest to be divided among their households.
On the north bank of the river, the *vecinos* held individual plots of varying size, forty-two suertes in all, while the *villa* retained eight suertes as
town property, subsequently divided into house lots. Their claims to this
land originated in their common entitlement to farmland and pastures
(*ejidos*) surrounding settled communities, as defined by Spanish legal tradition and colonial practice.[53] Once they came into possession of the
labores, the *vecinos* customarily recognized, worked, and bequeathed them
as private property.

The *hijuela* awarded to Josef Antonio Noriega in 1805 illustrates the
rationale behind the distribution of *labores* to townsmen and presidial
soldiers.[54] Noriega, born in San Miguel de Horcasitas, had established
permanent residence in Pitic four years before he petitioned Captain José
Fernández de Loredo for title to his land. During that time he had served
faithfully in the militia and cultivated "at his own expense and labor" a
solar measuring approximately four-fifths of an acre. Having personally
overseen the measurement of Noriega's plot and defined its boundaries
with adjoining properties, the presidial commander granted him title to
this small piece of land. Noriega fulfilled the requirements of permanent
residence, military service, effective possession, and the consensus of
his neighbors that his petition did not violate prior claims to arable land.

Haciendas and ranchos, private estates in the irrigable portions of the
river valley between settlements, constituted a different form of property. Not only was their size considerably greater than the *labores*—they
were measured in *sitios*, not in *suertes*—their origin was clearly more
private than communal.[55] These haciendas grew out of familial entre-
preneurship rather than residence in a given town, and legal title often
came considerably after de facto possession. Individual estates included
arable land for cultivation and rangeland for pasturing cattle. Private
property extended northeastward from Pitic along the Río San Miguel,
circumscribing the *labores* carved out of the alluvial banks surrounding Horcasitas, Nacameri, and Opodepe, and included resident families.

Table 7.5 Haciendas in the Valley of San Miguel Horcasitas, Sonora, 1803

	Owner	Sitios	Families
El Alamito	Fernando Iñigo Ruiz	9	20
El Zacatón	Juan Antonio Espinoza	1	2
Codórachi	José del Puerto	1	10
Mesteñas	José del Puerto	1	
El Pópulo	José Antonio Carranza	1	3
Chupisonora	Lona Pesqueira		
Agua Salada	Dionisio de Aguilar	2	4
De la Huerta	José Antonio Contreras	2	6
Chino Gordo	Julio Contreras	1	2

Source: BNFF 32/659.

Although it is unclear whether the families enumerated in Table 7.5 are tenants, sharecroppers, or resident laborers (*peones acasillados*), their inclusion in the description of these estates suggests forms of dependency markedly different from the sharecropping contracts analyzed above. Whereas Monteagudo, Estrada, Valencia, and Iñigo—*labradores* all—had entered into agreements basically among social equals, these tenants may have exercised usufruct rights to till the soil and care for a few animals of their own, but had no claim to the land. They probably worked for a share of the crop or a portion of the newborn calves, or they may have exchanged their labor for shelter and a wage paid in kind.[56]

Sonoran notables like Fernando Iñigo Ruiz, who held the title of "Administrador de Rentas, Teniente Contador de Menores, Tutelas y Albaceados" and who acquired title to Alamito in 1791, accumulated property during this period.[57] Some landowners divided and rented out portions of their estates. Several *vecinos* from Horcasitas, for example, rented parts of Agua de las Mesteñas. Chupisonora, principally grazing land, belonged to Doña Lona Pesqueira in name. However, she destined the income to religious charity and relied on *vecinos* from the tiny settlement of El Seri to check on her cattle each month. In several sections of the river, the alluvial floodplain narrowed and turned into a steep canyon. The "despoblado" indicated on the map (Figure 7.1) between Antúnez and

Hacienda de la Huerta lay unclaimed at this time, owing to topography and increasingly tenacious Apache raids that threatened all private herds.

Successful *labradores* acquired private lands in addition to the farming plots they tended in the *vecindario*.[58] The Valencia family, as noted above, expanded their holdings in the floodplain between the presidial lands of Pitic and Horcasitas. Luis Valencia and his son Thomás acquired title to Agua de las Mesteñas in 1788, defending their claim against the rival bid of Ambrosio López. The Valencias had bred their livestock on this site for nearly thirty years, and they had built a corral, house, and low tower there. Repeatedly they had kept armed men on their land to defend it against marauding Seris and Apaches. Sometime between 1790 and 1803, Ignacio Valencia sold both the Hacienda de Codórachi and Agua de las Mesteñas to José del Puerto, *vecino* and *teniente de justicia* in San Miguel de Horcasitas.[59]

Landholding families of Pitic purchased title to pasturelands in the arid range outside the *villa*. Concepción Pérez Serrano, born in Cucurpe but resident in Pitic, declared as her property a house and lot in the town, "with a small vineyard and fruit trees." In addition, she claimed half the ranch called "El Aguaje," nine leagues south of the presidio and measuring 3.5 sitios.[60] The Noriega family, associated with Juan José Buelna and Guadalupe Aros, bought 3 sitios of grazing land in the dry hilly country northwest of Pitic. They carved out a ranch called "El Pozo del Chino, San José," where José Antonio Noriega had built a corral and pastured his herd of horses. True to its name, El Pozo was valuable because underground water could be tapped by digging a well.[61]

A future generation of presidial descendants expanded northward into the Sonora river valley, buying small farming plots in what had been Opata mission lands. In 1836, Vicente Valencia, a *vecino* of Arizpe, then capital of the state of Sonora, paid Jesús Juraso, an Indian, twenty-six pesos for a small piece of land adjacent to his own *labor* in the floodplain at Bamori. Juraso had inherited the land from his godfather, Juan Semosegua. The sale contract stipulated that it was Juraso's private property, separate from the ancient village commons that the state was empowered to distribute. Thus, Juraso could dispose of it as he wished. Apparently the modest purchase price was sufficient to induce him to give the land to his neighbor.[62]

The formalization of property relations through legal title and land

sales during the early nineteenth century was not definitive: it was a process. Land rentals and customary use rights, as well as joint registration
of rustic property by a number of kinsmen or partners, created a varie-
gated landscape and blurred the distinction between outright ownership
and land tenancy. Sales contracts included a clause whereby the seller
waived his or her right, derived from colonial legislation, to reconsider
relinquishing tenure or to adjust the price. Although each sale of a farm
or town lot was, in fact, irrevocable, that could not be assumed; rather,
it had to be written into each transaction.[63] Furthermore, the appropriation of land took different forms. While the *labores* were derived from
colonial land grants issued by provincial authorities to local *vecinos*, individuals had recourse to the *denuncia* in order to expand their holdings or
to divide a common family patrimony among numerous heirs. The following cases illustrate the use of this legal instrument to solidify private
claims to land and water in the lower San Miguel and Sonora valleys.

When José Antonio Noriega and his associates from Pitic registered
a *denuncia* for "El Pozo del Chino" in 1810 (see above) Governor Alejo
García Conde commissioned Thomas Valencia to oversee the land survey. Noriega had pastured his horses there for five years, but "as Captain
José Fernando de Loredo will testify," he had taken his herd elsewhere
for lack of water. The corral he had left standing proved that he had used
the land. Three sitios were appraised at 50 pesos, for only one had any
source of water. Valencia summoned the townspeople of Pitic to the beat
of the presidial drum, and the town crier Dionisio Quate announced the
auction of El Pozo del Chino in favor of Noriega and his fellow bidders.
On the third "cry" (*pregón*), Manuel Palacios raised the bid to 160 pesos
but, when the original claimants met his price, Palacios retired his bid.
Noriega did not secure title to the land until November 1813 because, on
reviewing the case, Governor García Conde required Pitic authorities to
carry out all thirty *pregones* and to record testimony on the capacity of the
claimants to occupy the land.[64]

Northeast of Noriega's property in the middle San Miguel Valley, Josef
Constantino Robles petitioned in 1811 for title to 1.7 sitios adjoining his
own property as well as to the *ejidos* of Nacameri in the cordillera east of
the floodplain. Don Josef, lieutenant of justice and administrator of the
fiscal rents on tobacco and the *alcabala* sales tax, was a prominent *vecino*
of Nacameri. He found "that I have many head of cattle and no land on

which to raise them," and justified his claim to additional grazing land by his services to the king:

> For more than thirty years I have cooperated with what little I have in the defense of this territory against the enemy. Since our district (*partido*) is on the Apache frontier, they have not ceased to attack us in all that time and with unusual force during the last three or four years. In spite of the losses I have suffered from the stock they have carried off and killed, I have chosen to stay and serve our sovereign by managing the revenues from tobacco and *alcabalas* placed in my care.[65]

In due time Subdelegado Rafael Ortiz de la Torre ordered the land measured and appraised. The site had two springs which could supply well water. Robles's fellow townsmen set the minimum price at thirty pesos per sitio; but the *promotor fiscal* in Arizpe, Joseph Pérez, raised the value of the land to sixty pesos per sitio, giving a total price of sixty-seven pesos, four reales. Three *vecinos* from Nacameri who had helped brand Robles's cattle testified that he had more than 1,000 head of bovines and at least 100 head of horses and mules. A local town crier, "the Indian Xavier," shouted the *pregones* in Nacameri and San Miguel de Horcasitas in the spring of 1814. Two years later, the final auction was held in Arizpe (with no opposing bidders) and Robles took possession of his land.

During these same years, Dionisio de Aguilar expanded his holdings in the vicinity of San Miguel de Horcasitas. He bid for title to four sitios located fourteen leagues west of the *villa*, christening his property "San Antonio de Padua del Pozo." Aguilar had built a house on the site and dug several wells, successfully finding water. Several prominent *vecinos* served as witnesses and surveyors of the land: Francisco Noriega, Pedro Maytorena, Francisco Escobosa, and Joaquín de Islas. They established a just price of sixty pesos, considering that one of the plots was favored with water drawn from Aguilar's well. Final bidding took place in Arizpe during the spring of 1813; Aguilar faced no competition to secure title to the land he already occupied.[66]

Francisco Manuel Gómez del Campillo, a Spaniard established in Horcasitas, joined the growing number of proprietors in the valley. Campillo bred his cattle on the *ejidos*—common grazing land of the *villa*—and planted crops on floodplain land belonging to the community. He had tried his hand at mining, for he resided in the *bonanza* of San Francisco de

Asís in 1807, when he registered his claim to three sitios in La Palma. The property he chose had a well that drew water from the Arroyo de Taray which ran through the middle of it. Francisco Escobosa and Dionisio de Aguilar, called as witnesses, pointed out that Campillo had been ordered to take his herd of 2,000 head of cattle out of the *ejido*, after his neighbors had complained of crop damage. The final bidding occurred in Arizpe, in 1813, when Campillo paid seventy-eight pesos for La Palma and Taray.[67]

Three years later, Campillo joined with Ignacio Ramírez Arellano to expand his holdings. Campillo and Ramírez registered two more sitios in Taray and El Sauz, separate *realengos* that extended Campillo's property to the boundaries of Juan Contreras's Rancho de Saguibavi and the Rancho de Batobavi, held jointly by the López, Arvizu, and Landavazo families. The water table in El Sauz was high enough to provide a well and a watering hole for the cattle. All the parties concerned showed a tolerance for inexact measurements and accepted on good faith Campillo's assurances that he did not want to affect his neighbors' interests. Contreras was ill and could not be present at the land survey, but he sent a letter authorizing Ambrosio López, part owner of Batobavi, to safeguard his property. At a cost of forty-five pesos, Campillo and Ramírez made good their claim to El Sauz in less than four months and with no opposing bidders.[68]

Aguilar and Gómez del Campillo exemplified a predictable pattern of investing wealth obtained from mining and commerce in rural property. Campillo had used the communal lands of Horcasitas to build up his herds before acquiring land of his own. The proliferation of private holdings in the floodplain and grasslands between Horcasitas and Nacameri during the last two decades of colonial rule signified the accumulation of private wealth at the expense of the productive resources of these two communities. The *vecinos* of Nacameri found themselves surrounded by private ranches which had absorbed their common grazing lands. When one of their residents tried to register an additional *sitio* in his name, the *común* of Nacameri protested.

Antonio Gradillas, *vecino* of Nacameri and owner of "lo de Salas" denounced as *realengo* a strip of *agostadero* lying west of his ranch in 1809. When the land was measured, there were no adjacent properties other than his own, and apparently no one opposed his claim. The proceedings were delayed, however, because Subdelegado Juan José Padillas, who functioned as local magistrate, was among the presidial troops sent south to fight the rebel armies of the insurgency. Four years later, when Gradillas renewed his case, the *vecinos* of Nacameri presented a counter-claim to the same *sitio*. They found a sympathetic ear in the new *subdele-gado*, Rafael Ortiz de la Torre, who accepted their argument that Gradillas already owned two sitios, an area more than sufficient for his livestock.

Nacameri townspeople defended their claim on the dual basis of need and merit. They reminded Ortiz de la Torre that they and their forebears had defended "the *patria* against the enemy [Apaches]" and, at present, had no land for grazing their cattle and horses. Ortiz proposed measuring the same site in favor of the *común* of Nacameri, but Gradillas appealed to the intendant-governor in Arizpe. Having retrieved his papers, he returned to the Villa de Horcasitas to await the *ayuntamiento*'s decision. His efforts were rewarded, because this new municipal council upheld the original measurements for the *sitio*. Two years later, in the spring of 1816, public auction took place in Arizpe. The first round of three days' bidding awarded the *sitio* to the village of Nacameri for 32 pesos, the appraised value of the land. Gradillas's representative appealed, alleging that his client had not been informed opportunely, and demanded a second bidding. On that occasion the rival parties competed openly, raising the bid to 482 pesos, an unheard-of sum for land without permanent running water. The *común* of Nacameri could not outbid their rival. They lost the land to Gradillas, but had the satisfaction of knowing that he paid dearly for that additional *sitio*.[69]

In this dispute over relatively marginal grazing land the *común* of Naca-meri represented a *mestizo* community of smallholders. Their legal battle portended increased competition for land with ethnic overtones involving large landowners, Hispanized peasants, and a remnant population of Pimas during the decades following Mexican independence. Land tenure in Nacameri, as in many *serrano* communities, was further complicated by private land sales between Indians and *mestizos* and among the generalized population of *vecinos*. In 1827 local magistrates petitioned the state legislature of Occidente to change their status from pueblo to *villa*, arguing that the resident Pima population had fallen to only five families. The following year, the pueblo of Nacameri became the Villa de Rayón, with the provision that the remaining Indian families should receive land to be measured and distributed from the village commons.[70] During the better part of a decade, from 1829 to 1837, the Pimas of Rayón appealed to state authorities to carry out this *reparto*, but repeatedly they were told that the laws governing the distribution of Indian lands (particularly Law 89 of 1828) did not apply to them because Rayón was no longer a pueblo but a *villa*. Furthermore, there was no village *común* to give out: the *vecinos* held individual title to that land. In December 1837 a partial distribution of land was awarded to certain Indian families, drawing forth a chorus of protests from *vecinos* who claimed to have purchased their holdings from a former Pima governor, Juan Ignacio Grillo, or to have cleared the land by their own labor. The Robles and Contreras families led the appeal, since their lands were most directly affected by the redistribution of cropland to the Pimas and their kinfolk. At issue were several contested points: Who constituted bona fide native residents of Nacameri/Rayón? Did Pimas who had migrated elsewhere in search of work and returned for the *reparto* deserve an allotment? Could women, *mestizos*, or Yaquis appear in the Pima land rolls? The Hispanized *vecinos*, who included a minority of women proprietors such as María del Sí and María Inocencia Saenz, stuck tenaciously to the letter of the law, claiming that Law 89 excluded Indian women as potential smallholders.[71]

This protracted legal battle revealed deepening ethnic and class divisions as population pressure increased on the land. Hacendados led by the Aguilar, Robles, and Campillo clans expanded their properties at the expense of *mestizo* smallholders, who claimed traditional rights to village *ejidos* and took on the mantle of the *común*. Both these groups held themselves apart from the Pimas, who no longer constituted a recognized community but were relegated to marginal status in the Villa de Rayón. During the nineteenth century, true *realengos* became scarce as population growth and the expansion of grazing herds occupied ever larger areas of open range. Competitive bidding became more frequent than in years gone by, and prices rose accordingly. For example, in 1835, Ignacio Tomás de León and Antonio Moreno bid on four sitios in Los Arrieros, raising the purchase price from 60 to 200 pesos.[72] Prospective proprietors had to purchase land from former owners, as in San José de Pimas where María Josefa Salcedo obtained title to three sitios of grazing land for 65 pesos in 1835. Eight years later, she sold the property to Ramón López for 400 pesos.[73]

In a related process, second- and third-generation heirs of family holdings found it necessary to divide the original property or to sell out their individual shares either to one of their own or to an interested buyer outside the family. Thus, between 1841 and 1854 Francisco Alejandro Aguilar, a merchant established in the port of Guaymas, purchased eight separate shares of land in Los Arrieros and Jupanguaymas from the heirs of the Sánchez brothers, who had first registered the property in 1815. These three sitios originally cost 96 pesos; Aguilar paid a total of 820 pesos for the same ranch, more than eight times as much as the "just price" established for title in the original *denuncia*.[74]

The complicated history of Batobavi and Bacobavi, adjoining properties near San Miguel de Horcasitas, illustrates problems of inheritance among joint owners of rural estates over three generations. Some time prior to 1813 Juan Contreras sold Batobavi to four partners: José Miguel and Eugenio Arvizu, brothers; José Landavazo; and Ambrosio López. That year, the Arvizus and their fellow *parcioneros* (shareholders) bid on four sitios of *realengo* to expand their property westward, abutting several private ranches held by Francisco del Campillo, Joaquín de Islas, and the same Juan Contreras—all *vecinos* of the Villa de Horcasitas—who turned out to witness the land survey. The northeast corner of the square traced on the desert scrubland ended in a spring-fed pond, but the measurements left an undefined area to the southeast of the Batobavi annexation; for that reason, Joaquín de Islas refused to sign the papers. Despite his objections, Subdelegado Ortiz de la Torre proceeded with the bidding in Horcasitas and, three years later, the final auction took place in Arizpe, awarding the land to Arvizu and associates for sixty-seven pesos.[75]

The exact measurements of Batobavi and the assessed value continued to be a source of conflict among these kinsmen and neighbors. The titles were verified in 1825 and again in 1837, but the second generation of proprietors found the ambiguity intolerable. In 1834 Eugenio Arvizu and Manuel Landavazo filed a claim to untitled land between Batobavi and Chupisonora measuring four sitios, and in 1841 Francisco and Santiago Campillo petitioned the authorities in Horcasitas to measure the "huecos y baldíos" surrounding the ranchos of San José del Zanjón (La

Noria) and Batobavi. When advised of the projected survey, José Miguel Arvizu (son of Eugenio and nephew of the elder José Miguel, two of the original *parcioneros*) protested vigorously:

> In twenty-eight years of owning and occupying the land in good faith, no one in this department has allowed an operation to take place which so severely tramples on his rights. We feel a growing apprehension. Should this measurement take place (in which case it should be a general survey) for the greed of those [who question our titles], what security would we landowners have? This will be the beginning of discord in the pueblos and unending rivalry among families.[76]

Despite Arvizu's protest, Commissioner Ysidro Romero went ahead with the survey, citing legislation mandating the measurement of grazing land and the payment of state property taxes.[77] With the 1837 title in hand, Romero directed a team of surveyors, walking in the same direction as indicated in the documents, in order to confirm the previous land rights established by Arvizu and his shareholders. It turned out to be an arduous exercise, taking four days to complete the measurements. On the third day several members of the party, including the Campillo brothers, became separated from the main group. By following up on the boundaries indicated as the "corners" of the quadrant awarded to the *parcioneros* in 1837, Romero confirmed their title to the land, but showed that the four sitios estimated in the earlier survey turned out to be nineteen sitios and fifteen caballerías, indicating a substantial difference in the amount owed the state treasury. The proprietors and the surveyors in the field could not agree upon a just price, so the task of valuation was passed on to the Jefatura Superior de Hacienda. Romero's survey covered only the area annexed to Batobavi proper, because the Landavazo and Arvizu families refused to allow him to measure the ranch itself, arguing that it was not included in his commission.[78]

Not surprisingly, the Campillo brothers were dissatisfied with the results of the survey. They challenged the impartiality of the witnesses called to verify the boundaries of Batobavi and accused Romero of deliberately losing them in the desert brush in order to favor the Arvizus' interests. Both sides exchanged epithets of "greed and ambition."[79] A decade later, in the summer of 1852, two rival factions of these common shareholders petitioned the state government for exclusive title to the adjoining properties of Batobavi and Bacobavi. Taking advantage of the fact that the family had never paid the taxes corresponding to the 1841 measurement, Refugio Arvizu filed a *denuncia* in order to legalize his title to Bacobavi, purporting to speak for himself, his father Eugenio, and four daughters of José Miguel Arvizu (deceased). His claim was challenged by José Antonio Landavazo, Francisco Campillo (the former's son-in-law), Ramón Tapía (who represented his wife, Guadalupe Arvizu), and Miguel Islas (who held power of attorney for the four unmarried daughters of José Miguel Arvizu). They denied the legitimacy of Refugio's claim on the grounds that he and his father did not have enough cattle to occupy the land and accused him of stealing their unmarked cattle "in clandestine *corridas*," violating an agreement made earlier with his father. Landavazo and his associates showed their land titles and cited colonial and national legislation that protected them as legitimate communal owners (*una comunidad de accionistas*). They demanded that the municipal authorities of Horcasitas reject Refugio's claim and offered to enter into *composición* with the state concerning the amount owed on the entire area measured.[80]

This fourth survey described an area measuring twenty-two sitios and twenty-four caballerías; subtracting the four sitios of Batobavi proper, the *demasías* came to eighteen sitios and twenty-four caballerías, valued at 279 pesos. Faced with these results, José Antonio Landavazo formally renounced his claim to the extended area, reserving only his rights to the original four sitios. Eugenio Arvizu, Francisco Campillo, and Ramón Tapia, for their part, made arrangements to pay the tax. All the appropriate heirs and their representatives came together to claim separate parts of this extended (but arid) property under individual use rights. Campillo spoke for the four sitios on the eastern boundary with Batobavi in order to include his Rancho de Tavique, where he had built houses, corrals, and a small dam to water "three or four *milpas*" that his father had cleared. Tapia, Escobosa, and Arvizu objected, but finally ceded to Campillo's demands.[81]

The four-decade-long Batobavi land dispute developed out of the intricate relations of kinship and property that wove together the Arvizu, Landavazo, and Campillo lines; as such, it illustrates the conflicting norms of private and communal property that defined family patrimony. Population growth among the *vecinos* produced a larger number of heirs in each succeeding generation, even as their herds multiplied and depleted the natural grasslands on which their livelihood depended. The commercial interests personified by the Noriega, Arvizu, Aguilar, and Iñigo families in the San Miguel Valley sought grazing land for their expanding herds as part of their overall enterprises. These merchant landowners accumulated wealth and consolidated political power through the militias and local magistracies. Although they stood in a category apart from the *labradores* who tilled small plots of land, the economic interests of these elite families intersected with the peasant base of the Sonoran economy. They controlled the credit lines and dominated the commercial outlets for agrarian production in the region, even as the wealth they amassed flowed out of the productive capacity of smallholders and tenants. The relationships of dependency forged in towns like Pitic and San Miguel de Horcasitas contain a degree of interdependency. In order to maintain their social, economic, and political ascendancy these merchant landowners required the labor of muleteers, cultivators, herdsmen, and soldiers. Through judicial procedures such as the execution of wills, the issuance of powers of attorney, and the formalization of property boundaries, prominent families provided services and exercised their power in ways that weighed heavily on the daily life of small producers and laborers.

Conclusions

The foregoing analysis brings together two parallel processes of change in land tenure and in the economic structure of late-colonial Sonora. What emerges from this view of the central portion of the province is not a simple dichotomy between private and communal property, but overlapping claims to land ownership and usufruct. The *labores* distributed to households in the environs of the presidios, as noted for the *vecinos* of Pitic and San Miguel de Horcasitas, combined a communal rationale for claim to the land with a principle of individual proprietorship. Rustic stockmen alongside some of the provinces's leading merchant hacendados accelerated the enclosure of rangeland during the same period that peasant householders subdivided and sold portions of their farms. These smallholders paid increasingly higher prices for cropland, while ranchers extended their herds over the *agostadero* by paying minimum statutory prices. Both the subdivision of farmland and the enclosure of the *realengos* opened up a competitive land market in nineteenth-century Sonora.[82]

Overall, the history of transactions recorded here concerning landed property illustrates the complexity of a peasant economy in transition. Small but meaningful increments of technology led to changes in land use which intensified both the market orientation of direct producers and the stratification of their society. Differences in the possessions of peasant households, such as the sugar presses, distilling equipment, and mule teams noted above, bore directly on their ability to use the network of local markets to their advantage. In terms of grazing land, the frequent mention of wells to tap underground water in the appraisal of the *realengos* put up for auction indicates that enclosure meant both their privatization and their increased exploitation. Access to well water made new stretches of land susceptible to irrigation, either for marketable production or for the sustenance of resident laborers, and allowed ranchers to pasture ever larger herds of cattle.

The ways in which merchant capital dominated the commercialization of production, leading to the concentration of land ownership and the monetization of the economy, linked this frontier province to changes occurring over a wider area in late-colonial New Spain. As noted above, local merchants in the Villa de Pitic managed their neighbors' estates and held power of attorney for commercial houses based in Tepic. Their business transactions with professional merchants linked the web of indebtedness among local *vecinos* to larger networks of credit and exchange. Recent scholarship points to the uneven quality of economic growth throughout the viceroyalty, despite the dramatic crescendo of mining revenues up to the outbreak of the wars of independence.[83] Strong regional contrasts in the development of marketing systems and profound social inequalities marked the final decades of Spanish dominion in Mexico. Areas associated closely with mining, plantation agriculture, and the transatlantic trade—such as Guanajuato, Morelos, and Veracruz—sustained an export-oriented economy. Conversely, substantial zones in the Occidente, Norte, and Altiplano regions turned inward and developed interregional trading networks. Sonora fit this latter pattern, where direct producers were also itinerant traders who carried their goods across the Sierra Madre to Chihuahua and southward to Alamos and Sinaloa. Although it is difficult to trace the actual movement of goods between Sonora and the major viceregal centers of Mexico and Guadalajara, the presence of Tepic merchants in Pitic suggests that credit networks extended beyond the local routes used for the habitual exchange of merchandise.

The peasant economy of early nineteenth-century Sonora sustained a low level of the social division of labor. Most households produced grain and cattle as well as sugar and brandy, exhibiting both a clear orientation to the market and a concern for subsistence. Agropastoralists of the Sonora and San Miguel valleys tried their hand at mining and served in the presidial troops and civilian militias. Notwithstanding the apparent simplicity of the local economy, its growing complexity fueled a process of social stratification that divided hacendados and peasants.

The shifts in power and increments of wealth that favored certain families over others, when taken together, follow lines of class formation far more strongly than they follow lines of ethnic cleavage. Still, racial distinctions may have been blurred, but they were not obliterated. The families who left records in the notarial archives of Pitic counted themselves among the *gente de razón* in the parish baptismal records.[84] Nevertheless, a fair number of Pitiqueño *vecinos* came from mission villages and mining camps in the sierra, so that the *calidad* they recorded may have hidden Indian origins. Ties of fictive kinship linked prominent townsmen to the Pima and Seri families whose children they baptized. The parish priests' habitual failure to record Pima and Seri surnames as well as the names of grandparents (which they did note for Hispanic parishioners) suggests their bias concerning the social status of Indian residents in the *villa* and its environs. Pima, Guayma, and "coyote" families often appear as the servants of landowning households. Thus, the explicit racial terminology used to distinguish these sectors of the population carried connotations of economic and social standing. Some of the presidial soldiers at Pitic were Pimas; these militiamen and their families received the status of *vecinos* and had the right to a minimal portion of farmland in the *ejidos* assigned to the presidio, as did the Opata militiamen of Bavispe (see Chapter 6). In contrast, the resident *peones* who labored on the haciendas in the San Miguel Valley in exchange for subsistence, sometimes identified as Indians in the parish registers, lived in conditions of economic marginality and social dependency.

This portrait of Pitic society and rural landholding patterns in central Sonora illustrates the historical links between the political exercise of power and the social relations of production. In the transition from colonial to republican rule in this northern frontier, state authorities made their presence felt keenly in the formalization of property rights. Nevertheless, Sonoran proprietors both large and small had recourse to other sources of influence. Kinship and customary inheritance gave them access to land and the means of production. Those who aspired to wealth and power used market transactions as well as family ties to accumulate property and rise to public office. Merchant capital based outside the region accelerated class formation in Sonora, deepening inequalities produced by social stratification within the area. Conflicts that arose over material interests bespoke cultural divisions and increasingly divergent value systems in this frontier society.

The social configuration of the central Sonoran highlands had changed significantly along with the physical landscape by the mid-nineteenth century. Mission holdings as well as town commons and *ejidos* had vanished, converted to private *labores* and ranches. Together, this chapter and Chapter 6 document the dismemberment of the ethnic corporate communities after the dissolution of their landed base and the differentiation of the Hispanized peasantry. These processes generated conflict on different levels, expressed in both class and ethnic confrontation. Part Four of this book discusses the counterpoint of accommodation and resistance that defined relations between the Spanish and indigenous sectors of Sonoran society. It underscores the role of the state in this historic conflict during both the colonial and the national periods.

Part IV

Ethnogenesis and Resistant Adaptation

8

Cultural Endurance and Accommodation to Spanish Rule

Edward H. Spicer, whose work opened new avenues in the ethnohistory of northwestern Mexico and the U.S. Southwest, envisioned the cultural survival of native peoples in terms of *ethnic enclaves*. His perception of successive cycles of conquest emphasized the persistence of ethnic groups through language, ritual, and territorial defense, despite increasing pressures to assimilate into the dominant society.[1] *Ethnogenesis*, a term that denotes the birth or rebirth of ethnic identities in different historical moments, takes the processual quality of ethnic persistence a step further than Spicer's figure of ethnic enclaves.[2] The concept of ethnogenesis is used here not to trace the longevity of certain cultural traits or practices from pre-Hispanic to late-colonial times, but rather to underscore the changing historical quality of culture itself.[3] It places the ethnic component of Sonoran highland peoples within the context of their full historical experience under Spanish and Mexican rule. Opatas, Pimas, and Eudeves survived as ethnic entities well into the nineteenth century, but the political, economic, and social dimensions of their cultural identity were radically changed through their relations with the dominant society and through the internal articulation of their communities.

Ethnogenesis occurred through different modes of resistant adaptation to alien domination. Throughout the Americas, Indians developed creative methods for using colonial institutions to attain specific ends; in the process, however, they participated in their own subjugation by legitimating the intrusion of those very institutions into their ethnic polities.[4] The history of the *serrano* communities of Sonora illustrates the dependency of indigenous peoples on the colonial system that enveloped them. Yet it demonstrates, with equal significance, the ways in which their mobility forced the Spaniards to alter the colonial project. The asymmetry of power between Spaniards and Indians marked a tense counterpoint between accommodation and resistance. Although native leaders and commoners at times pursued different goals, the underlying principle that guided the Sonoras' strategies for cultural and material survival served to conserve their communities and to achieve a limited degree of autonomy.

Indigenous peoples used the political and cultural tools they had at hand to further their own interests, gain limited space in which to enhance their prestige, or claim control over their own time and labor power. They learned to manipulate Spanish legal institutions, appealing to rival authorities, in order to defend their material resources and a vestige of their traditional social order. Serrano communities became adept at petitioning local officials to accomplish specific goals, working through the church and the military. They moved within the parallel lines of authority personified by missionaries, presidial commanders, and provincial governors in order to secure particular advantages or defend traditional prerogatives. Highland peasants negotiated their labor services as mission cultivators, mineworkers, and presidial soldiers. However, their accommodation to the order imposed by the colonial state, evident in the skills they developed to maneuver within the system, masked different levels and degrees of resistance. Periodic flight, withdrawal, individual acts of defiance, and open rebellion punctuated Spanish–Indian relations on the Sonoran frontier. The present chapter and the next examine successive episodes of collaboration and confrontation among different native peoples, Spanish authorities, and Hispanic colonists in Sonora. Together they elucidate the dual theme of resistant adaptation and cultural persistence through the changing quality of relations between dominant and subordinate actors over an extended historical period.

The Politics of Accommodation

Indians had recourse most frequently to the petition as a means of redressing grievances in the missions, often achieving at least some of their aims. The "hijos del pueblo" allied with their missionary against the encroachments of vecinos on community resources; conversely, they appealed to Spanish magistrates and military authorities to prevail on religious superiors to keep an especially beloved missionary or to object to a missionary's actions not of their liking. The Opatas of Opodepe and Nacameri in the middle San Miguel Valley, for example, brought specific complaints before the *alcalde mayor* of Sonora, Joaquín Rivera, in 1777–79. In the first instance, the Opata captain-general Juan Manuel Varela charged that Fray Antonio Martínez interfered with his recruitment of militiamen and refused to supply native patrols with sufficient amounts of food from mission stores; Varela further accused the friar of selling mission grain without accounting for the proceeds. For his part the Franciscan commissary of Ures, writing on behalf of the aging Fray Antonio, argued that *vecinos* in Nacameri had incited the Indians to bring these charges. In particular, Teniente de Justicia Santiago Contreras had turned against Martínez because the friar had reclaimed a "small piece of land, the only plot left for the mission," land that Contreras had used (without benefit of title) for some years; the friar had also resisted pressures to sell grain cheaply to Contreras and to tolerate Contreras's sale of liquor in the pueblo.[5]

Two years later Governor Manuel Grijalba of Opodepe, in the name of all his villagers, petitioned Captain Pedro Tueros of the Presidio de San Miguel de Horcasitas, to overturn the Franciscan commissary's decision to remove Fray Antonio Oliva from his mission. Grijalba entoned the language of humility (as "poor Indians and loyal vassals of our sovereign") but warned that he would appeal to the higher authority of the commandant-general, if necessary. The Opatas defended the implicit right, if not to choose their missionary, at least to retain one of their liking; at the same time, they denounced the impoverishment of the pueblos owing to successive transfers and replacements of missionaries.[6] The Opatas showed that they understood the division of authority between religious and military hierarchies. The local commander Pedro Tueros responded well to their test: he sent letters immediately to the Commandancia General and to Franciscan superiors on behalf of the Indians' request. He commended the justice of the Indians' petition and even appealed the case to the provincial of Xalisco. In the end, Commandant Teodoro de Croix upheld Captain Tueros's actions and confirmed Oliva's permanence in Opodepe.

Petitions of a different nature revealed the growing pressures on arable land concomitant with the increase in the Hispanic population. With uneven success Indians and missionaries protested the alienation of village lands and sought to preserve the human and material resources of the *común*. In 1764, Jesuits in the Pimería Alta presented a formal complaint concerning the damages caused to native *milpas* and mission *labores* in the villages near the presidios of Altar and Tubac. They prevailed on Juan Claudio Pineda, governor of the province, to admonish Captains Bernardo de Urrea and Juan Bautista de Anza to manage presidial herds with greater care in order to avoid the destruction of the Indians' crops.[7]

Soldiers stationed in the presidios and a growing number of *vecinos* who gathered under the protective shadow of these garrisons were squatting on *realengos* and allowing their animals to wander onto mission land. A year after the Jesuit complaint, ten heads of household residing in Altar petitioned Governor Pineda for title to a strip of farmland, "by the gracious mercy of the king." The governor granted their request for individual plots to be measured and assigned within a square league of the presidio, justifying this division of the land in terms of the need to settle the frontier threatened by rebellious Apaches, Seris, and Pimas.[8] Farther east, in the vicinity of the Presidio de Terrenate and the Aguacaliente mines, local authorities intervened to halt the arbitrary measurement of land carried out by Joseph de Olave, a self-styled *comisario de tierras*. Olave was awarding land indiscriminately to the *vecinos*, without taking into account the area reserved for the presidio and the Pima missions, and it was feared that his actions might incite the Indians to rebel.[9]

The movement of different groups of Indians through the Pimería Alta increasingly concerned Bourbon authorities. This territory had always been an open frontier where Pimas, Athapaskans, and Hokanspeaking peoples along the lower Gila and Colorado rivers remained outside the effective control both of missions and presidios. The Jesuit *entradas* to populous *rancherías* in the upper San Pedro and Santa Cruz drainages during the 1730s had created new missions, but subsequent population movements and the spread of cattle *estancias* into the area had disrupted village life. The Pimas of northeastern Sonora, the Sobaípuris, inhabited a corridor of mountain passes and natural grasslands that were vulnerable to raiding by mounted bands of Apaches. Garrisons at Fronteras (1692) and Terrenate (1742), with troop detachments sent northward to San Bernardino and Santa Cruz, were not sufficient to contain the highland nomads. In 1756 the Sobaípuris requested missionaries for their pueblos in the San Pedro Valley; six years later, when their petitions went unanswered, they migrated westward to Santa María de Suamca, Dolores de Guebavi, and San Xavier de Bac, where they mingled with Hymeris, Sobas, and Tohono O'odham. The Sobaípuris of Bac formed a separate *ranchería* in the *visita* of Tucson.

Belatedly, Jesuits and military commanders alike realized the importance of the Sobaípuri aldeas to defend the frontier. Priests and captains exchanged proposals for resettling Pimas in Buenavista, San Luis, and Santa Barbara along the upper Santa Cruz river, and debated the pros and cons of transferring the Presidio of Tubac northward to Tucson. When proposals were aired to move the Sobaípuris with a military escort to Buenavista or, conversely, to send the Tohono O'odham to a site farther east in the Santa Cruz valley, the Sobaípuri leader in Tucson, called Chachalaca, approached Governor Juan Claudio de Pineda to negotiate the future of his community.[10]

Governor Pineda found his interlocutor to be "an Indian of great stature, uninhibited and well informed."[11] For all that Pineda tried to convince Chachalaca that he and his people would be far better off in a valley with fertile land and abundant water, the Sobaípuri governor made it clear that his *ranchería* would choose where they wanted to live. For the present, they would stay in Tucson. Chachalaca played to his advantage the Sobaípuris' independence from the missions and their loyalty to the colonial order. He reminded the governor that his people had not openly rebelled, and he defended their freedom of movement: "Sir, at the time of the last uprising [the Pima revolt of 1751] I and my kinsmen were good [remained at peace], and anywhere we live we will continue to be loyal."[12] Governor Pineda surmised that the Sobaípuris' "wandering spirit" could not be easily contained, and he openly admitted to the Jesuit Manuel Aguirre that the province did not have sufficient troops to force them to resettle elsewhere.

In both word and action the Sobaípuris and Tohono O'odham living in Tucson had resisted the missionary's efforts to control their movements and to enforce work discipline. Padre Alonso Espinoza called them a "ranchería volante": "During the summer growing season, they live in their *milpas*; when the crop is in, they go to other pueblos or to the sierra."[13] He reported that there was sufficient land at Tucson for both groups of Pimas, but water was scarce. The Tohono O'odham habitually complained that their crops withered for lack of water and, for the same reason, they planted but a few vegetables in the mission común. The Indian governor of Tucson asked to be relieved of planting anything at all in support of the mission. The Apaches raided the villages for horses and cattle, while the Pimas of Bac and Tucson took smaller livestock for their own use. Padre Espinoza met a firm wall of resistance when he tried to pasture 100 sheep and 50 calves in Tucson, even when Captain Anza intervened on his behalf. "It seems," concluded the aging missionary, "that if words were not sufficient to make me leave, they will accomplish their purpose with hunger." [14] Espinoza tacitly admitted that the Indians of Tucson maintained an independent stance toward the head village of Bac and set limits to the missionary's authority over their daily life.

The erosion of village resources during the latter half of the eighteenth century, owing in large measure to the *vecinos'* encroachments on mission land, acclerated Indian outmigration. In 1795, more than 100 Tohono O'odham from the *ranchería* of Aquituni were persuaded to settle in the vicinity of Bac. The *vecinos* of the Presidio de Tucson, however, were loath to share irrigation water with the Indians, and their unfenced cattle trampled native *milpas*. Friars Juan Bautista Llorens and Diego Bringas intervened with the commandant-general on their behalf, but to no avail. [15] When O'odham petitions failed to slow or reverse the process, increasing numbers of them retreated to the desert or settled on the margins of ranches and mining camps.

Conversely, in central Sonora, similar population movements spurred native governors to appeal for missionaries as a means of rebuilding their pueblos. Sibubapas, Pimas who had left mission life, alternated between foraging and raiding in order to survive. Their recurring nomadism was undoubtedly related to the ruinous condition of a number of highland missions at the close of the century. For example, Taraichi and Yécora, Pima villages surrounded by the mining *reales* of Trinidad, Tacupeto, San Javier, and Río Chico, scarcely held thirty households—all living at bare subsistence and in fear of the Apaches. Fray Juan Felipe Martínez reported in 1797 that most of the *hijos del pueblo* had left the mission and taken concubines or gone to work in the mining camps, refusing to head their governors' summons to return to their villages. [16] That same year, the Indian governors of Onavas, Tónichi, and Soyopa implored Fray Juan Felipe and Teniente de Justicia Juan Joseph Salcido in Ures to send them a resident missionary. Describing a state of spiritual abandonment in which their people lived without instruction and religious services, these Pima leaders lamented the economic, demographic, and cultural decline of their communities. The Franciscan commissary summarized their words, rendering the Indians' petition a defense of community:

> They [Pima governors] do not want to see their pueblos as they find them today. They are all very poor and could not support a parish priest, especially since they do not control even what is left of mission property. Their communities were not meant to be in the way that they are now. They want the missionaries who taught them and the old way of governing their villages. Otherwise they will not be content, because they feel they are losing their pueblos.[17]

Faced with a shrinking resource base, Pima and Opata peasants defended their way of life through what remained of the missions' communal structures and through the military. For Indians as well as *vecinos* military service, centered around the presidios, provided a means of social ascendancy. In a land where nobility-by-lineage was virtually unknown among either natives or Spaniards, the material benefits and social prestige associated with bearing arms could raise militiamen above the ordinary lot of peasants, albeit in unequal degree for different ranks of soldiers and officers. Spanish presidial captains with titles linking them to the royal military hierarchy had ample opportunity to manipulate company payrolls and to profit from regional commerce. Presidial infantrymen drew a suerte of farmland and grazed their herds in the common *ejidos* of these fortified towns.[18] At another level, Opata and Pima presidial auxiliaries found material benefit and political leverage in military service. Despite an unmistakable ethnic barrier, evident in the differential wages for Indians and *gente de razón* and in the placement of native soldiers in positions of greatest risk during campaigns, *serrano* men accommodated presidial life to their traditional norms of honor and prestige. The Opatas of Bacerác, Bavispe, and Bacoachi, as well as the Pimas of San Ignacio, who formed entire presidial companies, re-created the outlines of a native elite through this Spanish institution.

Actual military practice had important repercussions for the exercise of power and for Indian–Spanish relations in the province. Repeated punitive expeditions against the Seris of the desert coastland and the Apaches of the sierra deflected conflict outward against alien groups. Equally significant, these campaigns provided native and Spanish soldiers the opportunity for booty and for human captives to sell. The ongoing wars against the nomads gave rise to a parallel dimension in the opposition between conquerors and conquered in northern New Spain. From the mid-eighteenth century to the close of the colonial era and after independence, the fear of sporadic raids on the part of village dwellers and the heightened bitterness of retaliation on both sides became the focal point for policy makers and *vecinos* concerning mere survival in an ethnically mixed society. This war against the *bárbaros* may have reduced the probabilities for any successful sustained collective action by sedentary peoples against their Spanish overlords.

Indian Auxiliaries and Presidial Soldiers

Indians served in the colonial military structure both as presidial soldiers and as temporary recruits drawn from their pueblos. In the former capacity Opatas and Pimas became salaried auxiliaries assigned to a particular outpost, where they were entitled to a suerte of presidial land. Muster rolls available for the end of the eighteenth century offer a comparison of the relative costs of two presidios manned by Spaniards and "hijos del país," as shown in Table 8.1. The presidial company of Tubac moved northward to San Agustín de Tucson in 1775, taking over lands farmed by O'odham and Sobaípuri families, some of whom may have been absorbed into the new garrison. San Miguel de Bavispe in northeastern Sonora was composed entirely of Opata soldiers after 1781, under the command of a Spanish officer.

A common foot soldier in Tucson earned 240 pesos a year; his counterpart in Bavispe drew 3 reales a day, totaling only 136 pesos, 7 reales annually. The commander of San Miguel de Bavispe, Lorenzo Peralta, held the rank of *teniente* and, for that reason, earned considerably less than Captain José de Zúñiga of Tucson.[19] The lesser ranks of officers were notably thinner in Bavispe than in Tucson, reflecting the fact that native auxiliary companies were basically infantry who moved, lightly armed, through the sierra in search of Apache encampments.

Temporary recruits drafted from numerous *serrano* villages augmented

Table 8.1   *Plazas* Assigned to Two Frontier Presidios
in Sonora, 1797

Officers and Soldiers	Tucson		Bavispe	
	No.	Salary (Pesos)	No.	Salary (Pesos)
Capitán	1	3,000	1	700
Capellán	1	480	1	480
Teniente	1	700		
Alfereces	2	1,000	1	450
Sargentos	3	972	2	648
Tambor	1	144		
Cabos	6	1,656		
Carabineros	6	1,620		
Armero	1	272		
Soldados	84	20,160	86	11,747
Total	106	30,004	91	14,025

Source: Fray Diego Bringas, 1797 (AMH AD 1).

presidial troops. In 1777, Captain Juan Bautista de Anza ordered Captain General Juan Manuel Varela to supply seventy-five Opata warriors
to serve as auxiliaries in the presidios of San Bernardino, Santa Cruz,
Tubac, and San Ignacio de Buenavista in the Pimería Alta. Their recruitment was distributed as shown in Table 8.2. Each warrior would receive
three reales a day; he was required to take with him a bow with a double
string and fifty arrows or a lance and leather shield. Anza ordered that
these recruits be relieved every two months. Whether or not this system was carried out, frequent forays into the hills in search of Apaches
meant that the missions were relinquishing a significant part of their
adult labor force, some of whom would not return. Numerous ecclesiastical and military reports attest to their loss from native households
and communities.

   In the summer of 1777, for example, a delegation of Opata leaders led
by Captain-General Juan Manuel Varela confronted Captain Juan Bautista de Anza over payment of their salaries; their demands were ulti-
mately directed to Commandant-General Teodoro de Croix. Varela, who

Table 8.2   The Draft of Opata Auxiliaries in Sonora, 1777

Presidio	No.	Supplying Missions
San Bernardino	20	Bacadéguachi
		Bacerác
		Guásabas
Santa Cruz	20	Saguaripa
		Oposura
		Mátape
		Batuco
Tubac	20	Arizpe
		Banámichi
		Aconchi
San Ignacio	15	Opodepe
		Cucurpe

Source: BNFF 34/735.

had received his title from Commandant-Inspector Hugo O'Connor, achieved an artful combination of complaint and protestation of loyalty to the king. Captain Juan Manuel had no means to pay his warriors, except "by his personal labor to the detriment of his own family." The Opata warriors had to pay other men in their home communities to watch over their fields and herds when they went on patrol, because the fear of an Apache attack made it too dangerous for their women and children to go out to the fields alone. Had they known they would not receive a salary, however, they could have charged the village común with the care of their families and crops. Varela complained further that some missionaries and Spanish magistrates thwarted his functions, trying to limit his powers as they saw fit. Varela asked not to be held in subordination to any authority other than military officers and requested confirmation of his position as political governor of Bacerác, Bavispe, and Guachinera—his own district—like his grandfather, Captain Gerónimo Noperi, in his day. Finally, Varela demanded assurance of the full attributes of his post, "just as the king had conferred them on him."[20]

Captain Anza sympathized with the Opata leaders and wrote to the commandant-general and to the *alcalde mayor* of Sonora, Joaquín Rivera, in support of Varela's petition. From his own pocket, Anza gave Varela twenty pesos to have a uniform made and, thus attired, to meet Teodoro de Croix in Janos and accompany him on his first tour of Sonora; he gave an additional twenty pesos to distribute among the militiamen. Anza's monetary compensation, although hardly equal to the Opata soldiers' back pay, allowed Varela to distinguish himself from the common warriors and, at the same time, to redistribute material benefits among them. For his part, Varela promised to supply seventy-five Opata soldiers to reinforce presidial troops in return for Anza's assurances that they would not be sent on expeditions in such large numbers as to threaten the security of their pueblos (see Table 8.2).

The commandant-general acceded to Varela's demands within the year, perhaps because he was keenly aware that the Crown depended on Opata auxiliaries for the defense of the Apache frontier. Croix instructed Pedro de Corbalán, intendant-governor of Sonora, to extend the title of "Political Governor of Bacerác, Bavispe, and Guachinera" to Juan Manuel Varela, specifying that he should suffer no interference from Spanish magistrates. Moreover, he ordered the *caja real* in Alamos to pay Varela his annual salary of 400 pesos.[21] The issue of the political authority of captains-general in the pueblos and the precise limits of their power vis-à-vis village governors, however, was not resolved consistently over the years. If Croix gave Varela wide powers in 1777, Pedro Garrido y Durán attempted to restrict the Opata captain-general Ygnacio Noperi's functions in 1789, while a year later Commandant-General Enrique Grimarest allowed him greater latitude.

Two decades after Varela's successful negotiations with the newly established Comandancia General de Provincias Internas, Fray Juan Felipe Martínez underscored the dramatic decline of the Opata pueblos in the once prosperous valleys of Guásabas and Bavispe:

> The Opata nation, so famous for their loyalty and services to these provinces, are wearied and bent with the demands for their labor. These miserable Indians are reduced to fearsome poverty, their lands surrounded [by the *vecinos*]. What little they have left they cannot sow, because they are continually sent out as soldiers, escorts, and mail carriers, without recompense. Their families go hungry, and their villages and missions are falling into decline. For these reasons they are sorely discontent.[22]

Even if we allow for the friar's principal concern as Franciscan commissary for the maintenance of the mission churches, his statement corroborates the Opata complaints voiced twenty years earlier—that in the men's absence from the pueblos, their crops often went unharvested for lack of laborers and for fear of the Apaches. These unending military drafts took their toll on mission stores as well. When Opata captains objected that missionaries in Opodepe and Mátape, for example, refused to supply them with grain for military expeditions, Fray Juan Prestamero countered that the mission *común* no longer produced enough to provide for internal subsistence, let alone to provision military patrols.[23]

Presidial service and the material support for military patrols represented a kind of forced mobilization for *serrano* peoples, often carried out in conditions of hardship. Nevertheless, their participation in the defense of the province gave Indian auxiliaries a certain leverage to negotiate with colonial authorities and practice warfare on their own terms, as evidenced by Pima troops recruited to subjugate rebel Seris who had been dispossessed of their lands in Pópulo (see Chapter 5 above). During the summer of 1750 Colonel Diego Ortiz Parrilla, governor of Sonora, organized a major expedition to "punish" and eradicate Seri bands who had scattered along the desert coastline west of Pitic and fled to encampments on Tiburón Island, where natural water deposits ensured them a chance of survival.[24] Yaqui and Pima auxiliaries greatly outnumbered presidial troops and Spanish militiamen; altogether these auxiliaries, gathered in San Miguel de Horcasitas, made up a force of more than 600 soldiers.

In mid-September, Governor Ortiz ordered the first embarkment of men and horses to Tiburón Island. Forty-eight soldiers and 100 Pimas accompanied by 2 Seri leaders who had remained loyal to the Spaniards explored the island. They discovered that the Seris had poisoned the best mountain springs, and the invading force was forced to retreat to the beach. Ortiz sent two messages to the Seri leader, whose name in Spanish meant *Canta la flecha que mata* ("The arrow sings that kills"), exhorting him to allow the governor to visit his *ranchería* and to bring his people back to the Sonoran mainland. When "Canta la Flecha" rebuked these overtures, Ortiz gave the order to climb the Sierra de Tiburón and attack the Seris. None of the soldiers responded until the Pimas, who had explored some of the infested water holes and discovered that they could withstand the poison, answered (through an interpreter) in unequivocal terms: "We have come from far away to kill the Seris, who wandered through the *monte* causing damage. Since we arrived here, we have not done anything except eat, and now we want to go to the hills and find them."[25]

The Pimas' bravura galvanized the soldiers into action. For nearly two weeks they pursued the rebel Seris deep into the hills, finally destroying their *ranchería*. Seris and Pimas battled each other with stones, clubs, and poisoned arrows, moving through terrain they both knew well. After the final skirmish five Pimas returned to camp victorious, their quivers nearly empty of arrows but filled with the ears of their victims. At a cost of four wounded, these auxiliaries brought with them twenty-eight prisoners—all women and children. The Seri men, including "Canta la Flecha," had all died.

What does this episode reveal about the tactics and motives of Indian auxiliaries who fought with the Spaniards against other Sonoran peoples? First of all, these irregular forces were organized by pueblos, and each captain led the warriors from his own village. Secondly, for the Pimas war was both a ritual act and a deadly exercise. Their clothing and headgear set apart individual warriors according to rank and showed that all were prepared for combat. In their determination to attack the Seri *ranchería* they sought trophies that signified the material proof of their bravery and human captives who could be sold into slavery.

These general considerations apply, as well, to Pima and Opata troops who accompanied presidial forays against Apache *rancherías*. Juan de Mendoza of Horcasitas led a mixed expeditionary force as far north as the Gila Valley in 1757. Imploring the aid of his patron San Joaquín, Mendoza traversed "all the Gila River, in the Apache heartland." He counted among his achievements "having killed thirty brave *gandules* and taken prisoner two warriors and thirty-seven women and children," called *piezas*, evidently to sell or hold ransom in order to force the Apaches to return some of their captives.[26] Similarly, in 1766 Juan Bautista de Anza took a force of Pima auxiliaries and troops selected from the presidios of Tubac, Terrenate, and Fronteras and advanced north of Sonora, traveling through mountainous country from the San Pedro to the Gila rivers. Anza attacked various *rancherías* of Apaches and returned to Tubac with fifteen Apache women, some of whom had recently given birth, where he divided them and other booty "among the people who had

accompanied me, in equal parts, as you have instructed me to do."²⁷
Fifteen years later, after the expeditions of 1774–75 to Alta California
that brought Anza fame and the title of captain, he led a three-pronged
expedition through Nueva Vizcaya and Nuevo México. His forces comprised presidial soldiers, militiamen, and Opata auxiliaries. Anza's route
took his Indian troops far beyond their home communities in search
of a passable road between Sonora and the Río Grande settlements of
New Mexico. They encountered Gileños and "Apaches Navajoes," engaging them in a few skirmishes and exchanging prisoners.²⁸ In 1795 Indian
auxiliaries accompanied José de Zúñiga, commander of the Tucson presidio, whose expedition successfully traced a route between the two
provinces.²⁹ Lamentably, the route was not used consistently in the following years, owing largely to the unceasing movements of nomads
through the sierra.

At the close of the century, Lieutenant José Cortés of the Royal Corps
of Engineers praised the Opatas as brave soldiers and loyal subjects,
comparing them to the Tlaxcaltecas who had fought with the Spaniards during the conquest of Tenochtitlán. Armed both with their traditional weapons and the Spanish musket, Opatas were sent as far away
as Coahuila; some warriors had not returned to their families in more
than two years. Lieutenant Cortés pointedly observed that the Spaniards
would have had few victories against the Apaches without the Opatas,
remarking on both their agility in the sierra and their ferocity in battle.
He reported that the last troop review of the Opata presidial companies
of Bacoachi and Bavispe showed more than 1,000 men ready to fight,
and he confirmed the exemplary authority of the captain-general of the
Opata nation. Cortés recommended raising their wages to equal that of
regular troops and urged colonial authorities to conserve Opata communities and make their population grow.³⁰

Lieutenant Cortés's words of praise for the Opatas' battle valor contrasted sharply with Fray Juan Felipe Martínez's lament over the impoverishment of their communities during those same years. While the Sonoras' intent was to use the colonial institutions of presidio and mission
to rebuild their communities and create for themselves a political space
for negotiation, their collaboration with the Spanish military came at
a high price. Economically, their resources of land and labor diminished; politically, the overlapping spheres of authority between civilian

and military officers exacerbated internal divisions in the pueblos, and the colonial order circumscribed the autonomy of indigenous communities. During the transition from Bourbon to Mexican rule in the early nineteenth century, as the reciprocal component of the colonial pact withered, *serrano* peoples turned from accommodation to armed mobilization. "Resistant adaptation" took on the countenance of confrontation and gave rise to a new phase of ethnogenesis among the highland peoples of Sonora.

9

Patterns of Mobilization

The institutions and ideas through which daily life is expressed in periods of apparent quiescence contain also a perpetual resonance of . . . oppositional culture.

Gavin Smith, 1989 [1]

What constitutes resistance? In what ways do subordinate peoples confront those who hold power over them? Although resistance may encompass individual acts of rebellion or nonconformity, its historical significance points to the mobilization of dispossessed social classes, captives, slaves, or subjugated nations to lessen the burdens imposed on them and to ransom a part of their dignity. [2] The indigenous peasants of highland Sonora developed a culture of opposition in their struggle to maintain certain areas of their domestic and community lives outside Spanish surveillance and to create zones of refuge in the arid and mountainous terrain of their world. Their stance toward Spanish domination and the radical tenets of Mexican Liberalism sought to recover a vestige of their ethnic polities, to conserve their communal lands, and to reduce the demands made of them in labor and military service.

Specific forms of collective action and their relative efficacy were linked to native modes of organization. The Sonoras' identity and social bases of survival were eminently local in nature. Their households and *rancherías*, linked together through intricate strands of kinship, defined the criteria for membership in the ethnic community. When *serrano* peoples mobilized to take action, they turned to these same structures which held their societies together. Furthermore, village elders exercised authority over younger members of the community and held the power to incite rebellion or argue for accommodation and forbearance. Their decisions help to explain why and when native communities fought, negotiated, or ran away.

Indian communities defended the basic tenets of their way of life through a variety of strategies. Flight, in its different manifestations, constituted the most pervasive means of resistance. Individuals, extended families, and entire *rancherías* rejected the social control imposed in the mission villages and moved at will in the *monte*, working occasionally in the numerous mining camps scattered across the Sonoran terrain. While unpredictable and certainly unrelated to anything resembling a central native authority, these territorial migrations were not random. By shifting their residence from missions to mines and haciendas, or by alternating mission life with foraging in the desert, native peoples sustained one of their most cherished values: freedom of movement. Village Indians with serious grievances who deserted the missions turned flight into the first stage of rebellion. This was the case of the Sibubapas (Suvbàpas), scattered groups of Pimas from central Sonora who adopted the Seris' raiding tactics and even joined them in a rising tide of violence against the colonial order.

Frequent local rebellions occurred throughout the province, their rhythm measured in counterpoint to the intensity of state repression. The cost of open and armed resistance was high. Indian renegades usually moved in small groups; when forced to confront Spanish firearms, they suffered heavy casualties. Rebel leaders faced the very real threat of exemplary punishment ending in death, should they be defeated and captured alive. Less illustrious *cabecillas* might be spared their lives, but were subjected to public humiliation, enslavement, or imprisonment. Despite these deterrents, *serrano* peoples did resort to rebellion; even when stopping short of armed revolt, they sustained an undercurrent of opposition to Spanish domination through routine patterns of resistance.

Quotidian forms of collective action clustered around the negotiation and withdrawal of labor power. The pattern of seasonal migration from the missions was undoubtedly linked to avoidance of the missionaries' labor demands, and those Indians who settled permanently in the villages reduced their work in the mission fields to a minimum. By the end of the eighteenth century, some communities refused to work for the missionaries and ignored Bourbon rulings to pay the tithe. Moreover, colonial authorities never succeeded in imposing tribute collection on Sonoran pueblos. José de Gálvez's attempt to institute the head tax on Yaqui *comuneros*, in 1769, met with a clever rebuttal. Protesting their loyalty to the king, Yaqui leaders acquiesced, in theory, in a tribute payment linked to guarantees concerning their control over tribal lands, all the while lamenting a dual calamity of heavy floods followed by severe drought that ruined their harvests two years in a row and left them with nothing to pay. Using a Spanish discourse of loyalty and piety, they implored provincial officials join them in praying for steady rains and abundant harvests.[3]

The nuances of resistance and the values native peoples asserted are the core themes of this chapter, analyzed in subsequent sections on flight and zones of refuge, frontier wars, and major rebellions. The historical significance of these concurrent patterns of mobilization that conserved indigenous institutions and created new cultural expressions becomes evident through an overview of Indian, Spanish, and Mexican relations from the seventeenth to the nineteenth century. The *longue durée* reveals a constant tension between the subordinate and dominant strata of Sonoran society, tempered by bonds of interdependence that developed across racial and class lines.

In the 1640s, half a century after the initial stages of Jesuit evangelization in Sinaloa and southern Sonora, the full force of Spanish colonization came to bear on the territory north of the Yaqui River. Captain Pedro de Perea invaded the heartland of the Opatería; he installed Franciscan missionaries in the upper Sonora, Oposura, and Bavispe valleys and demanded labor and provisions from the Indian communities to support his ranching and mining enterprises. Perea's abortive captaincy-general (1641–45) sparked violent resistance from native villagers and gave rise to jurisdictional disputes between Jesuits and Franciscans in the province.[4] In the decades following Perea's brief passage through Sonoran history, however, the Spanish population of Sonora and Ostimuri increased. New *reales de minas* changed the regional landscape and created points of contention with the *serrano* peoples.

The closing years of the seventeenth century were tumultuous across

New Spain's northern frontier. The Río Grande Pueblos of New Mexico rose against the Spanish in 1680, forcing missionaries and colonists— nearly 2,000 strong, including some 500 Indian slaves—to flee the colony and retreat to El Paso del Norte.[5] The following year, even as Governor Antonio de Otermín failed in his attempted reconquest of New Mexico, the Opatas conspired to rebel and destroy Spanish settlements in northern Sonora. In 1684, an uprising of Janos, Jocomes, Sumas, Mansos, Chinarras and Conchos enflamed the mountain frontier between Sonora and Nueva Vizcaya.[6] During the 1690s the Tarahumaras launched a number of major revolts, in league with Jobas and Conchos, forcing the Spaniards to mobilize militias throughout the mining provinces of Cosihuiriáchic and Ostimuri for most of the decade.[7] Diego de Vargas restored Spanish rule to New Mexico in 1691–94, but Crown dominion over the greater Northwest was hardly secure. Rebellion erupted among the northern Pimas in 1695, with disturbing signs of new unrest in the Opatería.[8]

Eighteenth-century Sonora presented alternating periods of peace and warfare. During the early decades of the century, missionary activity waned in the Pimería Alta, after the energetic ministry of Padre Eusebio Francisco Kino (1687–1711), leaving much of northern Sonora beyond effective Spanish surveillance. Conversely, the spread of mining and ranching operations in central Sonora and Ostimuri augmented pressures on serrano ethnic territory. Parallel to the mounting intensity of Spanish military campaigns against the coastal Seris and the mountain Athapaskans, three major rebellions shook the province at midcentury. Cáhita and Pima peoples rose up in arms in 1739–41, shattering the administration of Governor Manuel de Huidobro and forcing the abandonment of many haciendas and reales de minas. Eight years later, Seris and Pimas who had settled in the mission of Pópulo in the San Miguel Valley revolted against the arbitrary measures of Spanish officials who took away their lands and sold their families into slavery. In 1751, the northern Pimas again rebelled, destroying mission compounds and Spanish settlements in the Altar and Magdalena valleys.

The expulsion of the Jesuits (1767) brought in its wake a period of renewed migrations and turbulence throughout highland Sonora. Opata, Pima, Eudeve, and Joba dialects became mixed and confused as ethnic populations shifted in mission pueblos such as Tonichi, Soyopa, Nácori,

Mátape, Alamos, Batuco, Cucurpe, Arivechi, and Bacanora.⁹ It was this period as well that saw an increase in the bands of Sibubapas and Suaquis who abandoned the missions and roamed through the countryside hunting and raiding livestock. The threat of rebellion could be as effective as an actual revolt, as the Yaquis demonstrated in their negotiations over tribute payment described above. Spanish military commanders feared these enemies within the colony even as they made war against the Apaches and Comanches beyond its borders. Increased presidial fortifications, the recruitment of indigenous auxiliaries, and the establishment of Apache peace encampments brought a reprieve of sorts along the eastern frontier during the 1780s and 1790s.

Following the wars of independence (1810–21), when supply routes were interrupted, presidial troops left the province to fight the insurgency, and Apache raiding increased, the nineteenth century opened a new chapter in the history of Indian–white relations in Sonora. The second quarter of the century saw renewed unrest that flaired into open rebellion by Cáhitas, Pimas, and Opatas who opposed the radical changes in land tenure and town governance imposed by Mexican state authorities. Their movements expressed elements of both ethnic and class conflict and revealed deepening divisions in the communities. The transitional period from 1790 to 1840 indelibly altered the history of Sonoran ethnic polities, centered on communal control over land and labor. The dissolution of the colonial pact between indigenous peasants and the state during this crucial half-century bore significantly on the culture of opposition that developed in northwestern Mexico.

Rancherías Volantes: Flight and Resettlement

Colonial authorities lamented over and over the compound problem of *gentiles*, native bands not yet reduced to mission life; rebellious Seris joined by apostate Pimas; and Apache raiders from the eastern sierra who penetrated ever deeper into Sonoran territory. The Jobas alternatively sought missionaries and fled from the settled villages of the Opatería, just as the movements of Sibubapas, Pápagos and Sobaípuris eluded Spanish subjugation. Missionaries and Bourbon administrators alike judged that, taken together, these wandering peoples outside the colonial order hindered commercial progress and kept the province in the shadow of poverty.[10]

Vagabonds became another nomadic element in the area. Following European legal and cultural norms, the term *vagabundo* signified individuals who had no visible means of support; they lacked a permanent dwelling, and they did not belong to a fixed community. In northern New Spain, *vagabundaje* referred to persons of different ethnic and social status, including unsettled *gambusinos* (prospectors) who moved from one mining bonanza to another, soldiers who had deserted their posts, and mission Indians who had left their pueblos and turned to raiding. When presidial commanders and priests referred to people of mixed race who wandered through the pueblos as "vagabonds," they were knowingly using an opprobrious term to describe what they saw as a threat to ordered society.[11] Yet it was the nature of the colonial enterprise itself which produced (or exacerbated) the phenomenon of vagabondage. Mining *reales* in Sonora of varying longevity, characterized by placer sites with little long-term investment, sustained a small core of permanent workers but gave rise to a mobile labor force that secured a livelihood from a variety of sources.[12] Presidial solders who tired of the risks and harsh living conditions on the frontier and, especially, convicted criminals sent to hard labor in these northern garrisons, sought opportunities to escape.[13]

Contemporary reports denounced the physical destruction wrought by the "enemies" (nearly always understood to be Apaches or Seris) and the abandonment of traditional villages, now reduced to a small fraction of their former population. Mission districts comprising three or four *visitas* at midcentury counted only one or two pueblos fifty years later, with less than half of their original population. Likewise, provincial officials could name dozens of ranches and mines that were either deserted or sustained by only a handful of subsistence farmers and *gambusinos*.[14] If, indeed, Apaches had set fire to Suamca and destroyed Guevavi in the Santa Cruz Valley, and rebellious Pimas and Seris had forced the abandonment of the Hacienda de la Soledad to the west of Cucurpe, the apparent desolation of highland Sonora at the close of the colonial period had other causes as well. It is clear that not all the "Apaches" were actually Apaches. The Athapaskan bands who lived by hunting, raiding, and long-distance trade were joined or mimicked by village Indians who chose to quit sedentary life under mission discipline and by renegade Spaniards for whom poverty and oppression made vagabondage a plausible alternative.

These wandering peoples developed divergent patterns of intraregional migration that became a means of conserving their splintered communities. In the face of land enclosures that threatened to destroy the agrarian base of established villages in nearly all the arable valleys of Sonora, dispossessed Indians and impoverished *vecinos* turned to squatting and pillaging as a means of survival. The "rancherías volantes" so named by Padre Manuel Aguirre in the 1760s included Indians as well as *gente de razón* by the end of the century. Flight and resettlement were not merely random movements or instinctive reactions to colonial pressures; rather, they created an alternative mode of existence in a province so sparsely settled and held within them the seeds of rebellion.

Colonial officials distinguished between the "old enemies" considered to be in open hostility to the regime—*gentiles* who had not been incorporated into the religious and economic structures of the colony—and the "new enemies," Indians once reduced to mission life who left the pueblos of central Sonora. While their reports focused on particular bands of rebels, such as the Seris of Cerro Prieto or the Apaches Mescaleros, presidial commanders and provincial governors saw this as a global problem of frontier defense. They never tired of voicing their fear of a generalized rebellion should the Pápagos, for example, join the Seris and Sibubapas, or should the Pimas Gileños find common cause with the Apaches. The fear of rebellion which guided colonial policy was grounded in a history of local uprisings.

Spanish field commanders became astute observers of different kinds of rebellion and of distinct forms of confederation among Sonoran Indians. Captain Lorenzo Cancio, commander of the Presidio de San Carlos de Buenavista, advised the viceroy of the seriousness of the revolt of Suvbàpas in the context of continual wars with the Apaches and Seris. In 1766, Cancio estimated that more than 100 families of fugitive Suvbàpas began hostilities in the sierra and then took refuge with "the old rebel nations" in Cerro Prieto. "All of these *regiones*," he noted, "are settled by reduced Indians who number in the thousands, but the Pimas Altos and Bajos that still remain at peace—believe, your excellency, an official who professes the truth—if we do not speedily punish the old and new enemies, I fear the domestic Indians of this province of Sonora, with the exception of the Opatas and Eudeves, will go the way of our enemies."[15]

Although Cancio spoke a hard line of "punishing the enemy," he and other presidial officers recognized the difficulty of engaging rebel bands in open combat and the danger of concentrating their troops in any one area. They had learned that it was foolhardy to mount a major assault against a rebel stronghold without leaving sufficient troops to guard the presidios and the pueblos. Given the slippery nature of the alliances among mission and non-mission Indians and their frequent migrations from the pueblos to Spanish settlements and the monte, "they gather intelligence from those who live among us, and they know our movements and campaign preparations."[16] Because the Spanish show of force was of limited efficacy, it was necessary to combine military action with negotiation, gifts, and reassurances of pardon in order to bring hostile Indians back to village life. Presidial commanders dealt with different capitancillos (leaders), who variously declared themselves "friends" and "enemies" of the Spanish and who controlled a following basically among their own kinfolk. Seasoned officers learned to distinguish different styles of arrowheads in order to identify particular bands of renegades and call on the appropriate Indian leaders to forestall further hostilities or persuade a rebellious ranchería to accept a peaceful settlement.

Numerous Sibubapa rebellions, like the incidents reported by Captain Cancio, were part of the general upheaval in the missions occasioned by the violent sudden and forced exodus of the Jesuits in 1767. Because cultivation was severely diminished and, in some pueblos, temporarily abandoned, the Indians turned in greater numbers to hunting and gathering ("mescaleando" and "panaleando"). Their habitual migrations to the desert and mountain canyons to gather beeswax and honey, agave leaves and hearts, and amaranthus seeds and greens, for example, raised suspicions among vecinos and presidial commanders concerning the theft of livestock and possible conspiracies to rebel. Heretofore "domestic Indians" gave voice to mounting grievances over depleted mission stores, the arrogance of civilian comisarios, disrupted lines of authority, and the arbitrary demands made of them by newly installed Franciscan missionaries.

The descendants of Pimas who, in 1717, had successfully petitioned local magistrates to obtain land and establish a pueblo in Buenavista, thus complained to Captain Juan Joseph Lumbreras, acting commander of the Presidio de San Carlos (in whose shadow they now lived) about the excessive labor demanded of them by their missionary, Fray Francisco Cordón.[17] In his zeal to finish building a new church, Fray Francisco compelled men and women to work daily hauling adobe bricks and clay mortar, to the point of losing their crops. Furthermore, he had personally flogged Indians with leather thongs and canes and even kicked them. Cordón violated the lines of authority established among native officers; he humiliated them by publicly whipping their wives for the "offense" of gathering nopal or grinding corn to feed their families instead of carrying clay to the church.

Captain Lumbreras took up the Pimas' cause. He admonished Fray Francisco not to force the Indians to work without pay or to keep them from harvesting their milpas, reminding him that "since this was one of the pueblos where the Indians had rebelled and fled, but have now returned to their houses and are faithful in their work, it is necessary to treat them with love, as the king commands us to do."[18] Lumbreras warned Cordón that the mission was under his jurisdiction as commander of the presidio and, to prove the point, he summoned the gobernador, alcalde, and alguacil of Buenavista to his quarters. There, he proceeded to lay out new ground rules for the Indians' work and freedom to travel. In defiance of Cordón's orders forbidding his neophytes to leave the mission, Lumbreras directed the Pimas to obtain a pass from him, in concurrence with their governor, when they wanted to leave the village. He told them that they should continue building the church by rotating the labor weekly among three "squadrons" so that they could dedicate the necessary time to their milpas. Lumbreras offered to lend them seeds to plant a new crop and, should it fail, to pardon their debt. He reported these events to Intendant-Governor Pedro de Corbalán and to Viceroy Marqués de Croix; the latter reproved Lumbreras's intervention in the conflict but, at the same time, warned the friar not to let the Indians perceive a serious cleavage between ecclesiastical and military authorities.[19]

Indeed, provincial governors and viceregal authorities were acutely aware of the restless movements of Indians in the highland terrain of Sonora and Ostimuri between the Mayo and Yaqui river valleys. This territory of Pima and Cáhita ethnic frontiers was significantly transformed by mining and ranching enterprises clustered around the *reales* of San Antonio de la Huerta, Trinidad, Río Chico, and Baroyeca which were linked, in turn, to the administrative center of Alamos. In February 1769, rebellious Indians murdered the priest of Baroyeca as he returned to the province from the Bishopric of Durango. Then, on Palm Sunday (March 19, 1769) a band of Pimas attacked the mission of Batacosa and the silver-refining hacienda of Tobaca. They carried off the mission's herd of horses and sacked the houses of resident laborers in Tobaca. There, they surrounded the church and, as Mass ended, a two-hour battle ensued, at the end of which seven of the Indians who had defended the hacienda lay mortally wounded and the Pimas fled south on fresh horses. Spanish militias and Indian warriors gathered in Tobaca that same day to pursue them, but while Lieutenant Manuel Campoy and Second Lieutenant Tadeo Padilla disputed the command of their improvised forces, their Indian allies lost interest and wandered off; the rebels terrorized the pueblo of Macoyagüi. Finding the village nearly deserted because most of the people had gone to the head village of Conicarit to celebrate the Feast of the Palms, the rebels galloped into the church, denuded and smashed religious statuary, then proceeded to the *casa de comunidad* where they stole the Indians' canes of office. Padilla's militia, augmented by twelve archers from Macoyagüi who vowed revenge against their attackers, gave chase and finally opened fire on the Pimas on a hillside deep in the Sierra Madre. Leaving behind their livestock and supplies, the Pimas eluded their pursuers by retreating further into the mountains. Two days later, these same rebels (or a different band of Pimas) attacked the mission of Tepagüi, leaving behind three dead, and moved downstream to the Rancho de la Cabeza near Camoa pueblo.[20]

It was not coincidental that highland Pimas rebelled over accumulated grievances in the spring of 1769 — precisely when most of the Sonoran presidial troops, commanded by Domingo de Elizondo, were concentrated in the coastal garrisons of Guaymas and Pitic to begin the offensive against the Seri stronghold in Cerro Prieto. Moreover, the movements of these renegade Sibubapas illustrated a familiar pattern of Indian revolt. They chose targets that were vulnerable and partly deserted; they destroyed or stole property, especially livestock, that was of value to the Spaniards and whose loss hindered their mobility; and they posted sentinels and messengers to inform them of the movements of

Spanish troops. The nature of their attacks also carried a strong element of revenge. For example, the leader of this band, estimated at about sixty warriors, was the deposed governor of a *ranchería* of Pimas that had settled in the Real de Sobia; the Indian who killed the priest of Baroyeca had been his servant. The rebels used their knowledge of the terrain to good advantage and more often than not escaped capture, retreating to zones of refuge in the desert or in the secluded peaks and canyons of the sierra, where mounted horsemen could not reach them and soldiers were loath to follow them on foot.[21] The capture of several of their leaders, however, weakened the movement. In the spring of 1770, some of the Sibubapas took refuge in the mission of Belén and negotiated the terms of their surrender to the Spanish *cuartel* in Guaymas through the offices of the priest assigned to the Yaqui pueblos and a woman, "la vieja Ursula." The Pimas insisted on staying in Belén until all their kinfolk should have come down from the mountains so that their families would be kept together.[22]

These peace agreements were fragile, and presidial officers readily admitted that they depended on Indian governors to control the movements of renegade bands. In 1772, Captain Lumbreras of Buenavista remonstrated with Diego, *gobernador* of Suaqui, to bring to account a band of Sibubapas accused of robbing and slaughtering presidial livestock. When confronted with the arrows, Diego at first admitted that the culprits were his people, but later vacillated, saying that they could have been Piatos or Yaquis. Lumbreras returned to Buenavista exasperated: "I accomplished nothing, even after I gave out all the tobacco I had brought along for the occasion." For his part, Diego argued that the missionary had stored all the harvest in the head village of Tecoripa, and that for want of food the Pimas of Suaqui had scattered far beyond the village. Of the ninety-two families registered at the mission, only seven remained there, sixty-eight were spread along the arroyo for more than five leagues (fifteen miles), ten had gone to Belén, and seven were living in different placer mines. Reports of isolated assaults and murders continued to arrive in Buenavista, and Lumbreras lamented that "it is irremediable, because [the Indians] are so dispersed."[23]

Even as the Sibubapas and their confederates confounded Spanish rule in southern Sonora and Ostimuri, the northern Pimas kept up a similar rhythm of flight–rebellion–negotiation in the Altar Valley. Ignacio

Tuburijipci, the governor of Pitiquito who had led a band of fifty-two men, women, and children away from the mission, surrendered peacefully to Captain Bernardo de Urrea in the Sierra del Mescal Amargoso, a place chosen by the Pima leader. This encounter between the Indian warrior and the Spanish presidial commander took place only after three prior meetings with "ambassadors" of Tuburijipci, the sending of gifts of food and tobacco, and assurances of good treatment and safe conduct. The final meeting was arranged by messengers who kept Tuburijipci in communication with the governors of the western pueblos of the Pimería Alta. On his return to the Presidio de Altar, Urrea received an "ambassador" from Marcos Siarihumar, the leader of a small band of Seris encamped in the Sierra de Caracagüi, who informed the captain that if he would grant them a royal pardon they would come down from the hills and live in their pueblo. Thus assured, a few days later they surrendered to Teniente Ignacio Miguel de Urrea and followed him to Pitiquito.[24] In subsequent events, however, Spanish officials again accused Tuburijipci and Bautista José of Oquitoa of inciting rebellion; the latter had stolen the horse herd from the Presidio de Altar and taken it to the Apaches. Local officials urged harsh punishment, but Viceroy Antonio María Bucareli commuted their death sentences to imprisonment.[25]

Episodes like these show us that the Indians' mode of low-scale, constant rebellion kept the frontier open and obliged the Spaniards to fight on Indian terms. Spanish forces encountered similar tactics in the wars they waged against the Seris and Apaches and in a number of major uprisings that threatened to break their dominion in Sonora.

Frontier Wars

These are the great endeavors of these barbarians, whose main objective is to steal.

Domingo Elizondo to Viceroy Marqués de Croix, 1768[26]

Bourbon officials intended to control the vast northern provinces of New Spain by militarizing the frontier. At midcentury, the royal visitor José Rafael Rodríguez Gallardo warned the Crown that the potential mining and commercial wealth of Sonora would be lost to the empire if the pervasive nomadism of its coastal and mountain tribes were not curbed. His message was echoed by presidial commanders and (ironically) by the last generation of Jesuits to serve in the province; it was put into action by José de Gálvez, who orchestrated a series of radical reforms in viceregal administration and military deployment in New Spain. Timed to coincide with the expulsion of Jesuit missionaries, the Sonora expedition commanded by Colonel Domingo Elizondo was sent to quash the rebellious Seris and their Pima allies ensconced in the Cerro Prieto. Elizondo led a combined force of 705 presidial troops and 150 Yaqui and Pima auxiliares, distributed in three *cuarteles* established in Pitic, Guaymas, and San José de Pimas.[27]

The Elizondo expedition arrived in two contingents by land and by sea during the late spring of 1768, the beginning of the hottest and driest season in the Sonoran Desert. Indigenous communities like the coastal Cáhitas, as well as the intended "enemies"—the Seris—anticipated their coming with trepidation. Colonel Elizondo reported to Viceroy Croix that his overland entry into the province, moving north from Tepic, had helped disabuse the Yaquis of their fear that the purpose of the expedition was "to kill all the Indian [men] and take away their women, children, and goods."[28] The Seris crippled the expedition from the outset by attacking its horse and mule herd in Guaymas; their escape demonstrated the "barbarians'" strategic advantage in their knowledge of the terrain. Suspecting from prior experience that the Spanish would search for them at the *aguajes* and *tinajas* that supplied water in the arid desolation of Cerro Prieto, the Seris had moved their *rancherías* away from these natural springs. Their objective was to draw the troops deeper into their refuge, where horses were useless and infantry would perish from thirst. The Seris prepared ambushes in places that both disguised their movements and provided an escape route through the thick and thorny desert scrub. When the expeditionaries came across Seri encampments, they found them deserted, sometimes with stolen livestock and gear left behind and their cooking fires barely extinguished.[29] Their "strange method of warfare" obeyed one overriding purpose: to maintain an open avenue of flight. Elizondo's plan for a three-pronged attack on the Seris' mountain fortress did not work out as he had hoped: he marched his troops and horses from one *ranchería* to another, taking only a few prisoners, but never finding the bulk of the rebellious Indians.[30]

The Sonora expedition never succeeded in subjugating the Seris, nor did it carry out its projected campaign against the Apaches. This pattern of assault-and-retreat exhausted the Spanish forces, but also took its toll on the embattled remnants of Seri and Pima rancherías which subdivided into ever smaller groups and were almost permanently on the run. Rebel leaders did sue for peace from time to time—a peace that bought them respite in an ongoing war—and some Seri rancherías returned to mission life in Pitic and El Carrizal.[31]

A similar war of endurance unfolded in the Sierra Madre, involving Apaches, Opatas, Pimas, and Spaniards. Distinct bands of Athapaskan hunter-gatherers—Mogollones, Gileños, Mimbreños, and Chiricaguas—maintained rancherías over a vast mountainous territory between Nueva Vizcaya, New Mexico, and Sonora that lay beyond the political control of the established colony. The sierra was for them a zone of refuge, as was the coastal desert for the Seris. The Apaches hunted, gathered, and herded the livestock they stole to trade with other Plains tribes to the north. Their migratory patterns brought them into peaceful as well as hostile encounters with serrano communities and Spanish mining and ranching settlements. The Apache wars had a long history of assaults, robberies, and punitive expeditions, including the capture and exchange of prisoners, when Commandant-General Jácobo Ugarte y Loyola instituted a policy of peace encampments in the environs of the northern presidios. Different bands of Apache kinsmen followed their leaders and agreed to settle in the peace camps near Fronteras, Bacoachi, Bavispe, and Janos, in Sonora and Chihuahua, in exchange for food, clothing, tools, and planting seed for cultivation of their own small maize plots.[32] Spanish officials envisioned these encampments as quasi-permanent settlements, a way of changing the Apaches' migratory habits. The Indians, for their part, accepted the inducements to be "reduced" to the lands set aside for them outside the presidios as an alternative resource, but they did not abandon their mountain refuge or their intricate web of political alliances. Thus, Apache capitancillos and their extended families came and went from the peace encampments (often taking with them unguarded livestock) to seek their sustenance in the sierra. Their movements led to continual rounds of military skirmishes and negotiated surrenders, in which the taking of captives played an important part. The expedition led by Don Manuel de Echeagaray to bring fugitive Apaches back to Bacoachi and Fronteras illustrates well this kind of frontier warfare.[33]

From September 24 to November 30, 1788, Captain Echeagaray led a mixed expedition of more than 400 troops, consisting of Spanish, Opata, and Pima presidial soldiers as well as Apache auxiliaries, who aided the Spanish in scouting out rancherías. His route passed through what had been the land of the Sobaípuris. With the help of these "Apaches amigos"—including 17 men and 4 women—Echeagaray's forces discovered a number of rancherías, but found them deserted because the Apaches were alerted to their movements and fled ahead of their arrival. The expeditionaries, however, did take a number of prisoners at each encounter, nearly always women and children. Their capture of the wives and widows of prominent Apache chieftains was a tactic to induce their menfolk to surrender to Spanish forces. Such was the case when Echeagaray took captive both the wife of the capitancillo Compá and the widow of the captain of the Chiricahuas: within a few days Compá and Capitancillo Chacho sought out Echeagaray and met his terms for surrender. They joined the expedition to seek out those rancherías that belonged to their people. In the following weeks, their kinfolk surrendered to the Spanish in small groups, a total of 53 persons. These were "reduced" Apaches, destined to be reincorporated into the peace encampments, and Echeagaray distinguished them from the "piezas," prisoners who would be distributed as slaves or servants among Spanish households. The latter numbered 149, of whom 28 died before the expedition was completed. Noting that it was too cumbersome to keep these prisoners on the campaign and feed them, Echeagaray sent them to Fronteras under armed guard. Their importance for the expedition is underscored by the exact accounting the captain made of the numbers of "gandules" and "piezas," indicating whether they were dead or alive and the place of their capture, which he annexed to the report.[34]

The expedition advanced as far as the Sierra de San Francisco, on the trail of Capitancillo Chiquito and his ranchería. On learning that Chiquito and Capitancillo Guegoca and their families had fled to New Mexico, Echeagaray halted the chase, because his troops (neither infantry nor cavalry) could withstand any further marches. The Apaches had learned that if they fled far enough, they could outrun the Spaniards and outlast their endurance. On the return trip, a last *capitancillo*, Uisaque, sent word to the Spanish captain that he wanted to surrender and bring his people to petition for peace; however, he could not go to Bacoachi until "four moons had passed." Although Echeagaray was inclined to disbelieve him, some of the recently reduced Apaches convinced him that the offer was sincere. He dispatched 200 soldiers to await the arrival of this *ranchería* and abandoned plans to press on to New Mexico.[35]

Captain Echeagaray observed the Apaches' habitual migratory patterns leading eastward from the Sierra de San Francisco to New Mexico, where they raided and obtained salt from the Zuni Pueblos, and westward into Sonora. He referred to knowledge gleaned from earlier expeditions, like the Zuni campaign of 1747, and identified various Apache bands according to their indigenous nomenclature and the names by which Spaniards knew them. For example:

Yutaquene = Mogollones
Chicon-ane = Gileños
Ay-agné = Mimbreños

That Apache ethnicity was complex—with many internal divisions and enmities exacerbated by the endemic warfare that raged on this frontier—is illustrated by Echeagaray's comment that the Apache auxiliaries sacked and destroyed the *rancherías* on which the expedition opened fire, taking their belongings and stores of piñon nuts and acorns.

The Spaniards became adept at manipulating different bands of Apaches, alternating harsh treatment with clemency, and using their prisoners to gain further knowledge of fugitive *rancherías*. In this regard, Captain Echeagaray singled out Joseph María González, a soldier-interpreter of Bacoachi, for special words of praise. The Indians, however, considered these expeditions to have invaded their territory; they maintained their own network of spies and messengers to apprise them of troop movements. In these frontier wars, fugitive *rancherías* moved together as extended families of men, women, and children who lived on the margins of the colony, but not completely isolated from it. Thus, their strategies combined flight with negotiation, returning periodically to settled life.

Mobilization for Rebellion

Serrano peasant communities, apparently incorporated into the colonial system, used similar tactics of guerrilla warfare in a number of major rebellions whose proportions threatened Spanish hegemony in the province. Their causes were many: the abuses of forced labor and enslavement, epidemics, land encroachments, grievances against particular missionaries, and the hostile environment created by the frontier wars. Their rhythm corresponded to the pace of Spanish colonization and to the movements of nomadic tribes that either threatened the livelihood of indigenous villagers or created opportunities for armed confrontation.

These conditions coalesced in 1681, when several Opata leaders conspired to rise up against Spanish settlements in their territory. Jesuit missionization had proceeded for three decades, and a number of *reales de minas* were firmly established in the heart of the Opatería—San Juan Bautista, Nacozari, Tepache, Bacanuche, San Juan—along with many more mining camps and livestock ranches. Planned to begin in October, the start of the cold dry months of winter, the Opatas had determined to draw the Spanish militias into an ambush, then attack their unprotected *reales* and haciendas disguised as Apaches. The *tlatole*, or call to arms, had traveled by messenger from pueblo to pueblo, implicating Opata villages and the Concho and Suma missions of Casas Grandes and Carretas, and the revolt was betrayed by a Spanish *vecino's ladino* servant before it could be carried out. His declaration before a war council in San Juan Bautista in early July led to an effective preemptive strike and the arrest of Indian *cabecillas* in most of the Opata communities of northeastern Sonora: Bacoachi, Cuquiárachi, Tebidéguachi, Cuchuta, Teuricachi, Guachinera, Bavispe, Bacerác, and Bacadéguachi. Dozens of suspects were interrogated, and their combined testimony left a picture of unrest and smoldering resentment in the region. Although inspired by the success of the Pueblo Revolt of 1680, and evidently in communication with Sumas, Conchos, Janos, and Sobaípuris, the Opata movement was indigenous to the Sonoran highlands.

The exemplary punishments for convicted leaders were severe: fifteen were condemned to death, four were sentenced to forced labor for up to ten years, and still others were flogged and tortured on the gibbet. These implicated conspirators had carried the titles of *gobernador*, *alcalde*, *topil*, *fiscal*, and even *capitán a guerra*, corresponding to the Spanish governing hierarchy established in the pueblos. What had incited them to rebel? They complained of whippings inflicted by the missionaries, hangings ordered by military captains, and excessive demands for *repartimiento* labor in the mines. Moreover, as in New Mexico, the province had suffered drought and famine, which the Indians blamed on the Spaniards' livestock "which dried up all the springs and ruined the land."[36]

New rumors of rebellion surfaced in October—in part, to avenge the executions of July. Amid a second round of arrests and forced confessions, the Opatas of Cuchuta, Cuquiárachi, and Tebidéguachi abandoned their pueblos and fled to the sierra. This time Francisco Cuervo, the *alcalde mayor* of San Juan Bautista offered clemency: if the Indians would return to their villages within six days, they would not be punished. Upon the arrival of 750 Opatas, Cuervo admonished them not to receive new *tlatoles*, but to obey their priests and tend their crops. The Indians agreed, presenting crosses as a sign of this new covenant; Cuervo, for his part, released the prisoners he had taken.

The agreement of 1681 created a fragile peace. Although Opata auxiliaries helped to quell the uprising of Janos, Jocomes, Sumas, Mansos, Chinarras, and Conchos that engulfed the missions of Soledad, Carretas, and Casas Grandes in 1684, the grievances that had provoked them to rebel remained and simmered. The Opata-Spanish alliance, which would endure for more than a century, was forged largely in the caldron of the frontier wars that divided nomadic and sedentary peoples, at the same time that the colonial economy opened new avenues for Opata laborers and direct producers. Political and economic forces emanating from the missions, mines, and presidios altered the contours of *serrano* ethnic territory and created conditions of interdependency between highland peasants and Spanish *vecinos*. From this interdependency, the Opatas, Eudeves, and the most settled of the Pima pueblos constructed the notion of a colonial pact, understood as a reciprocal exchange of labor and military service for recognition of their collective claim to land.[37]

The Opata-Spanish alliance was tested anew during the Pima Alta uprising of 1695. In this northernmost region of Sonora, only recently incorporated into the Jesuit mission program, the rebellion had multiple causes: Padre Kino's evangelization methods, the *vecinos'* cattle herds and demands for Pima laborers, and the arbitrary reprisals taken by military officers who often confused the northern Pimas with the nomadic raiders of the Sierra Madre. In 1688, the roving *compañía volante* of Fronteras destroyed the Pima *ranchería* of Mututicachi, sending twenty prisoners to forced labor in the mines of Alamos (Sinaloa) and mistreating some fifty others, accused of having stolen livestock. Acting on the same unfounded suspicions, a lieutenant of the Fronteras presidio had three Sobaipuri chieftains executed in 1692, and he threatened Soba leaders of Tubutama, saying that they had "conspired" against the Spanish.[38]

Padre Kino's innovative style of evangelization opened the Pimería Alta to Spanish colonialism beginning in 1687, albeit at the cost of altering the methods of indoctrination that the Jesuits had established in Sinaloa, Ostimuri, and Sonora. Early mission history (1591–1650) set a conservative pace of *reducciones*, advancing gradually from one valley or ethnic enclave to another. Unlike his confreres, Kino did not concentrate his efforts in any one village, but aspired to reach the entire Pimería Alta. Working northward from his base in Cucurpe and Dolores de Cosari, Kino traveled relentlessly through the region. Repeatedly he visited the Pima villages of the Magdalena and Altar-Asunción valleys, instilling in them a demand for missionaries. Seven years later, three priests arrived to bolster his solitary mission, taking up residence in pueblos that had responded favorably to Kino. Christened San Pedro y San Pablo de Tubutama, Nuestra Señora de la Asunción de Caborca, and San Ignacio de Cabórica, these *aldeas* became head villages whose influence radiated over a number of *rancherías*. Beginning in 1694, then, the Pimas confronted not merely an itinerant missionary, but resident ministers who obliged them to attend religious services, pressured them to conform to Christian norms of monogamy, and demanded their labor in mission fields under the supervision of Opata overseers—their traditional enemies.

These mounting pressures ignited the flame of rebellion. The Pima uprising occurred in two phases, in the spring and summer of 1695. It began in the western villages of the Altar and Asunción valleys, when a group of Pimas killed the Opata overseers that the Jesuits had brought to Tubutama. Their missionary (Daniel Januske) escaped, but the rebels swept through Oquitoa, Atil, and Caborca. In this last pueblo, the westernmost village of the Pimería Alta, they killed Padre Francisco Xavier Saeta, who only a few months earlier had taken charge of the mission. Severe reprisals taken against the Pimas by the commander of the Presidio de Fronteras served only to spread the rebellion further, into the San Ignacio and Cocóspera valleys. Kino labored to effect a cease-fire, and persuaded the headmen of various rancherías to meet in El Tupo to negotiate a peace agreement. He guaranteed their personal safety, and a general pardon, if they would turn over rebel leaders to Spanish officials. Once gathered in El Tupo, however, presidial troops and their Seri auxiliaries initiated a massacre of unarmed Pima cabecillas, a betrayal of their trust that gave rise to several months of bitter warfare. The Pima rebellion was suppressed only by the combined action of presidial troops from Janos and Fronteras.[39]

The uprising of 1695 thus flared in reaction to military excesses and to the initial stages of missionization in the Pimería Alta after the Pueblo Revolt, during the tumultuous period when Tarahumaras, Opatas, Pimas, Janos, Jocomes, Sumas, and Jinarras took up arms against Spanish domination. But the eighteenth-century rebellions that so seriously challenged Spanish policies in Sonora arose from a different set of pressures in which the political organization of the missions and the economic demands of the vecinos on Indian land and labor figured prominently. Outstanding in the memory of Spanish colonists and native villagers were the Yaqui rebellion of 1740, the Seri uprisings that began in 1748, and the Pima rebellion of 1751. The best documented and most carefully studied of these movements was the uprising of 1739–41 involving Mayos, Yaquis, and Pimas.[40] Their rebellion led to the temporary abandonment of nearly all mines and private estates in Ostimuri and southern Sonora, whose vecinos along with the first governor of Sonora and Sinaloa fled to the Real de Alamos. Its suppression required massive troop mobilization from the Sinaloa garrisons and several rounds of negotiation with Yaqui leaders. Vecinos and colonial officials feared a general uprising of serrano pueblos. Indeed, one of the major battles of this episode occurred in Tecoripa, a central village of the Pimería Baja west of the mining districts of San Miguel, Soyopa, San Xavier, and Río Chico. Rebel emissaries had traveled as far as Ures, on the Sonora River, to incite mission Indians to join their movement, but they were captured when the Pima governors of Pitic and San Francisco, a visita of Ures, refused to follow their call to arms.[41]

What had impelled the Cáhita peoples to rebel? From myriad claims and counterclaims, accusations, and petitions lodged by missionaries, colonial officials, *vecinos*, and Indians, several major issues emerged to clarify the origins of the 1740 uprising. The pueblos of the fertile Yaqui and Mayo deltas had lived under Jesuit tutelage for more than a century. In general, their villages had fared well under the mission regime—as attested by the stability of their population—but the Jesuits increasingly diverted labor, cattle, and surplus produce from the Cáhita pueblos to the struggling missions of Baja California. This issue reached critical importance in 1739–40, when alternating seasons of flood and drought devastated Yaqui harvests and when hunger stalked the land.

The Indians' colonial experience extended beyond the missions to civil society. Mining *reales* in Ostimuri and Sinaloa demanded workers through the *repartimiento* and contractual service (the latter often remunerated in cloth) and, at the same time, provided access to colonial merchandise and a market for indigenous foodstuffs. Thus, *vecinos* and missionaries engaged in open rivalry for Indian laborers, and a growing Spanish population on the eastern margins of Yaqui territory began to covet native land; nevertheless, labor remained the greater point of contention.

Prior to 1732, the Jesuits had exercised virtually singular control over Yaqui and Mayo territory through their resident missionaries. In that year, however, the establishment of the Gobierno de Sonora y Sinaloa (administratively separate from the Reino de Nueva Vizcaya) created a parallel secular authority to whom the Indians could and did address specific grievances. Indeed, one of the most striking features of the 1740 uprising is the deliberate use of different political offices by indigenous leaders to press their claims. Before, during, and after the revolt, Yaqui captains and governors who had served in Spanish militias, and who were well acquainted with the colonial order, articulated formal petitions before the *alcalde mayor* of Ostimuri, the governor of Sonora, and the viceroy of New Spain. Significantly, their grievances and proposed solutions underscored the following points: (1) the removal of specific Jesuits whose arbitrary discipline and interference in village elections had earned the Indians' wrath; (2) the expulsion of *mestizo* and mulatto (*coyote*) assistants who the missionaries had brought to some of the Yaqui pueblos; (3) confirmation of the Indians' right to carry their traditional arms; (4) termination of compulsory labor in the missions without pay;

(5) autonomous elections of their own officers; (6) respect for the Indians' land and subsistence crops; and (7) the freedom to sell their own produce and to work outside the missions.[42] The Yaquis defended simultaneously the integrity of their communities and access to colonial markets. They deeply resented the presence of outsiders in their pueblos, especially in positions of authority, at the same time that they sought commerce on their own terms with the *vecinos*.

Barely eight years after the suppression of the Yaqui rebellion, Spanish policies provoked the Seri rising of 1748, cutting short the Jesuits' patient labor of bringing nomadic bands to mission life in the pueblos of Nacameri, Pópulo, and Los Angeles. The hostilities of that year marked the beginning of a constant state of unrest in western Sonora, lasting well into the nineteenth century. By order of Visitor José Rafael Rodríguez Gallardo, the presidial garrison of Pitic was transferred upstream to the middle San Miguel Valley, appropriating mission land for the soldiers and *vecinos* who settled there. Spanish military officers met the protests of resident Seri and Pima families with violent repression.[43] The Seris took vengeance on specific Spanish targets, applying their considerable *arts de guerre* with deadly accuracy. They burned the Hacienda de Chupisonora, located across the river from Pópulo, because, they said, José de Mesa's cattle had destroyed their wheat crops. In subsequent years Seri warriors and their allies repeatedly attacked mines and ranches in the vicinity of Soledad and Santa Ana, carrying off or destroying cattle and forcing the *vecinos* to flee. They "annihilated" the entire herd of range-fed horses bred by Nicolás Bohórquez and Agustín de Vildósola in Pitic; their assaults in the lower Sonora Valley left the *reales* of Las Animas and Gavilán, the pueblos of San Francisco and Santa Rosalía, and the Aguajito ranch (property of Juan Thomás Beldarraín, who led militiamen in the punitive campaign of 1750) in ruins. With few exceptions, the Seris avoided the missions and turned their wrath against Spanish settlements that invaded their territory.[44]

Even as the Seris maintained a smoldering "low intensity" war, successfully repelling two major expeditions launched against them, the northern Pimas rebelled in 1751; the fury of their movement fell against the mission pueblos. As many as 1,000 warriors from the Altar and Concepción valleys and the Papaguería, moving in separate bands, attacked numerous villages and small mining and ranching settlements.

They burned and sacked churches and other mission property, stole or destroyed entire herds of cattle, and murdered two missionaries: Tomás Tello of Caborca and Enrique Rúhen of Sonoitac. Pima rebels held the Spanish military at bay for more than two months, until a combined force of presidial troops and militiamen defeated them at Aribac, leaving more than 100 warriors dead. A similar number of *vecinos* had perished over the course of the rebellion, and Spanish property was reduced to ashes.[45]

In the ensuing investigation, it was alleged that rebel leaders had vowed to "finish off the Spanish nation and live alone in the land that belonged to them."[46] Their anger is striking in view of the fact that at this time the Pimería Alta was not heavily settled by *gente de razón*. Santa Ana and Soledad constituted the only *reales de minas* of any importance, although the area from Oquitoa to Bac was dotted with small mines and ranches that were the Pimas' principal targets. The destruction or theft of the *vecinos'* cattle — as with the Seris' warcraft — constituted both a tactic and an objective. By killing off the *ganado mesteño*, the Indians defended their own territory, attacked Spanish property, and reduced their adversaries' mobility.

It is equally significant that the Pimas singled out two missionaries for death, considering them *españoles* and, as such, among the enemy. Padres Tello and Rúhen may have fallen victim to the Indians' wrath because of their relative isolation in Caborca and Sonoitac. The latter friar had only recently arrived at his post; as occurred with Padre Saeta half a century earlier, the Tohono O'odham of this remote *ranchería* rejected the demands that a resident priest made on their daily lives and his interference in the intimate details of their familial organization. The Pimas' testimony before Governor Ortiz Parrilla expressed their resentment against work discipline, corporal punishment, and other burdens of mission life.[47] Notwithstanding the Indians' articulate protest, the reason for the uprising went beyond these immediate grievances to questions of power and leadership within the Pima community.

Luis Oacpicagigua, governor of Sáric and captain-general of the Pima nation, played a central role in the rebellion of 1751. In his home village, Luis at one time enjoyed the confidence of the missionaries stationed downstream in Tubutama. Furthermore, he curried favor with the Spanish military during the campaign of 1750 against the Seris, to the point that Governor Ortiz Parrilla conferred on him the extraordinary title of captain-general, bringing with it a personal guard and the privilege of carrying a sword and musket. Luis used the honors he received from the Spaniards to enhance his prestige with his own people. He controlled a considerable extension of arable land and bred his own herds of live-stock. He harvested each year bountiful surpluses of maize, wheat, and cotton to distribute to a growing number of dependents and followers. His generosity was proverbial in the area, extending from gifts of food, tools, and weapons to frequent feasts and *borracheras*.[48]

Why, then, did Luis Oacpicagigua turn against the colonial struc-ture that had apparently served his purposes so well? It may be that the increasing presence of missionaries and colonists in the Pimería Alta at midcentury threatened to diminish the elevated status that Luis had worked so hard to attain. Mines and *estancias*, however small and scat-tered, grew in number at the same time that (albeit slowly and gradually) the Jesuits placed resident missionaries in pueblos like Caborca, Sonoíta (Sonoitac), and Sáric. The pressure of an expanding colonial frontier severely limited Luis's freedom of movement and invaded the relative autonomy which the northern Pimas had enjoyed. Particularly abrasive were the missionaries' disciplinary measures that limited the polyga-mous largesse of a *cacique* like Luis and impinged on the dignity of Pima commoners.[49]

Luis of Sáric was not the only rebel leader, nor was he the supreme commander of a unified army. There were numerous *cabecillas* of separate bands of rebellious warriors; in preparation for the uprising, Luis had to negotiate with the leaders of different villages and *rancherías*.[50] After the movement was quelled, some Pimas returned to their pueblos, but others fled to the *monte* to forage for subsistence beyond the control of soldiers and priests. Bands of western Pimas remained allied with Seris; others imitated the Apaches in their assault on colonial settlements in the upper Santa Cruz drainage.

The Indians' tactics of guerrilla warfare effectively thwarted Spanish military policies and set undeniable limits on the colonial project. Im-perial designs to develop Sonora's potential mineral wealth remained substantially unfulfilled, and the Indians' destruction of property cut short the ambitions of individual miners and ranchers to accumulate wealth and establish a family patrimony.[51] If, however, as the frightened *vecinos* claimed, rebellious Indians pretended to eliminate all Spaniards from the province, their organization was not equipped to accomplish this, nor to sustain political autonomy over a wide territory. Although the Sonoran uprisings and military campaigns to the Cerro Prieto had reverberations in Sinaloa and Nueva Galicia, where the expulsion of the Jesuits created an upheaval in native communities as well, there were no lasting organic links among these different movements.[52] Alliances between *cabecillas* were fleeting, and each had limited authority over his followers. Moreover, the constant movement of scattered renegade bands, over time, weakened corporate institutions in the pueblos. Indian governors found themselves presiding over *aldeas* with a greatly reduced core of resident households; the dispersal of so many families in small *rancherías* dispelled the efficacy of their leadership and dissipated their control over the productive resources of the community. This process intensified during the critical period of transition from the colony to the republic.

The Opata Defense of Ethnic Space, 1790–1840

The Opatas' sense of territorial integrity gave rise to their collective claim to arable land and to their staunch defense of the internal governance of their communities. Their insistence on the indissoluble link between the material and political dimensions of their ethnic space led to an escalation of confrontations between the Opatas and the Spanish and Mexican authorities as well as to divisive conflicts within their pueblos. The 1790 confrontation in Bacerác, although quickly diffused, brought to the fore tensions that simmered beneath the Opatas' persistence as an ethnic nation.

On July 9, 1790, a crowd of Opatas had gathered in Tetahueca, a mission field where the wheat harvest was in progress. Juan Ignacio Gil Samaniego, *juez comisario*, advanced toward the Indians in his character as acting civil magistrate for the three villages of Bacerác, Bavispe, and Guachinera. Anticipating trouble, he had brought an escort—two Indian officials from Bavispe; the Opata troop commander, Josef de Tona, and two presidial soldiers, Manuel Pacheco and Juan Mazón; and the Spanish lieutenant of the Presidio de Bavispe, Lorenzo Peralta. In the village, Gil was joined by two *vecinos* who had settled in the valley and by Ygnacio Noperi, captain-general of the Opata nation. Together they walked to Tetahueca, where Bacerác's governor Josef Antonio Mascorta awaited them.

At "a full meeting of nearly the whole community," Gil questioned one of their members, Atanasio Zorrilla. He demanded to know if, the day before, Zorrilla had in fact rebuked and threatened Governor Mascorta and his *alguacil*, Nicolás Sánchez, while working in the field. When Zorrilla admitted that it was true, Gil ordered him to be tied and whipped. As the punishment was being administered, Captain Noperi asked: "What crime has this man committed for him to be punished so?" The magistrate rejoined, "Is it not enough for him to have offended his governor?" At that, Noperi turned to the crowd, raised his cane of office, and called out: "My people, what are you waiting for? Why do you not free this man? In the name of the king, let him go!"[53]

Captain Noperi's words galvanized the crowd. Manuel Pacheco rushed forward to cut the ropes that bound Zorrilla. When Gil tried to stop him, Pacheco brushed him aside and declared: "Where the king's name is heard, no one else commands." Gil called to Lorenzo Peralta for aid, but the lieutenant was nowhere to be found. As the people grew angrier, Governor Mascorta proffered his cane of office to the magistrate, but Gil refused to accept it. Rather, he made a judicious retreat, but not without remarking to Noperi: "You have fulfilled your obligation." Juez Comisario Gil and his party returned to Bacerác and from there proceeded to Bavispe, where he appealed to his superior, Teniente de Alcalde Mayor Gregorio Ortiz Cortés. Captain Noperi and his followers rode to Arizpe to lodge their complaint with the intendant-governor, Enrique de Grimarest, who reprehended Gil's actions and upheld Noperi's privileges and authority.

Teniente Ortiz's on-site investigation one month later clarified the accusations made by each of the contenders. Captain Noperi had embellished his petition to the intendant-governor by accusing Gil Samaniego of abusing the terms of employment for Indian laborers drawn from the pueblos. Bacerác residents including Governor Mascorta, however, exonerated Gil of any wrongdoing. In the course of the hearings, charges of a different nature mounted against Captain Noperi. Only a year earlier, the former intendant-governor Pedro Garrido y Durán had sternly reminded Noperi that his authority extended only to the military command of Opata militias recruited from the villages to patrol the area and forestall the threat of Apache raids. He was not to interfere in the internal governance of the pueblos. This reprimand came in the wake of several arbitrary acts committed by Noperi. He had humiliated a former governor of Bacerác and attempted to take away his cane of office. More recently, he had taken over the office of *juez de agua*—the office in charge of distributing irrigation water, traditionally reserved for village officials—and he had physically threatened Governor Mascorta in a public meeting of Bacerác *comuneros*.

The attempted flogging of Atanasio Zorrilla occurred because Governor Mascorta had prevailed on his missionary, Fray George Loreto, to request Gil Samaniego's intervention in order to discipline Zorrilla's insolence. Zorrilla seemed to defy all authority, whether native or Spanish, on principle. A year earlier, Gil Samaniego reported, when Captain Noperi had political authority in Bacerác, Zorrilla had challenged him publicly. At that time, Noperi himself had appealed to Gregorio Ortiz who, in turn, had ordered Zorrilla punished. While Zorrilla's behavior did not typify village attitudes, these events suggest that Opata commoners resented the exemptions their officials enjoyed from field labor on mission land. Furthermore, whipping, whether ordered by their own governors or by Spanish officers, was humiliating.[54]

The conflicts that surfaced in Bacerác stemmed from the convergence of overlapping spheres of authority on native highland communities. Figure 9.1 illustrates the areas of potential conflict among civilian, military, and religious authorities. At the center stands the Indian *cabildo*, established in the pueblos through the institution of the Spanish mission. Indian political officers (the village governors, alcaldes, and fiscales) were elected annually in the pueblos and received their canes of office from the missionary or the Spanish magistrate.[55] Elevated above the individual pueblos, the captain-general of the Opata nation represented a military authority subordinate to Spanish officers. The captain-general received his title from the Comandancia General de las Provincias Internas; he commanded the Opata captains of each pueblo and all native troops when on patrol. When the captains-general pressured Spanish authorities to grant them political authority in the villages from which they drew soldiers, they came into conflict with village governors. The Opata presidial companies established in Bavispe and Bacoachi

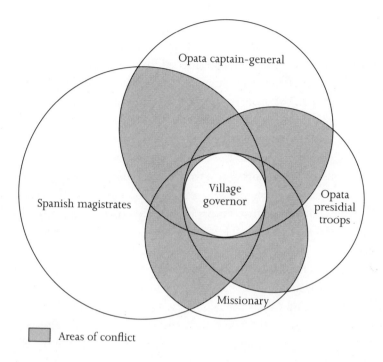

Figure 9.1. Overlapping spheres of authority: missionaries, villages, and military command

gave these soldiers *vecino* status and created yet another sphere of authority that enveloped the native pueblos.

Overshadowing the indigenous sectors of authority were the Spanish magistrates and the missionaries. The *alcaldes mayores, tenientes de justicia,* and *jueces comisarios* were local *vecinos* who, more often than not, lived in the mission pueblos. Although accountable to the intendant-governor, they exercised noticeable pressure on the communities. These magistrates assumed prerogatives that diminished the stature of native governors and undermined the moral authority of the resident priest. The missionaries who dealt with these increasingly complex layers of command repeatedly voiced their resentment at losing control over the "hijos del pueblo," even as they were held accountable for the administration of the mission economy. They came into open conflict with Spanish officials and local landowners who demanded Indian labor and with Opata captains over food supplies requisitioned for their military patrols.

Spanish colonialism superimposed all these spheres of authority on aboriginal political structures, which rested on kinship, respect for elders, and local chieftaincies. It is difficult to ascertain how Sonoran indigenous polities intersected with the colonial hierarchy. *Serrano* peoples personified leadership, as seen in the *caciques* who led hunting parties and commanded warriors drawn from clusters of villages, redistributed food and gifts, and negotiated with Spanish authorities. The canes of office bestowed on native officers by their colonial overlords were intended to legitimate their election under the rules established by the Iberian order. In practice, however, they elevated the persona of the governors and captains so distinguished and could either confirm indigenous political culture or signal their dependency on the colonial realm.[56]

The ambiguity surrounding political leadership of the *común* intensified after Mexican independence, when new legislation ordered the division of communal lands and questioned the legitimacy of village authorities. Sonoran state authorities created new legal precedents and took action to distribute village lands among individual households, reserving a "surplus" of arable land for auction to the *vecinos*.[57] Land tenure itself became embroiled in a new source of contention created by the distinction between *hijos de pueblo* and citizens, a legal separation that defined opposing avenues to acquiring property. Village holdings were further complicated by land rentals to non-Indians, arranged through contracts with individual residents or with the *común*. These combined pressures, added to the increasing burden of Apache patrols on Opata pueblos during the 1820s and 1830s, when the state government failed to support the peace encampments, pushed *serrano* leaders to petition the governors of Occidente and Sonora for redress, appealing their cause to the president of Mexico. When negotiations failed, the Opatas turned to armed rebellion.

In the final years of the intendancy system, Opata warriors reversed their celebrated loyalty to the colonial regime and defied orders to send them on a military mission to Baja California. Minor skirmishes occasioned by the arrest of these soldiers and the retaliation of a faction of Opatas who held the Presidio de Bavispe for a week in 1818, flared into open warfare two years later. Armed Opata bands occupied Mobas, Tónichi, and the mining placers of San Antonio de la Huerta; they turned Tónichi into a fortified base from which they threatened the entire region of eastern Sonora. It took the combined royalist troops of Durango, Sonora, and Chihuahua to defeat the Opatas in the battle of Arivechi, November 16, 1820, leaving 100 Indians dead and taking 240 prisoners.[58]

After the formal constitution of the state of Occidente in 1824, hostilities erupted again between the Opatas and local militias of *vecinos*. Although Opata warriors still served in the presidial rolls maintained to patrol the Apache frontier, *vecinos* like Ygnacio Samaniego, the *alcalde* of Bavispe, openly questioned their efficacy and complained of the Indians' "arrogance," presumably because they were permitted to carry arms. Samaniego went so far as to propose disbanding the Opata presidial company at Bavispe—in effect, abandoning the colonial pact that had endured between the Spanish Empire and the Opata nation. The Indians, for their part, withdrew from state and ecclesiastical institutions. Opatas of Guachinera, where no *vecinos* lived, refused to pay the tithe and ignored their priest's entreaties to send for him with a military escort in order to celebrate Mass and hear their confessions. Town officials in a wide corridor from Bavispe and Guásabas to Saguaripa and Mulatos (Chihuahua) nervously exchanged communications during the spring and early summer of 1825, surveying the movements of Opata bands led by Juan Dórame and Francisco Solano. The *vecinos* anticipated armed assaults against ranches and mines in Sonora and Chihuahua, and were especially fearful of an allied movement of Opatas and Tarahumaras. If, in fact, the Opatas were planning a revolt, they dispersed and returned to their pueblos in July, after the arrest of Solano near Oposura, although Dórame remained at large.[59]

From 1825 to 1833, bands of Opata and Yaqui rebels engaged presidial troops under the authority of the Comandancia Militar de Occidente in numerous skirmishes. These uprisings, occurring simultaneously with new Apache incursions through the sierra, seriously shook the fledgling government, but state troops suppressed the Indians' movement by capturing and executing their leaders. The Opata warriors Juan Dórame, Dolores Gutiérrez, Luis Calderón, Juan Güiriso, Antonio Baiza, and Miguel and Bautista Sol joined forces with the famed Yaqui *cabecilla* Juan Banderas in a call to arms to form an autonomous ethnic state in the Sonoran highlands. Militantly opposed to the division of communal lands and to new taxes imposed by the state government, they sought to restore the colonial mission regime in their villages and, with it, the traditional *común*.[60]

During this same period, state authorities eliminated the office of captain-general of the Opata nation, thereby diminishing the Opatas' military status on the frontier.[61] Of more profound significance, Sonoran governors implemented a radical division of village lands in the Sonora river valley and the districts of Saguaripa and Arivechi. Law 89 (1828) of the state of Occidente and subsequent legislation enacted by the state of Sonora brought irrevocable changes to Opata and Eudeve villages, separating peasant cultivators into classes of *vecinos* and Indians, smallholders and landless "proletarians."[62] The severity of the schism created in the *serrano* pueblos is evident in the language of the Opatas' formal protests directed to state and national authorities. While some Indian cultivators requested the partition of village lands in order to acquire legal title to the *milpas* they had in cultivation, sensing the growing pressures of *vecinos* who demanded ever larger portions of cropland and pastures, a number of traditionalist leaders pressed the government to restore to them the power to distribute farming plots and exercise authority in their pueblos as was the custom under the colonial regime. Rebellious *cabecillas* like Juan Güiriso, one of the last Opata captains-general, emerged from these divided communities and rose to power on the momentum of intravillage conflict.[63]

Opata leaders protested the loss of village land, the disintegration of the *común*, and the corrosion of their authority as parts of the same process. They denounced the bitter divisions between "indios de campana" and "indios ciudadanos" that arose as a result of legislation permitting Indians to seek the status of citizenship, obtain title to individual farming plots, and opt out of the communal obligations that had sustained their communities. Land rentals provoked further discord in the pueblos, yet the conventions regulating their cost and distribution illustrate the values that Indians ascribed to the land. Opatas in the Sonora Valley, for example, proposed renting small arable plots to *vecinos* according to quotas set by the amount of wheat that could be sown in them, rather than by auction, as was the custom. The price for larger tracts of land, however (viz., more than ten fanegas de sembradura), would be bid in public auction. They distinguished between poor peasants who, like themselves, sought access to land, and landowning vecinos who used village resources to expand their operations beyond their own properties.[64]

In 1831, Opata representatives met with President Anastasio Bustamante, who granted them an executive order directing the governor of Sonora to recognize their communities' fundo legal and to restore alienated land to their villages. But state authorities ignored the president's ruling: the partition of village lands continued apace, often with recourse to violence. The villages of Cumpas and Oposura, for example, fell victim to the commercial ambitions of their priest, Don Julián Moreno. Notwithstanding their colonial title to mission land and effective occupation of the last remaining irrigated labor the Indians of Cumpas had under cultivation, Moreno enlisted the support of state troops to force the Opatas to give up their claim to this field.[65]

In July 1836, José Anrríquez, the governor of Cumpas, and Juan Ysidro Bohórquez, "a native of Oposura representing himself and thirty-six pueblos that constitute the Opata nation," presented two formal petitions to the secretary of state and the Congress in Mexico City. Their reasoning linked the core problem of the land with their own status as leaders of their people. They upheld a holistic sense of peasant autonomy, a political order that receded from their grasp in this time of transition marked by changing agrarian structures and a new configuration of power. Both leaders gave a detailed account of the violent usurpation of arable land in Cumpas; they staunchly defended the village's claim to communal holdings and underscored the Indians' need for irrigated land. First, let us hear Anrríquez:

> More than 500 souls live in this pueblo and its outlying rancherías, and it is impossible for so many people to subsist solely on dryland dependent on rainfall (tierras de temporal). . . . Father Moreno [in contrast] has no need of this little piece of land, since he owns three or four ranches, an area so large that he has much more than he can use. . . . By dint of Law 89, [state authorities] have forced us to leave the field we have referred to and move to other land so dry that it is good only

for pasturing cattle. But what we want is to sow our crops in land having permanent water.[66]

Bohórquez, for his part, denounced the corruption of the Sonoran executive, which served only the interests of the governor's extended family and friends. Naming the leading families of the regional oligarchy, he asked rhetorically who had benefited from Mexico's independence:

> We Indians, in the epoch of liberty, live more oppressed than when we were subjugated [to colonial rule]. There was independence for the Morenos, Escalantes, Morales and Escobosos, but not for us. I say this because in those times they never took away our property, but now the communities are deprived of their land and do not receive justice.[67]

In the Opatas' view, the material base of their agrarian communities was necessarily linked to the religious and social foundations of their ethnic polity.[68] Accompanying the appeals by Anrríquez and Bohórquez were equally vehement letters from three representatives of Aconchi, who lamented the division of communal lands and the acrimonious separation of villagers into "vecinos" and "los de campana." They petitioned the federal government to send them a minister "favorable to our salvation" who would observe the Holy Doctrine integrally; to restore their village lands, observing colonial landmarks; to ensure that their elected officers be persons of their own nation and pueblo, not *vecinos* or strangers; to allow them to use corporal punishment; to exempt them from paying ecclesiastical fees; and to provide that Indians who had chosen citizenship be obliged to leave their pueblos.[69] In effect, what they demanded was a return to the mission regime that had crumbled in the previous decade, to be replaced by the new political order of municipalities.

The secretary of state responded to the Opata demands with a new order, reiterating Bustamante's directive of 1831, but in ambiguous terms referring merely to compliance with the law.[70] By midcentury, the Opatas had lost their communal lands, and within a few decades their ethnic territory was considerably eroded. The Opata nation suffered disintegration not because they lacked a sense of their own history or political acumen, but rather because the power structure they confronted had surpassed economically and militarily the resources they could marshal in defense of their ethnic community.

A parallel drama unfolded during these same years in northwestern Sonora, where Tohono O'odham leaders articulated a defense of community in terms that recalled the temporal and religious order established by the missions. Captain Tegeda and the *alcaldes* of Caborca and Pitiquito described the deplorable state of their pueblos in a letter they penned to the last remaining friar in the Pimería Alta who, in turn, forwarded it to Governor Manuel Escalante y Arvizu.[71] They denounced the illusory equality between Indians and *vecinos* that accelerated the Indians' flight from their pueblos. As O'odham farmer-gatherers seized the freedom to wander or work wherever they wished, "their lands are taken over by all who care to enter our villages." For this same reason the Pima missions of San Ignacio, Sáric, Tubutama, and Oquitoa were devoid of Indians. As their communal irrigation systems fell into disrepair, foraging populations turned to robbery, preying on the cattle herds of missions, presidios, and ranches.

During the winter of 1834–35, unusual flooding had destroyed canals and arable fields in the Altar-Asunción-Concepción drainage. Because their repair required a manpower which the villages could no longer muster, Captain Tegeda and the *alcaldes* prevailed on the state governor (through their missionary) to allow them to recall Indian peones who worked on the haciendas to come to their pueblos, and to restrain hacendados from preventing their return. This would bring wandering Tohono O'odham back to Caborca to build irrigation weirs, reclaim sufficient land for their support, and live once more in their villages. Tegeda demanded that native governors be authorized to determine which lands could be rented of those which had been left vacant through death or migration, offering them first to Indians "who were learning Christian doctrine and contemplating baptism" and secondly to "good *vecinos* who will work the land and live there permanently." Echoing the Opatas' scale of values noted above, he suggested that Indian officers charge a "just rent" to ranchers who grazed cattle on mission land and distribute the harvests gathered each year among native residents. Captain Tegeda both assured Governor Escalante that "in Caborca, there are Indians capable of good administration" and warned him that "wandering Pápagos, who have no pueblo and live like vagabonds," were forced to steal livestock from the Presidio de Altar and nearby ranches. Escalante, however, rejected the Indians' petition, arguing that returning hacienda workers to their pueblos would have altered "the natural course of events."[72] The governor's words had a hollow ring five years later, when repeated fractious accusations of cattle theft by Tohono O'odham and Mexicans alike led to skirmishes and armed revolt in the mining camps between Sonoíta and Quitobac, northwest of Caborca. In the early 1840s the northern Pima pueblos continued to crumble, the last of their missionaries left the zone, and the Hiach'eD and Tohono O'odham retreated further into the desert, living effectively beyond the control of Sonoran authorities.[73]

Conclusions

These divergent patterns of mobilization over two centuries of Sonoran history reveal multiple layers of conflict within and across the Indian/ Spanish divide that embroiled *serrano* communities in the struggle for material and cultural survival. Tribal entities such as the Opatas, Pimas, Apaches, Seris, and Yaquis alternatively allied and fought with one another, joined forces with Spanish and Mexican presidial troops, or rebelled against the colonial and national states. Inter- and intravillage strife punctuated political relations among different indigenous pueblos and between them and the dominant society. Notwithstanding the strong correlation between ethnic rebellion and Spanish and Mexican encroachments on Indian lands, this condition by itself is not sufficient to predict episodes of armed revolt.[74]

Sonoran highland and desert peoples expressed contradictory responses to the missions, combining hostility with guarded allegiance. The numerous skirmishes and desertions reported for the Sibubapas, as well as the major uprisings of Yaquis and Pimas chronicled above, show that Indians resented the personal (and occasionally despotic) authority of the missionaries. At times, they vented their anger by destroying or desecrating religious imagery and even by murdering their priests. More striking, over the long run, was their adaptation of mission structures to the ongoing enterprise of community. The traditional order that Opatas and Tohono O'odham struggled to conserve against the tide of Mexican

Liberalism during the nineteenth century was firmly rooted in the colonial mission.

Because the *serrano* peoples' vision was focused on the community, their notions of polity were linked to village governance. During the Yaqui revolt of 1740 and the Opata political movements of the 1820s and 1830s, Indians demanded the freedom to elect their own officers and to banish outsiders from their pueblos. "Outsiders" were non-Indians— Spaniards, *castas*, and *mestizos* who were socially and racially distinct from indigenous *comuneros*—as well as their own brethren who had chosen to be citizens and therefore no longer shared in the work required to maintain the *común*. Ambiguity blurred the differences between "insiders" and "outsiders" and diminished the power of Indian leaders as the ethnic communities became more and more entwined with the colonial order and, following independence, with the Mexican state. Conflicting spheres of authority—military, ecclesiastical, and civilian— impinged on village governance and set the conditions for armed revolt.

Indigenous and peasant rebellions do not suddenly erupt from an otherwise peaceful landscape: they emerge from a context of ongoing resistance. Oppressed peoples mobilize at different levels of intensity and display a wide variety of overt actions; in Sonora, these included flight, small localized revolts, and regional uprisings. The present chapter has outlined a chronology of conflict and resistance from the mid-seventeenth to the mid-nineteenth century in order to discern the values that *serrano* peoples defended over the long term of historical change. Their cultural "goods," rooted in kinship and territory and linked to the internal structures of household and community, defined the basic elements of ethnic consciousness. The transition from colonial to national rule marked a critical juncture for collective action, one at which the opposing discourses of indigenous communities and propertied elites clashed in an open struggle for power.[75]

To what ends did Sonoran peoples mobilize? What did they seek to accomplish when they assumed the risks of rebellion? The Seris, desert-dwelling Cunca'ac, wanted autonomy. They defended zones of refuge beyond the limits of the established colony, where they maintained a nomadic way of life until the mid-twentieth century.[76] The Opatas, Eudeves, and highland Pimas, agricultural communities that were both exploited and supported by the colonial economy, upheld what they considered to be a pact of reciprocal services and obligations, defended their village lands, and claimed certain privileges connected with military service and the missions (e.g., the right to bear arms and exemption from paying tribute and the tithe). *Serrano* pueblos articulated a number of interrelated demands at different historical moments, bringing together issues of polity, religion, and material subsistence. At times their content was transmuted—as, for example, in the Opatas' parallel appeals for restoration of communal lands, observance of Catholic ritual, and local autonomy.[77]

Sonoran patterns of mobilization marked a set of political actions and a mode of warfare calculated to force concessions from the colonial regime and to weaken the Spaniards' hold over their territory. Accommodation and mobilization were two related dimensions of the "arts of resistance" that highland peasants developed under domination. The degrees of freedom they accomplished, however, were limited. Autonomous Indian communities faded from the Sonoran landscape by mid-nineteenth century, even before the Juárez–Lerdo legislation (1854–57) radically changed the legal framework for land tenure at the national level. Peasant families of Pima, Opata, and Eudeve ancestry persisted in the *ranchero* economy of nineteenth-century Sonora, but community institutions lost control over basic resources and were absorbed into larger political structures.

This "history from below" illustrates unforeseeable and, at times, contradictory outcomes of ethnogenesis and cultural change. The *serrano* peoples of mid nineteenth-century Sonora had not retreated into ethnic enclaves, nor were they mere relics of an "authentic" indigenous past. Their story did not move in linear progression; rather it combined elements of both continuity and change, persistence and loss. And through its twists and turns, the Sonoran highlanders refashioned their identity in response to concrete historical conjunctures. Their choices did not clearly embrace accommodation or resistance, but alternated between these two polarities.

The Indians participated in their own subjugation by assimilating to colonial institutions and practices, as seen in their accommodation to mission life, in their use of legal petitions, and in their military service in defense of the imperial realm. In numerous occasions we have seen that Indian governors, holding aloft the canes of office that invested them with authority, voiced an eloquent tribute to the religious and political structures established by the missions in order to salvage their communities in the face of undeniable material and human impoverishment. Governor Bohórquez of Oposura and Captain Tegeda of Caborca, in their reasoned opposition to the aggressive policies of Mexican Liberalism, turned the symbols of the old Jesuit order to a staunch defense of ethnic territory.

Military service provided another point of intersection between the *serrano* indigenous polities and the Spanish state. The Bourbon regime used Indian auxiliaries and presidial foot soldiers as a means of lowering the costs of frontier defense, while Opata and Pima warriors fought alongside the presidials to regain (or conserve) the insignia of military ranking and prestige. Nomadic frontiers that remained porous through the incessant wars against the Apaches and the Seris opened avenues of negotiation with the colonial powers for the *serrano* communities living within the orbit of Spanish dominion. Moreover, the lines between nomadism and sedentarism became blurred, as illustrated by the Sobaípuris, Pápagos, and Sibubapas—different groups of Pima-speakers ranging in area from the desert to the highlands—who moved in and out of the mission communities. Their patterns of flight, rebellion, and negotiation pointed away from accommodation to armed resistance for those who accepted the harsh life of foraging in the *monte*.

Sonoran peoples articulated a subaltern discourse through their actions, in search of autonomy and more advantageous terms of negotiation. That Spanish control over these disperse and varied peoples was tenuous, at best, is revealed in the candid testimony of presidial captains like Bernardo de Urrea and Lorencio Cancio, who knew the province well. They admitted the futility of their military campaigns against mobile bands of guerrilla rebels. The enemy was numerous and fleet of foot, and often well-informed of the Spaniards' movements. The Indians' resistance was rooted in the land itself, sustained by their intimate knowledge of the terrain and by the bonds of kinship that connected scattered bands of fugitives in ever-wider networks of *parientes*. The same historical actors tested both alternatives of accommodation and resistance, and their choices had important implications for the ecological and cultural boundaries of their world.

Conclusions: Contested Space

Those who go through the desolate valley will find it a place of springs, for the early rains have covered it with pools of water.

Psalms 84:1–6

Serrano peoples depended on the confluence of land, water, and labor to grow their crops and harvest the desert. Their livelihood required spatial mobility and a wide range of wild and cultivated resources in the semiarid environment of northwestern Mexico. Spanish colonialism worked long-term structural changes in the ecological and social relations of production that diverted labor from essential subsistence tasks and shrank the resource base on which Sonoran communities relied for their own reproduction. The expansion of a market economy in this frontier province during the second half of the eighteenth century prompted a conjuncture of events that deepened the crisis of survival for indigenous peasants. Not only did Bourbon policies increase the burdens placed on Indian communities, but they altered the mode of exploitation by commodifying land and labor. The period of transition between colonial and national rule witnessed the impoverishment of native pueblos, leading to economic dependency and a dispersal of the cultural nuclei of household and community.

Social ecology provides a conceptual framework for analyzing the full import of these processes of change, encompassing both the colonial policies to which peasant communities were subjected and the responses they developed to adapt and resist. Understood as a complex web of relations among different indigenous peoples and between them and their Spanish overlords in reference to the land they occupied, the concept gives meaning to the values that *serrano* pueblos espoused and to the political struggles in which they engaged. Their discourse in defense of the *común*—reiterated in written petitions, ritualized in syncretic religious ceremonialism, and politicized in the internal governance of the pueblos—was concerned as much with the economic components of subsistence as with the social and cultural parameters of community. The Sonoras' holistic sense of livelihood conflicted with the demands for surplus product and labor emanating from the colonial system. At issue was a basic question: To what ends should the productive energy of peasants be applied? How could physical survival and the ceremonial and political needs of their communities be reconciled to the taxable surpluses required by Church and Crown?

The durability of the mission system played no small role in the ecological and economic relations that bound highland villages to the colonial structures gradually imposed in Sonora. Jesuit and Franciscan administration of the *temporalidades* was intended to support a corporate system of agrarian production. To that end, missionaries marketed the surpluses generated by the Indians' labor and invested the income in church construction and in merchandise that was redistributed in the pueblos. The ecclesiastical and secular commercial circuits that linked the missions with colonial settlements were closely intertwined, and their combined networks of exchange defined the regional contours of northwestern Mexico.

The collapse of the mission economy during the last quarter of the eighteenth century had serious implications for peasant livelihood, despite the Sonoras' ambivalent stance toward the missions. Highland villagers had accepted the mission system as a way of rebuilding their communities after the destructive phase of conquest, but they never depended solely on the missions for their own sustenance. *Serrano* pueblos combined agriculture with foraging and sought out colonial markets to sell their grains and obtain seasonal work. The missions raised overall levels of production in the riverine villages, but burdened individual households with increased demands for their labor to such an extent that the missionaries' market orientation undermined the corporate nature of the agrarian economy they so resolutely tried to maintain. Nevertheless, the communal administration of peasant labor by the missionaries and Indian governors provided a fundamental rationale for the ongoing effort to sustain the *común*. And that rationale, in itself, helped to mediate the conflict between livelihood and surplus in the pueblos. In this light, Opata and Tohono O'odham appeals to Sonoran state governors in the 1830s—to respect communal landholdings and endorse the return of hacienda laborers to their communities—implied nothing less than the restoration of work regimes first established under the auspices of the missions.

In their dealings with the missions and Spanish enterprises, *serrano* peoples both embraced and resisted the commodification of village production, so closely tied to the ecological roots of their subsistence economy. If, indeed, native peasants approached the market desirous of colonial trade goods (especially cloth), they sought out new avenues for selling their grain and their own labor in the mines and haciendas *as an alternative means of survival.* Highland villagers developed partial linkages to the market, but the minimum requirements for sustaining their households came from their own *milpas*, foraging, and nonmarket trade with nomadic Indian groups from beyond the confines of the established colony. The accumulation of wealth that had monetary value in the colonial market, such as stored grain, livestock, processed food and fibers, tanned hides, pottery, and woven cloth, altered the orientation of peasant economy, but not its baseline objective: subsistence.

The colonial economy propelled indigenous pueblos toward modified forms of simple commodity production. Bourbon policies changed the allocation of labor, undermining the rotational work obligation that was consonant with village custom and mission discipline, and replacing it with wage labor (paid mostly in kind). Yaqui leaders negotiating with Governor Manuel Bernal de Huidobro, in 1740, demanded the freedom to sell their crops independently of the missionary and to leave their pueblos and work in the mines for periods of time of their own choosing. Not infrequently, mission Indians sold their grain through itinerant merchants (*rescatadores*) who controlled the terms of exchange. Furthermore, we have seen that during the final decades of the eighteenth century Opata warriors relied increasingly on their salaries as presidial soldiers to support their families and communal obligations. It is equally significant that following the expulsion of the Jesuits, under Franciscan administration, Indians demanded a wage for any skilled labor they performed in the missions.

Simple commodity production, together with labor remunerated in commodities or in money which could be exchanged for goods in the colonial market, led to the internal differentiation of household and village units and to the stratification of the Sonoran peasantry by gender, race, and economic status.[1] *Serrano* men were drawn into wage labor as mineworkers, muleteers, hacienda peones, and soldiers. Indigenous women, by contrast, worked in the *milpas*, ground corn, prepared food, and wove cloth in the missions. They, too, left the villages, but not as wage earners; rather, they foraged and hunted small game in the *monte*. Children of working age participated in all domestic tasks and probably were "lent" to *vecino* households as servants.[2] These gendered work patterns generally held true, notwithstanding the migration of entire *rancherías* to the *reales de minas* where their subsistence strategies became even more closely tied to the colonial economy.

Peasants and Indians in Sonora

The individualization and commodification of *serrano* labor and production deepened racial and economic divisions among peasant smallholders. In Sonora, as in other rural contexts, peasants were not a singular class; rather, they were historical actors who figured collectively in a complex process of class formation. Peasants *and* Indians were defined in terms of their relationship to the land and to their communities. Intra- and interethnic conflicts, working in counterpoint to European conquest and colonization, altered the material conditions of peasant life and changed the very meaning and internal structure of indigenous communities.

The analysis of property relations, corporate villages, and individual peasant units presented in Chapters 6 and 7 prompts us to ask: What were the linkages between Indian and Hispanized peasants? What were the barriers that separated them? Are we dealing with two distinct strata of, on the one hand, indigenous commoners relegated to a diminished land base and increasingly dependent on the sale of their labor for survival and, on the other hand, Hispanic households of simple commodity producers who regularly sold a portion of their crops and livestock, solicited credit, and grappled with land values set by the market?

It is clear that by the late eighteenth century, *serrano* pueblos were racially mixed villages of peasant smallholders with competing claims to material resources. Rival notions of property—the ancestral holdings of the *común* and individually held land grants and purchases—infused the very meaning of community and fueled conflict in the pueblos, as evidenced by the acerbic confrontations between "hijos de campana" and "indios vecinos" recounted in Chapter 9. That land itself became a commodity only toward the end of the period under study is reflected by sharply rising prices in recorded sales at mid-nineteenth century. Notwithstanding the accumulation of wealth by a small network of notable families and the concomitant dispossession of Indian and mestizo smallholders, this secular process created linkages of dependency and interdependency among the provincial elite, Hispanized labradores, and the remnants of serrano communities vis-à-vis access to cropland, pastures, and seasonal labor.

Indigenous leaders displayed considerable tenacity in defending their corporate landholdings, and their arguments concerning the integrity of communal property reiterated the concept of ethnic territory in the face of powerful economic and political opponents. The political discourse that emerged in the nineteenth century reinterpreted the serrano peoples' basic cultural values in new social circumstances. Their claims to an ethnic patrimony rested on the principles of kinship, reciprocity, and redistribution in order to ensure the reproduction of households and communities. Within an ethic of reciprocity it was understood that los parientes were precisely those persons who could both demand and give food and labor when needed. Thus, the Sonoras' basic social unit— the extended family, or ranchería de parientes—had a flexible size and composition. It expanded and contracted according to need and specific circumstances.[3]

The cyclical nature of household formation in Sonora, as evidenced in the reconstitution of domestic units through exogamy and miscegenation, reflected the enduring cultural values of serrano peoples as well as the impact of colonial domination on indigenous society. If, indeed, the pueblo de indios recognized by law and incorporated into the missions was a creation of the colonial order,[4] and if formal community institutions had declined in Sonora by the late eighteenth century, highland villagers re-created their communities in new ways. Migration stimulated both spatial and social mobility as Indians moved from one pueblo to another, shuttled from the missions to mines and ranches, and formed breakaway rancherías in the sierra. The displacement of cooperative labor arrangements by commodified forms of production and wage dependency led to the impoverishment and dispersal of the serrano pueblos. In a parallel process, however, these same pueblos reconstituted their ethnicity in smaller village units.

A Contested Hegemony

Indian leaders transposed the cultural values of reciprocity and redistribution that governed village life to a wider political plane in their effort to articulate the terms of a colonial pact with the Spanish Crown. There was no denying that any notion of a compact between the Spanish Imperium and the indigenous polities began with the basic condition of colonialism itself: conquest and subordination. Colonial authorities and provincial elites saw the indigenous peoples as an inferior social stratum, confined to the juridical category of *indio* and destined to perform physical labor.[5] *Serrano* village governors and militia captains saw their communities as *naciones* subordinate to, but recognized within, the colonial matrix and having guarantees of autonomy and material subsistence.

Following the juridical and economic innovations introduced under Mexican rule, *serrano* pueblos attempted to redefine their relation to the state and mounted a concerted opposition to the accumulation of property by landed entrepreneurs who undermined their communal patrimony. Indian pueblos were divided among themselves even as they defended their claim to the basic resources of land and water. The arguments voiced by the Opata governors of Oposura and Cumpas when they addressed state and national authorities in the 1830s did not express the unanimous opinion of the thirty-six pueblos they claimed to represent. Rather, theirs was an alternative political stance forged out of discordant voices within the Indian communities.[6] Two opposing sets of principles were at war in the formulation of a subaltern discourse, related to different means of gaining access to land and to the very identity of the community. While traditionalists upheld the corporate nature of local polities and affirmed their redistributive functions, a significant minority of villagers viewed themselves as individual citizens and recipients of an exclusive *hijuela* to a plot of cropland.

If the highland peoples developed a "hidden transcript" in their refuges beyond Spanish and Mexican surveillance, we are not privy to

those discussions nor did they leave a written record.[7] We can, however, discern from their public statements the cultural norms and values
that bound their ethnic identity to the community. Serrano leaders confronted the Sonoran ruling elite by ascribing alternative meanings to a
common lexicon, as illustrated by their use of terms like nación and libertad. Juan Ysidro Bohórquez defended a holistic concept of ethnic space
when he claimed to speak for the Opata nation, an entity distinct from
the Mexican nation-state.[8] While the Sonoran notables construed liberty
as the unrestricted freedom for individuals to accumulate wealth, Opata
leaders rendered it as a collective liberty, the security needed for the reproduction of their communities. In their perception, the state should
serve as a protective adjudicator in recognition of reciprocal obligations
between those who hold power through the institutions of government
and subordinate ethnic peoples. In that spirit, wrote Bohórquez:

> Filled with confidence, the Opata pueblos of Sonora have sent me to
> ask Your Excellency to take measures to return their lands to the vil-
> lages that have been dispossessed [of them], and to make those who
> rule in Sonora understand that Your Excellency, as the Supreme Chief
> of the Mexican Nation, order them to treat us well and not to take
> away our properties.
>
> I entreat Your Excellency to send a person of confidence from the
> high government to Sonora, to recognize the titles that the Opata
> pueblos hold to their fundo legal, so that once Your Excellency is in-
> formed of the usurpations they have suffered, their lands shall be re-
> turned to them.

Bohórquez addressed President Anastasio Bustamante in words that his
forebears might have directed to the viceroy: he used the colonial honor-
ific "Your Excellency," and closed his petition with assurances of respect
for the president of the Mexican Republic "as the sovereign father of all
[his] subjects."[9] His language bespoke a hierarchical triad that bound
together the Opata pueblos, the Sonoran state government, and Mexican
national institutions within an implicitly gendered model of patriarchy.
His insistence on nación reinforced the Opatas' claim to their communal
lands and to political autonomy.

Borhorquez defended the corporate territorial community, notwithstanding the fact that nineteenth-century serrano pueblos were hetero-

geneous, comprising a mixed population of *castas*, *criollos*, and Indians. Furthermore, many of them were recently settled *rancherías*, shifting in location and composition without continuous links to their indigenous past.[10] The Opata defense of community combined traditionalist and innovative elements. While their cultural nucleus focused on the pueblos as corporate bodies, the Opatas sought political alliances that extended beyond the confines of the community. Facing the pressures exerted by Sonoran notables and state authorities to usurp their communal lands and invalidate their village polity, Indians appealed to the national government and tried to forge a regional web of leadership under the rubric of the "Opata nation." Although defeated militarily and outmaneuvered politically, *serrano* peoples like the Opatas and Yaquis attempted to redefine their ethnic territory under the conditions imposed on them by the emerging Mexican state.

These central themes of community, ethnicity, and class illustrate the secular process of long-term structural change under colonial and post-colonial regimes. This study shows how one frontier colony, slowly and unevenly, was integrated into a commercial economy that was itself moving toward capitalist forms of commodity production. Both the structural and the agential components of change documented here for Sonora point to the confrontational nature of the process and bear comparison with other European colonies in the Americas. The alteration of cultural norms and economic practices at the micro level of provinces, with its attendant process of class formation, is necessarily related to changing modes of production at the macro level of empires and world systems. The envelopment of Mexico's major industries and distributive circuits by European metropoles—typified by the Spanish fiscal and mercantile extraction of wealth from New Spain and the British penetration of the Mexican economy during the formative years of the Republic—both required and accelerated radical changes in communities and provinces, moving in the direction of higher levels of commercialization.

These global processes set in motion multiple dimensions of conflict at the provincial level. The social ecology of peasant survival linked the materialist concerns of livelihood to the politics of resistance.[11] *Serrano* peoples' cultural responses to economic and political changes created new expressions of ethnic as well as class consciousness and ascribed alternative meanings to the central concepts of community and property. Their survival strategies and modes of resistance retarded and altered the projects of economic expansion and political domination advanced by Spanish colonialists and Mexican landed elites. The analysis of Sonoran peasant economy, in turn, bears on the wider spectrum of Mexican history at the close of the colonial era. This purposefully detailed focus on the Sonoran highlands affords a clear perspective of the structural changes that underlay the political upheavals of the early nineteenth century.[12]

Our view from the periphery opens new avenues of research on the transition to modernity and the development of the capitalist world system. Social ecology provides a conceptual framework that balances the structural approach of global capitalist models by underscoring the complexity of the process and highlighting the ways in which the human agency of diverse social groups influenced the outcome.[13] It integrates the dual process of class formation and ethnogenesis by bringing together diverse elements of socioeconomic differentiation and cultural production.[14] The genre of peasant studies in Latin America, both for the colonial and the national period, has developed impressively in recent years, contributing new empirical data and fresh interpretations of class and ethnic relations in widely heterogeneous societies. The methodology employed in this study bears comparison with research both on densely settled areas and on frontier provinces that recognizes the strategic importance of mobility for subordinate peoples in changing physical environments and that explores new meanings for the themes of community, livelihood, and nation.[15]

Notes

Preface

1 Sweet, "The Ibero-American Frontier Mission"; Bolton, "The Mission as a Frontier Institution in the Spanish-American Colonies."

2 The "school of borderlands studies," whose beginnings are associated with Herbert Eugene Bolton, now represents several generations of scholars. In U.S. academia the field of borderlands teaching and research, although traditionally treated as a subsection of U.S. history, is more recently forging ties to Latin American, Chicano/a, and Latino/a studies. See admirable summaries of both the history and the historiography by David J. Weber: *The Spanish Frontier in North America*; *The Mexican Frontier, 1821–1846*; and *Myth and History of the Hispanic Southwest*. The *Journal of the Southwest* (University of Arizona), among other regionally based journals, provides an important forum for critical writing on the discursive reinvention of "Southwest." INAH Sonora publishes the Noroeste de México series of original treatises on the history and anthropology of the region.

3 This discussion (perforce brief) is informed, in part, by recent essays and critiques represented by the following authors and works: Van Young, "To See Someone not Seeing: Historical Studies of Peasants and Politics in Mexico," "The Cuautla Lazarus: Double Subjectives in Reading Texts on Popular Collective Action," and "Dreamscape with Figures and Fences: Cultural Contention and Discourse in the Late Colonial Mexican Countryside"; Seed, "Colonial and Postcolonial Discourse" and "More Colonial and Postcolonial Discourses"; Mignolo, "Colonial and Postcolonial Discourse: Cultural Critique or Academic Colonialism?"; Adorno, "Reconsidering Colonial Discourse for Sixteenth- and Seventeenth-Century Spanish America"; Vidal, "The Concept of Colonial and Postcolonial Discourse"; Mallon, "The Promise and Dilemma of Subaltern Studies: Perspectives from Latin American History"; Prakash, "Subaltern Studies as Postcolonial Criticism" and "Introduction: After Colonialism"; Klor de Alva, "The Postcolonization of the (Latin) American Experience: A Reconsideration of 'Postcolonialism,' and 'Mestizaje' "; Silverblatt, "Becoming Indian in the Central Andes of Seventeenth-Century Peru."

4 Indeed, these very terms are open to debate. Mignolo ("Colonial and Postcolonial Discourse," p. 124) warns against confusing fields of study and

perspectives. Mallon ("The Promise and Dilemma of Subaltern Studies," pp. 1492) and Klor de Alva ("The Postcolonization of the [Latin] American Experience," p. 247–48) caution that the transference of postcolonial paradigms from the British sphere of colonization in southern Asia and Africa to the postindependence histories of Latin America is unwarranted without considerable contextualization. Likewise, Adorno ("Reconsidering Colonial Discourse," p. 144–45) argues that the Spanish conquest and early colonial period are qualitatively different from the Anglo-European "worlds of colonialism and postcolonialism."

5   This is what Mallon, for example, calls "riding many horses" ("The Promise and Dilemma of Subaltern Studies," pp. 1514–15), referring to the internal tension in subaltern studies between postmodernist criticism—implying a fragmentation of knowledge—and a politically committed project. Vidal ("The Concept of Colonial and Postcolonial Discourse," pp. 117–18) argues strongly for the unification of the "technocratic" and the "political" and warns against ignoring established categories or reducing the "political dimension of cultural analysis . . . to the textual deconstruction of authority under the guise of a crisis in the notion of social subjectivity."

6   Klor de Alva ("The Postcolonization of the [Latin] American Experience," pp. 254–63) points to the complex derivations of *colony* in Spanish America and underscores the ambivalent stance of the Hispanized elites toward the metropole and toward the indigenous and racially mixed *castas* they sought to control and exploit.

7   Prakash, "Subaltern Studies as Postcolonial Criticism," p. 1477; Mallon, "The Promise and Dilemma of Subaltern Studies," p. 1494. They both cite Ranajit Guha, "Preface," in Ranajit Guha & Gayatri C. Spivak, eds., *Selected Subaltern Studies* (New York: Oxford University Press, 1988, pp. 35–36).

8   Seed, "Colonial and Postcolonial Discourse," p. 183. Adorno ("Reconsidering Colonial Discourse," pp. 138–40) insists that documents are not merely descriptive but convey "assertive and interpretive values" and that they should be read with the same scrutiny as literary texts. Van Young ("Cuautla Lazarus," pp. 3–5) writes cogently of the skeptical reading of texts, with heightened awareness of the circumstances in which they were produced.

9   Van Young begins his essay "Dreamscape with Figures and Fences" with a challenge to reverse the "man–land" dyad and view the human presence in the New World (or anywhere else) as a cultural project. I would characterize my own work as "ecological history" rather than as "historical ecology," following the principles of cultural geography established by such accomplished practitioners as Carl O. Sauer and Robert West. In what may be yet another example of the differences between Anglo-American and Latin American historiographic traditions, I depart somewhat from the ap-

proach to environmental history developed by U.S. historians like William Cronon and Donald Worcester. Notwithstanding the magisterial quality of their work, their frame of reference cannot be simply transferred to the ecology of preindustrial northwestern Mexico. In a similar vein, Elinor Melville's *A Plague of Sheep*, on sixteenth-century central Mexico, is inspirational for my work, although our subject matter and time periods diverge.

Introduction: The Social Ecology of the Sonoran Frontier

1 Martínez-Alier, "Ecology and the Poor: A Neglected Dimension of Latin American History," p. 623.
2 In this work, I have defined the region of study in terms of the ethnic peoples who comprise its subjects and the territories they occupied. The methodology of regional history—ordering political, cultural, and economic systems within spatial and temporal frameworks—is a topic of lively discussion among scholars of different disciplines. See Van Young, ed., *Mexico's Regions. Comparative History and Development*; Sergio Ortega Noriega, "Reflexiones sobre metodología de la historia regional en México," paper presented at the Congreso de Historia Regional (Taxco, Guerrero, May 1993).
3 Sheridan, "The Limits of Power: The Political Ecology of the Spanish Empire in the Greater Southwest," pp. 153–71.
4 Frontiers exist in the mind and on the ground, as Peter Sahlins has shown for the peasants of Cerdanya in "The Nation in the Village," pp. 234–63. Weber, *The Spanish Frontier in North America*, p. 11, defines frontiers as "zones of interaction between two different cultures."
5 Powell, *La guerra chichimeca (1550–1600)*, pp. 165–78 et passim; González y González, *Pueblo en vilo*; Tutino, *From Insurrection to Revolution in Mexico. Social Bases of Agrarian Violence, 1750–1940*, pp. 47–60; Brading, *Haciendas and Ranchos in the Mexican Bajío: León, 1680–1860*; Bakewell, *Silver Mining and Society in Colonial Mexico: Zacatecas, 1546–1700*; Jiménez Pelayo, *Haciendas y comunidades indígenas en el sur de Zacatecas*, pp. 23–38.
6 Griffen, *Culture Change and Shifting Populations in Central Northern Mexico*; John, *Storms Brewed in Other Men's Worlds: The Confrontation of Indians, Spanish and French in the Southwest, 1540–1795*; Hall, *Social Change in the Southwest, 1350–1880*; Sheridan, "The Limits of Power," pp. 153–57.
7 Kirchhoff, "Mesoamérica: Sus límites geográficos, composición étnica, y caracteres culturales," pp. 92–107; Kirchhoff, "Gatherers and Farmers in the Greater Southwest: A Problem in Classification," pp. 529–50; Riley, *Frontier People*; Di Peso, *Casas Grandes: A Fallen Trading Center of the Gran Chichimeca*; Guevara Sánchez, *Arqueología del área de las Cuarenta Casas, Chihuahua*; Hedrick,

Kelley, and Riley, eds., *The North Mexican Frontier*; Riley and Hedrick, eds., *Across the Chichimec Sea*; Mathien and McGuire, eds., *Ripples in the Chichimec Sea. New Considerations of Southwestern–Mesoamerican Interactions*; McGuire and Villalpando, "Prehistory and the Making of History in Sonora," pp. 159–77.

8 Martínez-Alier, "Ecology and the Poor," pp. 622, 630–35, argues this same point in reference to peasant agriculture in the Andes. The notion of a language of resistance, discussed further below and developed at length in Chapter 9 below, is argued eloquently by James C. Scott in *Domination and the Arts of Resistance*.

9 Sheridan, in "The Limits of Power," uses the term *political ecology* to emphasize the limits placed on the advance of the Spanish Empire in the northern periphery of Mexico (see note 3 above). I use *social ecology* to connote the seeds of conflict over control of basic resources in the region. Our different meanings are not in opposition, but complement each other.

10 These three terms refer to non-Indians of different racial categories in colonial society. *Vecinos* were landholding residents of a given locality; whether or not they were literally of Spanish origin, they were Hispanic in their cultural and political orientation. *Gente de razón* ("people of reason") were distinguished from Indians in their civil status and legal obligations; racially they could be Spanish, *criollo* (American-born "whites"), or *mestizo* (a mixture of white and Indian). *Castas*, a term that appeared frequently in colonial documents generated in Sonora, included persons of mixed racial composition with Amerindian, European, and African antecedents.

11 Mallon, *The Defense of Community in Peru's Central Highlands*, pp. 3–11; Scott, *Domination and the Arts of Resistance*, pp. 14–23 et passim.

12 Wright, *Classes*, pp. 10–14; Smith, *Livelihood and Resistance*, passim.

13 In order to address the complexity of class formation, *mode of production* is used in this work to indicate the particular means of procuring resources and distributing them within a given society. This concept comprehends the organization of material life to mean both production in the literal sense—for example, agriculture, stockraising, and extractive industries—and resource procurement from hunting and gathering. Of interest here is the particular combination of social organization, technology, and natural conditions that determines levels of productivity, as well as the ways in which human societies direct labor power and apportion the means of production and the social product among their individual units. Relations of production involve ownership, possession, usufruct, and appropriation of both the means of survival and surplus wealth. In peasant societies the forces of production are closely related to the man–land relationship within specific ecosystems.

14 Collier, *Marriage and Inequality in Classless Societies*, esp. chap. 4, "Understand-

ing Inequality." Schryer, in *Ethnicity and Class Conflict in Rural Mexico*, pp. 17–26, discusses the intersection of class and ethnicity within a Marxist framework of analysis.

15 Collins, "Labor Scarcity and Ecological Change," pp. 19–37; Deere, "The Differentiation of the Peasantry and Family Structure: A Peruvian Case Study," pp. 422–37.

16 Wolf, *Peasant Wars of the Twentieth Century*; Orlove, "Against a Definition of Peasantries," pp. 22–35; Orlove and Custred, "Agrarian Economies and Social Processes in Comparative Perspective: The Agricultural Production Unit," pp. 13–29; Shanin, "Introduction," in Shanin, ed., *Peasants and Peasant Societies*, p. 6; Edleman, *Proletarian Peasants*, pp. 13–25. Warman, in *"We Come to Object,"* p. 5, argues that peasant identity "does not depend so much on the concrete job as on the nature of the relationships that regulate it."

17 *Rancheros* are a meaningful social category, closely related to that of peasants, for diverse regions of Latin America. Authoritative studies include González y González, *Pueblo en vilo*; Schryer, *The Rancheros of Pisaflores*; Craig, *The First Agraristas*; Lloyd, *El proceso de modernización capitalista en el noroeste de Chihuahua (1880–1910)*; Gudmundson, "Peasant, Farmer, Proletarian: Class Formation in a Smallholder Coffee Economy, 1850–1950," pp. 221–58; Gelman, "Producción campesina y estancias en el Río de la Plata colonial. La región de colonia a fines del siglo XVIII," pp. 41–65; and Gelman, "Los caminos del mercado: Campesinos, estancieros y pulperos en una región del Río de la Plata colonial," pp. 89–118.

18 This discussion of culture and ethnicity in changing historical contexts is based largely on the following authors: Geertz, *La interpretación de las culturas*; White, *Ethnological Essays*; Bourdieu, *Sociología y cultura*; Ortiz, *The Tewa World. Space, Time, Being and Becoming in a Pueblo Society*; Gosner, "Las élites indígenas en los altos de Chiapas (1524–1714)," pp. 405–23; Gosner, "Critical Perspectives on the Construction of Ethnic Identity: Debating 'Indian-ness' in Colonial Central America"; Merrill, *Rarámuri Souls. Knowledge and Social Process in Northern Mexico*; Alvarsson, "Ethnicity—Some Introductory Remarks," pp. 7–14; Mörner, "Etnicidad, movilidad social y mestizaje en la historia colonial hispanoamericana," pp. 29–44.

19 Andean scholars in particular have used the term *ethnogenesis* to express the reconstitution of ethnic identity in different historical moments: Stern, *Peru's Indian Peoples and the Challenge of Spanish Conquest. Huamanga to 1640*; Powers, *Andean Journeys*. See also Hobsbawm, "Introduction: Inventing Traditions," in Hobsbawm and Ranger, eds., *The Invention of Tradition*, pp. 1–14.

20 Pauline Turner Strong, in "Captivity in White and Red," applies the notion of cultural convergence and commingling to her discussion of Indian–white relations in North America.

21 Richard White defines *nation* in similar terms for the Mississippian Choctaw peoples (*The Roots of Dependency*, p. 2).

22 Pérez de Rivas, *Historia de los triunfos de nuestra santa fé*, vol. 2, p. 199.

23 Similar interpretations of the Pueblos of New Mexico and the Maya of
Yucatán are set forth by Gutiérrez, *When Jesus Came, the Corn Mothers Went Away*,
pp. xxi–xix, 22; and by Farriss, "Nucleation versus Dispersal," pp. 187–216.

24 Farriss, in *Maya Society under Colonial Rule*, pp. 117–46, observes both centrifugal and centripetal forces at work in Yucatecan communities and argues
for the essentially religious nature of social bonding among the lowland
Maya. Kessell, in *Kiva, Cross, and Crown*, observed repeated instances of centrifugal pressures in Pecos. I assert that social bonding followed perceived
ecological and cosmic necessities among the Sonoran peoples of northwestern Mexico.

25 Carmagnani, *El regreso de los dioses*, chaps. 1 and 2, esp. pp. 13–16, 69–72.

26 Ibid., p. 49.

27 Urban and Sherzer, "Introduction," pp. 8–9; Warman, *"We Come to Object,"*
p. 4.

28 The works listed here inform the main contours of the historiography
concerning Indians and the colonial state in New Spain: Gibson, *Tlaxcala
in the Sixteenth Century* and *The Aztecs under Spanish Rule*; Farriss, *Maya Society under
Colonial Rule*; García Martínez, *Los pueblos de la sierra. El poder y el espacio entre
los indios del norte de Puebla hasta 1700*; MacLeod and Wasserstrom, eds., *Spaniards and Indians in Southwestern Mesoamerica: Essays on the History of Ethnic Relations*;
Borah, *Justice by Insurance: The General Indian Court of Colonial Mexico*; Chance,
Conquest of the Sierra. Spaniards and Indians in Colonial Oaxaca; Lockhart, *Nahuas and
Spaniards. Postconquest Central Mexican History and Philology*; Lockhart, *The Nahuas
after the Conquest: A Social and Cultural History of the Indians of Central Mexico, Sixteenth
through Eighteenth Centuries*; Harvey, ed., *Land and Politics in the Valley of Mexico. A
Two Thousand Year Perspective*; Kellogg, *Law and the Transformation of Aztec Culture*;
Taylor, *Landlord and Peasant in Colonial Oaxaca*.

29 On the articulation of the colonial pact, see Jacobsen, "Campesinos y
tenencia de la tierra en el altiplano peruano en la transición de la colonia
a la república," pp. 25–93. Platt, in *Estado boliviano y ayllú andino*, pp. 27–30 et
passim, links the political role of the Andean *curacas* as mediaries between
the *ayllus* and the colonial state to the economic *"modelo cacical* of agrarian
mercantilism."

30 On the Yaquis, see Spicer, *Cycles of Conquest* and *The Yaquis. A Cultural History*;
Hu-Dehart, *Missionaries, Miners, and Indians*; Gouy-Gilbert, *Une résistance indienne*;
Figueroa Valenzuela, *Los que hablan fuerte*; and McGuire, *Politics and Ethnicity on
the Río Yaqui*.

31 Voss, "Northwest Mexico," pp. 79–128 in Diane Balmori, Stuart Voss, and

Miles Wortman, *Notable Family Networks in Latin America*. Romano, "Algunas consideraciones alrededor de nación, estado (y libertad) en Europa y América centro-meridional," pp. 1–24.

32 Weber, *Economía y sociedad*, pp. 315–27. Benedict Anderson's *Imagined Communities* is only tangentially applicable to the distinction that I make here. His phrase "a horizontal comradeship" (p. 16), to describe a nation imagined as a community of equals, reinforces my use of "ethnic polity" to distinguish particular "nations" from the nation-state. I argue that the Sonoran landed elite and *serrano* community leaders ascribed opposing meanings to a common lexicon of "freedom" and "nation."

33 Wolf, *Europe and the People without History*, p. x.

34 Ibid., pp. 1–19.

35 Scott, *Weapons of the Weak*, chap. 8; Scott, *Domination and the Arts of Resistance*, pp. 1–44.

36 Mallon, "The Promise and Dilemma of Subaltern Studies," pp. 1492–93.

37 Ibid., p. 1502.

38 See, for example, Klor de Alva, "The Postcolonization of the (Latin) American Experience," p. 253; Silverblatt, "Becoming Indian in the Central Andes," pp. 284–86.

39 See Mignolo, "Colonial and Postcolonial Discourse," pp. 126–27. Griffith, in *Beliefs and Holy Places*, develops this theme for the Pimería Alta. Schwartz, ed., in *Implicit Understandings*, foregrounds the dialogic element of colonial encounters. Davis, in *Women on the Margins*, explores in great detail the importance of stories as vessels to convey moral values.

40 On the use of metonymy, see Urban and Sherzer, "Introduction," in *Nation-States and Indians in Latin America*, p. 10; Penney, "Metonym and Metaphor: Public and Private Meanings in Sculpture, Engraving, and Painting," in Penney *Art of the American Indian Frontier*, pp. 55–65.

41 Irene Silverblatt ("Becoming Indian," pp. 288–89; *Moon, Sun, and Witches: Gender Ideologies and Class in Inca and Colonial Peru* [Princeton: Princeton University Press, 1987]) relates witchcraft and Spanish extirpation of idolatry to the construction of "indianist ideologies."

42 Melville, in *A Plague of Sheep*, discusses the dramatic consequences of "ungulate irruptions" in central Mexico.

43 Stern, "New Approaches to the Study of Peasant Rebellion and Consciousness: Implications of the Andean Experience," pp. 3–28.

44 Mitchell, "Everyday Metaphors of Power," pp. 545–77; Van Young, "Cuautla Lazarus," pp. 3–26; John Gaventa, *Power and Powerlessness. Quiescence and Rebellion in an Appalachian Valley* (Urbana: University of Illinois Press, 1980), passim.

1 Ethnic Frontiers in the Sonoran Desert

1 *Estado de la provincia de Sonora, 1730,* a Jesuit document attributed to Padre Cristóbal de Cañas, edición y estudio de Flavio Molina Molina (Hermosillo: Molina (private ed.) 1979), p. 7, based on an earlier edition in *Documentos para la historia de México* (Mexico City, 1856) and cited in Reff, "The Location of Corazones and Señora: Archaeological Evidence from the Río Sonora Valley, Mexico," p. 105 (translation mine).

2 Pérez Bedolla, "Geografía de Sonora," pp. 111–72; West, *Sonora. Its Geographical Personality,* pp. 1–15.

3 Barnes, Naylor, and Polzer, *Northern New Spain, A Research Guide,* pp. 76–93; Spicer, *Cycles of Conquest,* pp. 8–23.

4 Crosswhite, "Desert Plants, Habitat, and Agriculture in Relation to the Major Pattern of Cultural Differentiation in the O'odham People of the Sonoran Desert," pp. 47–76; Fontana, "Pima and Papago: Introduction" and "History of the Papago," pp. 125–48.

5 In this latter context, *alto* and *bajo* did not mean "higher" and "lower," but "north" and "south."

6 Gerhard, *The North Frontier of New Spain,* pp. 279–81; West, *Sonora. Its Geographical Personality,* p. 21; Pennington, *The Pima Bajo of Central Sonora, Mexico,* vol. 1: *The Material Culture,* p. 2.

7 Pennington, *The Pima Bajo of Central Sonora, Mexico,* vol. 2: *Vocabulario en la lengua nevome,* p. 42; Riley, *Frontier People,* p. 50. Opata and Pima rivalry, which seems to be borne out in the archaeological and documentary evidence of the contact period, figured in the history of Sonoran missions.

8 Barnes, Naylor, and Polzer, *Northern New Spain, A Research Guide,* pp. 81–87; Spicer, *Cycles of Conquest,* p. 23; Riley, *Frontier People,* pp. 50, 295–98.

9 Pennington, ed., *Arte y vocabulario de la lengua dohema, heve o eudeva. Anónimo (siglo XVII);* Pennington, *La cultura de los eudeve del noroeste de México.*

10 Spicer, *Cycles of Conquest,* pp. 9–12; Sauer, *Aboriginal Population of Northwestern Mexico;* Gerhard, *The North Frontier of New Spain,* pp. 244, 279–81; Doyel, "The Transition to History in Northern Pimería Alta," p. 141.

11 Riley, *Frontier People,* p. 297; Griffen, *Indian Assimilation in the Franciscan Area of Nueva Vizcaya,* p. 42; Reff, *Disease, Depopulation, and Culture Change in Northwestern New Spain, 1518–1764,* p. 54.

12 Spicer, *Cycles of Conquest,* pp. 229–61. Ethnohistorical sources on the Apaches are voluminous. Outstanding among them are these: Lumholtz, *Unknown Mexico;* Lange, Riley, and Lange, eds., *The Southwestern Journals of Adolph F. Bandelier;* Lejeune, *La guerra apache en Sonora;* Zúñiga, *Rápida ojeada al estado de Sonora;* Griffen, *Culture Change and Shifting Populations in Central Northern Mexico;* Griffen, *The Apaches at War and Peace.*

13 Montané Martí, "Desde los orígenes hasta 3000 años antes del presente"; Alvarez Palma, "Sociedades agrícolas." Doolittle, in *Canal Irrigation in Prehistoric Mexico. The Sequence of Technological Change*, pp. 79–92, argues that Southwestern canal irrigation systems developed independently of Mesoamerica.

14 Alvarez Palma, "Sociedades agrícolas," pp. 232–43; Ballereau, "A Complete Survey of Petroglyphs from Cerros La Proveedora and Calera, Sonora."

15 McGuire and Villalpando, "Prehistory and the Making of History in Sonora," pp. 165–66; Alvarez Palma, *Huatabampo. Consideraciones sobre una comunidad agrícola prehispánica en el sur de Sonora*.

16 McGuire and Villalpando, "Prehistory and the Making of History in Sonora," p. 166; Villalpando, *Los que viven en las montañas*; Spicer, *Cycles of Conquest*, pp. 10–11; Felger and Moser, *People of the Desert and Sea*.

17 McGuire and Villalpando, "Prehistory and the Making of History in Sonora," pp. 167–68; Doyel, "The Transition to History in Northern Pimería Alta," pp. 139–58. West, in *Sonora. Its Geographical Personality*, p. 24, suggests that the trincheras belong to an earlier phase of settlement (A.D. 800–1100), basing his judgment on earlier archaeological surveys: Johnson, "The Trincheras Culture of Northern Sonora"; Sauer and Brand, "Prehistoric Settlements of Sonora, with Special Reference to Cerros de Trincheras."

18 Amsden, *Archaeological Reconnaissance in Sonora*, coined the term *Río Sonora* culture. See also Pailes, "The Río Sonora Culture in Prehistoric Trade Systems," pp. 134–43; Doolittle, *Pre-Hispanic Occupance in the Valley of Sonora, Mexico*; West, *Sonora. Its Geographical Personality*, pp. 18–20; and McGuire and Villalpando, "Prehistory and the Making of History in Sonora," pp. 169–71.

19 Doolittle, "Settlements and the Development of 'Statelets' in Sonora, Mexico," pp. 13–24; Doolittle, *Oasis in the Gran Chichimeca: Pre-Hispanic Occupance in the Valley of Sonora*; Reff, "The Location of Corazones and Señora: Archaeological Evidence from the Río Sonora Valley, Mexico," pp. 102–4.

20 Wilcox, "A Historical Analysis of the Problem of Southwestern–Mesoamerican Connections," pp. 34–35 in Wilcox and Masse, eds., *The Protohistorical Period in the North American Southwest, A.D. 1450–1700* (Tempe: Arizona State University, Anthropological Research Papers 24, 1981.; Guevara Sánchez, *Arqueología del área de las Cuarenta Casas, Chihuahua*, p. 11.

21 Di Peso, *Casas Grandes: A Fallen Trading Center of the Gran Chichimeca*; Braniff, *La frontera protohistórica Pima-Opata en Sonora, Mexico. Proposiciones arqueológicas preliminares*; Riley, *Frontier People*, pp. 39–96; Reff, *Disease, Depopulation, and Culture Change in Northwestern New Spain, 1518–1764*, pp. 53–68. Reff argues for hierarchically ranked, patrilineal chiefdoms among the protohistoric Opata, but his interpretation of *serrano* polities based on the early exploration chronicles is questioned by McGuire and Villalpando, "Prehistory and the

Making of History in Sonora," pp. 172–73, and by Sheridan, "The Limits of Power," p. 157.

22   Villalpando, "¿Significaba para ellos prestigio? El uso de la concha en Sonora," pp. 21–33.

23   Pfefferkorn, *Descripción de la provincia de Sonora*, bk. 1, p. 22 et passim.

24   Gerhard, *The North Frontier of New Spain*, pp. 244–45; Riley, *Frontier People*, p. 78; Reff, *Disease, Depopulation, and Culture Change*, pp. 20–27. Quotation from Cabeza de Vaca, *Naufragios*, p. 85.

25   Riley, *Frontier People*, pp. 15–17, 77–78; Di Peso, "Discussion of Masse, Doelle, Sheridan, and Reff Papers from Southwestern Protohistory Conference," p. 113.

26   Cabeza de Vaca, *Naufragios y relación de la jornada que hizo a la Florida con el adelantado Pánfilo de Narváez*, pp. 81–92. The compelling story of Cabeza de Vaca has attracted many scholars. See, for example, Weber, *The Spanish Frontier in North America*, pp. 42–45; Cleve Hallenbeck, *Alvar Núñez Cabeza de Vaca: The Journey and Route of the First European to Cross the Continent of North America, 1534–36* (Glendale, Calif.: Arthur H. Clark, 1940); Basil C. Hedrick and Carroll L. Riley, eds. and trans., *The Journey of the Vaca Party* (Carbondale: Southern Illinois University, 1974); Carl O. Sauer, *Sixteenth Century North America: The Land and the Peoples as Seen by the Europeans* (Berkeley: University of California Press, 1971); and Donald E. Chipman, "In Search of Cabeza de Vaca's Route across Texas: An Historiographical Survey," *Southwest Historical Quarterly* 91, 1987: 127–48.

27   Riley, *Frontier People*, p. 19; Kessell, *Kiva, Cross, and Crown*, pp. 1–28. The major source in English for the history of the Coronado expedition is Hammond and Rey, eds., *Narratives of the Coronado Expedition, 1540–1542*. Scholars continue to debate the explorers' routes. Conventional wisdom places "Corazones" in the Sonora Valley; however, Coronado's army may have passed through the Oposura or Bavispe drainages. His failed colony was probably razed by Opata or Eudeve villagers.

28   The principal source for the Ibarra expedition is Hammond and Rey, eds., *Obregón's History of 16th Century Exploration in Western America*. Also see Riley *Frontier People*, pp. 21–23; Gerhard, *The North Frontier of New Spain*, pp. 165, 245; and Reff, *Disease, Depopulation, and Culture Change*, pp. 84–89. On the mining industry of Zacatecas, see Bakewell, *Silver Mining and Society in Colonial Mexico*; Jiménez Pelayo, *Haciendas y comunidades indígenas en el sur de Zacatecas*, pp. 125–37. *Real de minas* refers to a licensed center for mining, comprising a town site and numerous encampments for extracting and processing the ore.

29   Jones, *Nueva Vizcaya. Heartland of the Spanish Frontier* pp. 22–75; Naylor and Polzer, eds., *The Presidio and Militia on the Northern Frontier of New Spain, 1570–1700*, pp. 36–40, 486–87; Ortega Noriega, "El sistema de misiones jesuíticas: 1591–1699," pp. 31–42.

30 Royal patronage of the church's evangelizing mission in the Americas was formalized by the papal bull *Universalis Ecclesiae Regiminis*, issued by Pope Julian II in favor of King Ferdinand in 1508. Ortega Noriega, "La iglesia católica en la conquista española," p. 37.

31 Pérez de Rivas, *Historia de los triunfos de nuestra santa fé*, vol. 2, pp. 246–58; Mange, *Diario de las exploraciones en Sonora. Luz de tierra incógnita*; Kino, *Las misiones de Sonora y Arizona. Comprendiendo la crónica titulada: "Favores celestiales" y la "Relación diaria de la entrada al noroeste"*; Polzer, *Rules and Precepts of the Jesuit Missions of Northwestern New Spain*, pp. 1–58; González R., *Etnología y misión en la Pimería Alta, 1715–1740*.

32 Gerhard, *The North Frontier of New Spain*, pp. 161–74; Jones, *Nueva Vizcaya. Heartland of the Spanish Frontier*, pp. 97–116; Deeds, "Rural Work in Nueva Vizcaya: Forms of Labor Coercion on the Periphery," pp. 425–50; Reff, *Disease, Depopulation, and Culture Change*, pp. 243–51; González R., *Tarahumara: La sierra y el hombre*; Sheridan and Naylor, eds., *Rarámuri. A Tarahumara Colonial Chronicle, 1607–1791*; Merrill, *Rarámuri Souls*, pp. 30–35; Pennington, *The Tepehuan of Chihuahua*, pp. 1–26.

33 Naylor and Polzer, eds., *The Presidio and Militia on the Northern Frontier of New Spain, 1570–1700*, p. 417, n. 22; West, *Sonora. Its Geographical Personality*, pp. 45–46.

34 West, *Sonora. Its Geographical Personality*, pp. 44–50, 53–55. Although these population counts list only militiamen, some women did come to the Sonoran frontier. Pedro de Perea's widow, María Ibarra, lived in the Opata village of Banámichi after her husband's death. In the 1670s one of the most productive mines of the Real de San Miguel de Arcángel belonged to Juana de Jaziola.

35 Ibid., pp. 55–58, fig. 19. The quotation is from AGN AHH *Temporalidades* 278, exp. 36, 1671: "Ropa es la moneda que corre entre los indios."

36 West, *Sonora. Its Geographical Personality*, pp. 80–91; Velasco, *Noticias estadísticas del estado de Sonora, 1850*, pp. 165–96.

37 West, *Sonora. Its Geographical Personality*, pp. 50–53.

38 Gerhard, *The North Frontier of New Spain*, pp. 157–59, 218; Bakewell, *Silver Mining and Society in Colonial Mexico*, pp. 122–24; West, *The Mining Community of Northern New Spain*, p. 53.

39 Río, "Repartimientos de indios en Sonora y Sinaloa," pp. 11–16; West, *Sonora. Its Geographical Personality*, pp. 62–66, p. 140 (app. D); West, *The Mining Community of Northern New Spain*, p. 118, n. 9. As late as 1715, Opata *tapisques* received wages of six to eight pesos a month (Archivo Municipal de Parral 1715, Administración y Guerra, cited in West, ibid.).

40 Río, "Repartimientos de indios en Sonora y Sinaloa," p. 17. The *partido* is well researched for the major silver centers of Mexico and Peru, where it

was known as the *corpa*. See Bakewell, *Silver Mining and Society in Colonial Mexico*, p. 125; Stern, "Feudalism, Capitalism, and the World-System in the Perspective of Latin America and the Caribbean," p. 852. In Mexican mines the *partido* was combined with other forms of payment: Flores Clair, "Minas y mineros: Pago en especie y conflictos, 1790–1880," pp. 51–68; West, *The Mining Community of Northern New Spain*, p. 49.

41 Reff, *Disease, Depopulation, and Culture Change*, pp. 160–78.

42 Gerhard, *The North Frontier of New Spain*, p. 316; Sheridan and Naylor, eds., *Rarámuri. A Tarahumara Colonial Chronicle, 1607–1791*, pp. 39–70; Naylor and Polzer, eds., *The Presidio and Militia on the Northern Frontier of New Spain, 1570–1700*, pp. 483–720.

43 Hu-Dehart, in *Missionaries, Miners and Indians*, emphasizes the role of conflicting authorities in the Yaqui rebellion of 1740.

44 Porras Muñoz, *Iglesia y estado en Nueva Vizcaya (1562–1821)*, p. 46; Río, "El noroeste novohispano y la nueva política imperial española," pp. 193–219.

45 Viveros, ed., *Informe sobre Sinaloa y Sonora*, pp. 21–45, 47–48.

46 AGN Historia 316, exp. 12, f. 456v, and AGI Patronato 232, ramo I, ff. 203–6, cited in West, *Sonora. Its Geographical Personality*, p. 62, n. 8.

47 Escandón, "Economía y sociedad en Sonora: 1767–1821," pp. 287–98.

48 Gálvez's decree of 1769 is found in BNFF 34/740, 741. Also see Río, "El noroeste novohispano y la nueva política imperial española," pp. 209–19; Escandón, "La nueva administración misional y los pueblos de indios," pp. 258–64; Kessell, *Friars, Soldiers, and Reformers*, pp. 42–55; and Weber, *The Spanish Frontier in North America*, pp. 224–29, 236–42.

49 Moorhead, *The Presidio: Bastion of the Spanish Borderlands*; Weber, *The Spanish Frontier in North America*, pp. 204–35; Kessell, "The Puzzling Presidio San Phelipe de Guevavi, Alias Terrenate," pp. 21–46. The Terrenate garrison was transferred to Quiburi in 1775, later moved to Las Nutrias after disastrous encounters with the Chiricahua Apaches, and finally relocated at Suamca in 1787.

50 Río and López Mañón, "La reforma institucional borbónica," pp. 223–40.

51 Vidargas del Moral, "La intendencia de Arizpe en la independencia de Nueva España: 1810–1821," pp. 307–9; Kessell, *Friars, Soldiers, and Reformers*, p. 238. On popular participation in the insurgency of the Bajío, see Tutino, *From Insurrection to Revolution in Mexico*; Van Young, "To See Someone Not Seeing: Historical Studies of Peasants and Politics in Mexico," pp. 133–59. On the Apache peace camps, see Griffen, *The Apaches at War and Peace*; Griffen, *Utmost Good Faith: Patterns of Apache-Mexican Hostilities in Northern Chihuahua Border Warfare, 1821–1848*.

52 Kessell, "Friars versus Bureaucrats," pp. 151–59; Radding, *Las estructuras socioeconómicas de las misiones de la Pimería Alta, 1768–1850*, pp. 13–20.

2   Amerindian Economy in Sonora

1   Quoted in Shanin, ed., *Peasants and Peasant Societies*, p. 21.

2   Chayanov, *The Theory of Peasant Economy*, pp. 70–89; Scott, *The Moral Economy of the Peasant*, pp. 34–40; Sahlins, *Stone-Age Economics*, pp. 41–100.

3   Riley, *Frontier People*, pp. 48, 68, 76–85; Braniff, *La frontera protohistórica Pima-Opata en Sonora*, vol. 1, passim.

4   AGN *Temporalidades* 325, exp. 69, cited in West, *Sonora: Its Geographical Personality*, p. 62. Fanega = 1.5 bushels of grain (Van Young, *Hacienda and Market*, p. 360). See glossary.

5   Castetter and Bell, *Pima and Papago Agriculture*, pp. 48–63, 74–113; Nabhan, *The Desert Smells Like Rain*, pp. 75–86; Nabhan, *Gathering the Desert*, pp. 93–184; Nabhan, "Papago Indian Desert Agriculture and Water Control in the Sonoran Desert, 1697–1934," pp. 43–59; Nabhan, "Ak-ciñ and the Environment of Papago Indian Fields," pp. 61–76; Di Peso, *The Upper Pima of San Cayetano*, pp. 450–55. Fray Pedro Font, in his *Diario* [of the Anza expedition, September 29, 1775–June 2, 1776] written in Tubutama in 1777 (ms. in the John Carter Brown Library, f. 18a), reported that the Pápagos channeled water by means of irrigation ditches (acequias) built outward from the mouths of arroyos during the rainy season. I am grateful to Julio Montané and to Kieran R. McCarty for this reference.

6   Castetter and Bell, *Pima and Papago Agriculture*, pp. 8–9, 48–49, 62–63; Fontana, *Of Earth and Little Rain*, p. 40; MacDougal, *Across Papaguería*, p. 5.

7   Castetter and Bell, *Pima and Papago Agriculture*, pp. 40–42, 55–58, 124–26; Rodríguez and Silva, *Etnoarqueología de Quitovac, Sonora*; Di Peso, *The Upper Pima*, pp. 450–55.

8   Pennington, *The Pima Bajo of Central Sonora*, vol. 1, pp. 141–43.

9   Ibid., pp. 143–47; Boserup, *The Conditions of Agricultural Growth*, pp. 15–22. Although fallowing was less essential to Sonoran cultivation than in tropical areas, Pima agricultural practices strongly suggest a form of short fallow adapted to seasonal rainfall and hillside gradients. See recent research on swidden agriculture and fallowing for western, central, and southeastern Mexico, in Rojas Rabiela, ed., *Agricultura indígena: pasado y presente*, passim.

10 Pennington, *The Pima Bajo of Central Sonora*, vol. 1, pp. 145–46; Doolittle, *Pre-Hispanic Occupance in the Valley of Sonora, Mexico*, p. 9.

11 Doolittle, "Pre-Hispanic Occupance in the Middle Río Sonora Valley," pp. 94–102, 130–34; Doolittle, "Agriculture in North America on the Eve of Contact: A Reassessment," pp. 386–401; Sheridan, *Where the Dove Calls*, pp. 54–56; Sheridan and Nabhan, "Living with a River: Traditional Farmers of the Río San Miguel," pp. 1–16. Spores, in "Settlement, Farming Technology, and Environment in the Nochixtlan Valley," pp. 557–69, describes similar irrigation techniques for the Mixtec culture of Oaxaca.

12   Pfefferkorn, *Descripción de la provincia de Sonora*, vol. 1, p. 57 (quotation), vol. 2, pp. 61–63; Nentvig, *Descripción geográfica, natural y curiosa de la provincia de Sonora*, p. 141; Pennington, *The Pima Bajo of Central Sonora*, vol. 1, p. 147.

13   Di Peso, *The Upper Pima*, p. 458; Pennington, *The Pima Bajo of Central Sonora*, vol. 1, pp. 147–55; Molina Molina, *Diccionario de flora y fauna indígena de Sonora*, p. 18.

14   Nabhan, "Amaranth Cultivation in the U.S. Southwest and Northwest Mexico," pp. 129–33; Sauer, "The Grain Amaranths and their Relatives," pp. 103–37.

15   Pennington, *The Pima Bajo of Central Sonora*, vol. 1, pp. 148–49, 165–78; Nentvig, *Descripción . . . de Sonora*, pp. 140–41; Pfefferkorn, *Descripción . . . de Sonora*, vol. 1, pp. 57–67.

16   Di Peso, *The Upper Pima*, p. 458; Pennington, *The Pima Bajo of Central Sonora*, vol. 1, pp. 159–60. *Tasoleras* are still a part of the *serrano* landscape today.

17   Pfefferkorn, *Descripción . . . de Sonora*, vol. 2, pp. 55–57; Pennington, *The Pima Bajo of Central Sonora*, vol. 1, pp. 179–84.

18   Pennington, *The Pima Bajo of Central Sonora*, vol. 1, pp. 149–50, 252–7; Johnson, "The Piman Foot Drum and Fertility Rites," pp. 140–41, cited in Pennington, ibid. *Venado* is the deer dance, accompanied by the masked *pascola*, or ritual clown, performed by the Yaqui and Mayo Indians of southern Sonora to the present day.

19   Di Peso, *The Upper Pima*, pp. 434–37. Gutiérrez, in *When Jesus Came, the Corn Mothers Went Away*, pp. 3–7, interprets the Acoma origin myth to emphasize the link between plant germination and human sexuality.

20   Di Peso, *The Upper Pima*, p. 458; Ruth Underhill, *Singing for Power: The Song Music of the Papago Indians of Southern Arizona* (Berkeley: University of California Press, 1938), cited in Fussell, *The Story of Corn*, pp. 113–14.

21   Pennington, *The Pima Bajo of Central Sonora*, vol. 1, p. 150.

22   Di Peso, *The Upper Pima*, p. 443; Underhill, *Papago Woman*, pp. 17–26; Fontana, "The *Vikita*: A Biblio History," pp. 259–72.

23   Pennington, *The Pima Bajo of Central Sonora*, vol. 1, pp. 304–6; Pfefferkorn, *Descripción . . . de Sonora*, vol. 1, p. 67, and vol. 2, p. 59.

24   Pfefferkorn, *Descripción . . . de Sonora*, vol. 1, p. 67, and vol. 2, p. 53; Pennington, *The Pima Bajo of Central Sonora*, vol. 1, pp. 297–99; Di Peso, *The Upper Pima*, pp. 450–51, 455.

25   Di Peso, *The Upper Pima*, p. 445; Pfefferkorn, *Descripción . . . de Sonora*, vol. 2, pp. 61–63.

26   Jones, "The Wi'gita of Achi and Quitobac"; Underhill, *Papago Woman*, pp. 81–82; Fontana, "The *Vikita*: A Biblio History," pp. 259–72; Hayden, "The Vikita Ceremony of the Papago," pp. 273–324.

27   Nabhan, *The Desert Smells Like Rain*, pp. 25–38, poem on p. 26–27; Underhill,

Papago Woman, pp. 17, 27, 69–71; Garcés, *Diario de exploraciones en Arizona y California en los años de 1775 y 1776*, pp. 6, 87.

28 Castetter and Bell, *Pima and Papago Agriculture*, pp. 6–7; Sahlins, *Stone-Age Economics*, pp. 149–84. White, in *Roots of Dependency*, pp. 36–47, explains eloquently the differences between European commerce and Choctaw gift alliances.

29 Castetter and Bell, *Pima and Papago Agriculture*, pp. 45–46; Crosswhite, "The Annual Saguaro Harvest and Crop Cycle of the Papago," pp. 47–76; Crosswhite, "Desert Plants, Habitat, and Agriculture," pp. 47–76.

30 Nentvig, *Descripción . . . de Sonora*, p. 118. Chapter 5 of this book discusses the Jobas' relationship to the missions.

31 Pfefferkorn, *Descripción . . . de Sonora*, vol. 2, p. 58.

32 Ibid., pp. 106–8. "Economy of abundance" is from Sahlins, *Stone-Age Economics*, p. 1–39. On the difference between exchange and commerce, see Halperín and Dow, eds., *Peasant Livelihood*; Polanyi, Arensbert, and Pearson, eds., *Comercio y mercado en los imperios antiguos*; Lehmann, ed., *Ecology and Exchange in the Andes*. The effect of colonial commerce on Amerindian economy is discussed more fully in Chapter 3 below.

33 Pfefferkorn, *Descripción . . . de Sonora*, vol. 2, p. 61.

34 Jácobo Sedelmayr, 1749, UASP Az 370; Pfefferkorn, *Descripción . . . de Sonora*, vol. 2, pp. 49–53, 61–65, 144.

35 See Nabhan, *The Desert Smells Like Rain*, pp. 101–10, on the metabolism of traditional O'odham gatherers contrasted with the eating habits of the reservation Pápago.

36 Pfefferkorn, *Descripción . . . de Sonora*, vol. 1, p. 64, and vol. 2, pp. 106–8. Mayo women of southern Sonora today weave woolen rugs on a simple loom made of a wooden frame placed over four stakes driven into the ground.

37 Nentvig, *Descripción . . . de Sonora*, p. 117.

38 Pfefferkorn, *Descripción . . . de Sonora*, vol. 2, p. 65.

39 Nabhan and Sheridan, "Living Fencerows of the Río San Miguel, Sonora, Mexico," pp. 97–111.

40 The preservation of indigenous *altepeme* (s. *altepetl*, city-state) and their political hierarchies under the domination, first, of *encomiendas* and, later, of *corregimientos* in the Mexican altiplano was directly related to the control of labor. Gibson, *The Aztecs under Spanish Rule*, pp. 220–56; Lockhart, *The Nahuas after the Conquest*, pp. 96–114; García Martínez, *Los pueblos de la sierra*, pp. 72–83. In Oaxaca, commercialization of cotton and cochineal coupled with the *repartimiento de efectos* brought income to Indian communities, but radically altered their internal social relations. See Chance, *Conquest of the Sierra*, pp. 90, 97–122.

41 Farriss, *Maya Society under Colonial Rule*; Jones, *Maya Resistance to Spanish Rule*;

Cook, "Quichean Folk Theology and Southern Maya Supernaturalism," pp. 139–54; Ortiz, *The Tewa World.* "Made People" in Tewa Culture had the power to carry out ritual ceremonies (Ortiz, ibid., p. 79–119).

42 Gutiérrez, *When Jesus Came,* pp. 3–38.

43 Bauer, "Millers and Grinders," pp. 1–17.

3 Native Livelihood and the Colonial Economy

1 Newberry Library, Ayer Collection, vault no. 871: *Doctrina christiana y pláticas doctrinales, traducidas en lengua ópata por el R. Manuel Aguirre de la Compañía de Jesús,* impressas en la Imprenta del Real y más antiguo Colegio de San Ildefonso de México, 1765, p. 108, ¶ 6.

2 Weber, *The Spanish Frontier in North America,* pp. 107–12, 119–21, 145–55, 191–95, 241–64. Weber, citing Spanish officials' disdain for the missions in Florida, California, and New Mexico, argues that the missionaries competed poorly against English and French trade goods for the Indians' loyalty, especially in colonial Florida. See also Erick Langer, "Missions and the Frontier Economy: The case of the Franciscan Missions among the Chiriguanos, 1845–1930," pp. 49–76, in Langer and Jackson, eds., *New Latin American Mission History;* Juan Carlos Garavaglia, "Un modo de producción subsidiaria. La organización económica de las comunidades guaranizadas durante los siglos XVII–XVIII en la formación regional altoperuana rioplatense." In *Modos de Producción en América Latina,* Cordoba: Siglo Veintiuno Editores, Cuadernos de Pasado y Presente, 1973.

3 Spicer, *Cycles of Conquest,* p. 292; Spicer, *The Yaquis. A Cultural History,* p. 30.

4 BNFF 32/662: Padre Joseph Roldan, "Luz con que se deben mirar las sementeras que los Jesuitas hacen en sus missiones." Also see Nentvig, *Descripción . . . de Sonora,* p. 141; Pfefferkorn, *Descripción . . . de Sonora,* vol. 2, p. 57. For relative surface measurements of a *fanega,* see note 39 below.

5 Spicer, *The Yaquis. A Cultural History,* pp. 21–32; Pfefferkorn, *Descripción . . . de Sonora,* vol. 2, pp. 144–46; BNFF 32/663 [c. 1772]. For an interesting discussion of mission discipline, see Ortega Noriega, "La misión jesuítica como institución disciplinaria (1610–1721)," pp. 169–80.

6 AGN Jesuitas IV-10, exp. 201, f. 235v.

7 AGN Jesuitas IV-10, exp. 142, f. 176v.

8 Pfefferkorn, *Descripción . . . de Sonora,* vol. 2, pp. 142–43.

9 AGN Jesuitas IV-10, exp. 10, f. 38 (Pitic, June 4, 1754).

10 AGN Jesuitas IV-10, exp. 189, ff. 222–23, 240 (1766–67).

11 See Chapter 1, note 39, above.

12 AGN Jesuitas IV-10, exp. 11, f. 39 (1757).

13 AGN Jesuitas IV-10, exp. 177, 188 (1766).

14 Brading, *Mineros y comerciantes en el México borbónico* (1763–1810), pp. 143–44; Pérez Herrero, *Plata y libranzas*, pp. 33–55, 209–53. Garner, in "Prices and Wages in Eighteenth-Century Mexico," pp. 73–77, confirms the widespread use of *libranzas* and comments on the problem of determining commodity values in view of the fact that bookkeepers recorded prices without an actual exchange of money. Van Young, in *Hacienda and Market in Eighteenth-Century Mexico*, pp. 71–74, refers to commissioned sales of wheat between merchants and hacendados in the Guadalajara area, a comparable situation, but not the same as the system of barter-on-credit which operated in the Northwest. See also, Chamoux, *et al, Prestar y pedir prestado*, p. 19–109.

15 AGN *Jesuitas* IV-10, exp. 130, f. 164 (1764); exp. 174, f. 208 (1766).

16 AMH AS 1, 1666–1828, folios unnumbered.

17 AGN *Jesuitas* IV-10, exp. 69, 71, 80 (1764); exp. 220, 221 (1767); exp. 86, f. 118; exp. 208, f. 242.

18 AGN *Jesuitas* IV-10, exp. 171–72; exp. 4, f. 2 (1762–66); exp. 201, f. 235v.

19 *Capital* is used here to denote an accumulated stock of productive resources in a given economic unit (e.g., a peasant farm or village) without implying a capitalist mode of production. See Chayanov, *The Theory of Peasant Economy*, pp. 11, 20–103.

20 AMH AS 1, 1666–1828.

21 Ground flour was sold by the *carga*; whole grains were sold in *fanegas*. By weight, 1 carga = 4 fanegas of wheat and 3 fanegas of maize; by volume, 1 carga = 2 fanegas of grain. Judging from the correlation of prices to amounts in the Jesuit records, we may conclude that it is probable that the missionaries sold their grain by volume. See Barnes, Naylor, and Polzer, *Northern New Spain, A Research Guide*, pp. 69–73.

22 AGN *Jesuitas* IV-10, exp. 8, f. 36; exp. 80, f. 112; exp. 185, f. 218a, b.

23 One marco of silver was worth seven pesos, two reales.

24 AMH AS 1, 1666–1828.

25 AMH AS 1, 1666–1828.

26 West, *Sonora: Its Geographical Personality*, p. 61.

27 Ibid., p. 62, citing Pfefferkorn, *Descripción . . . de Sonora*, and AGN *Historia* 316, exp. 12, f. 456.

28 BNFF 38/854, ff. 1–3. Corbalán, a Gálvez appointee and relative of the Viceroy Marqués de Croix, served as intendant and governor of Sonora in 1770–72 and 1777–87. See Barnes, Naylor, and Polzer, *Northern New Spain*, p. 112; Kessell, *Friars, Soldiers, and Reformers*, p. 125.

29 Regional studies published over the past two decades and colony wide syntheses of data series on grain prices and tithe records provide a good baseline of comparison with Sonora. Nevertheless, we lack systematic price analyses of the Sonoran data, which are scattered and far less complete than

for areas like Michoacán, the Bajío, and the Valley of Mexico. See Gibson, *The Aztecs under Spanish Rule*; Florescano, *Precios del maíz y crisis agrícolas en México* (1708–1860); Morin, *Michoacán en la Nueva España del siglo XVIII*; Rabell Romero, *Los diezmos de San Luis de la Paz*; Chowning, "The Consolidación de Vales Reales in the Bishopric of Michoacán," pp. 541–78; Van Young, *Hacienda and Market in Eighteenth-Century Mexico*; Garner, "Price Trends in Eighteenth-Century Mexico"; Garner, "Prices and Wages in Eighteenth-Century Mexico"; and Garner, *Economic Growth and Change in Bourbon Mexico*, pp. 1–71.

30   Garner, "Prices and Wages in Eighteenth-Century Mexico," pp. 73–85. During the colonywide famine of 1749–50 in New Spain, maize prices reached thirty-two reales (four pesos) per fanega.

31   Van Young, *Hacienda and Market in Eighteenth-Century Mexico*, pp. 59–74; Garner, "Wages and Prices in Eighteenth-Century Mexico," pp. 90–91, citing Flor de María López, *Dolores Hidalgo: Estudio económico, 1740–1790* (Mexico City, 1974); Garner, *Economic Growth and Change in Bourbon Mexico*, pp. 31–32, 98, 267–68.

32   Swann, *Tierra Adentro*, pp. 54–55.

33   Garner, "Prices and Wages in Eighteenth-Century Mexico," p. 80, table 4.1.

34   West, *Sonora: Its Geographical Personality*, p. 61.

35   Morin, in *Michoacán en la Nueva España del siglo XVIII*, pp. 141–42, 188–90, observes that wheat flour from Valladolid was in demand in Mexico City, where its price was as much as twenty reales per carga more than flour from Toluca, owing to transportation costs. Morin warns us, however, that "price is only one variable among many others" and that, consequently, its significance is tempered by the prevailing conditions of commodity exchange. In this context, it is well to remember that comparisons between Sonora and New Spain at large must take into account different marketing systems. Historians working on Zacatecas, Jalisco, the Bajío, or the Valley of Mexico compile their tables from municipal *alhóndigas* and *pósitos* and from tithe and *alcabala* records, which were inoperative in Sonora. See Garner, *Economic Growth and Change in Bourbon Mexico*, pp. 85–86, 91–97.

36   BNFF 35/761.

37   BNFF 35/762.

38   BNFF 34/736: "Estado que manifiesta el número de poblaciones correspondientes a esta jurisdicción, distancias y rumbos de la capital, bienes que poseen sus habitantes, y lo demás que se expresa en las casillas."

39   One suerte = 10.5 hectares, or 26.5 acres; 1 fanega = 3.5 hectares, or 8.5 acres. This land measurement originally was not fixed but referred to the area that could be sown with 1 fanega, or 1.5 bushels, of maize. See Brading, *Haciendas y Ranchos del Bajío*, p. 21; Van Young, *Hacienda and Market in Eighteenth-*

Century Mexico, p. 361; Barnes, Naylor, and Polzer, Northern New Spain, A Research Guide, p. 69; and Plan de Pitic, AGN Tierras 2773, 22, f. 243.

40   Kessell, Friars, Soldiers, and Reformers, pp. 29–53.

41   McCarty, A Spanish Frontier in the Enlightened Age, pp. 53–72; Radding, Las estructuras socioeconómicas de las misiones, pp. 13–16.

42   West, Sonora: Its Geographical Personality, p. 62.

43   AMH (UA microfilm 811, roll 3).

44   AMH AD 1 (UA 811, roll 2); BNFF 35/762.

45   To borrow Scott's phrase (for a different time and place), the missions failed to provide serrano peasants "risk insurance" in late colonial Sonora (Moral Economy of the Peasant, pp. 40–58).

4   Sexuality, Marriage, and Family Formation in Sonora

1   Pedro de Leyva was thirty-three years of age when he penned his report to the bishop on September 25, 1800 (AMH AD 2, exp. unnumbered, ff. 1–8). Real de la Santísima Trinidad was founded in 1754. During the ensuing decade it was the principal commercial center of Ostimuri, closely followed by the reales of Río Chico and San Antonio de la Huerta, Sonora. The rich silver lodes of Trinidad were not fully exploited, owing to disputes over their ownership. Nentvig, Descripción . . . de Sonora, p. 170.

2   Padre Leyva, AMH AD 2, 1800; B. Joaquín Antonio Flores and Lic. Manuel María Moreno in San Xavier, 1797, AMH AD 1 (1744–94). Indios volantes y sin pié fijo means, roughly, "Indians on the run and without firm footing."

3   Padre Leyva, AMH AD 2, 1800; Padre José María Paz y Goicochea to Bishop Rouset, Real de la Cieneguilla, May 12, 1797, AMH AD 1.

4   Naborías were Indians who had left their communities and lived by wage labor or service tenantry. The term came from Arawak, appropriated by the Spaniards in the sixteenth century to mean dependents of a native ruler who were severed from community rights and obligations. See Lockhart, The Nahuas after the Conquest, p. 609. Laboríos were Indian laborers in a Spanish labor, or hacienda, similar to gañanes. See Gerhard, The North Frontier of New Spain, p. 370; Florescano, "La formación de los trabajadores en la época colonial, 1521–1750," pp. 100–14; and González Sánchez, "Sistemas de trabajo, salarios y situación de los trabajadores agrícolas, 1750–1810," pp. 135–50.

5   AMH AD 2, 1800, Padre Leyva to Bishop Rouset; BNFF 32/663; Burguière, "La historia de la familia en Francia. Problemas y recientes aproximaciones," pp. 17–23; Gutiérrez, "Honor Ideology, Marriage Negotiation, and Class-Gender Domination in New Mexico, 1690–1846," pp. 81–104; Seed, "The

Church and the Patriarchal Family," pp. 284–93; Matson and Fontana, eds., *Friar Bringas Reports to the King*, pp. 25–33, 138–49; Merrill, "Conversion and Colonialism in Northern Mexico," pp. 129–63; Radding, "En la sombra de la sierra," pp. 13–44. On Jesuit *padrones*, see AGN Jesuitas IV-10, exp. 5, f. 33 (Tecoripa, 1737, Padre Rector Diego Gudiño).

6   AMH AD 1; AMH AS 22; Franciscan *estados* in BNFF 36/100, 802, 803, 815, 797, 798, and 37/829, 40/912.

7   Spicer, "People on the Desert," pp. 3–59.

8   Archetti and Stölen, *Explotación familiar y acumulación de capital en el campo argentino*, pp. 50–51; Sahlins, *Stone-Age Economics*, p. 77; Cook and Borah, *Essays in Population History*, vol. 1, chap. 3; Henry, *Manual de demografía histórica*, p. 31; Meillassoux, "From Reproduction to Production," pp. 93–105, and *Maidens, Meal and Money*, passim; Boserup, *The Conditions of Agricultural Growth*, pp. 45–54; Quale, *Families in Context*, pp. 34–35; Smith, "Introduction," in Smith, ed., *Kinship Ideology and Practice in Latin America*, pp. 3–27.

9   Johnson, "The Opata: An Inland Tribe of Sonora," pp. 169–99.

10 Ibid., p. 187. Naming ceremonies, in which children receive sponsors and become members of the community, are described for the Río Grande Tewa Pueblos by Ortiz, *The Tewa World*, pp. 31–41.

11 Johnson, "The Opata," pp. 182, 188. Nentvig, *Descripción . . . de Sonora*, p. 114 (¶139), refers to gift exchanges among *noraguas*. Indians incurred debts with their missionaries to procure the items to exchange, a development which suggests that native customs had been altered by their exposure to the commodity market.

12 Sahlins, *Stone-Age Economics*, pp. 101–48; Chayanov, *The Theory of Peasant Economy*, pp. 53–69; Kandiyoki, *Women in Rural Production Systems*, p. 18.

13 Giraud, "De las problemáticas europeas al caso novohispano: Apuntes para una historia de la familia mexicana," pp. 58–64; Ortega Noriega, "El discurso teológico de Santo Tomás de Aquino sobre el matrimonio, la familia, y los comportamientos sexuales," pp. 15–78; Lavrin, "Introduction," in *Sexuality and Marriage in Colonial Latin America*, pp. 1–46.

14 Sauer, *The Distribution of Aboriginal Tribes and Languages in Northwestern Mexico*; Sauer, *Aboriginal Population of Northwestern Mexico*; Beals, *The Comparative Ethnology of Northern Mexico before 1750*; West, *The Mining Community in Northern New Spain*; West, *Sonora. Its Geographical Personality*; Gerhard, *The North Frontier of New Spain*.

15 Dobyns, "Indian Extinction in the Middle Santa Cruz River Valley," pp. 163–81; Dobyns, *Spanish Colonial Tucson*; Jackson, "Demographic and Social Change in Northwestern New Spain"; Jackson, "Demographic Change in Northwestern New Spain," pp. 462–79; Reff, *Disease, Depopulation, and Culture Change in Northwestern New Spain, 1518–1764*; Radding, *Las estructuras socioeconómicas de las misiones de la Pimería Alta*. Ignacio del Río applies this same methodology in

his *Conquista y aculturación en la California jesuítica*. See also Swann, "The Demographic Impact of Disease and Famine in Late Colonial Northern Mexico."

16   See the thoughtful discussions of acculturation in Río, *Conquista y aculturación en la California jesuítica*, pp. 51–21; and Spicer, *Cycles of Conquest*, pp. 567–86. Reff, *Disease, Depopulation, and Culture Change*, pp. 243–49, and Jackson, *Indian Population Decline*, pp. 139–43, 163–66, emphasize the destructive component of acculturation.

17   Riley, *Frontier People*; Doolittle, *Pre-Hispanic Occupance in the Valley of Sonora, Mexico*; Braniff, *La frontera protohistórica Pima-Opata en Sonora*; McGuire and Villalpando, "Prehistory and the Making of History in Sonora."

18   [Padre Manuel Aguirre], 1765, and reports gathered by Padre José de Utrera, in W. B. Stevens Collection 66, 67, 68 (University of Texas–Austin).

19   Padre Ignacio Lizassoaín, *Visita* of 1761, W. B. Stevens Collection 47; Cook and Borah, *Essays in Population History*, vol. 1, pp. 263–71.

20   AGN AHH 17, exp. 32 (1766), Padre Rapicani of Batuc; AMH AD 1 (1796), "Informes sobre Ures, Cucurpe y Oposura."

21   On race and class in colonial New Spain, see Cook and Borah, *Essays in Population History*, vol. 2, chap. 2, pp. vi, 180–82, et passim; Brading, "Los españoles in México hacia 1792," pp. 126–44; Anderson, "Race and Social Stratification," pp. 209–44; debate among John K. Chance, William B. Taylor, Robert McCaa, Stuart Schwartz, Arturo Grubessick, Patricia Seed, and Philip F. Rust, published in *Comparative Studies in Society and History* (1977–83); Seed, *To Love, Honor, and Obey in Colonial Mexico*; and Gutiérrez, *When Jesus Came, the Corn Mothers Went Away*, pp. 176–206. For ethnic terms commonly used in Sonora, see Barnes, Naylor, and Polzer, *Northern New Spain, A Research Guide*, pp. 90–3; Jackson, *Indian Population Decline*, pp. 195–96.

22   Gómez Canedo, ed., *Sonora hacia fines del siglo XVIII*; Radding, *Las estructuras socioeconómicas de las misiones de Pimería Alta*, pp. 74–80; Dobyns, "Indian Extinction in the Middle Santa Cruz River Valley," pp. 163–81; Jackson, "Demographic Change in Northwestern New Spain," pp. 462–79; Villalpando, "Algunas consideraciones demográficas sobre la Pimería Alta a fines del siglo XVIII"; "Informes de los frailes Canales, Diez de Josef, Santiestéban al obispo Rouset de Jesus" (1796), AMH AD.

23   Bishop Antonio de los Reyes, BNFF 34/759, f. 31 (1784).

24   The population counts from primary sources, used to calculate general trends, often do not include children. See Cecilia Andrea Rabell, "La población novohispana a la luz de los registros parroquiales," pp. 17–48 (Mexico City: Instituto de Investigaciones Sociales, Universidad Nacional Autonoma de México, Cuadernos de Investigación Social No 21, 1990).

25   Jackson, in *Indian Population Decline*, pp. 118–26, emphasizes the impact of high infant mortality on mission population in both epidemic and non-

epidemic periods. On the Indians' reproductive capacity in other regions of Spanish colonial America, see Farriss, *Maya Society under Colonial Rule*, pp. 57–85; Newson, "Los sistemas de trabajo y demografía en América Española durante la colonia: Patrones de mortalidad y fertilidad," pp. 289–97.

26 Reff, *Disease, Depopulation, and Culture Change in Northwestern New Spain*, pp. 97–242. Jackson, in *Indian Population Decline*, argues that recovery did not occur in the Pimería Alta.

27 See Cook and Borah, *Essays in Population History*; Rabell Romero, "Los estudios de demografía histórica novohispana; Malvido, "Cronología de epidemias y hambrunas en la población colonial" and "Efectos de las epidemias y hambrunas en la población colonial de México (1519–1810)," pp. 171–78; Cook, "La viruela en la California española y mexicana, 1770–1845," pp. 257–94; Calvo, "Demografía y economía: La coyuntura en Nueva Galicia en el siglo XVII," pp. 579–614; and Reher, ¿Malthus de nuevo? Población y economía en México durante el siglo XVIII," pp. 615–64. References to disease in Sonoran missions are culled from AGN *Jesuitas* IV-10, exp. 166, f. 200; AMH AS caja 1, 1666–1828; UASP Az 370, 1749.

28 See Malvido, "Factores de despoblación y de reposición de la población de Cholula (1641–1810)," pp. 52–110. Langer and Jackson, in "Colonial and Republican Missions Compared: The Cases of Alta California and Southeastern Bolivia," pp. 286–311, emphasize infant mortality as the major cause of population decline in the California missions.

29 Crosby, *The Columbian Exchange*, pp. 122–64.

30 BNFF 36/802.

31 Malvido, "Factores de despoblación y de reposición de la población de Cholula (1641–1810)," pp. 55–58; Florescano, *Origen y desarrollo de los problemas agrarios de México, 1500–1821*; Le Roy Ladurie, *Historia del clima desde el año mil*.

32 BNFF 36/802.

33 Sedelmayr to Balthasar, 1749, UASP Az 370. *Non est abbreviata manus Domini*, "the hand of God is not short" may be interpreted to mean, "the hand of God reaches very far."

34 BNFF 37/829, Fray Dávalos to Intendente García Conde, 1806.

35 The model for Figures 4.2–4.7 comes from Archetti and Stölen, *Explotación familiar y acumulación de capital en el campo argentino*. Examples of second nuptials for Indians and *vecinos* are found in AGN *Jesuitas* IV-10, exp. 6, f. 34, 1747; exp. 149–50, 1764.

36 *Padrón* from AMH AS *Información Matrimonial* 1780–1801, caja 22. In the discussion of the data used for the tables and figures derived from this source, *family* denotes parents and children, i.e., persons related to one another over two or three generations; *household* refers to those persons who reside together.

NOTES TO CHAPTER FOUR 333

37 San José de Tacupeto, founded more than a century earlier in 1675, came under the jurisdiction of the Alcaldía de Ostimuri, centered in Río Chico and later in Trinidad. See Gerhard, *The North Frontier of New Spain*, pp. 264–69.

38 This hypothesis is supported in part by the family compounds observed in the Yaqui villages of Sonora today. See Spicer, *The Yaquis. A Cultural History*, p. 242 et passim.

39 AMH AS, bk. 1, 1783–1828; AGN *Jesuitas* IV-10, exp. 97, f. 129, 1764: Father Francisco Xavier de Noriega, a priest at San José de Gracia, married a Yaqui couple with Yaqui witnesses, following the instructions of Father Andrés Michel, the Jesuit missionary of Ures. These patterns in Sonora are reminiscent of similar communities created within haciendas in central Mexico. See, for example, Tutino, "Family Economies in Agrarian Mexico, 1750–1910," p. 258–71. Taylor, "Haciendas coloniales en el valle de Oaxaca," pp. 71–104.

40 On comparable family strategies of hacienda tenants, see Tutino. Susan Kellogg argues for the significance of complex households, defined as laterally or vertically extended families in coresidence, in order to question the apparent simplicity of population projections based on aggregate data for late pre-Hispanic and early colonial Tenochtitlán-Tlatelolco: "Households in Late Prehispanic and Early Colonial Mexico City: Their Structure and Its Implications for the Study of Historical Demography," pp. 483–94.

41 On the position of women and the vulnerability of dependents in a large mining center of northern Mexico, see McCaa, "Women's Position, Family and Fertility in Mexico: The Case of Parral, 1777–1930," pp. 8–9. On children raised outside the parental home, see Smith, "The Family and the Modern World System: Some Observations from the Caribbean," p. 353. Jackson, in *Indian Population Decline*, p. 108, notes the high numbers of orphans taken in by family members in the Pimería Alta.

42 Long, "Introduction," in *Family and Work in Rural Societies*, pp. 1–30.

43 Swann, in *Tierra Adentro*, pp. 90, 171–271, et passim, emphasizes the importance of ethnic and spatial exogamy in the marriage patterns of late eighteenth-century Nueva Vizcaya. His study combines careful demographic research at the parish (micro) level with regional comparative analysis. During this period, Swann argues, people of different racial groupings increasingly "selected marriage partners from outside their own settlements and parishes" and, further, "the growth of the mixed races was more likely the result of local increases in the rate of racially exogamous marriages than the outcome of any sizeable influx of mixed-race migrants" (p. 189).

44 Lavrin, "Introduction," in *Sexuality and Marriage in Colonial Latin America*, pp. 4–7; Ortega Noriega, "De amores y desamores," pp. 17–19.

45   Spicer, *Cycles of Conquest*, p. 471.

46   Ibid., pp. 470–75. For comparable observations among slave families in the United States and the Caribbean, see Gutman, "Marital and Sexual Norms among Slave Women," pp. 300–302. Robert McCaa found similar attitudes in late eighteenth-century Parral: "Women's Position, Family and Fertility in Mexico," pp. 233–43.

47   AMG AD 1: Fray Juan Felipe Martínez, *Padrón e inventario de la nueva misión de los seris*, 1796. On the ambiguous meanings of "illegitimacy" in Iberian law and custom, see Kuznesof, "The History of the Family in Latin America: A Critique of Recent Work," pp. 168–86; Lewin, "Natural and Spurious Children in Brazilian Inheritance Law from Colony to Empire: A Methodological Essay," pp. 351–96; McCaa, "Women's Position, Family and Fertility in Mexico"; and Calvo, *La Nueva Galicia en los siglos XVI y XVII*, pp. 19–94.

48   This interpretation of the Sonoran material is based on Chayanov, *The Theory of Peasant Economy*; Deere, "The Differentiation of the Peasantry and Family Structure," pp. 422–37; Gutman, *The Black Family in Slavery and Freedom*; Gutman, "Marital and Sexual Norms among Slave Women"; and Collier, *Marriage and Inequality in Classless Societies*, esp. chap. 4 ("Understanding Inequality"). On patriarchy in northern New Spain, with emphasis on political and social elites, see Gutiérrez, *When Jesus Came, The Corn Mothers Went Away*, pp. 227–97, 327–36; Martin, *Governance and Society in Colonial Mexico*, pp. 149–83.

49   Burguière, "La historia de la familia en Francia. Problemas y recientes aproximaciones," pp. 17–19; Le Roy Ladurie, *Montaillou. The Promised Land of Error*, pp. 24–52.

5   "Gypseys" and Villagers: Shifting Communities and Changing Ethnic Identities in Highland Sonora

1   See Spicer, *Cycles of Conquest*; McGuire, *Politics and Ethnicity on the Río Yaqui*; Meillassoux, *Maidens, Meal and Money*; Wolf, *Peasants*; Mallon, *The Defense of Community in Peru's Central Highlands* and *Peasant and Nation*; Collier, *Marriage and Inequality in Classless Societies*; and Ouweneel, *"Altepeme and Pueblos de Indios"*.

2   Spicer, in *Cycles of Conquest*, characterizes all the agricultural tribes of pre-Hispanic Sonora as "ranchería peoples" to distinguish them from the "band" nomads of the desert coastland and from the "village" people of New Mexico. For Sonora, however, I use *aldea* and *ranchería* to distinguish both the size and relative permanence of native settlements. In the colonial documentation, *ranchería* indicates a group of families who settled in a given place or moved together. AGN Jesuitas I-6, exp. 11, ff. 189–210, 1770.

3   Sauer, *Aboriginal Population of Northwestern Mexico*; Doolittle, "Aboriginal Agri-

cultural Development in the Valley of Sonora, Mexico"; Riley, Frontier People; Braniff, La frontera protohistórica Pima-Opata en Sonora, México.

4 Polzer, Rules and Precepts of the Jesuit Missions, p. 37; BL M-M 1716, vols. 1–77, "Informe sobre Guásabas," 1744.

5 AGN AHH leg. 17, exp. 24, 31, 1765–66; BNFF 36/800, 802, 806; 34/759. Also see Chapter 6 below on land tenure.

6 BL M-M 1716, vols. 1–77, "Informe sobre Tecoripa," 1744; AGN Jesuitas IV-10, exp. 5, f. 33; Viveros, ed., Informe sobre Sinaloa y Sonora, pp. 105–6; BNFF 32/674, "Informe sobre Ures," 1744. Also see the padrón for San Joséph de Pimas, 1796, AMH AD 1.

7 BL M-M 1716, vols. 1–77, "Informe sobre Santos Reyes de Cucurpe," 1744; Vara, La creciente. Dobyns, in From Fire to Flood, makes similar observations on the Gila, San Pedro, and Santa Cruz drainages of Arizona.

8 AGN Misiones 26. Father Juan Ortiz Zapata (b. Zacatecas, 1620) visited the entire Jesuit mission field of northwestern Mexico in 1678 and wrote a set of regulations following his visitation that same year (Polzer, Rules and Precepts, pp. 81–82).

9 AGN Jesuitas II-29, exp. 19: Padres Joseph Roldán, Thomas Pérez, and Manuel Aguirre to Padre Ignacio Lizassoaín, 1762, DRSW R III-C-4.

10 AGN Jesuitas II-29, exp. 19; AGN AHH leg. 17, exp. 35, 1744, and exp. 33, 1766. The population of Santa Catarina may refer to the Jobas of Nátora and San Matheo who, as Roldán reported earlier, had moved to the mission of Arivechi. The "branches" (ramos) associated with three different hamlets may correspond to bands or other kin segments of the ethnic group.

11 AGN Jesuitas II-29, exp. 19. One fanega = 55.5 liters, or 1.5 bushels; it also refers to the extent of land in which that amount of grain could be planted. See Barnes, Naylor, and Polzer, Northern New Spain, A Research Guide, pp. 69–72. (See Chapter 3, note 39 above.)

12 Padrón of Arivechi mission, 1796, AMH AS caja 22.

13 Dobyns, "Indian Extinction in the Middle Santa Cruz River Valley"; Velarde in Mange, Diario de las exploraciones en Sonora, pp. 91–94, 126; Crosswhite, "The Annual Saguaro Harvest and Crop Cycle of the Papago," pp. 69–75.

14 AGN Jesuitas IV-10, exp. 82, f. 114, 1764; Gerhard, The North Frontier of New Spain, pp. 174–78.

15 UASP Az 370, Padre Jacobo Sedelmayr to Visitador Padre Balthasar, 1749; AGN Jesuitas IV-10, exp. 119, f. 153, 1764, and IV-10, exp. 116, f. 180, 1764.

16 AGN Jesuitas IV-10, exp. 227, f. 262, 1767; Nentvig, 1767, BL M-M 1716, vols. 1–77; Nentvig, Descripción . . . de Sonora, pp. 220, 224.

17 AGN AHH leg. 278, exp. 20, 1748–49.

18 UASP ms. 40, 1799; John, Views from the Apache Frontier.

19 Viveros, ed., Informe sobre Sinaloa y Sonora, pp. 38–39, 106–11, 116–17; AGN AHH

278, exp. 17, 1748, and exp. 20: "Visita al rectorado de San Francisco Borja," 1749. Rodríguez Gallardo governed the province during his visit, having the power to investigate and remove local officials and to carry out administrative orders.

20   Padre Ortiz Zapata, 1678, AGN Misiones 26; AGN AHH 278, exp. 19, 1749; Viveros, ed., Informe sobre Sinaloa y Sonora, pp. 85, 107–8.

21   AGI Guadalajara 135, I.2, ff. 17–18, 29–33, 40–42; I.3a., ff. 48–54.

22   Officer, Hispanic Arizona, p. 40; Kessell, Friars, Soldiers, and Reformers, pp. 35 (map), 7, 40, 78; Viveros, ed., Informe sobre Sinaloa y Sonora, pp. 85, 104.

23   UASP ms. 145, 1767, "Gabriel Antonio de Vildósola, capitán del presidio y juez político de Fronteras, vende a su esposa María Rosa Bezerra Nieto, la hacienda Santa Bárbara compuesta de dos labores" (1756); AHGES TP 15, 192, 1801–14; AGN Tierras 1421, 8, 1814; 1423, 16, 1818.

24   AGI Guadalajara 188, ff. 277–356, 1749–50.

25   Spicer, Cycles of Conquest, pp. 105–12; Viveros, ed., Informe sobre Sinaloa y Sonora, pp. 44–55, 59–61, 102–4; UASP Az 370; AGN AHH 278, exp. 18 (Jesuit missionaries P. Segesser, C. Rojas, and T. Miranda protested the usurpation of Pima lands in Nacameri). See Sheridan, "Cross or Arrow?" pp. 317–34.

26   Fray Antonio de los Reyes, "Noticia del actual estado de las misiones que en la gobernación de Sonora administran los PP. del Colegio de Propaganda Fide de la Santa Cruz," July 6, 1772, AGN Historia 16, exp. 8, ff. 229–62v.

27   Fray Mattheo Diez de Josef and Fray Francisco Canales to Bishop Rouset de Jesús, 1796, UA 811, roll 2. This film was made by UA, but I consulted it in INAH, Centro Sonora.

28   Kessell, Friars, Soldiers, and Reformers, pp. 161–63; Gerhard, The North Frontier of New Spain, pp. 284–85. On Indians who went to the presidios for short periods of time, see AGN Jesuitas IV-10, exp. 72, f. 103, 1764.

29   AGI Guadalajara 505, ff. 377–78.

30   Francisco Antonio Crespo to Viceroy Antonio María Bucareli, 1774, AGN Provincias Internas 247, ff. 359–61 (reproduced in McCarty, ed. and trans., Desert Documentary, pp. 19–24).

31   AGN Minería 11, f. 119, Pedro Corbalán to Viceroy Bucareli (cited in Gutiérrez, "Estado, comercio, y minería en Sonora de 1769–1782," pp. 24–25).

32   Pineda, "The Baroyeca Mine in Spanish Sonora," pp. 192–205.

33   BNFF 32/659, Juan Gortari, Real de Aigame, 1803; BNFF 36/815, Pedro de Villaescusa, San Carlos de Buenavista, 1803. On Villaescusa's military career, see Almada, Diccionario, p. 727.

34   Bishop Reyes to Viceroy Matías de Gálvez, 1784, BNFF 34/759.

35   BNFF 36/800; Kessell, Friars, Soldiers, Reformers, pp. 170–77.

36   Fray Juan de Santiestéban to Bishop Rouset, 1796, AMH AD 1; Felger and Moser, People of the Desert and Sea, p. 10; Crosswhite, "The Annual Saguaro

Harvest and Crop Cycle of the Papago"; Bell, Anderson, and Stewart, *The Quitobaquito Cemetery.*

37 Kessell, *Friars, Soldiers, and Reformers*; Officer, *Hispanic Arizona*; Voss, *On the Periphery of Nineteenth-Century Mexico,* pp. 24–32.

38 See García Martínez, "Pueblos de Indios, Pueblos de Castas," on central New Spain.

39 AMH AS 1, 1666–1828 (baptism). The early Aconchi records are fragmentary and conserved together with other mission accounts and inventories.

40 AGN Jesuitas IV-10, exp. 142, f. 176; exp. 146, f. 180; exp. 149–50, ff. 183–84; exp. 158, f. 192.

41 AGN Jesuitas IV-10, exp. 172, f. 206 (Ures, 1766). Two fanegas = 3 bushels; 2 almudes = 8.2 quarts.

42 AGN AHH leg. 17, exp. 32, 1766.

43 AMH AD 1, Pedro Galindo Navarro, 1785; Kessell, *Friars, Soldiers, and Reformers,* p. 165. Galindo Navarro referred to Law 21, title 3, book 6 of the *Recopilación de leyes de los reynos de las Indias* (1680).

44 AGN Jesuitas IV-10, exp. 231, f. 266 (Governor Pineda, San Miguel de Horcasitas, 1767).

45 Robinson, "Patrones de migración en Michoacán en el siglo XVIII," pp. 169–73. Favre, in "The Dynamics of Indian Peasant Society and Migration," pp. 253–67, documents a comparable process of community fission in the Peruvian puna. Wightman, in *Indigenous Migration and Social Change,* examines Andean migrations and the absorption of *forasteros* into alien communities. Farriss, in *Maya Society under Colonial Rule,* pp. 200–223, identifies three related patterns of "drift, dispersal, and flight" in Yucatán.

46 Hawkins, "Ethnicity in Mesoamerica," pp. 23–27; Radding, *Las estructuras socioeconómicas de la misiones de la Pimería Alta,* pp. 47–48; Stoler, "Rethinking Colonial Categories," pp. 134–61.

47 Deere, in "The Differentiation of the Peasantry and Family Structure," pp. 428–29, 436, emphasizes the particular social relations of production arising from the peasant–landlord relationship in highland Peru.

6   Land and the Indian Común

1 BPEJ ARAG RC 27-9-359, 1716, 15 folios: "Los pimas de Xecatacari y Obiachi a Thomas de Esquivel, teniente de justicia mayor del Real de San Miguel Arcángel y su jurisdicción en la Provincia de Sonora."

2 BPEJ ARAG RC 27-9-359, f. 13v. "Despoblado" in this context refers to the absence both of livestock and people. Buena Vista was probably occupied by Pimas from numerous *rancherías* of the middle Yaqui River until mid-century; following the Cáhita and Pima rebellion of 1739–41, the Spanish

built the Presidio de San Carlos de Buena Vista on or near the site of the Pimas' village. By the turn of the nineteenth century, "El Jacatecare" appeared as a ranch belonging to a military captain's widow (BNFF 36/815). For further references to Xecatacari, see Daniel Januske, S.J., *Informe del estado presente en que se hallan las misiones de Sonora*, AHH Temporalidades leg. 17, exp. 2, 1722. I thank Fritz Jandrey of Documentary Relations of the Southwest, University of Arizona, for this archival citation.

3   AGN AHH leg. 278, exp. 10 (18 folios), and AHP UA microfilm 318, roll 1723B (31 folios). See Sheridan, *Where the Dove Calls*, pp. 15, 150.

4   Real de la Soledad, located west of Cucurpe, was abandoned in 1757 (Nentvig, *Descripción . . . de Sonora*, p. 182). The Jesuit Francisco Eusebio Kino used Cucurpe as his base of operations to support mission expansion into the Pimería Alta. The ranch (*estancia*) to which the Indian witnesses of Cucurpe referred supplied cattle to the Pima missions of Dolores and Remedios northeast of Cucurpe.

5   On the conventional meaning of "desde tiempo inmemorial" and its legal ambiguities, see Van Young, *Hacienda and Market in Eighteenth-Century Mexico*, p. 326, n. 28.

6   AHP UA 318, roll 1723B, f. 8v.

7   Carmagnani, *El regreso de los dioses*, pp. 13–16; García Martínez, "Jurisdicción y propiedad," pp. 47–60.

8   *Recopilación de leyes de los reynos de las Indias* (1680), Libro IV Título XII: De la venta, composición y repartimiento de tierras, solares y aguas, Ley V. See Rivera Marín de Iturbe, *La propiedad territorial en México, 1301–1810*.

9   *Recopilación* (1680), Libro IV Título XII, Ley V.

10   Meyer, *Water in the Southwest*, pp. 123–28.

11   AGN AHH Temporalidades leg. 1165, "Medidas de tierras y modo de medirlas que están en uso según las ordenanzas"; YSMA LAMC group 307, series I, box 3, folder 57, "Método de medir tierras y aguas segun la costumbre y uso en las Provincias de N.E. arreglado a la ordenanza de la materia"; Meyer, *Water in the Southwest*, p. 122, n. 28, and pp. 128–30; Barnes, Naylor, and Polzer, *Northern New Spain, A Research Guide*, pp. 69–72.

12   Meyer, *Water in the Southwest*, pp. 117–20.

13   Ibid., pp. 133–43.

14   Avalos, "The Colonial Period of Mexico and Its Legal Personality," p. 3; Ebright, "Introduction," in *Spanish and Mexican Land Grants and the Law*, pp. 3–11.

15   *Recopilación* (1680). The relevant sections for this chapter are Libro IV, Títulos VII, XII; Libro VI, Título III.

16   AGN Tierras 1424, exp. 9; Río, "El noroeste novohispano y la nueva política imperial española," pp. 193–219. García Martínez, in "Jurisdicción y

propiedad," analyzes the circumscription of Indian pueblos' jurisdictional space by the Spanish state in sixteenth-century Mesoamerica.

17 Ebright, "Introduction," p. 4.

18 Gálvez's decree is in BNFF 34/740, 741; Río, "El noroeste novohispano," pp. 209–10; Escandón, "La nueva administración misional y los pueblos de indios," pp. 258–64. Efforts to collect tribute and the tithe in Sonora met with failure (see Chapter 3 above).

19 Pedro de Corbalán, Informe, 1772, AHGES; Informe reservado, 1778, BNFF 34/738.

20 Pedro de Nava, 1794, AGI Guadalajara 586.

21 During the wars of independence, Sonora remained nominally under the administration of the Intendencia de Arizpe and the Comandancia de Provincias Internas de Occidente. After 1821, the northwestern provinces sent delegates to the Diputación Provincial convened under the auspices of Iturbide. In 1824, Sonora and Sinaloa became part of the constitutional Republic of Mexico as the unified Estado de Occidente, but they divided into two separate states in 1831.

22 Radding, Las estructuras socioeconómicas de las misiones, pp. 28–29, 88–90; Romero, "La privatización de la tenencia de la tierra," pp. 150–58; Juan de Gándara, Protector de Indios de Opodepe, to Fiscal Protector General de Indios, July 24, 1818, BPEJ ARAG RC 264-5-3600; Fernando Ma Grande, Visitador de las Misiones de la Pimería Alta, to Gobernador del Estado de Occidente, 1828 (I consulted a copy of this document through the courtesy of Kieran R. McCarty).

23 Sonoran state decrees were consulted in AHGES caja 36-1, exp. 1052. Laws directly concerning land tenure are no. 3 (1833), no. 10 (1834), and nos. 41, 47, 62, 75 (1835).

24 The evidence on which this statement is based comes from the Archivo de Instrumentos Públicos de Jalisco (AIPJ), Ramos de Tierras y Aguas (RTA) and Libros de Gobierno de la Audiencia (LGA). See, for example, measurements of the landholdings of the Murrieta and Valenzuela families in four different localities in the vicinity of Baroyeca: AIPJ RTA 1a. Colección, libro 10, exp. 157, ff. 410v–17.

25 AIPJ LGA 47G, ff. 218–20.

26 AIPJ LGA 47G, ff. 220v–22v: "Título de confirmación de la merced y composición al pueblo común y naturales de Santa Anna de Nuri en el Reyno de la Nueva Vizcaya . . ."

27 AHP UA microfilm 318, roll 1723A, B.

28 BL M-M 1716, Padre Carlos de Roxas, 1744; Archivo Eclesiástico de Arizpe, Libro de Bautismos, 1740–90.

29 BNFF 34/733, 9 folios, 1778: "Descripción de Arizpe."

30 AMH AS 1, 1666–1828, Aconchi/Baviácora account books, 1726.

31 BNFF 34/759, f. 23, 1784.

32 Nentvig, Descripción . . . de Sonora, pp. 137, 177–78.

33 Tamarón y Romeral, Descripción de la diócesis de Nueva Vizcaya, p. 1013. Nentvig, Descripción . . . de Sonora, p. 174, reported smaller numbers for Tonibabi and Tepache. The discrepancy in the figure for these two reports of 1761 and 1762 is no doubt owing to demographic fluctuations in the mining centers of Sonora.

34 AGN Tierras 474, exp. 2, ff. 1–161. Captain Alvarez Tuñón y Quiroz was commander of the compañía volante stationed at the Presidio de Fronteras and served as alcalde mayor of the province in 1719. Prudhom's full title was "Alcalde Mayor Gabriel de Prudhom, Butrón y Mújica, Barón de Heijder." Almada, Diccionario, pp. 46–49; Mirafuentes Galván, "Elite y defensa," pp. 419–21.

35 AMH AD 1, exp. 1–30, 1765; BNFF 37/833, 1807. Moreno was the executor of Grijalba's will. The Morenos followed a pattern of criollo behavior which was widely observed in other regions of New Spain, but which occurred less frequently in this frontier province. This is the only capellanía I have found for Sonora, although numerous such liens were registered in the districts of Alamos, Culiacán, and Rosario to the south. On capellanías and censos, see Bauer, La iglesia en la economía de América Latina and "The Church and Spanish American Agrarian Structures," pp. 78–98; Van Young, Hacienda and Market in Eighteenth-Century Mexico, pp. 182–91; and Florescano, "The Hacienda in New Spain," pp. 250–85.

36 AHGES TP leg. IV, exp. 44, ff. 1091–1123, 1773–1808.

37 BNFF 35/722, 1790; AHGES leg. VII, exp. 87, 1833–34; AGN Gobernación caja 3, año 1837.

38 BNFF 34/736. See Table 3.10 above.

39 BNFF 34/763, 764.

40 Fray Núñez Fundidor, "Relación de Bacerác" (1777), BNFF ms. 1762, ff. 88–142.

41 Fundidor, "Relación de Bacerác"; Polzer, "The Franciscan Entrada into Sonora, 1646–1652: A Jesuit Chronicle," pp. 253–78; McCarty, A Spanish Frontier in the Enlightened Age, p. 43. Franciscans began missions in this valley in 1646; in 1650 the Society of Jesus received jurisdiction over the area, and the Jesuits administered these pueblos until 1767. In 1768 the Franciscan Provincia de Jalisco took charge of Opata missions.

42 Fundidor, "Relación de Bacerác"; BNFF 35/722, 1790, ff. 3–6.

43 BNFF 35/722, f. 5. One vara = 83 centimeters, or 2.7 feet.

44 BNFF 35/722, ff. 2v–3. Caballero Teodoro de Croix was the first "Coman-

dante de Provincias Internas," arriving in Arizpe in 1779; Ugarte y Loyola was "Comandante General de las Provincias Internas" in 1786.

45 BNFF 35/763; Gómez Canedo, ed., *Sonora hacia fines del siglo XVIII*, pp. 64–69, 106–10. After the ephemeral and unlamented *custodia* of San Carlos de Sonora imposed by Bishop Reyes (1783–87), five of the principal missions administered by the Franciscan province of Xalisco were secularized in 1791: Aconchi, Banámichi, Ures, Mátape, and Onavas.

46 Sheridan, *Where the Dove Calls*, pp. 84–88. Mesquite and *encinas* dominate different altitudes. *Encinas* grasslands are highly valued as natural pasture, and mesquite pods nourish cattle.

47 *Real cédula* of February 14, 1805, cited by Intendant-Governor Alexo Carcía Conde in AGN *Tierras* 1422, 6.

48 For similar observations on the early nineteenth-century United States concerning the absence of competitive bidding, see Hahn, *The Roots of Southern Populism*, pp. 76–85; and Faragher, *Sugar Creek*, pp. 55–56.

49 AHGES TP tomo IV, exp. 40, ff. 899–947.

50 AHGES TP leg. 1, exp. 1, 1831. Vicente Ybarra may be the son of José Vicente Ybarra, named as Indian governor in the previous case. The younger Ybarra is identified only as "ciudadano."

51 BNFF 35/722; AMH AD 1, "Padrón de Batuc," 1796.

52 AHGES TP leg. 7, exp. 87, ff. 1304–50.

53 AHGES TP leg. 7, exp. 83, ff. 1188–1218.

54 AHGES TP leg. 7, exp. 84–85, ff. 1219–89.

55 AHGES TP leg. 9, exp. 114, ff. 955–1014, 1847.

56 In subtropical zones of Indoamerica, the shifting quality of the *milpa* is associated with swidden agriculture and rotating fields. See Farriss, *Maya Society under Colonial Rule*, pp. 125–28; Boserup, *The Conditions of Agricultural Growth*, pp. 15–17.

57 AGN *Tierras* 1423, exp. 16, 29 folios (1818–19).

58 AGN *Tierras* 1423, exp. 14, 22 folios.

59 AGN *Tierras* 1423, exp. 16.

60 AGN *Tierras* 1421, exp. 8, 26 folios (1814–18). San Bernardino and Santa Rosa de Corodéhuachi were two different presidios referred to as "Fronteras."

61 AHGES TP leg. 15, exp. 192, 1819–21. Escalante actually paid only 164 pesos, 6 reales, claiming damages for the loss of the original title awarded to his father.

62 AGN *Tierras* 1423, exp. 15, 22 folios (1818–19). José Desiderio was no doubt a brother or cousin of José Manuel de Vildósola, the mining deputy of Arizpe named above.

63 AGI *Guadalajara* 135, I, 3, ff. 48–54 (1731–32); Viveros, ed., *Informe sobre Sina-*

loa y Sonora, pp. 38–39, 106–11, 116–17; AGN AHH 278, exp. 17 (1748); Kessell, *Mission of Sorrows*, p. 43.

64   Bartlett, *Personal Narrative*, vol. 1, pp. 260, 273.

65   Dobyns, *From Fire to Flood*; Van Young, "Conflict and Solidarity in Indian Village Life"; White, *The Roots of Dependency*, pp. 29–33.

66   For similar observations concerning the moderate size of late-colonial private estates and the subdivision of large haciendas into smaller units which were rented out through various tenancy and sharecropping arrangements, see Van Young, *Hacienda and Market in Eighteenth-Century Mexico*, pp. 110–13 et seq.; Brading, *Haciendas y ranchos del Bajío*, p. 65 et passim; and Cuello, "El mito de la hacienda colonial en el norte de México," pp. 186–205. Jacobsen, in *Mirages of Transition*, pp. 201–26, shows that nineteenth-century highland Peruvian haciendas were formed by purchasing numerous peasant holdings.

67   AHGES TP leg. 2, exp. 18, 1835. Ignacio Elías González was commandant of the Presidio de Tubac. He and Juan Rafael were probably third-generation descendants of Francisco Elías González de Zayas, who had emigrated from Spain and settled in Alamos, a prosperous mining *real* in the province of Sinaloa in the 1720s. Twenty years later, Francisco received a commission in the Spanish army, serving in Janos (Chihuahua) and Terrenate (Sonora). His personal and family interests were centered in northern Sonora (see Officer, *Hispanic Arizona*, pp. 317–24).

68   Deeds, "Land Tenure Patterns in Northern New Spain," p. 448. See Robinson, ed., *Social Fabric and Spatial Structure*, esp. Robinson, "Introduction," and Swann, "Spatial Dimensions of a Social Process," pp. 117–80; West, *The Mining Community of Northern New Spain*; Florescano, "The Hacienda in New Spain," pp. 250–85; Van Young, *Hacienda and Market in Eighteenth-Century Mexico*; Van Young, "Mexican Rural History since Chevalier," p. 26; Van Young, "Conflict and Solidarity in Indian Village Life"; Cuello, "Saltillo in the Seventeenth Century"; Morin, *Michoacán en la Nueva España del siglo XVIII*; and Bakewell, *Silver Mining and Society in Colonial Mexico*.

69   Ouweneel, "The Agrarian Cycle," pp. 399–417; Melville, *A Plague of Sheep*; García Martínez, *Los pueblos de la sierra*; Chance, *Conquest of the Sierra*; Richard Garner, *Economic Growth and Change in Bourbon Mexico*.

70   Enrique Florescano, Claude Morin, and David Brading have shown dramatic cycles of grain prices in central and western Mexico during the eighteenth century, linking them to subsistence crises. Garner's detailed statistical analysis of maize prices across a number of regions points to a modest secular rise in prices, having noticeable impact after the "great hunger" of 1785–86.

71 Ouweneel, "The Agrarian Cycle."

72 Gibson, *The Aztecs under Spanish Rule*; Tutino, *From Insurrection to Revolution*; Brading, *Haciendas y ranchos del Bajío*; Van Young, *Hacienda and Market in Eighteenth-Century Mexico*; Taylor, *Landlord and Peasant in Colonial Oaxaca*; Chance, *Race and Class in Colonial Oaxaca*; Carmagnani, *El regreso de los dioses*.

73 West, *The Mining Community of Northern New Spain*; West *Sonora. Its geographical personality*, pp. 44–59; Swann, *Tierra Adentro*, pp. 22–25, 49–53; Deeds, "Land Tenure Patterns in Northern New Spain."

74 Contrast, for example, Schwartz, *Sugar Plantations*; Florescano, ed., *Haciendas y plantaciones*; Jacobsen, *Mirages of Transition*; and Ramírez, *Provincial Patriarchs*, pp. 95–206.

75 See Chapter 7 below on property sale and inheritance among non-Indian smallholders in Sonora. Also see Van Young, "Mexican Rural History since Chevalier," pp. 27–28.

76 Cuello, "The Persistence of Indian Slavery and Encomienda," pp. 683–700; Deeds, "Rural Work in Nueva Vizcaya," pp. 425–50.

77 Bazant, *Cinco haciendas mexicanas*; González Sánchez, "Sistemas de trabajo, salarios y situación de los trabajadores agrícolas, 1750–1810," pp. 125–72; Bauer, "Rural Workers in Spanish America," pp. 34–65; Tutino, "Life and Labor on North Mexican Haciendas"; Moreno García, *Haciendas de tierra y agua*; Nickel, *Morfología social de la hacienda mexicana*.

78 Semo, *Historia mexicana. Economía y lucha de clases*; Cuello, "El mito de la hacienda colonial"; Radding, "Acumulación originaria en el agro sonorense"; Deeds, "Land Tenure Patterns in Northern New Spain," p. 450; Van Young, "Mexican Rural History since Chevalier," pp. 13–27; Van Young, *Hacienda and Market in Eighteenth-Century Mexico*, pp. 343–57.

7 Peasants, Hacendados, and Merchants: The Cultural Differentiation of Sonoran Society

1 AHGES TP leg. 6, exp. 66, f. 91.

2 A NO book E-17 A-2, doc. 44, 1817. The *alcalde de barrio* was a neighborhood official. *Vecinos* were citizens with established residency and implicit property rights, subject to taxation and military service.

3 A NO doc. 46047, ff. 94–99, 1817. I have translated *vecinos criadores* (breeders) as "stockmen" or "pastoralists."

4 A NO doc. 47, f. 97.

5 Rivera Marín de Iturbe, *La propiedad territorial en México*, pp. 210–11.

6 A NO doc. 46, f. 94: ". . . hecho donación a la iglesia parroquial de este presidio de los bienes de ganado mayor que al tiempo de las recogidas para

los herraderos se hallase orejano como propio de todos los vecinos." On the collective labor for cattle drives and corporate rangeland in the San Miguel Valley, see Sheridan, *Where the Dove Calls*, pp. 47, 83–105.

7   Molina Molina, *Historia de Hermosillo antiguo*, pp. 17–87; Rodríguez Gallardo, *Informe*; J. Sedelmayr to Juan Antonio Balthasar, UASP Az 370, 1749, ff. 1–4; Joseph de Urrutia, *Plan del Real Presidio de San Miguel de Horcasitas* (1767) British Museum K 19929.

8   Molina Molina, *Historia de Hermosillo*, pp. 115–37; BNFF 32/659, "Nota individual y comprensiva de las suertes de tierra repartidas en la Villa de Pitic"; "Plan de Pitic," AGN *Tierras* 2773, exp. 22, 1785.

9   UA microfilm 811, roll 2; Molina Molina, *Historia de Hermosillo*, pp. 120–23.

10   AMH: Fray Juan Felipe Martínez, *Padrón e inventario de la nueva misión de los seris* (1796). Also see Felger and Moser, *People of the Desert and Sea*, pp. 9–13; Gerhard, *The North Frontier of New Spain*, pp. 283–84. The Guaymas, also referred to as Huimas, were brought into the Yaqui mission of Belén a century earlier, where some remained in the 1790s. Captain Loredo (BNFF 37/822) reported in 1804 only 166 persons in Pueblo de Seris, counting men, women, and children.

11   AMH, Fray Pascual Lucas Hernández, 1796, "Relación del Real Presidio del Pitic" (cited in Molina Molina, *Historia de Hermosillo*).

12   Barnes, Naylor, and Polzer, *Northern New Spain, A Research Guide*, p. 69; "Plan de Pitic" (see note 8 above), f. 243.

13   A NO doc. 19, ff. 42–43, January 29, 1811 ($\frac{1}{4}$ suerte = 6.6 acres).

14   A NO doc. 12, 1793.

15   A NO doc. 73, ff. 136–37, April 21, 1819.

16   Fernández de Loredo, 1804, BNFF 36/819.

17   Dionisio de Aguilar, hacendado and merchant in Horcasitas, enjoyed the financial backing of Manuel Rodríguez to bid for the sale of tobacco, gunpowder, and playing cards in 1817 (A NO doc. 50, ff. 106–7). See also BNFF 32/652, an anonymous report on the difficulties of establishing the *estanco de tabaco* at mid-eighteenth century.

18   Loredo, 1804 (see note 16 above); BNFF 37/822, ff. 1–3. One cuartillo was half a liter, worth three reales.

19   A NO doc. 6, 14, ff. 29–32, 1790; AHGES TP 1, 9, ff. 487–510.

20   A NO doc. 17, ff. 37–39, 1809.

21   A NO doc. 9, ff. 19–20, 1808.

22   A NO doc. 7, ff. 15–16, 1808.

23   A NO doc. 57, ff. 118–19, 1817.

24   A NO doc. 17, 37–39. Vidal's widow indicated that the land in question measured six cordeles by two cordeles (*cordel* is the coiled rope used for measuring land). If each cordel was 50 varas, the standard length, then the plot

comprised 30,000 square varas, or one-fifth of a suerte (approximately five acres). In her will she explained that José María had not consulted María Josefa's siblings at the time he gave her the land, because they were very young, and "although he asked my opinion, I left the decision up to him."

25 A NO doc. 14, ff. 29–32, 1790.

26 A NO doc. 31, ff. 63–65, 1816. Palacios's references to "plata labrada" indicate silverware.

27 See Courturier, "Women and the Family in Eighteenth-Century Mexico: Law and Practice"; Lavrín and Couturier, "Dowries and Wills: A View of Women's Social and Economic Role in Colonial Guadalajara and Puebla"; Nazzari, *Disappearance of the Dowry* (referring to Brazil).

28 Couturier, "Women and the Family," p. 296. See below for examples of *mejoras* and the *quinta* awarded to heirs of Sonoran estates. Some of the private land claims that conflicted with the customary communal land use discussed in Chapter 6 above had to do with siblings who sold or ceded their shares to one heir in the vicinity of Mátape, Batuc, or Cumpas.

29 A NO doc. 14, ff. 29–32, 1790.

30 See Nazzari, *Disappearance of the Dowry*, pp. xviii–xx.

31 A NO doc. 84, ff. 153–54, 1820.

32 A NO doc. 84, ff. 153–54, 1820. Uruchurtu appears in a number of credit transactions during the latter years of the decade of 1810–20: A NO doc. 76, 82, 83.

33 A NO doc. 49, ff. 102–4, 1817.

34 A NO doc. 28, ff. 57–58, 1816.

35 A NO doc. 42, ff. 84–85, 1817; doc. 72, ff. 134–35, 1819.

36 On the intersection of gender and class relations, see Mallon, "Patriarchy in the Transition to Capitalism."

37 A NO doc. 41, ff. 82–83, April 5, 1817. Velasco was a prominent hacendado and merchant in Pitic. He had a distinguished career in Sonora following Mexican independence: he was a deputy in the First General Congress, 1822; as state legislator, he helped draft the constitutions of Occidente (1825) and Sonora (1831). Early in his career, he was administrator of the placer mines of Cieneguilla in northwestern Sonora. A member of the Sociedad Mexicana de Geografía y Estadística, he wrote *Noticias estadísticas del estado de Sonora*, published first by the Sociedad (1860–65) and now a classic source on nineteenth-century Sonora (Antochiw, "Introduccíon," in Velasco, *Noticias*, p. 8.

38 BNFF 32/659, 1785; A NO doc. 1, 1783. On Monteagudo's antecedents, see AGN Jesuitas IV-10, exp. 72, f. 103.

39 A NO doc. 5, December 1, 1790.

40 A NO doc. 2, ff. 3–6, March 23, 1786.

41   A NO doc. 20, f. 44, 1803–9.

42   Smith, "How Marketing Systems Affect Economic Opportunity in Agrarian Societies"; Bath, "Dos modelos referidos a la relación entre población y economía en Nueva España y Perú durante la época colonial."

43   These observations exemplify simple commodity production and different forms of exchange in peasant economies. See, for example, Lehmann, ed., *Ecology and Exchange in the Andes*; Larson, *Colonialism and Agrarian Transformation in Bolivia*; Jacobsen, *Mirages of Transition*; Halperin and Dow, eds., *Peasant Livelihood*; Sheridan, *Where the Dove Calls*; Faragher, *Sugar Creek*; and Smith, *Livelihood and Resistance*.

44   A NO doc. 27, ff. 55–56, 1816. *Beatas* are devout laywomen who clean the church and care for the saints.

45   A NO doc. 55, ff. 115–16, 1817. Terms like "la china" and "el coyote" are local ethnic labels indicating mixed racial types. Mendibel "del yaqui" may have been an Indian from the Yaqui Valley.

46   A NO doc. 27, ff. 55–56, 1816.

47   This statement is based on A NO book E-17, A-2, thirty-one cases from 1801 to 1820.

48   A NO doc. 23, 1801.

49   A NO doc. 34, f. 70, 1816; doc. 40, ff. 80–81, 1816; doc. 45, ff. 92–93, 1817; doc. 77, f. 144, 1819.

50   A NO doc. 76, ff. 142–45, 1819.

51   A NO doc. 72, ff. 134–35, 1819.

52   See Smith, "Reflections on the Social Relations of Simple Commodity Production"; Chevalier, "There Is Nothing Simple about Simple Commodity Production"; Meillassoux, *Maidens, Meal and Money*; Orlove, "Against a Definition of Peasantries"; Chayanov, *The Theory of Peasant Economy*; Hahn, *The Roots of Southern Populism*; Hahn and Prude, eds., *The Countryside in the Age of Capitalist Transformation*; Mallon, *The Defense of Community in Peru's Central Highlands*; Merrill, "Cash Is Good to Eat."

53   Brusone, "Problemas del régimen de apropiación de la tierra"; Van Young, *Hacienda and Market in Eighteenth-Century Mexico*, pp. 107–13.

54   A NO doc. 22, ff. 47–48, September 27, 1805. *Hijuela*, in this case, is a title to a small rustic property; it can also mean an inheritance.

55   One sitio = 1 square league, or approximately 4,300 acres. Barnes, Naylor, and Polzer, *Northern New Spain, A Research Guide*, p. 69.

56   See Juan Gortari, *subdelegado*, "Haciendas y ranchos en el río de Horcasitas" (Real del Aygame, July 20, 1803), BNFF 32/659.

57   AHGES TP leg. 3, exp. 24.

58   See Brading, *Haciendas y ranchos del Bajío*, pp. 123–72 et seq. The labor of early eighteenth-century Guanajuato was much larger than the property which

went by that same term in nineteenth-century Sonora. In addition, see Rodolfo Fernández, "Ambito regional, haciendas y grupos de intereses," pp. 33–50; María Eugenia García Ugarte, "La transición de hacendados a rancheros en Querétaro," pp. 69–75; and Luis González, "Del hombre a caballo y la cultura ranchera," pp. 111–20 — all in *Las formas y las políticas del dominio agrario: Homenaje a François Chevalier.*

59 On the Valencia holdings, see AHGES TP leg. 1, exp. 9, ff. 487–510, 1788; A NO doc. 14, ff. 29–32, 1790.

60 A NO doc. 66, December 29, 1818.

61 AGN *Tierras* 1422, 6, (35 folios), 1805–19.

62 Mauricio Carrillo, *alcalde* of Arizpe, certified a land sale between Vicente Valencia and Jesús Juraso on July 15, 1836 (private archive, courtesy of Marco Antonio Valencia Arvizu, Hermosillo).

63 Legal provisions for reconsidering land sales cited in the Hermosillo notarial archives are based on "Ley 4 del título 7, libro 5° del ordenamiento real, establecida en Alcalá de Emares, que es la primera del título 11, libro 5° de la recopilación" (A NO doc. 19, ff. 42–43, 1811).

64 AGN *Tierras* 1422, 6 (1805–13) 35f.

65 AGN *Tierras* 1416, 11 (1811–19) 18f.

66 AGN *Tierras* 1422, 3, 1810; also see Table 7.5 above. Víctores and Dionisio de Aguilar, brothers, were Spanish immigrants. See as well Voss, *On the Periphery*, p. 28.

67 AGN *Tierras* 1424, 10 (1807–13).

68 AGN *Tierras* 1424, 7, 1816. See below on the combined properties of Batobavi and Bacobavi.

69 AGN *Tierras* 1424, 9 (1809–19). The *ayuntamiento* of the Villa de Horcasitas was one of the first to be established in the province of Sonora. Its members were prominent landowners and merchants in the community: Víctores de Aguilar (*alcalde constitucional*), Francisco de Campillo (*peninsular* and owner of El Sauz and La Palma), Francisco Escobosa, and Joaquín de Islas. Ignacio Colosio led the townsmen of Nacameri in their struggle to keep the land.

70 "Decreto 51 del Gobierno del Estado de Occidente," February 17, 1828, AHGES caja 331, Ramo de Tierras, tomo 1098 (cited in Romero, "La privatización de la tenencia de la tierra," p. 159).

71 Romero, "La privatización de la tenencia de la tierra," pp. 160–78.

72 AHGES TP leg. 5, exp. 48, 1835.

73 AHGES TP leg. 5, exp. 52–53, ff. 1573–1643 (1830–43).

74 AHGES TP leg. 5, exp. 47, 49, ff. 1279–1322, 1419–72 (1814–54). On Francisco Alejandro Aguilar, see Voss, *On the Periphery*, pp. 108, 139.

75 AGN *Tierras* 1422, 1, 1813–19.

76 AHGES TP leg. 7, exp. 82, ff. 1150–85; leg. 6, exp. 66, ff. 74–308 (quotation

on f. 91). In the centralist regime of that time the states were called "departments."

77 AHGES TP leg. 6, exp. 66: "Ley Orgánica de Hacienda #26, 1834" and "Reglamento para la Medida de Terrenos de Cría de Ganado Mayor y Caballada No. 30, 1835, Decreto No. 51, 1835."

78 AHGES TP leg. 6, exp. 66, ff. 102–5.

79 AHGES TP leg. 6, exp. 66, ff. 110–13.

80 AGHES TP leg. 6, exp. 66, ff. 141–44.

81 AGHES TP leg. 6, exp. 66, ff. 281–86.

82 Van Young, Hacienda and Market in Eighteenth-Century Mexico, pp. 271–342, and Brading, Haciendas y ranchos del Bajío, show an active market for landed estates in Guadalajara and the Bajío, areas dominated by urban markets. On peasant acquisition and rental of land, see Chayanov, The Theory of Peasant Economy, pp. 90–117; Martínez-Alier, "Relations of Production in Andean Haciendas," pp. 141–64; Chevalier, "There Is Nothing Simple about Simple Commodity Production," pp. 164–66; Shanin, "The Nature and Logic of the Peasant Economy," pp. 75–6; Wolf, Peasants, pp. 50–59; Caballero, Economía agraria de la sierra peruana, pp. 316–25; and Lenin, El desarrollo del capitalismo en Rusia, pp. 70–82.

83 Jacobsen and Puhle, eds., The Economies of Mexico and Peru; Ouweneel, "Raíces del 'chiaroscuro' en México," pp. 1–14; Van Young, "A modo de conclusión: El siglo paradójico," pp. 206–31; Garner, "Price Trends in Eighteenth-Century Mexico."

84 AMH AS I (1783–1822).

8 Cultural Endurance and Accommodation to Spanish Rule

1 Spicer, Cycles of Conquest, pp. 581–86; Spicer, The Yaquis. A Cultural History, pp. 337–62.

2 See, for example, Carmagnani, El regreso de los dioses; Gosner, "Critical Perspectives on the Construction of Ethnic Identity: Debating 'Indian-ness' in Colonial Central America"; Powers, Andean Journeys, passim; and Schwartz, "Introduction," in Schwartz, ed., Implicit Understandings, pp. 2–7.

3 Farriss, in "Indians in Colonial Yucatan: Three Perspectives," pp. 1–39, argues that acculturation is too limiting a term because it assumes the assimilation of Indians into the dominant culture, and suggests that "much more common may be the transformation of old forms into something that never existed in either of the original cultures" (p. 2). Also see Clendinnen, Aztecs. An Interpretation, p. 2.

4 Stern, Peru's Indian Peoples and the Challenge of Spanish Conquest, pp. 138–57; Stern,

"Introduction to Part I," pp. 29–30, and "The Age of Andean Insurrection, 1742–1782: A Reappraisal," pp. 34–93, in Stern, ed., *Resistance, Rebellion, and Consciousness in the Andean Peasant World*.

5 BNFF 34/735, 1777. Named to investigate the case were the following three *vecinos*: Buenaventura de Guandurraga, former *alcalde mayor*; Agustín de Asóstegui, former *juez comisario* of Ures; Rafael de la Estrella, then *juez comisario* of Ures.

6 BNFF 40/912, 1779.

7 BNFF 38/844, ff. 9–10.

8 BNFF 38/843, ff. 5–6, 1765.

9 BNFF 38/842. The document is undated, but by internal evidence this incident seems to have occurred on the heels of the Pima revolt of 1751.

10 BNFF 38/867, f. 3, 1764.

11 BNFF 38/867, f. 5. It is interesting to compare Pineda's description of the Sobaípuri *cacique* Chachalaca with Pérez de Rivas's admiring portrait of the Eudeve leader Sisibotari, more than a century earlier, in *Historia de los triunfos de nuestra santa fe*, bk. 6, chap. 13 [*Páginas para la historia de Sonora*], vol. 2, pp. 233–34.

12 BNFF 38/867, f. 5.

13 BNFF 38/867, f. 4v.

14 BNFF 38/867, ff. 4–4v.

15 Matson and Fontana, eds., *Friar Bringas Reports to the King*, p. 66; Officer, *Hispanic Arizona*, p. 72.

16 AMH AD 1, 1797, Fray Juan Felipe Martínez to Bishop Rouset de Jesús; BNFF 36/806, Martínez to Comandante Pedro de Nava.

17 AMH AD 1, 1797.

18 Mirafuentes Galvána, "Elite y defensa en la provincia de Sonora, siglo XVIII," pp. 411–28.

19 Officer, *Hispanic Arizona*, p. 68.

20 BNFF 34/734, f. 4.

21 BNFF 34/737, ff. 5–14.

22 AMH AD 1; BNFF 36/806, f. 26.

23 BNFF 34/735, f. 5; 40/912, ff. 1–2, 1777–79.

24 The following account is based on AGN *Jesuitas*, leg. 2–5, exp. 2: "Diario de lo acaesido y practicado en la entrada que se hizo a la Ysla del Tiburón este año de 1750. Escrito por P. Francisco Pimentel, capellán de la expedición encabezada por el Coronel Diego Ortiz Parrilla." Juan Thomas Beldarraín, first commanding officer of the Presidio de Tubac, died in 1759 (Officer, *Hispanic Arizona*, p. 38). My main interest in this discussion is to interpret the actions of Indians sent to fight the Seris; in Chapter 9 below, I focus on the Seris' resistance to Spanish domination. Tiburón, the largest island

in Mexican territory, approximately 600 square miles, has two mountain ranges which are separated by the Agua Dulce Valley.

25 Pimentel account (see note 24 above), f. 21.

26 BNFF 38/846, ff. 4–5, Mendoza to [Gov. Pineda]. *Gandules*, originally referring to Moorish soldiers, came to mean "vandals" or "vagabonds"; in Sonora, it referred to male Apache warriors taken captive.

27 Anza to Governor Pineda, 1766, BNFF 36/855.

28 AGI Guadalajara 272, exp. 628.

29 Officer, *Hispanic Arizona*, p. 68; Zúñiga, *Rápida ojeada al estado de Sonora*.

30 UASP no. 40, ff. 6–7, 12–13; John, ed., *Views from the Apache Frontier*.

9   Patterns of Mobilization

1 Smith, *Livelihood and Resistance*, p. 77.

2 Tilly, *From Mobilization to Revolution*.

3 AGI Guadalajara 505, ff. 359–97; Río, "Proceso y balance de la reforma tributaria del siglo XVIII en Sinaloa y Sonora," pp. 161–78.

4 See Chapter 1, note 33, above; and Navarro García, *Sonora y Sinaloa en el siglo XVII*, pp. 251–53.

5 Kessell, *Kiva, Cross, and Crown*, pp. 229–98; Gutiérrez, *When Jesus Came, the Corn Mothers Went Away*, pp. 130–40.

6 Navarro García, *Sonora y Sinaloa en el siglo XVII*, pp. 265–86.

7 Sheridan and Naylor, eds., *Rarámuri. A Tarahumara Colonial Chronicle, 1607–1791*, pp. 41–70; Navarro García, *Sonora y Sinaloa en el siglo XVII*, pp. 291–308.

8 Kessell, *Kiva, Cross, and Crown*, pp. 243–62; Kessell, ed., *Remote beyond Compare*, pp. 50–61; Navarro García, *Sonora y Sinaloa en el siglo XVII*, pp. 316–17; Naylor and Polzer, eds., *The Presidio and Militia on the Northern Frontier of New Spain, 1570–1700*, pp. 483–718.

9 Pennington, ed., *Arte y vocabulario*, pp. 31–50.

10 Nentvig, *Descripción . . . de Sonora*; Rodríguez Gallardo, *Informe sobre Sinaloa y Sonora*; Fray Antonio de los Reyes, "Breve descripción de la gobernación de Sonora y sus missiones, y los medios que parecen proporcionados para su restaurazión, Colegio de San Fernando y Mexico, 20 de abril de 1772" and "Memorial y estado actual de las missiones de la Pimería Alta y Baxa presentado al excmo. sr. virrey dn. Frey Antonio Maria Bucarelli y Ursua, 6 de julio de 1772" (AGN Misiones vol. 14, exp. 3); "Plan que por orden del rey ha formado fray Antonio Reyes para arreglar el gobierno espiritual de los pueblos y missiones en las provincias septentrionales de Nueva España y para que a este fin puedan tomarse las providencias que acuerde el Consejo Supremo de Indias, Sonora y 15 de septiembre de 1784" (AGN Misiones, vol. 14, exp. 5), published in *Misioneros valencianos en indias* (Valencia: Gener-

alitat Valenciana, 1989 [1784]), vol. 2, pp. 323–419 as Reyes, *Observaciones sobre el obispado de Sonora*. On the movements of Jobas and Sibubapas, see Chapters 5 and 8 above.

11 Stern, "Social Marginality and Acculturation on the Northern Frontier of New Spain," pp. 58–64. Thus the Jesuit Manuel Aguirre referred to poor squatters who moved from mission to mission as "zambaigos" and "vagabundos" (AGN AHH 17, 32, 1766).

12 Río, "Auge y decadencia de los placeres y el Real de la Cieneguilla, Sonora (1771–1783)," pp. 81–98.

13 Stern, "Social Marginality and Acculturation," pp. 117–19; Stern and Jackson, "Vagabundaje and Settlement in Colonial Northern Sonora," pp. 461–81.

14 BNFF 32/611, 622; BNFF 36/806; Revillagigedo, *Informe sobre las misiones*, 1793.

15 Lorenzo Cancio to Marqués de Croix, October 28, 1766, San Carlos de Buenavista, AGN *Provincias Internas* 48, 1, ff. 27–36.

16 AGN *Provincias Internas* [PI] 48, 1, f. 14; AGN Historia 17, 19, ff. 105–31.

17 On the petition of Pimas from Xecatacari and Buenavista, see Chapter 6, notes 1 and 2 above. The Pimas' complaints to Captain Lumbreras are summarized in his report to Viceroy Marqués de Crois, AGN PI 81, 4 (1771), ff. 122–27.

18 AGN PI 81, 4, f. 122. At the time of the Pimas' petition for land in Buenavista in 1717, their census showed 88 households and 305 persons; half a century later, the governor of Buenavista reported 82 families in the community—of whom, he said, only 5 had gathered a harvest.

19 AGN PI 81, 4, f. 129.

20 Subdelegado E. V. Beleña to Marqués de Croix, March 25, 1769, AGN PI 68, 1, ff. 33–38. The priest of Baroyeca killed by the Pimas was Don Ildefonso Felix.

21 AGN PI 48, 1, f. 87.

22 AGN Historia 18, 12 (1770), ff. 258–61: "Correspondencia entre el Bachiller Francisco Joaquín Valdés y José Antonio de Vildósola [comandante de las fuerzas acuarteladas en Guaymas]."

23 AGN PI 81, 4, ff. 150–64.

24 AGN PI 82, 1, ff. 180–205: "Diario que yo el capitán don Bernardo de Urrea formo para salir a la solicitud de Ygnacio Tuburijipci y su cuadrilla, indios que faltan por rendirse desde el día 3 de mayo de 1771." Bernardo de Urrea had long experience dealing with Pápagos, Seris, and Apaches. He was the first commander of the Presidio de Altar, founded in 1752; in 1767, he was assigned to carry out the expulsion of the Jesuits from Sonora. Miguel de Urrea, his son, was killed by Apaches in 1780. See Officer, *Hispanic Arizona*, pp. 46, 55–56.

25 Bohórquez to Grimarest, 1792, BNFF 35/787, ff. 4–5.

26 AGN PI 48, 3, f. 353.

27 Kessell, Friars, Soldiers, and Reformers, p. 18; AGN PI 48, 3, ff. 398–99.

28 AGN PI 48, 3, f. 338.

29 AGN PI 48, 3, ff. 391–97.

30 AGN PI 48, 3, ff. 410–17, 426–29.

31 AGN PI 235, exp. 4–6, ff. 209–91.

32 Hall, Social Change in the Southwest, 1350–1880, pp. 118–19; Griffen, "Apache Indians and the North Mexican Peace Establishments," pp. 183–95.

33 "Diario de la expedición verificada desde la Provincia de Sonora a las ordenes del Capitan D. Manl. de Echeagaray," Santa Cruz, November 30, 1788, AGN PI 235, 2, ff. 67–87v.

34 AGN PI 235, 2, ff. 73–74, 82.

35 AGN PI 235, 2, ff. 77v–78.

36 Navarro García, Sonora y Sinaloa en el siglo XVII, pp. 166, 265–75.

37 In central New Spain and the Andean highlands, tribute was the centerpiece of a similar kind of colonial pact. See Jacobsen, "Campesinos y tenencia de la tierra en el altiplano peruano"; Platt, Estado boliviano y ayllú andino.

38 Spicer, Cycles of Conquest, p. 124; Kino, Las misiones de Sonora y Arizona, p. 39.

39 Naylor and Polzer, eds., The Presidio and Militia on the Northern Frontier of New Spain, 1570–1700, pp. 583–718 (this is an edited translation of the campaign journal kept by the commanding officer of Janos, General Juan Fernández de la Fuente, from AHP microfilm 1695, frame 5–208).

40 Navarro García, La sublevación yaqui de 1740, is a carefully narrated account of the uprising based on documents in AGI. Hu-Dehart, in Missionaries, Miners and Indians, pp. 59–87, analyzed a similar corpus of manuscripts, as copied and microfilmed in the Pastells Collection, Vatican Library of St. Louis University, St. Louis, Missouri. The heated controversy between Jesuits and colonials that followed the Yaqui uprising created an abundant documentary record. Spicer examines this rebellion carefully in Cycles of Conquest and The Yaquis. A Cultural History.

41 BNFF 35/787, f. 1v, Subdelegado Juan María Bohórquez to Intendente Enrique Grimarest, 1792.

42 Hu-Dehart, Missionaries, Miners, and Indians, pp. 82–83; Navarro García, La sublevación Yaqui de 1740, pp. 44–45, citing AGI Escribanía 244A, cuaderno 23, ff. 207–19 (Declaraciones de Tacocay).

43 Spicer, Cycles of Conquest, pp. 107–8; AGN AHH Jesuitas leg. 2–5, exp. 2, f. 27; BNFF 35/787, f. 2v. Also see Chapter 5, note 25, above.

44 BNFF 35/787, ff. 6–7. Mirafuentes, "Seris, apaches y españoles en Sonora," argues that Seris learned from the Apaches the tactic of slaughtering horses in order to cripple Spanish militias, although the Seris (unlike the Apaches)

had not incorporated the horse into their own culture. See also Sheridan, "Cross or Arrow? The Breakdown of Spanish–Seri Relations, 1729–1750."

45   Spicer, *Cycles of Conquest*, pp. 129–30; Mirafuentes, "Seris, apaches y españoles en Sonora," p. 106.

46   BNFF 35/787, f. 6. Mirafuentes, "Seris, apaches y españoles en Sonora," offers a similar quotation from AGI *Guadalajara* 419A.

47   As in the Yaqui revolt a decade earlier, Jesuits were called to defend their actions following the Pima leaders' accusations. See the depositions by Padre Ignacio Keller of Suamca and Padre Juan Nentvig of Sáric, as well as a summary by the Jesuit provincial of New Spain, in BNFF 33/692, 693, 696.

48   Mirafuentes Galván, "El 'enemigo de las casas de adobe,' " pp. 103–24.

49   Ibid., pp. 111–14.

50   See, for example, Padre Keller, who claimed that Luis entered his mission of Suamca on the pretext of leading a patrol against the Apaches, but with the intention of inciting rebellion (BNFF 33/696).

51   BNFF 35/787, ff. 6–7. Bohórquez cataloged numerous *vecinos* whose fortunes were ruined by successive Indian uprisings.

52   Mirafuentes Galván, "Identidad india, legitimidad y emancipación política en el noroeste de México (Copala, 1771)."

53   BNFF 35/767, ff. 3–11. All direct quotations used here are drawn from this *expediente*. Gil Samaniego, Atanasio Ortiz, and Gregorio Ortiz Cortés, *teniente de alcalde mayor* for the Bavispe and Oposura valleys, were all landowning *vecinos* in the fertile stretch between Bacerác and Bavispe. Atanasio and Gregorio were *compadres* and related by marriage (see BNFF 35/722). Captain Ygnacio Noperi was related by blood to Captains Gerónimo Noperi and Juan Manuel Varela before him. See BNFF ms. 1762, ff. 88–142, Fray Nuñez Fundador, "Relación de Bacerác," 1777; AGN AHH leg. 278, exp. 20.

54   On whippings and shame among slaves, see Genovese, *Roll, Jordan, Roll*, pp. 120–23.

55   The cane of office (*bastón de mando*) was the Indians' insignia of power under colonial rule. These were carved wooden canes, passed along to the individuals who held office. Spicer, *The Yaquis. A Cultural History*, pp. 28–29.

56   Farriss, in *Maya Society under Colonial Rule*, pp. 227–55, reconstructs the ways in which Maya elites rebuilt their ascendancy through colonial political office.

57   See Chapter 6, notes 22–25, above.

58   Vidargas del Moral, "La intendencia de Arizpe en la independencia de Nueva España: 1810–1821," pp. 314–15; Kessell, *Friars, Soldiers, and Reformers*, p. 238. Archival sources for the 1820 uprising are in AGN *Provincias Internas* vols. 225, 251, 252.

59   BL HHB, M-M 495, 6–13; AHGES *Opatas* caja 361, tomo 1162, 1.

60 Spicer, *Cycles of Conquest*, pp. 61–64, 100–103; AGN *Gobernación* caja 3, exp. s/c, s/n, 1837.

61 AHGES *Opatas* caja 361, tomo 1162, exp. 1: "Dictamen del Consejo de Gobierno, Arizpe," 1832.

62 BNFF 32/659, 1803. Governor Manuel Escalante y Arvizu, writing to the president of Mexico on June 4, 1836, used the term *proletario* in this context (AGN *Gobernación* caja 3, exp. s/n.

63 See disputed elections for the captaincy-general of the Opata nation in 1833: AHGES *Opatas* caja 361, tomo 1162, exp. 1.

64 Escalante to Ministro de Estado y del Despacho de lo Interior, Arizpe, 1837, AGN *Gobernación* caja 3. *Fanega de sembradura* refers to the measurement of land in which 1 fanega (approx. 1.5 bushels) can be sown. Van Young indicates that 1 fanega de sembradura of maize was about 9 acres (*Hacienda and Market in Eighteenth-Century Mexico*, p. 360). These equivalences changed for different crops and in different regions.

65 Juan Ysidro Bohórquez to Presidente de la República, and José Anrríquez to the Cámaras Generales, 1836, AGN *Gobernación* caja 4, exp. s/c, fojas 1–5; Quijada Hernández, *Cumpas*, pp. 99–112.

66 Anrríquez to the Cámaras Generales, AGN *Gobernación* caja 4, exp. s/c, ff. 3–5.

67 AGN *Gobernación* caja 4, exp. s/c, f. 2.

68 I use "foundations" to convey the social networks sustained by religious and cultural practices, a concept not unrelated to Eric Wolf's phrase, "integument of custom," referring to the cultural inroads of capitalism in peasant communities (Wolf, *Peasant Wars of the Twentieth Century*, p. 279).

69 Juan Angel Piri, Gerónimo Velasco, and Josef Barbastro to Secretaría de Estado y Despacho del Interior, 1836, AGN *Gobernación* caja 4, exp. s/c, s/n.

70 Rough draft of a communication sent to the governor of Sonora, AGN *Gobernación* caja 4, exp. s/c, s/n, ff. 8–9v.

71 Captain Tegeda, Alcalde Juan Antonio Valenzuela of Pitiquito, and the *alcalde* of Caborca to Fray José María Pérez Llera, Presidente de las Misiones de la Pimería Alta, February 28, 1835, and Pérez Llera to Governor Escalante y Arvizu, March 12, 1835, in AHGES 1–2, 95.

72 ACQ AM doc. 16: Governor Manuel Escalante y Arvizu to Fray José María Pérez Llera, Arizpe, 1835; Pérez Llera, *Apuntes 1844*, 16. I consulted transcripts of these documents through the courtesy of Father Kieran McCarty, O.F.M., University of Arizona, Tucson.

73 AHGES leg. 4, exp. 2, 1832–56; Fontana, *Of Earth and Little Rain*, pp. 57–60.

74 Van Young, "Conflict and Solidarity in Indian Village Life," pp. 55–79.

75 On the use of multiple time frames in historical analysis, see Stern, "New Approaches to the Study of Peasant Rebellion and Consciousness," pp. 11–13.

76 Felger and Moser, *People of the Desert and Sea*; Sheridan, "Cross or Arrow?";
 Mirafuentes, "Seris, apaches y españoles en Sonora."
77 Van Young, "Agrarian Rebellion and Defense of Community," pp. 245–70.

Conclusions: Contested Space

1 Smith, *Livelihood and Resistance*, pp. 155–58; Friedmann, "Household Production and the National Economy"; Chevalier, "There Is Nothing Simple
 about Simple Commodity Production"; Merrill, "Cash Is Good to Eat."
2 The tiny Hispanic elite of Sonora acquired domestic service through the
 trade in *nijoras* more consistently than they did from the Opata, Eudeve,
 and Pima pueblos. (On *nijoras*, captive Indian children taken from the Yuma
 and other tribes northwest of the Pimería Alta, see Chapter 5 above.)
3 See Spalding, *De indio a campesino*, for a similar assessment of Andean families and ayllus.
4 See Heraclio Bonilla, "Presentación," in Spalding, *De indio a campesino*, p. 12;
 Spalding, ibid., p. 106; and García Martínez, "Pueblos de Indios, Pueblos
 de Castas," pp. 103–16.
5 Spalding, *De indio a campesino*, pp. 160–72.
6 Smith, *Livelihood and Resistance*, p. 159. Mallon, in *Peasant and Nation*, pp. 11–12,
 writes of "communal hegemony" to emphasize that rural communities
 are, themselves, contested arenas.
7 Scott, *Domination and the Arts of Resistance*, pp. 183–201.
8 AGN *Gobernación* caja 3, July 2, 1836.
9 Bohórquez, 1836, in AGN *Gobernación* caja 3, f. 2v.
10 García Martínez, "Pueblos de Indios, Pueblos de Castas"; Mentz, *Pueblos de
 indios, mulatos y mestizos, 1770–1870*.
11 Smith, *Livelihood and Resistance*, pp. 11–18.
12 See, for example, Rodríguez, ed., *Patterns of Contention in Mexican History*;
 Mallon, *Peasant and Nation*.
13 Stern, "Feudalism, Capitalism, and the World-System."
14 Smith, *Livelihood and Resistance*, pp. 218–28.
15 Representative works include Stern, *Peru's Indian Peoples and the Challenge of
 Spanish Conquest*; Mallon, *The Defense of Community in Peru's Central Highlands* and
 Peasant and Nation; Farriss, *Maya Society under Colonial Rule*; Chance, *Conquest of
 the Sierra*; García Martínez, *Los pueblos de la sierra*; Carmagnani, *El regreso de los
 dioses*; Jacobsen, *Mirages of Transition*; Langer, *Economic Change and Rural Resistance*;
 Spalding, *Huarochirí*; Wightman, *Indigenous Migration and Social Change*; Larson,
 Colonialism and Agrarian Transformation in Bolivia; Block, *Mission Culture on the Upper
 Amazon*; and Schryer, *Ethnicity and Class Conflict in Rural Mexico*.

Glossary

acequia   Irrigation ditch

agostadero   Uncultivated rangeland

agregados   Children not the off-spring of the head of household

aguajes   Natural water sources

ák-ciñ   (Pima) Field prepared for farming

akimel   Pima riverine farmers

albacea   Executor of a will

alcabala   Sales tax

alcalde de barrio   Neighborhood official

alcalde   Judge and *cabildo* officer

alcaldía mayor   Magistrate; colonial administrative office

aldea   Settled agrarian village

alguacil   Constable; elected official of mission governance

alhóndiga   Municipal granary; also *pósito*

almoneda pública   Public auction; also *remate*

almud   Volume measure = 4.6 liters or 4.1 quarts

apoderado   Person who holds power of attorney for another

aquiguat   Name that Opata mothers used to call their daughters

arrendatario   Tenant farmer who pays rent to the landowner either in money or in produce.

arriero   Muleteer

athapaskan   Language of the Apaches

baldío   Vacant or public land

barranca   Mountainous canyon

bastimentos   Supplies; basic grains of wheat and maize

batequis   Shallow holes dug in *arroyos* to find water

bayeta   Flannel

beata   Devout lay woman who cleans the church and cares for the saints

borrachera   Ritual drinking; implies excessive social drinking

bretaña   Linen

caballería   Area measure = 43 hectares and 105 acres

cabecera   Head village of a mission district

cabildo   Town council

cáhitas   Agricultural peoples of southern Sonora and northern Sinaloa

caja real   Provincial treasury

cantera   Quarry; sandstone used for building

cantora   Singer

capellanía   Chantry fund; lien on a rural estate to generate income for the support of a priest

capitancillos   Indian military leaders

carga   Volume measure that varies by product. Equal to approximately 111 liters or 3.1 bushels.

casados   Married couples

castas   Mixed races of Spanish, Indian, or African origins.

cimarrones Indians who fled the
missions

coa Digging stick; also *cupiara*
(Pima)

comisario de tierras Provincial
official who awarded land titles
under the terms of *composición*

comisario NonIndian administrator in a larger mission

compadrazgo Relationship through
godparents

compañía volante Itinerant Spanish military patrol

composición Legalization of land
title

común Mission communal land;
also refers to common wealth

comunero Indians who share
rights and obligations of belonging
to a community

comunicantes Those who receive
Christian communion

confesantes Those who receive
Christian confession

congregación Nucleation of Indians reorganized on the model of
Iberian towns

cordel Linear measure of 50 varas
(standard length) = 41.8 meters

corrida Seasonal cattle drives off
the range and into central corrals

coyote Indian and African racial
mixture; in Sonora, signified *mestizo*

creciente Flood

criadero Area for breeding livestock

criado Servant or child raised in
household service

criador Stockman

criollo Person of Spanish descent
born in the Americas

cuadrilla de peones Group of field
laborers

cuartillo Volume measure = half a
liter

cunca'ac Seri, nomadic bands of
the Sonoran Gulf coast (*kunka'ak*)

dagüinemaca (Opata) Public ritual
of formalized friendship

demasía Unclaimed land or extra
footage outside formal property
lines

denuncia Accusation or statement
of land claim

despoblado Area without livestock
and people

ejido Common land surrounding
settled communities

elotes Roasted ears of fresh corn

encomienda Grants of Indians for
tribute

entrada First missionary entry into
Indian communities

equipatas Winter rains

esquites Whole roasted grains of
corn

estado Ecclesiastical census sum-
marizing numbers of Indians by
category

estancia Ranch

estanco Monopoly for the sale and
taxation of tobacco, gun powder,
and playing cards

eudeves Highland villagers of
central Sonora

fanega Volume of grain equal to
55 liters or 1.5 bushels. Land measurement equivalent to the area
sown with 1 *fanega*, approximately
3.5 hectares or 8.5 acres

fundo legal Minimal allotment to
Indian pueblos and Spanish towns

as municipal property, conventionally a square league

galera Strip of raised land

gambusino Small-scale mining
prospector

ganado criollo Locally bred cattle

ganado mayor Cattle, oxen, horses,
and mules

ganado menor Sheep, goats, and
pigs

ganado mesteño Communal cattle,
or cattle grazed in common lands

gañan Hacienda laborer; also *jorna-
lero*

gandules Vandals, vagabonds; in
Sonora, it referred to male Apache
warriors taken captive

géneros Goods, unspecified merchandise

gente de razón Hispanic or mixed
races distinguished from the Indians

gentiles Unbaptized Indians

granos Measurement of silver; 12
granos = 1 real

guayma Indian peoples of Sonoran
Gulf coast, a band of Seris

heves Tegüima-speaking people;
later identified as Opata

hiach-ed S-ohbmakam: Pima
desert nomads

hijo natural Child born outside the
sacramental definition of marriage

hijos de la campana "Children of
the bell": Indians that lived under
permanent missionary supervision; also *hijos del pueblo, indios de
administración*

hijos del país Indians of the province used as presidial soldiers

hijuela Title to a small rustic

property; it also can mean an
inheritance

hohokam Pre-Hispanic agricultural settlements of Gila valley
and southern Arizona, related to
Historic Pima

hornos castellanos Adobe or stone
furnaces used in silver refining

indios conversos Indians who
accepted baptism

indios volantes Nomadic Indians;
also *ranchería volante*

jacal Hut, generally with a straw
roof

jobas Semi-nomadic Indians of
eastern Sonora

juez de agua Spanish officer in
charge of distributing irrigation
water

juez económico Elected native
official of Indian pueblos under
Sonoran state law of 1831.

juez político Spanish local judge;
also *alcalde*

justicias Elected officials of Indian
villages

labor Irrigated field

laboríos Indians who left their villages and hired out their labor; also
naborías

labrador Planter or farmer

ladino Spanish-speaking or accul-
turated Indian

libranza Mercantile letters of credit

lobo Mixed race of Indian and
African origins

malacate Water lift installed in
mines to control flooding

mano Native tool used to grind
maize kernels and seeds

manta Length of cotton cloth

maragua (Opata) Female ritual of confidence and support; also the name fathers used to call their daughters.

marcos Measurement of silver = 8.5 pesos

matlazáhuatl Epidemic disease

mayordomo Foreman

mediannata Tax paid for a *composición* of land or for a bureaucratic office

memorias Missionary annual lists of provisions

mercader viandante Merchant-creditor licensed to operate in different localities

merced de agua Water rights added to an existing land grant

merced de tierra Land grant awarded by the king

mescal Fermented liquid made from the heart of the *Agave yaquiana*

mestizaje Racial or ethnic mixture

mestizos Mixed races of Hispanic and Indian origins

metate Native tool used to grind maize kernels and seeds

milpa Cultivated peasant plot, either swidden or irrigated

miriguat (Opata) Name that mothers used to call their sons

monte Desert or transitional scrub forest; area for hunting and gathering

moreno Dark skinned person of mixed ancestry

mulato Mixed race of Hispanic and African origins

nación Ethnic polity distinguished from the modern nation-state

naturales Native people

nawait Tohono o'odham ceremony associated with the creation of rain-filled clouds

nebomes Pima farmers of the middle Yaqui River in eastern central Sonora

nixtamal Moist dough made from ground maize

noguat (Opata) Name that fathers used to call their sons

noragua (Opata) Male ritual of mutual obligations and friendship

noria Well

o'odham Pima

obrajes Mills or shops that produced cheap textiles and ceramics for colonial markets

oidag (Pima) Fields

olas ki: (Pima) Round house used for ceremonial purposes

opatas Tegüima-speaking villagers of highland Sonora

operario Mining laborer

padrón Official house-to-house census

papawi co'odham Tohono o'odham: "bean eaters"

parcionero Shareholder in a plot of land; also *accionista*

partido Amount of ore which the workers sold on their own account; also Jesuit mission districts

párvulos Infant or child, category used in missions *estados*

pascola Ritual clown

patronato real Royal patronage of the Catholic Church in the Americas

péchita Mesquite pod

peninsular   Spaniard

peón acasillado   Resident laborer on a hacienda

peri   Native birth ritual

piloncillo   Loaves of boiled sugar syrup

Pimería Alta   Northwestern territory of Pimas in Sonora

Pimería Baja   Nebomes of eastern central Sonora

pinole   Basic corn meal ground from roasted kernels

piscador   Wooden stick

plancha   Amalgamated silver plate

poblazones   Small settlements or hamlets

pozole   Stew made with *esquite* and boiled kernels

pregonero   Town crier

presidio   Fort, military fixed installation

promotor fiscal   Fiscal officer of the intendancy who reviewed land titles

propios   Landholding *vecinos*

quintal   Weight measurement for grains, approximately = 138 kg or 304 lb

ramada   Structure of forked posts and woven thatch

ranchería   Hamlet smaller than a village, often semi-nomadic

ranchero   Small private landholder who used extrafamilial labor

real cédula   Royal order, edict

realengas   Unappropriated or royal lands

reales de minas   Mining centers

reales   Monetary unit; 8 reales = 1 peso

rectorado   Jesuit supervisory district that combined several missions

recua de mulas   Muletrain

reducción   *Congregación;* concentration of *rancherías* in mission towns

repartimiento   Forced labor recruited from native villages, and sent to Spanish estates and mines for stipulated periods of time

rescatador   Itinerant grain merchant that acted as intermediary between Indian producers and regional markets

salina   Salt deposit

sayal   Woolen cloth

serrano   Peoples of the piedmont of eastern Sonora

sibubapas   Pimas of central Sonora who fled the missions (suvbàpas)

sitio   Grazing land

sobaípuris   Pimas of northeastern Sonora

sobras   Secondary rights to the water "left over" from the primary owner's use of a given amount of water

solar   Area measure = 70 hectares and 173 acres

soltero/a   Adolescent or unmarried person

stole   Pudding made with *esquite* and boiled kernels of corn

suaquis   Particula band of *sibubapas*

subdelegado   Local Spanish official with administrative duties

suerte   Small landholding of 10.5 hectares or 26.5 acres

tahona   Millstone moved with animal or human power

tapisque Worker drafted for harvest labor on private haciendas

tasajo de calabazas Dried strip of squash

tasolera Open corral where stalks were piled and weathered

tegüimas Opatas, also refers to their language

temporalidades All assets pertaining to the missions

teniente Local Spanish official with administrative and magisterial duties

tesgüino Fermented maize; *tesqüinadas*, ritual drinking

tierra de labrantío Arable land

tierras de agostadero Pasturage; also *tierras de paso*

tierras de pan coger Arable land dependent on rainfall, but susceptible to irrigation

tierras de pan llevar Arable land that required irrigation

tierras de pan sembrar Drylands with sufficient moisture for planting

tierras de temporal Dryland dependent on rainfall

tinaja Natural reservoir filled with water seepage from hillside springs

tlatole Native call to arms

tohono o'odham Desert-dwelling Pima of the western lowlands of Sonora

topil Native minor official for law and order

trapiche Sugar press

trinchera Fortified hilltop site

usiabagu (Pima) Women's ceremony that marked the time of planting

vaquero Cowboy or cattle guard

varas Linear measure = 0.8 meters or 2.7 feet

vecindario Neighborhood; also referred to nonIndian residents of a mission

vecino Hispanic landholding resident of a given place

visita Tour of inspection

visitador Inspector

vocal Electors for municipal councils, or unspecified council member

wahia (Pima) Wells

wi:kita Ceremony that gathered o'odham kinsmen and concerned the hunt, the onset of rains, and good health

yaqui Cahitan-speaking peoples of the Yaqui valley

zambaigo "Zambo": mixed races of African and Indian origins

Select Bibliography

Primary Sources

Aguirre, Manuel, S.J. *Doctrina christiana y pláticas doctrinales traducidas en lengua ópata*. Mexico City: Colegio de San Ildefonso, 1765.

Anza, Juan Bautista de. *Diario del primer viaje a la California, 1774*. Ed. Julio César Montané Martí. Hermosillo: Sociedad Sonorense de Historia, 1989.

Bartlett, John Russell, *Personal Narrative of Explorations and Incidents in Texas, New Mexico, California, Sonora, and Chihuahua, Connected with the United States and Mexico Boundary Commission during the years 1850, '51, '52, and '53*. New York: D. Apple & Company, 1854.

Burrus, Ernest J., and Félix Zubillaga, eds. *El noroeste de México. Documentos sobre las misiones jesuíticas, 1600–1769*. Mexico City: Universidad Nacional Autónoma de México, 1986.

Cabeza de Vaca, Alvar Núñez. *Naufragios y relación de la jornada que hizo a la Florida con el adelantado Pánfilo de Narváez*. Madrid: Espasa-Calpe, 1971 [1555].

Font, Fray Pedro. *Diario* [of the Anza expedition, September 29, 1775–June 2, 1776]. Tubutama, 1777 [ms. in the John Carter Brown Library].

Garcés, Fray Francisco. *Diario de exploraciones en Arizona y California en los años de 1775 y 1776*. Mexico City: Universidad Nacional Autónoma de México, 1968.

Gómez Canedo, Lino, ed. *Sonora hacia fines del siglo XVIII. Un informe del misionero franciscano fray Francisco Antonio Barbastro con otros documentos complementarios*. Guadalajara: Librería Font, 1971.

Hammond, George P., and Agapito Rey, eds. *Narratives of the Coronado Expedition, 1540–1542*. Albuquerque: University of New Mexico Press, 1940.

———, eds. *Obregón's History of 16th Century Exploration in Western America*. Los Angeles: Wetzel Publishing Co., 1928.

Ives, Ronald L., ed. *Sedelmayr's "Relación" of 1746*. Washington, D.C.: Smithsonian Institution, 1939. Bureau of American Ethnology Bulletin 123, Anthropological Papers, no. 9: 97–117.

Kino, Eusebio Francisco. *Las misiones de Sonora y Arizona. Comprendiendo la crónica titulada: "Favores celestiales" y la "Relación diaria de la entrada al noroeste."* Mexico City: Porrúa, 1989 [1702].

Lange, Charles H., Carroll L. Riley, and Elizabeth M. Lange, eds. *The Southwestern Journals of Adolph F. Bandelier, 1883–1884*. Albuquerque: University of New Mexico Press, 1970.

Lejeune, Louis. *La guerra apache en Sonora*. Trans. Michel Antochiw. Hermosillo: Gobierno del Estado de Sonora, 1984.

Lumholtz, Carl. *Unknown Mexico. Explorations in the Sierra Madre and Other Regions*, 1890–1898. Vols. 1, 2. New York: Charles Scribner's Sons, 1902.

Mange, Juan Mateo. *Diario de las exploraciones en Sonora. Luz de tierra incógnita*. Hermosillo: Gobierno del Estado de Sonora, 1985 [1720].

Naylor, Thomas H., and Charles W. Polzer, S.J., eds. *The Presidio and Militia on the Northern Frontier of New Spain, 1570–1700*. Tucson: University of Arizona Press, 1986.

Nentvig, Juan, *Descripción geográfica, natural y curiosa de la provincia de Sonora*. Mexico City: Archivo General de la Nación, 1971 [1764].

Pennington, Campbell, ed. *Vocabulario en la lengua dohema, heve o eudeve. Anónimo (siglo XVII)*. Mexico City: Universidad Nacional Autónoma de México, 1981.

Pérez de Rivas, Andrés. *Historia de los triunfos de nuestra santa fé entre gentes las más bárbaras y fieras del nuevo orbe*. Vols. 1, 2. Hermosillo: Gobierno del Estado de Sonora, 1985 [1645].

Pesqueira, Fernando, ed. *Documentos para la historia de Sonora*. Hermosillo: Universidad de Sonora.

Pfefferkorn, Ignaz. *Descripción de la provincia de Sonora*. Ed. and trans. Armando Hopkins Durazo. Hermosillo: Gobierno del Estado de Sonora, 1983 [1794–95].

Poma de Ayala, Guaman. *El primer nueva corónica y buen gobierno*. Ed. John V. Murra and Rolena Adorno. Mexico City: Siglo XXI, 1980 [1615].

Recopilación de leyes de los reynos de las Indias. Madrid, 1973 [1680].

Revillagigedo, Conde de. *Informe sobre las misiones, 1793 e Instrucción reservada al marqués de Branciforte, 1794*. Introduction and notes by José Bravo Ugarte. Mexico City: Editorial Jus, 1966.

Reyes, Antonio de los. *Observaciones sobre el obispado de Sonora*. Prologue by Vicent Ribes Iborra. In *Misioneros valencianos en indias*. Vol. 2. Valencia: Generalitat Valenciana, 1989 [1784]: 323–419.

Rodríguez Gallardo, José Rafael *Informe sobre Sinaloa y Sonora, 1750*. Germán Viveros, ed. Mexico City: Archivo General de la Nación, 1975.

Smith, Buckingham. *Grammar of the Pima or Nevome. A Language of Sonora from a Manuscript of the XVIII Century*. New York: Cramoisy Press, 1862.

———. *A Grammatical Sketch of the Heve Language*. New York: Cramoisy Press, 1861.

Tamarón y Romeral, Pedro. *Descripción de la diócesis de Nueva Vizcaya*. Madrid: Aguilar, Biblioteca Indiana, 1958 [1765].

Velasco, José Francisco. *Noticias estadísticas del estado de Sonora, 1850*. Hermosillo: Gobierno del Estado de Sonora, 1985 [Sociedad Mexicana de Geografía y Estadística, 1860–65].

Zúñiga, Ignacio. *Rápida ojeada al estado de Sonora*. Hermosillo: Gobierno del Estado de Sonora, 1985 [Mexico City, 1835].

Secondary Sources

Adorno, Rolena. *Guaman Poma. Writing and Resistance in Colonial Peru.* Austin: University of Texas Press, 1986.

———. "Reconsidering Colonial Discourse for Sixteenth- and Seventeenth-Century Spanish America." *Latin American Research Review* 28, 3, 1993: 135–45.

Almada, Francisco R. *Diccionario de historia, geografía y biografía sonorenses.* Hermosillo: Gobierno del Estado de Sonora, 1983.

Altman, Ida, and Reginald D. Butler. "The Contact of Cultures: Perspectives on the Quincentenary." *American Historical Review* 99, 2, 1994: 478–503.

Alvarez Palma, Ana María. *Huatabampo. Consideraciones sobre una comunidad agrícola prehispánica en el sur de Sonora.* Hermosillo: Instituto Nacional de Antropología e Historia, Noroeste de México 9, 1989.

———. "Sociedades agrícolas." In *Historia general de Sonora.* Vol. 1: *Período prehistórico y prehispánico.* Mexico City: Gobierno del Estado de Sonora, 1985: 225–62.

Alvarsson, Jan-Åke. "Ethnicity—Some Introductory Remarks." In Jan-Åke Alvarsson and Hernán Horna, eds., *Ethnicity in Latin America.* Uppsala: University of Uppsala, CELAS, 1990: 7–14.

Amsden, Monroe. *Archaeological Reconnaissance in Sonora.* Los Angeles: Southwestern Museum, Southwestern Museum Papers 1, 1928.

Anderson, Benedict. *Imagined Communities. Reflections on the Origin and Spread of Nationalism.* London: Verso, 1983.

Anderson, Rodney. "Race and Social Stratification: A Comparison of Working-Class Spaniards, Indians, and Castas in Guadalajara, Mexico, 1821." *Hispanic American Historical Review* 68, 2, 1988: 209–44.

Archetti, Eduardo P., and Kristi Anne Stölen. *Explotación familiar y acumulación de capital en el campo argentino.* Buenos Aires: Siglo Veintiuno Editores, 1975.

Avalos, Francisco. "The Colonial Period of Mexico and Its Legal Personality: A Bibliographical Essay." Tucson: University of Arizona College of Law Library, Bibliography Series 12, 1986.

Avila Palafox, Ricardo, Carlos Martínez Assad, and Jean Meyer, eds. *Las formas y las políticas del dominio agrario: Homenaje a François Chevalier.* Guadalajara: Universidad de Guadalajara, 1992.

Bakewell, Peter. *Silver Mining and Society in Colonial Mexico: Zacatecas, 1546–1700.* Cambridge: Cambridge University Press, 1971.

Ballereau, Dominique. "A Complete Survey of Petroglyphs from Cerros La Proveedora and Calera, Sonora." In Ken Hedges, ed., *Rock Art Papers.* San Diego: San Diego Museum Papers 23, 1987 [Special edition of SDMP].

Balmori, Diane, Stuart F. Voss, and Miles Wortman. *Notable Family Networks in Latin America.* Chicago: University of Chicago Press, 1984.

Barnes, Thomas C., Thomas H. Naylor, and Charles W. Polzer. *Northern New Spain, A Research Guide.* Tucson: University of Arizona Press, 1981.

Bath, Slicher van B.H. "Dos modelos referidos a la relación entre población y economía en Nueva España y Perú durante la época colonial." In A. Ouweneel and C. Torales, eds., *Empresarios, indios y estado.* Amsterdam: CEDLA [Centre for Latin American Research and Documentation], 1988: 15–44.

Bauer, Arnold J., "The Church and Spanish American Agrarian Structures." *The Americas* 28, 1, 1971: 78–98.

———. *La iglesia en la economía de América Latina.* Mexico City: Instituto Nacional de Antropología e Historia, 1986.

———. "Millers and Grinders: Technology and Household Economy in Meso-America." *Agricultural History* 64, 1, 1990: 1–17.

———. "Rural Workers in Spanish America: Problems of Peonage and Oppression." *Hispanic American Historical Review* 59, 1, 1979: 34–65.

Bazant, Jan. *Cinco haciendas mexicanas. Tres siglos de vida rural en San Luis Potosí.* Mexico City: El Colegio de México, 1975.

Beals, Ralph L. *The Comparative Ethnology of Northern Mexico before 1750.* Berkeley: University of California Press, Ibero-Americana 2, 1932.

Behar, Ruth. "Sexual Witchcraft, Colonialism, and Women's Powers: Views from the Mexican Inquisition." In Asunción Lavrín, ed., *Sexuality and Marriage in Colonial Latin America.* Lincoln: University of Nebraska Press, 1989: 178–206.

Bell, Fillman, Keith M. Anderson, and Yvonne G. Stewart. *The Quitobaquito Cemetery and Its History.* Tucson: National Park Service, 1980.

Block, David. *Mission Culture on the Upper Amazon. Native Tradition, Jesuit Enterprise and Secular Policy in Moxos, 1660–1880.* Lincoln: University of Nebraska Press, 1994.

Bolton, Herbert E. "The Mission as a Frontier Institution in the Spanish-American Colonies," *American Historical Review* 23, 1 1917: 42–61.

Borah, Woodrow. *Justice by Insurance: The General Indian Court of Colonial Mexico.* Berkeley: University of California Press, 1983.

Boserup, Esther. *The Conditions of Agricultural Growth.* Chicago: New Aldine Publishing Co., 1965.

Bourdieu, Pierre. *Sociología y cultura* [*Questions de sociologie*, 1984]. Mexico City: Grijalbo, 1990.

Bradby, Barbara, "'Resistance to Capitalism' in the Peruvian Andes." In David Lehmann, ed., *Ecology and Exchange in the Andes.* Cambridge: Cambridge University Press, 1982: 97–122.

Brading, David. "Los españoles en México hacia 1792." *Historia Mexicana* 23, 1, 1973: 126–44.

———. *Haciendas and Ranchos in the Mexican Bajío: León, 1680–1860.* Cambridge: Cambridge University Press, 1978. [Sp. ed. *Haciendas y ranchos del Bajío, Leon.* Mexico: Fondo de Cultura Económica, 1986].

————. *Mineros y comerciantes en el México borbónico* (1768–1810). Mexico City: Fondo de Cultura Económica, 1975.

Braniff, Beatriz. *La frontera protohistórica Pima-Opata en Sonora, México. Proposiciones arqueológicas preliminares.* Vols. 1–3. Mexico City: Universidad Nacional Autónoma de Mexico, 1985.

Brusone, Julio le Reverend. "Problemas del régimen de apropiación de la tierra." In Bernardo García Martínez, ed., *Historia y sociedad en el mundo de habla española.* Mexico City: El Colegio de México, 1970: 79–85.

Burguière, André. "La historia de la familia en Francia. Problemas y recientes aproximaciones." In *Familia y sexualidad en Nueva España.* Mexico City: Fondo de Cultura Economica, 1982: 17–23.

Caballero, José María. *Economía agraria de la sierra peruana antes de la reforma agraria de 1969.* Lima: Instituto de Estudios Peruanos, 1981.

Calvo, Thomas. "Demografía y economía: La coyuntura en Nueva Galicia en el siglo XVII." *Historia Mexicana* 41, 4, 1992: 579–614.

————. *La Nueva Galicia en los siglos XVI y XVII.* Mexico City: Centro de Estudios Mexicanos y Centroamericanos, el Colegio de Jalisco 1989.

Carmagnani, Marcello. *El regreso de los dioses. El proceso de reconstitución de la identidad étnica en Oaxaca. Siglos XVII y XVIII.* Mexico City: Fondo de Cultura Económica, 1988.

Castetter, Edward F., and Willis H. Bell. *Pima and Papago Agriculture.* Albuquerque: University of New Mexico Press, 1942.

Chamoux, Marie-Noëlle, Danièle Dehouve, Cécile Gouy-Gilbert, Marielle Pepin Lehalleur, coords. *Prestar y pedir prestado. Relaciones sociales y crédito en México del siglo XVI al XX.* México: Centro de Investigaciones y Estudios Superiores en Antropología Social, 1993.

Chance, John K. *Conquest of the Sierra. Spaniards and Indians in Colonial Oaxaca.* Norman: University of Oklahoma Press, 1989.

————. *Race and Class in Colonial Oaxaca.* Stanford: Stanford University Press, 1978.

Chayanov, A. V., *The Theory of Peasant Economy.* Madison: University of Wisconsin Press, 1986.

Chevalier, Francois. *Land and Society in Colonial Mexico. The Great Hacienda.* Berkeley: University of California Press, 1970.

Chevalier, Jacques M. "There Is Nothing Simple about Simple Commodity Production." *Journal of Peasant Studies* 10, 4, 1983: 153–86.

Chowning, Margaret. "The Consolidación de Vales Reales in the Bishopric of Michoacán." *Hispanic American Historical Review* 69, 3, 1989: 541–78.

Clendinnen, Inga. *Aztecs. An Interpretation.* Cambridge: Cambridge University Press, 1991.

Collier, Jane Fishbourne. *Marriage and Inequality in Classless Societies.* Stanford: Stanford University Press, 1988.

Collins, Jane, "Labor Scarcity and Ecological Change." In Peter D. Little and Michael Horowitz, eds., *Lands at Risk in the Third World. Local Level Perspectives.* Boulder: Westview Press, 1987: 19–37.

Cook, Garrett. "Quichean Folk Theology and Southern Maya Supernaturalism." In Gary H. Gossen, ed., *Symbol and Meaning beyond the Closed Community. Essays in Mesoamerican Ideas.* Albany: State University of New York, Institute for Mesoamerican Studies, 1986: pp. 139–53.

Cook, Sherburne F. "La viruela en la California española y mexicana, 1770–1845." In Enrique Florescano and Elsa Malvido, eds., *Ensayos sobre la historia de las epidemias en México.* Vol. 1. Mexico City: Instituto Mexicano de Seguro Social, 1982: 257–94.

Cook, Sherburne F., and Woodrow Borah. *Essays in Population History.* 3 vols. Berkeley: University of California Press, 1974–80.

Corcuera de Mancera, Sonia. *El fraile, el indio y el pulque. Evangelización y embriaguez en la Nueva España (1523–1548).* Mexico City: Fondo de Cultura Económica, 1991.

Couturier, Edith. "Women and the Family in Eighteenth-Century Mexico: Law and Practice." *Journal of Family History* 10, 3, 1985: 294–303.

Craig, Ann L. *The First Agraristas: An Oral History of a Mexican Agrarian Reform Movement.* Berkeley: University of California Press, 1983.

Cronon, William. "A Place for Stories: Nature, History, and Narrative," *Journal of American History* 78, 3 (1992): 1347–76.

Crosby, Alfred. *The Columbian Exchange. Biological Consequences of 1492.* Westport: Greenwood Publication Company, 1972.

Crosswhite, Frank. "The Annual Saguaro Harvest and Crop Cycle of the Papago, with Reference to Ecology and Symbolism." *Desert Plants* 2, 1, 1980: 47–76.

———. "Desert Plants, Habitat, and Agriculture in Relation to the Major Pattern of Cultural Differentiation in the O'odham People of the Sonoran Desert." *Desert Plants* 3, 2 (1981): 47–76.

Crumrine, Ross. *The Mayo Indians of Sonora. A People Who Refuse to Die.* Tucson: University of Arizona Press, 1977.

Cuello, José. "El mito de la hacienda colonial en el norte de México." In A. Ouweneel and C. Torales, comps., *Empresarios, indios y estado. Perfil de la economía mexicana (siglo XVIII).* Amsterdam: CEDLA [Centre for Latin American Research and Documentation], 1988: 186–205.

———. "The Persistence of Indian Slavery and Ecomienda in the Northeast of Colonial Mexico, 1577–1723." *Journal of Social History* 21, 4, 1988: 683–700.

———. "Saltillo in the Seventeenth Century: Local Society on the North Mexican Frontier." Ph.D. diss., University of California, 1981.

Davis, Natalie Zemon. "Iroquois Women, European Women." In M. Hendricks and P. Parker, eds., *Women, "Race," and Writing in the Early Modern Period.* London: Routledge, 1994: pp. 243–58.

————. *Women on the Margins. Three Seventeenth-Century Lives.* Cambridge: Harvard University Press, 1995.

Deeds, Susan M. "Indigenous Responses to Mission Settlement in Nueva Vizcaya." In Erick Langer and Robert H. Jackson, eds., *The New Latin American Mission History.* Lincoln: University of Nebraska Press, 1995: 77–108.

————. "Land Tenure Patterns in Northern New Spain." *The Americas* 41, 4, 1985: 446–61.

————. "Rural Work in Nueva Vizcaya: Forms of Labor Coercion on the Periphery." *Hispanic American Historical Review* 69, 3, 1989: 425–50.

Deere, Carmen Diana. "The Differentiation of the Peasantry and Family Structure: A Peruvian Case Study." *Journal of Family History* 3, 4 (1978): 422–37.

Di Peso, Charles. *Casas Grandes: A Fallen Trading Center of the Gran Chichimeca.* Vols. 1–8. Dragoon, Ariz.: Northland Press, 1974.

————. "Discussion of Masse, Doelle, Sheridan, and Reff Papers from Southwestern Protohistory Conference." In D. R. Wilcox and W. B. Masse, eds., *The Protohistoric Period in the North American Southwest, AD 1450–1700.* Tempe: Arizona State University, Antropological Research Papers 24, 1981: 113–22.

————. *The Upper Pima of San Cayetano of Tumacacori.* Dragoon, Ariz.: Amerind Foundation, 1956.

Dobyns, Henry F. "Do-It-Yourself Religion: The Diffusion of Folk Catholicism on Mexico's Northern Frontier, 1821–46." In Alan Crumrine and N. Ross Morinis, eds., *Pilgrimage in Latin America.* Westport: Greenwood Press, 1991: 53–70.

————. *From Fire to Flood.* Socorro, N. Mex.: Ballena Press, 1981.

————. "Indian Extinction in the Middle Santa Cruz River Valley." *New Mexico Historical Review* 38, 2, 1963: 163–81.

————. *Spanish Colonial Tucson.* Tucson: University of Arizona Press, 1976.

Doolittle, William E., "Aboriginal agricultural development in the Valley of Sonora, Mexico," *Geographical Review* 70, 3, 1980: 328–42.

————. "Agricultural Expansion in a Marginal Area of Mexico," *Geographical Review*, Vol. 73, No. 3 (1983) 301–313.

————. "Agriculture in North America on the Eve of Contact: A Reassessment." *Annals of the Association of American Geographers*, Vol. 82, No. 3 (1992) 386–401.

————. *Canal Irrigation in Prehistoric Mexico: The Sequence of Technological Change.* Austin: University of Texas Press, 1990.

————. "Pre-Hispanic Occupance in the Middle Río Sonora Valley: From an Ecological to a Socioeconomic Focus." Ph.D. diss., University of Oklahoma, 1979.

————. *Pre-Hispanic Occupance in the Valley of Sonora, Mexico. Archeological Confirmation of Early Spanish Reports.* Tucson: University of Arizona Press, Anthropological Papers 48, 1988.

————. "Settlements and the Development of 'Statelets' in Sonora, Mexico." *Journal of Field Archaeology* 11, 1984: 13–24.

Doyel, David E. "The Transition to History in Northern Pimería Alta." In David Hurst Thomas, ed., *Columbian Consequences*. Vol. 1: *Archaeological and Historical Perspectives on the Spanish Borderlands West*. Washington, D.C.: Smithsonian Institution Press, 1989: 139–58.

Ebright, Malcolm, ed. *Spanish and Mexican Land Grants and the Law*. Special Issue of *Journal of the West* 27, 3, 1988. 2nd ed. Yuma: Sunflower University Press, 1989.

Edleman, Robert. *Proletarian Peasants. The Revolution of 1905 in Russia's Southwest*. Ithaca: Cornell University Press, 1987.

Escandón, Patricia. "Economía y sociedad en Sonora: 1767–1821." In *Historia general de Sonora*. Vol. 2: *De la conquista al estado libre y soberano de Sonora*. Mexico City: Gobierno del Estado de Sonora, 1985: 275–98.

————. "La nueva administración misional y los pueblos de indios." In *Historia general de Sonora*. Vol. 2: *De la conquista al estado libre y soberano de Sonora*. Mexico City: Gobierno del Estado de Sonora, 1985: 249–74.

Faragher, John Mack. *Sugar Creek: Life on the Illinois Prairie*. New Haven: Yale University Press, 1986.

Farriss, Nancy M. "Indians in Colonial Yucatan: Three Perspectives." In Murdo J. MacLeod and Robert Wasserstrom, eds., *Spaniards and Indians in Southeastern Mesoamerica. Essays on the History of Ethnic Relations*. Lincoln: University of Nebraska Press, 1983: 1–39.

————. *Maya Society under Colonial Rule. The Collective Enterprise of Survival*. Princeton: Princeton University Press, 1984.

————. "Nucleation versus Dispersal: The Dynamics of Population Movement in Colonial Yucatán." *Hispanic American Historical Review* 58, 2 1978: 187–216.

Favre, Henri. "The Dynamics of Indian Peasant Society and Migration to Coastal Plantations in Central Peru." In K. Duncan and I. Rutledge, eds., *Land and Labour in Latin America*. Cambridge: Cambridge University Press, 1977: 253–67.

Felger, Richard Stephen, and Mary Beck Moser. *People of the Desert and Sea. Ethnobotany of the Seri Indians*. Tucson: University of Arizona Press, 1985.

Figueroa Valenzuela, Alejandro. *Los que hablan fuerte. El desarrollo de la sociedad yaqui*. Hermosillo: Instituto Nacional de Antropología e Historia, Noroeste de México 7. 1986.

Flores Clair, Eduardo. "Minas y mineros: Pago en especie y conflictos, 1790–1880." *Historias* 13, 1986: 51–68.

Florescano, Enrique. "La formación de los trabajadores en la época colonial, 1521–1750." In *La clase obrera en la historia de México. De la colonia al imperio*. Mexico City: Universidad Nacional Autónoma de México, 1980: 9–124.

————. "The Hacienda in New Spain." In Leslie Bethell, ed., *Colonial Spanish America*. Cambridge: Cambridge University Press, 1987: 250–85.

———, ed. *Haciendas, Latifundios y plantaciones en America Latina* Mexico City: Siglo Veintiuno Editores, 1975.

———. *Origen y desarrollo de los problemas agrarios de México, 1500–1821.* Mexico City: Ediciones Era, 1976.

———. *Precios del maíz y crisis agrícolas en México (1708–1860).* Mexico City: El Colegio de México, 1971.

Fontana, Bernard L. *Of Earth and Little Rain. The Papago Indians.* Flagstaff, Ariz.: Northland Press, 1981.

———. "Pima and Papago: Introduction" and "History of the Papago." In William C. Sturtevant, ed., *Handbook of North American Indians.* Vol. 10: Alfonso Ortiz, ed., *Southwest.* Washington, D.C.: Smithsonian Institution, 1983: 125–48.

———. "The Vikita: A Biblio History." *Journal of the Southwest* 29, 3, 1987: 259–72.

Friedmann, Harriet. "Household Production and the National Economy: Concepts for the Analysis of Agrarian Formations." *Journal of Peasant Studies* 7, 2, 1980: 158–84.

Fussell, Betty. *The Story of Corn. The Myths and History, the Culture and Agriculture, the Art and Science of America's Quintessential Crop.* (New York: Alfred A. Knopf, 1992).

García Martínez, Bernardo. "Jurisdicción y propiedad: Una distinción fundamental en la historia de los pueblos de indios del México colonial." *European Review of Latin American and Caribbean Studies* 53, 1992: 47–60.

———. "Pueblos de Indios, Pueblos de Castas: New Settlements and Traditional Corporate Organization in Eighteenth-Century New Spain." In Arij Ouweneel and Simon Miller, eds., *The Indian Community of Colonial Mexico. Fifteen Essays on Land Tenure, Corporate Organizations, Ideology and Village Politics.* Amsterdam: CEDLA [Centre for Latin American Research and Documentation], Latin American Studies 58, 1990: 103–16.

———. *Los pueblos de la sierra. El poder y el espacio entre los indios del norte de Puebla hasta 1700.* Mexico City: El Colegio de México, 1987.

Garner, Richard L. "Price Trends in Eighteenth-Century Mexico." *Hispanic American Historical Review* 65, 2, 1985: 279–326.

———. "Prices and Wages in Eighteenth-Century Mexico." In Lyman L. Johnson and Enrique Tandeter, eds., *Essays on the Price History of Eighteenth-Century Latin America.* Albuquerque: University of New Mexico Press, 1990: 73–108.

Garner, Richard L., with Spiro E. Stefanou. *Economic Growth and Change in Bourbon Mexico.* Gainesville: University Press of Florida, 1993.

Gaventa, John. *Power and Powerlessness: Quiescence and Rebellion in an Appalachian Valley* Urbana: University of Illinois Press, 1980.

Geertz, Clifford. *La interpretación de las culturas.* Barcelona: Geidsa Eds., 1989 [New York, 1973].

Gelman, Jorge. "Los caminos del mercado: Campesinos, estancieros y pulperos en una región del Río de la Plata colonial." *Latin American Research Review* 28, 2, 1993: 89–118.

————. "Producción campesina y estancias en el Río de la Plata colonial. La región de colonia a fines del siglo XVIII." *Boletín del Instituto de Historia Argentina y Americana "Dr. E. Ravignani,"* 3rd ser., 6, 1992: 41–65.

Genovese, Eugene D. *Roll, Jordan, Roll. The World the Slaves Made.* New York: Vintage Books, 1976.

Gerhard, Peter. *The North Frontier of New Spain.* [Princeton: Princeton University Press, 1982] rev. ed., Norman: University of Oklahoma Press, 1993.

Gibson, Charles. *The Aztecs under Spanish Rule.* Stanford: Stanford University Press, 1964.

————. *Tlaxcala in the Sixteenth Century.* New Haven: Yale University Press, 1952.

Giraud, François. "De las problemáticas europeas al caso novohispano: Apuntes para una historia de la familia mexicana." In *Familia y sexualidad en Nueva España.* Mexico City: Fondo de Cultura Económica, 1982: 56–80.

Gonzalbo Aizpuru, Pilar. *Historia de la educación en la época colonial. El mundo indígena.* Mexico City: El Colegio de México, 1990.

González R., Luis. *Etnología y misión en la Pimería Alta, 1715–1740.* Mexico City: Universidad Nacional Autónoma de México, 1977.

————. *Tarahumara: La sierra y el hombre.* Mexico City: Fondo de Cultura Económica, 1982.

González Sánchez, Isabel. "Sistemas de trabajo, salarios y situación de los trabajadores agrícolas, 1750–1810." In *La clase obrera en la historia de México. De la colonia al imperio.* Mexico City: Universidad Nacional Autónoma de México, 1980: 125–72.

González y González, Luis. *Pueblo en vilo: Microhistoria de San José de Gracia.* Mexico City: El Colegio de México, 1968.

Gosner, Kevin. "Critical Perspectives on the Construction of Ethnic Identity: Debating 'Indian-ness' in Colonial Central America." American Historical Association Annual Meeting, Chicago, 1991.

————. "Las élites indígenas en los altos de Chiapas (1524–1714)." *Historia Mexicana* 34, 1984: 405–23.

Gossen, Gary H. "The Chumula Festival of Games: Native Macroanalysis and Social Commentary in a Maya Carnival." In Gossen, ed., *Symbol and Meaning beyond the Closed Community.* Albany: State University of New York, Institute for Mesoamerican Studies, 1986: 227–54.

Gouy-Gilbert, Cécile. *Une résistance indienne. Les yaquis du Sonora.* Lyons: Fédérop, 1983.

Griffen, William B. "Apache Indians and the North Mexican Peace Establishments." In Charles Lange, ed., *Southwestern Culture History: Collected Papers in Honor of Albert H. Schroeder.* Santa Fe: Ancient City Press, 1985: 183–95.

————. *The Apaches at War and Peace: The Janos Presidios, 1750–1858.* Albuquerque: University of New Mexico Press, 1988.

————. *Culture Change and Shifting Populations in Central Northern Mexico.* Tucson: University of Arizona Press, Anthropological Papers 13, 1969.

————. *Indian Assimilation in the Franciscan Area of Nueva Vizcaya.* Tucson: University of Arizona Press, Anthropological Papers 33, 1979.

————. *Utmost Good Faith: Patterns of Apache–Mexican Hostilities in Northern Chihuahua Border Warfare, 1821–1848.* Albuquerque: University of New Mexico Press, 1988.

Griffith, James S. *Beliefs and Holy Places. A Spiritual Geography of the Pimería Alta.* Tucson: University of Arizona Press, 1992.

Gruzinski, Serge. "Individualization and Acculturation: Confession among the Nahuas of Mexico from the Sixteenth to the Eighteenth Century." In Asunción Lavrín, ed., *Sexuality and Marriage in Colonial Latin America.* Lincoln: University of Nebraska Press, 1989: 96–117.

————. "Normas cristianas y respuestas indígenas: Apuntes para el estudio del proceso de occidentalización entre los indios de Nueva España." In *Del dicho al hecho . . . Transgresiones y pautas culturales en la Nueva España.* Mexico City: Instituto Nacional de Antropología e Historia, Colección Científica, 1989: 109–22.

Gudmundson, Lowell. "Peasant, Farmer, Proletarian: Class Formation in a Smallholder Coffee Economy, 1850–1950." *Hispanic American Historical Review* 69, 2, 1989: 221–58.

Guevara Sánchez, Arturo. *Arqueología del área de las Cuarenta Casas, Chihuahua.* Mexico City: Instituto Nacional de Antropología e Historia, 1986.

Gutiérrez, Edgar Omar. "Estado, comercio, y minería en Sonora de 1769–1782." Ms. INAH Centro Sonora, 1990.

————. "La organización de los mineros sonorenses al transitar de los siglos XVIII al XIX." In *Memoria. XVII Simposio de Historia y Antropología de Sonora.* Hermosillo: Universidad de Sonora, 1992: 317–32.

Gutiérrez, Ramón A. "Honor Ideology, Marriage Negotiation, and Class-Gender Domination in New Mexico, 1690–1846." *Latin American Perspectives* 12, 1, 1985: 81–104.

————. *When Jesus Came, the Corn Mothers Went Away. Marriage, Sexuality, and Power in New Mexico, 1500–1846.* Stanford: Stanford University Press, 1991.

Gutman, Herbert G. *The Black Family in Slavery and Freedom,* New York: Pantheon Books, 1976.

————. "Marital and Sexual Norms among Slave Women." In Nancy F. Cott and Elizabeth H. Pleck, eds., *A Heritage of Her Own.* New York: Simon and Schuster, 1979: 298–310.

Hahn, Steve. *The Roots of Southern Populism. Yeoman Farmers and the Transformation of the Georgia Upcountry, 1850–1890.* New York: Oxford University Press, 1983.

Hahn, Steve, and Jonathan Prude, eds. *The Countryside in the Age of Capitalist Transformation. Essays in the Social History of Rural America.* Chapel Hill: University of North Carolina Press, 1985.

Hall, Thomas D. *Social Change in the Southwest, 1350–1880.* Lawrence: University of Kansas Press, 1989.

Halperin, R., and J. Dow, eds. *Peasant Livelihood.* New York: St. Martin's Press, 1977.

Harris, Olivia. "Labor and Produce in an Ethnic Economy: Northern Potosí, Bolivia." In David Lehmann, ed., *Ecology and Exchange in the Andes.* Cambridge: Cambridge University Press, 1982: 70–97.

Harvey, H. R., ed. *Land and Politics in the Valley of Mexico. A Two Thousand Year Perspective.* Albuquerque: University of New Mexico Press, 1991.

Hawkins, John P. "Ethnicity in Mesoamerica: A Statistical Test of Economic versus Ideological Theories of Ethnic Change." *Boletín de Estudios Latinoamericanos y del Caribe* 40, 1986: 23–35.

Hayden, Julian D. "The Vikita Ceremony of the Papago." *Journal of the Southwest* 29, 3, 1987: 273–324.

Hedrick, Basil C., J. Charles Kelley, and Carroll L. Riley, eds. *The North Mexican Frontier.* Carbondale: Southern Illinois University Press, 1971.

Henry, Louis. *Manual de demografía histórica.* Barcelona: Grijalbo, 1983.

Hobsbawm, Eric. "Peasants and Politics." *Journal of Peasant Studies* 1, 1 (1973): 3–22.

Hobsbawm, Eric, and Terence Ranger, eds. *The Invention of Tradition.* Cambridge: Cambridge University Press, 1983.

Hu-Dehart, Evelyn. *Missionaries, Miners and Indians. Spanish Contact with the Yaqui Nation of Northwestern New Spain, 1533–1820.* Tucson: University of Arizona Press, 1981.

Jackson, Robert H. "Demographic Change in Northwestern New Spain." *The Americas* 41, 4, 1985: 462–79.

———. "Demographic and Social Change in Northwestern New Spain: A Comparative Analysis of the Pimería Alta and Baja California." M.A. thesis, University of Arizona, 1982.

———. *Indian Population Decline. The Missions of Northwestern New Spain, 1687–1840.* Albuquerque, University of New Mexico Press, 1994.

Jacobsen, Nils. "Campesinos y tenencia de la tierra en el altiplano peruano en la transición de la colonia a la república." *Allpanchis* 23, 37, 1991: 25–93.

———. *Mirages of Transition. The Peruvian Altiplano, 1780–1930.* Berkeley: University of California Press, 1993.

Jacobsen, Nils, and Hans-Jürgen Puhle, eds. *The Economies of Mexico and Peru during the Late Colonial Period.* Berlin: Colloquium Verlag, 1986.

Jiménez Pelayo, Agueda. *Haciendas y comunidades indígenas en el sur de Zacatecas.* Mexico City: Instituto Nacional de Antropología e Historia, 1989.

John, Elizabeth A. H. *Storms Brewed in Other Men's Worlds: The Confrontation of Indians,*

Spanish and French in the Southwest, 1540–1795. College Station: Texas A & M University Press, 1975.

———, ed. *Views from the Apache Frontier. Report on the Northern Provinces of New Spain by José Cortés,* Trans. John Wheat. Norman: University of Oklahoma Press, 1989 [1799].

Johnson, Alfred. "The Trincheras Culture of Northern Sonora." *American Antiquity* 29, 1963: 174–86.

Johnson, Jean B. "The Opata: An Inland Tribe of Sonora." In Basil C. Hedrick, J. Charles Kelley, and Carroll L. Riley, eds. *The North Mexican Frontier.* Carbondale: Southern Illinois University Press, 1971: 169–99.

Jones, Grant D. *Maya Resistance to Spanish rule. Time and History on a Colonial Frontier.* Albuquerque: University of New Mexico Press, 1989.

Jones, Oakah L. *Nueva Vizcaya. Heartland of the Spanish Frontier.* Albuquerque: University of New Mexico Press, 1988.

Jones, Richard. "The Wi'gita of Achi and Quitobac." *The Kiva* 36, 4, 1971: 1–29.

Kandiyoki, Deniz. *Women in Rural Production Systems: Problems and Policies.* Paris: UNESCO, 1985.

Kellogg, Susan. "Households in Late Prehispanic and Early Colonial Mexico City: Their Structure and Its Implications for the Study of Historical Demography." *The Americas* 44, 4, 1988: 483–94.

———. *Law and Transformation of Aztec Culture.* Norman: University of Oklahoma Press, 1995.

Kessell, John L. "Friars versus Bureaucrats: The Mission as a Threatened Institution on the Arizona-Sonora Frontier, 1767–1842." *Western Historical Quarterly* 5, 1974: 151–62.

———. *Friars, Soldiers, and Reformers. Hispanic Arizona and the Sonora Mission Frontier, 1767–1856.* Tucson: University of Arizona Press, 1976.

———. *Kiva, Cross, and Crown. The Pecos Indians and New Mexico, 1540–1840.* Washington, D.C.: National Park Service, U.S. Department of the Interior, 1979.

———. *Mission of Sorrows: Jesuit Guevavi and the Pimas.* Tucson: University of Arizona Press, 1970.

———. "The Puzzling Presidio San Phelipe de Guevavi, Alias Terrenate." *New Mexico Historical Review* 41, 1, 1966: 21–46.

———, ed. *Remote beyond Compare. Letters of Don Diego de Vargas to His Family from New Spain and New Mexico, 1675–1706.* Albuquerque: University of New Mexico Press, 1989.

Kirchhoff, Paul. "Gatherers and Farmers in the Greater Southwest: A Problem in Classification." *American Anthropologist* 54, 4, 1954: 525–50.

———. "Mesoamérica: Sus límites geográficos, composición étnica, y caracteres culturales." *Acta Americana* 1, 1943: 92–107.

Klor de Alva, J. Jorge. "The Postcolonization of the (Latin) American Experience: A Reconsideration of 'Colonialism,' 'Postcolonialism,' and 'Mestizaje.' " In Gyan Prakash, ed., *After Colonialism. Imperial Histories and Postcolonial Displacements*. Princeton: Princeton University Press, 1995: 241–75.

Kuznesof, Elizabeth. "The History of the Family in Latin America: A Critique of Recent Work." *Latin American Research Review* 29, 2, 1989: 168–86.

Langer, Erick D. *Economic Change and Rural Resistance in Southern Bolivia, 1830–1930.* Stanford: Stanford University Press, 1989.

Langer, Erick, and Robert H. Jackson. "Colonial and Republican Missions Compared: The Cases of Alta California and Southeastern Bolivia." *Comparative Studies in Society and History* 30, 2, 1988: 286–311.

Larson, Brooke. *Colonialism and Agrarian Transformation in Bolivia. Cochabamba, 1550–1900.* Princeton, Princeton University Press, 1988.

Lavrín, Asunción, ed. *Sexuality and Marriage in Colonial Latin America.* Lincoln: University of Nebraska Press, 2nd ed. 1992 [1989].

Lavrín, Asunción, and Edith Couturier. "Dowries and Wills: A View of Women's Social and Economic Role in Colonial Guadalajara and Puebla." *Hispanic American Historical Review* 59, 2, 1979: 280–304.

Lehmann, David, ed. *Ecology and Exchange in the Andes.* Cambridge: Cambridge University Press, 1982.

Lenin, V. I. *El desarrollo del capitalismo en Rusia. Proceso de la formación del mercado interior para la gran industria.* Moscow: Editorial Progreso, 1981 [1908].

Le Roy Ladurie, Emmanuel. *Historia del clima desde el año mil* [Histoire du climat depuis l'an mil, 1983]. Mexico City: Fondo de Cultura Económica, 1990.

———. *Montaillou. The Promised Land of Error.* New York: Vintage, 1979 [1978, George Braziller, Inc.]

Lewin, Linda. "Natural and Spurious Children in Brazilian Inheritance Law from Colony to Empire: A Methodological Essay." *The Americas* 48, 3, 1992: 351–96.

Lloyd, Jane-Dale. *El proceso de modernización capitalista en el noroeste de Chihuahua (1880–1910).* Mexico City: Universidad Ibero-Americana, 1987.

Lockhart, James. *The Nahuas after the Conquest: A Social and Cultural History of the Indians of Central Mexico, Sixteenth through Eighteenth Centuries.* Stanford: Stanford University Press, 1992.

———. *Nahuas and Spaniards. Postconquest Central Mexican History and Philology.* Stanford: Stanford University Press, UCLA Latin American Center Publications, 1991.

Long, Norman, ed. *Family and Work in Rural Societies. Perspectives on Non-wage Labour.* London: Tavistock Publications, 1984.

Macdougal, D. T. "Across Papaguería." *American Geographical Society,* 40, 1908: 1–21.

MacLeod, Murdo J., and Robert Wasserstrom, eds. *Spaniards and Indians in Southwestern Mesoamerica: Essays on the History of Ethnic Relations.* Lincoln: University of Nebraska Press, 1983.

Mallon, Florencia E. *The Defense of Community in Peru's Central Highlands*. Princeton: Princeton University Press, 1983.

―――. "Patriarchy in the Transition to Capitalism," *Feminist Studies* 13, 2, 1987: 379–407.

―――. *Peasant and Nation. The Making of Postcolonial Mexico and Peru*. Berkeley, University of California Press, 1995.

―――. "The Promise and Dilemma of Subaltern Studies: Perspectives from Latin American History." *American Historical Review* 99, 5, 1995: 1491–1515.

Malvido, Elsa. "Cronología de epidemias y hambrunas en la población colonial." In Enrique Florescano and Elsa Malvido, eds., *Ensayos sobre la historia de las epidemias en México*. Vol. 1. Mexico City: Instituto Mexicano de Seguro Social, 1982: 171–78.

―――. "Efectos de las epidemias y hambrunas en la población colonial de México (1519–1810)." In Enrique Florescano and Elsa Malvido, eds., *Ensayos sobre la historia de las epidemias en México*. Vol. 1. Mexico City: Instituto Mexicano de Seguro Social, 1982: 179–200.

―――. "Factores de despoblación y de reposición de la población de Cholula (1641–1810)." *Historia Mexicana* 23, 1, 1973: 52–110.

Martin, Cheryl English. *Governance and Society in Colonial Mexico: Chihuahua in the Eighteenth Century*. Stanford: Stanford University Press, 1996.

Martínez-Alier, Juan. "Ecology and the Poor: A Neglected Dimension of Latin American History." *Journal of Latin American Studies* 23, 2 (1991): 621–39.

―――. *Haciendas, Plantations, and Collective Farms. Agrarian Class Societies—Cuba and Peru*. London: Frank Cass 1977.

―――. "Relations of Production in Andean Haciendas, Perú." In K. Duncan and Ian Rutledge, eds., *Land and Labour in Latin America*. Cambridge, Cambridge University Press, 1977: 141–64.

Mathien, Frances Joan, and Randall H. McGuire, eds. *Ripples in the Chichimec Sea. New Considerations of Southwestern–Mesoamerican Interactions*. Carbondale: Southern Illinois University Press, 1986.

Matson, Daniel S., and Bernard L. Fontana, eds. *Friar Bringas Reports to the King. Methods of Indoctrination on the Frontier of New Spain 1796–97*. Tucson: University of Arizona Press, 1977.

Mayer, Enrique, "A Tribute to the Household: Domestic Economy and the Encomienda in Colonial Peru." In R. T. Smith, ed. *Kinship Ideology and Practice in Latin America*, 85–117, 1988.

McCaa, Robert. "Women's Position, Family and Fertility in Mexico: The Case of Parral, 1777–1930." *Annales de Démographie Historique*, n.v., 1989: 233–43.

McCarty, Kieran, ed. and trans. *Desert Documentary*. Tucson: Arizona Historical Society, 1976.

―――. *A Spanish Frontier in the Enlightened Age. Franciscan Beginnings in Sonora and Ari-*

zona, 1767–1770. Washington, D.C.: Academy of American Franciscan History, 1981.

McGuire, Randall H., and M. Elisa Villalpando. "Prehistory and the Making of History in Sonora." In David H. Thomas, ed., *Columbian Consequences: Archaeological and Historical Perspectives on the Spanish Borderlands West*. Vol. 1. Washington, D.C.: Smithsonian Institution Press, 1989: 159–77.

McGuire, Thomas R. *Politics and Ethnicity on the Río Yaqui: Potam Revisited*. Tucson: University of Arizona Press, 1986.

Meillassoux, Claude. "From Reproduction to Production." *Economy and Society* 1, 1972: 93–105.

———. *Maidens, Meal and Money. Capitalism and the Domestic Community*. Cambridge: Cambridge University Press, 1981.

Melville, Elinor. "Environmental and Social Change in the Valle de Mezquital, Mexico, 1521–1600." *Comparative Studies in Society and History* 32, 1990: 24–53.

———. *A Plague of Sheep. Environmental Consequences of the Conquest of Mexico*. Cambridge: Cambridge University Press, 1994.

Mentz, Brígida von. *Pueblos de indios, mulatos y mestizos, 1770–1870. Los campesinos y las transformaciones protoindustriales en el poniente de Morelos*. Mexico City: CIESAS [Centro de Investigaciones y Estudios Superiores en Antropología Social], Ediciones de la Casa Chata 30, 1988.

Merrill, Michael. "Cash Is Good to Eat: Self-Sufficiency and Exchange in the Rural Economy of the United States." *Radical History Review* 3, 4, 1976: 42–71.

Merrill, William. "Conversion and Colonialism in Northern Mexico. The Tarahumara Response to the Jesuit Mission Program, 1601–1767." In Robert W. Hefner, ed., *Conversion to Christianity. Historical and Anthropological Perspectives on a Great Transformation*. Berkeley: University of California Press, 1989: 129–63.

———. *Rarámuri Souls. Knowledge and Social Process in Northern Mexico*. Washington, D.C.: Smithsonian Institution Press, 1988.

Meyer, Michael. *Water in the Southwest. A Social and Legal History*. Tucson: University of Arizona Press, 1984.

Mignolo, Walter D. "Colonial and Postcolonial Discourse: Cultural Critique or Academic Colonialism?" *Latin American Research Review* 28, 3, 1993: 120–34.

Mirafuentes Galván, José Luis. "Elite y defensa en la provincia de Sonora, siglo XVIII." In *Memoria del XI Simposio de Historia y Antropología de Sonora*, Hermosillo, Sonora: Universidad de Sonora, 1987: 411–28.

———. "El 'enemigo de las casas de adobe,' Luis de Sáric y la rebelión de los pimas altos en 1751." In *Memoria del XIII Simposio de Historia y Antropología de Sonora*. Vol. 1. Hermosillo: Universidad de Sonora, 1989: 103–24.

———. "Identidad india, legitimidad y emancipación política en el noroeste de México (Copala, 1771)." Jaime E. Rodríguez O., ed., *Patterns of Contention in Mexican History*. Wilmington: Scholarly Resources, 1992: 49–67.

————. "Seris, apaches y españoles en Sonora. Consideraciones sobre su confrontación militar en el Siglo XVIII." *Históricas* 22, 1987: 18–29.

Mitchell, Timothy. "Everyday Metaphors of Power." *Theory and Society* 19, 5, 1990: 545–77.

Molina Molina, Flavio. *Diccionario de flora y fauna indígena de Sonora*. Hermosillo: Gobierno del Estado de Sonora, 1989.

————. *Historia de Hermosillo antiguo. En memoria del aniversario doscientos de haber recibido el título de Villa de Pitic (1783–1983)*. Hermosillo: Molina, 1983.

Montané Martí, Julio César. "Desde los orígenes hasta 3000 años antes del presente." In *Historia general de Sonora*. Vol. 1: *Período prehistórico y prehispánico*. Mexico: Gobierno del Estado de Sonora, 1985: 177–223.

Moorhead, Max. *The Presidio: Bastion of the Spanish Borderlands*. Norman: University of Oklahoma Press, 1975.

Moreno García, Heriberto. *Haciendas de tierra y agua*. Michoacán: Colegio de Michoacan: 1989.

Morin, Claude. *Michoacán en la Nueva España del siglo XVIII. Crecimiento y desigualdad en una economía colonial*. Mexico City: Fondo de Cultura Económica, 1979.

Morinis, Alan, and N. Ross Crumrine. "*La Peregrinación:* The Latin American Pilgrimage." In Crumrine and Morinis, eds., *Pilgrimage in Latin America*. Westport: Greenwood Press, 1991: 1–17.

Mörner, Magnus. "Etnicidad, movilidad social y mestizaje en la historia colonial hispanoamericana." In Jan-Åke Alvarsson and Hernán Horna, eds., *Ethnicity in Latin America*. Uppsala: University of Uppsala, CELAS, 1990: 29–44.

Murra, John V. "The Mit'a Obligations of Ethnic Groups to the Inka State." In George A. Collier, Renato I. Rosaldo, and John D. Wirth, eds., *The Inca and Aztec States, 1400–1800. Anthropology and History*. New York: Academic Press, 1982.

Nabhan, Gary. "*Ak-ciñ* and the Environment of Papago Indian Fields." *Applied Geography* 6, 1, 1986: 61–76.

————. "Amaranth Cultivation in the U.S. Southwest and Northwest Mexico." *Amaranth Proceedings*, 1979: 129–33.

————. *The Desert Smells Like Rain. A Naturalist in Papago Indian Country*. San Francisco: North Point Press, 1982.

————. *Gathering the Desert*. Tucson: University of Arizona Press, 1985.

————. "Papago Indian Desert Agriculture and Water Control in the Sonoran Desert, 1697–1934." *Applied Geography* 6, 1, 1986: 43–59.

Nabhan, Gary, and Thomas E. Sheridan. "Living Fencerows of the Río San Miguel, Sonora, Mexico: Traditional Technology for Floodplain Management." *Human Ecology*, 5, 2, 1977: 97–111.

Navarro García, Luis. *Sonora y Sinaloa en el siglo XVII*. Seville: Escuela de Estudios Hispano-Americanos, 1967.

————. *La sublevación yaqui de 1740*. Seville: Escuela de Estudios Hispano-Americanos, 1966.

Naylor, Thomas, and Charles W. Polzer, eds. *The Presidio and Militia on the Northern Frontier of New Spain, 1570–1700*. Tucson: University of Arizona Press, 1986.

Nazzari, Muriel. *Disappearance of the Dowry. Women, Families, and Social Change in São Paulo, Brazil, 1600–1900*. Stanford: Stanford University Press, 1991.

Newson, Linda. "Los sistemas de trabajo y demografía en América Española durante la colonia: Patrones de mortalidad y fertilidad." *Histórica e Populaçao. Estudos sobre a América Latina*. São Paulo: ABEP, IUSSP, CELADE, 1990: 289–97.

Nickel, Herbert J. *Morfología social de la hacienda mexicana*. Mexico City: Fondo de Cultura Económica, 1988.

Nolan, Mary Lee. "The European Roots of Latin American Pilgrimage." In N. Ross Crumrine and Alan Morinis, eds., *Pilgrimage in Latin America*. Westport: Greenwood Press, 1991: 19–49.

Officer, James E. *Hispanic Arizona, 1536–1856*. Tucson: University of Arizona Press, 1987.

Orlove, Benjamin S. "Against a Definition of Peasantries: Agrarian Production in Andean Peru." In R. Halperin and J. Dow, eds., *Peasant Livelihood*. New York: St. Martin's Press, 1977: 22–35.

Orlove, Benjamin S., and Glynn Custred. "Agrarian Economies and Social Processes in Comparative Perspective: The Agricultural Production Unit." In Orlove and Custred, eds., *Land and Power in Latin America. Agrarian Economies and Social Processes in the Andes*. New York: Holmes & Meier, 1980: 13–29.

Ortega Noriega, Sergio, "De amores y desamores." In Sergio Ortega Noriega, Lourdes Villafuerte García, Teresa Lozano Armendares et al, eds. *Amor y desamor. Vivencias de parejas en la sociedad novohispana*. México: Instituto Nacional de Antropología e Historia, 1992: 9–26.

————. "El discurso teológico de Santo Tomás de Aquino sobre el matrimonio, la familia, y los comportamientos sexuales." In *El placer de pecar y el afán de normar*. Mexico City: Joaquín Mortiz and Instituto Nacional de Antropología e Historia, 1987: 15–78.

————. "La iglesia católica en la conquista española," in Sergio Ortega Noriega and Ignacio del Río, eds., *Historia General de Sonora. II. De la Conquista al Estado Libre y Soberano de Sonora*. Hermosillo: Gobierno del Estado de Sonora, 1985: 37–41.

————. "La misión jesuítica como institución disciplinaria (1610–1720)." In *Memoria. XVII Simposio de Historia y Antropología de Sonora*. Vol. 1. Hermosillo: Universidad de Sonora, 1992: 169–80.

————. "El sistema de misiones jesuíticas: 1591–1699." In *Historia General de Sonora*. Vol. 2: *De la conquista al estado libre y soberano de Sonora*. Mexico City: Gobierno del Estado de Sonora, 1985: 37–78.

Ortiz, Alfonso. *The Tewa World. Space, Time, Being and Becoming in a Pueblo Society.* Chicago: University of Chicago Press, 1969.

Ouweneel, Arij. "The Agrarian Cycle as a Catalyst of Economic Development in Eighteenth-Century Central Mexico. The Arable Estate, Indian Villages, and Proto-Industrialization in the Central Highland Valleys." *Ibero-Amerikanisches Archiv,* N.F. Jg. 15, H. 3, 1989: 399–417.

———. "*Altepeme* and *Pueblos de Indios.* Some Comparative Theoretical Perspectives on the Analysis of the Colonial Indian Communities." In A. Ouweneel and S. Miller, eds., *The Indian Community of Colonial Mexico.* Amsterdam: CEDLA [Centre for Latin American Research and Documentation], 1990.

———. "Raíces del 'chiaroscuro' en México. Algunas consideraciones acerca de esta compilación." In A. Ouweneel and C. Torales, comps., *Empresarios, indios y estado. Perfil de la economía mexicana (siglo XVIII).* Amsterdam: CEDLA, 1988: 1–14.

Ouweneel, Arij, and Simon Miller, eds. *The Indian Community of Colonial Mexico. Fifteen Essays on Land Tenure, Corporate Organizations, Ideology, and Village Politics.* Amsterdam, CEDLA, 1990.

Pailes, Richard A. "The Río Sonora Culture in Prehistoric Trade Systems." In Carroll Riley and Basil Hedrick, eds., *Across the Chichimec Sea.* Carbondale: Southern Illinois University Press, 1978: 134–43.

Painter, Muriel Thayer. *A Yaqui Easter.* Tucson: University of Arizona Press, 1971.

Penney, David W., et al., ed., *Art of the American Indian Frontier.* Seattle: University of Washington Press, for Detroit Institute of the Arts, 1992.

Pennington, Campbell, W., ed. *Arte y vocabulario de la lengua dohema, heve o eudeva. Anónimo (siglo XVII).* Mexico City: Universidad Nacional Autónoma de México, 1981.

———. *La cultura de los eudeve del noroeste de México.* Hermosillo: Instituto Nacional de Antropología de México, Noroeste de México 6, 1982.

———. *The Pima Bajo of Central Sonora, Mexico.* Vol. 1: *The Material Culture.* Salt Lake City: University of Utah Press, 1980.

———. *The Pima Bajo of Central Sonora, Mexico.* Vol. 2: *Vocabulario en la lengua nevome.* Salt Lake City: University of Utah Press, 1979.

———. *The Tepehuan of Chihuahua. Their Material Culture.* Salt Lake City: University of Utah Press, 1969.

Pérez Bedolla, Raúl Gerardo. "Geografía de Sonora." In *Historia General de Sonora.* Vol. 1: *Período prehistórico y prehispánico.* Mexico City: Gobierno del Estado de Sonora, 1985: 111–72.

Pérez Herrero, Pedro. *Plata y libranzas. La articulación comercial del México borbónico.* Mexico City: El Colegio de México, 1988.

Pickens, Buford, ed. *The Missions of Northern Sonora. A 1935 Field Documentation.* Tucson: University of Arizona Press, 1993.

Pineda, Nicolás. "The Baroyeca Mine in Spanish Sonora: Ownership, Management, and Labor, 1701–1850." *Journal of the Southwest* 32, 2, 1990: 192–205.

Platt, Tristan. *Estado Boliviano y Ayllú Andino: Tierra y Tributo en el Norte de Potosí*, Lima: Instituto de Estudios Pervanos, 1982.

Polanyi, Karl, Conrad M. Arensberg, and Harry W. Pearson, eds. *Comercio y mercado en los imperios antiguos.* Barcelona: Editorial Labor, S.A., 1976 [New York: Free Press, 1957].

Polzer, Charles W. "The Franciscan Entrada into Sonora, 1646–1652: A Jesuit Chronicle." *Arizona and the West* 14, 3, 1972: 253–78.

———. *Rules and Precepts of the Jesuit Missions of Northwestern New Spain.* Tucson: University of Arizona Press, 1976.

Porras Muñoz, Guillermo. *Iglesia y estado en Nueva Vizcaya, 1562–1821.* Mexico City: Porrúa, 1980.

Powell, Philip W. *La guerra chichimeca (1550–1600).* Mexico City: Fondo de Cultura Económica, 1977 [*Soldiers, Indians, and Silver.* Berkeley: University of California Press, 1952].

Powers, Karen. *Andean Journeys: Migration, Ethnogenesis, and the State in Colonial Quito.* Albuquerque, University of New Mexico Press, 1995.

Prakash, Gyan. "Introduction: After Colonialism." In G. Prakash, ed., *After Colonialism. Imperial Histories and Postcolonial Displacements.* Princeton: Princeton University Press, 1995: 3–17.

———. "Subaltern Studies as Postcolonial Criticism," *American Historical Review* 99, 5, 1994: 1475–90.

Pryor, Frederic L. *The Origins of the Economy. A Comparative Study of Distribution in Primitive and Peasant Economies.* New York: Academic Press, 1977.

Quale, G. Robina. *Families in Context. A World History of Population.* New York: Greenwood Press, 1992.

Quijada Hernández, Armando. *Cumpas. Fragmentos de su historia.* Hermosillo: Gobierno del Estado de Sonora, 1992.

Rabell Romero, Cecilia. *Los diezmos de San Luis de la Paz. Economía en una región del Bajío en el siglo XVIII.* Mexico City: Universidad Nacional Autónoma de México, 1986.

———. "Los estudios de demografía histórica novohispana: Una revisión crítica." Seventh Conference of Mexican and United States Historians, Oaxaca, 1985.

Radding, Cynthia. *La acumulación originaria de capital agraria en Sonora. La comunidad indígena y la hacienda en Pimería Alta y Opatería, 1768–1868.* Hermosillo: Instituto Nacional de Antropología e Historia, Noroeste de México, 5, 1981: 13–46.

———. "En la sombra de la sierra. La etnicidad y la formación del campesinado en el noroeste de Nueva España." *HISLA* 11, 1988: 13–44.

———. *Las estructuras socioeconómicas de las misiones de la Pimería Alta, 1768–1850.*

Mexico City: Instituto Nacional de Antropología e Historia, Noroeste de México 3, 1979.

————. "The Function of the Market in Changing Economic Structures in the Mission Communities of Pimería Alta, 1768–1821." *The Americas* 34, 2, 1977: 155–69.

————. "Población, tierra y la persistencia de comunidad en la provincia de Sonora, 1750–1800." *Historia Mexicana* 41, 4, 1992: 551–78.

Ramírez, Susan. *Provincial Patriarchs. Land Tenure and the Economics of Power in Colonial Peru.* Albuquerque: University of New Mexico Press, 1986.

Reff, Daniel T. *Disease, Depopulation, and Culture Change in Northwestern New Spain, 1518–1764.* Salt Lake City: University of Utah Press, 1991.

————. "The Location of Corazones and Señora: Archaeological Evidence from the Río Sonora Valley, Mexico." In David R. Wilcox and W. Bruce Masse, eds., *The Protohistoric Period in the North American Southwest, AD 1450–1700.* Tempe: Arizona State University, Anthropological Research Papers 24, 1981: 94–112.

————. "Old World Diseases and the Dynamics of Indian and Jesuit Relations in Northwestern New Spain, 1520–1660." In Ross Crumrine and Phil C. Weigand, eds., *Ejidos and Regions of Refuge in Northwestern Mexico,* Anthropological Papers of the University of Arizona 46, Tucson: University of Arizona Press, 1987: 85–94.

Reher, David S. "¿Malthus de nuevo? Población y economía en México durante el siglo XVIII." *Historia Mexicana* 41, 4, 1992: 615–64.

Riley, Carroll L. *The Frontier People. The Greater Southwest in the Protohistoric Period.* Albuquerque: University of New Mexico Press, 1987.

Riley, Carroll L., and Basil C. Hedrick, eds. *Across the Chichimec Sea.* Carbondale: Southern Illinois University Press, 1978.

Río, Ignacio del. "Auge y decadencia de los placeres y el Real de la Cieneguilla, Sonora (1771–1783)." *Estudios de Historia Novohispana* 8. Mexico City: Universidad Nacional Autónoma de México, 1985: 81–98.

————. *Conquista y aculturación en la California jesuítica.* Mexico City: Universidad Nacional Autónoma de México, 1984.

————. "El noroeste novohispano y la nueva política imperial española." In *Historia general de Sonora.* Vol. 2: *De la conquista al estado libre y soberano de Sonora.* Mexico City: Gobierno del Estado de Sonora, 1985: 193–219.

————. "Proceso y balance de la reforma tributaria del siglo XVIII en Sinaloa y Sonora." In *Memoria del XIII Simposio de Historia y Antropología de Sonora.* Vol. 1. Hermosillo: Universidad de Sonora, 1989: 161–78.

————. "Repartimientos de indios en Sonora y Sinaloa." In *Memoria del VII Simposio de Historia de Sonora.* Hermosillo: Universidad de Sonora, 1982: 7–22.

Río, Ignacio del, and Edgar López Mañón. "La reforma institucional borbónica."

In *Historia general de Sonora*. Vol. 2: *De la conquista al estado libre y soberano de Sonora*. Mexico City: Gobierno del Estado de Sonora, 1985: 223–48.

Rivera Marín de Iturbe, Guadalupe, *La propiedad territorial en México, 1301–1810*. Mexico City: Siglo XXI, 1983.

Robinson, David, ed. *Migration in Colonial Spanish America*. Cambridge: Cambridge University Press, Cambridge Studies in Historical Geography 16, 1990.

———. "Patrones de migración en Michoacán en el siglo XVIII: Datos y metodologías." In Thomas Calvo and Gustavo López, coords., *Movimientos de población en el Occidente de México*. Mexico City: Centro de Estudios Mexicanos y Centroamericanos, 1988: 169–206.

———, ed. *Social Fabric and Spatial Structure in Colonial Latin America*. Published for the Dept. of Geography, Syracuse University, by University Microfilms International, Ann Arbor, 1979.

Rodríguez, François, and Nelly Silva. *Etnoarqueología de Quitovac, Sonora*. Mexico City: Centro de Estudios Mexicanos y Centroamericanos and Instituto Nacional de Antropología e Historia, two reports published in 1985 and 1986.

Rodríguez, O., Jaime E. *Patterns of Contention in Mexican History*. Wilmington: Scholarly Resources, 1992.

Rojas Rabiela, Teresa, ed. *Agricultura indígena: pasado y presente*. México: Centro de Investigaciones y Estudios Superiores en Antropología Social, 1994.

Romano, Ruggiero. "Algunas consideraciones alrededor de nación, estado (y libertad) en Europa y América centro-meridional." In Antonio Annino et al., eds., *America Latina: Del estado colonial al estado nación (1750–1940)*. Vols. 1, 2. Milan: Franco Angeli, 1987: 1–24.

Romero, Saúl Jerónimo. "La privatización de la tenencia de la tierra en Sonora, 1740–1860." M.A. thesis, Universidad Nacional Autónoma de México, 1991.

Roseberry, William. *Anthropologies and Histories: Essays in Culture, History, and Political Economy*. New Brunswick: Rutgers University Press, 1989.

Saeger, James Schofield. "Another View of the Mission as a Frontier Institution: The Guaycuruan Reductions of Santa Fe, 1743–1810." *Hispanic American Historical Review* 65, 3, 1985: 493–518.

Sahlins, Marshall. *Stone-Age Economics*. New York: Aldine, 1972.

Sahlins, Peter. "The Nation in the Village: State-building and Communal Struggles in the Catalan Borderland during the Eighteenth and Nineteenth Centuries." *Journal of Modern History* 60, 1988: 234–63.

Sauer, Carl O. *Aboriginal Population of Northwestern Mexico*. Berkeley: University of California Press, Ibero-Americana 10, 1935.

———. *The Distribution of Aboriginal Tribes and Languages in Northwestern Mexico*. Berkeley: University of California Press, Ibero-Americana 5, 1934.

Sauer, Carl O., and Donald Brand. "Prehistoric Settlements of Sonora, with Special Reference to Cerros de Trincheras." *University of California Publications in Geography* 5, 3, 1931: 67–148.

Sauer, Jonathan D. "The Grain Amaranths and Their Relatives: A Revised Taxonomic and Geographic Survey." *Annals of the Missouri Botanical Garden*, 54, 2, 1967: 103–37.

Schryer, Franz J. *Ethnicity and Class Conflict in Rural Mexico*. Princeton: Princeton University Press, 1990.

———. *The Rancheros of Pisaflores: The History of a Peasant Bourgeoisie in Twentieth-Century Mexico*. Toronto: University of Toronto Press, 1980.

Schuetz, Mardith K. "Professional Artisans in the Hispanic Southwest." *The Americas* 40, 1, 1983: 17–71.

Schwartz, Stuart B., ed. *Implicit Understandings: Observing, Reporting, and Reflecting on the Encounters between Europeans and Other Peoples in the Early Modern Era*. Cambridge: Cambridge University Press, 1994.

———. *Sugar Plantations in the Formation of Brazilian Society. Bahia, 1550–1835*. Cambridge: Cambridge University Press, 1985.

Scott, James C. *Domination and the Arts of Resistance*. New Haven: Yale University Press, 1990.

———. *The Moral Economy of the Peasant. Rebellion and Subsistence in Southeast Asia*. New Haven: Yale University Press, 1976.

———. *Weapons of the Weak. Everyday Forms of Peasant Resistance*. New Haven: Yale University Press, 1985.

Seed, Patricia. "The Church and the Patriarchal Family: Marriage Conflicts in Sixteenth- and Seventeenth-Century New Spain." *Journal of Family History* 10, 3, 1985: 284–93.

———. "Colonial and Postcolonial Discourse." Review Essay. *Latin American Research Review* 26, 3, 1991: 181–200.

———. "More Colonial and Postcolonial Discourses." *Latin American Research Review* 28, 3, 1993: 146–52.

———. *To Love, Honor, and Obey in Colonial Mexico. Conflicts over Marriage Choice, 1574–1821*. Stanford: Stanford University Press, 1988.

Semo, Enrique. *Historia mexicana. Economía y lucha de clases*. Mexico City: Editorial Era, 1978.

Shanin, Teodor, ed. *Peasants and Peasant Societies*. Oxford: Oxford University Press, 1987.

Sheridan, Thomas E. "Cross or Arrow? The Breakdown of Spanish–Seri Relations, 1729–1750." *Arizona and the West* 21, 1979: 317–34.

———. "The Limits of Power: The Political Ecology of the Spanish Empire in the Greater Southwest." *Antiquity* 66, 1992: 153–71.

———. "Prelude to Conquest: Yaqui Population, Subsistence, and Warfare during the Protohistoric Period." In D. R. Wilcox and W. B. Masse, eds., *The Protohistoric Period in the North American Southwest, AD 1450–1700*. Tempe: Arizona State University, Antropological Research Papers 24, 1981.

————. *Where the Dove Calls. The Political Ecology of a Peasant Corporate Community in Northwestern Mexico*. Tucson: University of Arizona Press, 1988.

Sheridan, Thomas E., and Gary Nabhan. "Living with a River: Traditional Farmers of the Río San Miguel." *Journal of Arizona History* 19, 1, 1978: 1–16.

Sheridan, Thomas E., and Thomas H. Naylor, eds. *Rarámuri. A Tarahumara Colonial Chronicle, 1607–1791*. Flagstaff, Ariz.: Northland Press, 1979.

Silverblatt, Irene. "Becoming Indian in the Central Andes of Seventeenth-Century Peru." In G. Prakash, ed., *After Colonialism. Imperial Histories and Postcolonial Displacements*. Princeton: Princeton University Press, 1995: 279–98.

Simmons, Marc. *Witchcraft in the Southwest. Spanish and Indian Supernaturalism on the Río Grande*. Lincoln: University of Nebraska Press, 1980.

Smith, Carol. "How Marketing Systems Affect Economic Opportunity in Agrarian Societies." In R. Halperin and J. Dow, eds., *Peasant Livelihood*. New York: St. Martin's Press, 1977: 117–46.

Smith, Gavin. *Livelihood and Resistance. Peasants and the Politics of Land in Peru*. Berkeley: University of California Press, 1989.

————. "Reflections on the Social Relations of Simple Commodity Production." *Journal of Peasant Studies* 13, 1, 1985: 99–108.

Smith, Raymond T. "The Family and the Modern World System: Some Observations from the Caribbean." *Journal of Family History* 3, 4, 1978: 337–60.

————. *Kinship Ideology and Practice in Latin America*. Chapel Hill: University of North Carolina Press, 1984.

Soboul, A. "The French Rural Community in the Eighteenth and Nineteenth Centuries." *Past and Present* 10, 1956: 78–95.

Spalding, Karen. *De indio a campesino. Cambios en la estructura social del Perú colonial*. Lima: Instituto de Estudios Peruanos, 1974.

————. *Huarochirí: An Andean Society under Inca and Spanish Rule*. Stanford: Stanford University Press, 1984.

————. "Social Climbers: Changing Patterns of Mobility among the Indians of Colonial Peru." *Hispanic American Historical Review* 50, 4, 1970: 645–64.

Spicer, Edward H. *Cycles of Conquest. The Impact of Spain, Mexico, and the United States on the Indians of the Southwest, 1533–1960*. Tucson: University of Arizona Press, 1963.

————. *The Yaquis. A Cultural History*. Tucson: University of Arizona Press, 1980.

Spicer, Rosamond B. "People on the Desert." In Alice Joseph, R. B. Spicer, and Jane Chesky, *The Desert People*. Chicago: University of Chicago Press, 1974 [1949]: 3–59.

Spores, Ronald. "Settlement, Farming Technology, and Environment in the Nochixtlan Valley." *Science* 166, 3905, 1969: 557–69.

Stavig, Ward. "Ethnic Conflict, Moral Economy, and Population in Rural Cuzco on the Eve of the Thupa Amaro II Rebellion." *Hispanic American Historical Review* 68, 4, 1988: 737–70.

———. "The Past Weighs on the Minds of the Living: Culture, Ethnicity, and the Rural Lower Class." *Latin American Research Review* 26, 2, 1991: 225–46.

Stern, Peter. "Social Marginality and Acculturation on the Northern Frontier of New Spain." Ph.D. diss., University of California, 1984.

Stern, Peter, and Robert H. Jackson. "Vagabundaje and Settlement in Colonial Northern Sonora." *The Americas* 44, 4, 1988: 461–81.

Stern, Steve J. "Feudalism, Capitalism, and the World-System in the Perspective of Latin America and the Caribbean." *American Historical Review* 93, 4, 1988: 829–72.

———. "New Approaches to the Study of Peasant Rebellion and Consciousness: Implications of the Andean Experience." In Stern, ed., *Resistance, Rebellion, and Consciousness in the Andean Peasant World, 18th to 20th Centuries*. Madison: University of Wisconsin Press, 1987: 3–28.

———. "Paradigms of Conquest: History, Historiography, and Politics." *Journal of Latin American Studies* 24 (Quincentenary Supplement, ed. Tulio Halperín Donghi), 1992: 1–34.

———. *Peru's Indian Peoples and the Challenge of Spanish Conquest. Huamanga to 1640*. Madison: University of Wisconsin Press, 1982.

Stoler, Ann Laura. "Rethinking Colonial Categories: European Communities and the Boundaries of Rule." *Comparative Studies in Society and History* 31, 1, 1989: 134–61.

Strong, Pauline Turner. "Captivity in White and Red: Convergent Practice and Colonial Representation on the British Amerindian Frontier, 1606–1736." In Daniel Segal, ed., *Crossing Cultures. Essays in the Displacement of Western Civilization*. Tucson: University of Arizona Press, 1992: 33–104.

Swann, Michael M. "The Demographic Impact of Disease and Famine in Late Colonial Northern Mexico," *Geoscience and Man* 21, 1980: 97–109.

———. "Spatial Dimensions of a Social Process: Marriage and Mobility in Late Colonial Northern Mexico." In David Robinson, ed., *Social Fabric and Spatial Structure in Colonial Latin America*. Ann Arbor, 1979: 117–80.

———. *Tierra Adentro. Settlement and Society in Colonial Durango*. Boulder: Westview Press, Latin American Studies 10, 1982.

Sweet, David. "The Ibero-American Frontier Mission in Native American History." In Erick Langer and Robert H. Jackson, eds., *The New Latin American Mission History*. Lincoln: University of Nebraska Press, 1995: 1–48.

Taylor, William B., *Drinking, Homicide, and Rebellion in Colonial Mexican Villages*. Stanford: Stanford University Press, 1979.

———. "Haciendas coloniales en el valle de Oaxaca." In Enrique Florescano, ed., *Haciendas, latifundios y plantaciones en América Latina*. Mexico City: Siglo Veintiuno Editores, 1975.

———. *Landlord and Peasant in Colonial Oaxaca*. Stanford: Stanford University Press, 1972.

Tilly, Charles. *From Mobilization to Revolution*. New York: Newberry Award Records, 1978.

Toor, Frances. *A Treasury of Mexican Folkways*. New York: Crown Publishers, 1947.

Tutino, John. "Family Economies in Agrarian Mexico, 1750–1810." *Journal of Family History* 10, 3, 1985: 258–71.

———. *From Insurrection to Revolution in Mexico. Social Bases of Agrarian Violence, 1750–1940*. Princeton: Princeton University Press, 1986.

———. "Life and Labor on North Mexican Haciendas: The Querétaro–San Luis Potosí Region." In Elsa Frost, Michael C. Meyer, and Josefina Vázquez, eds., *El trabajo y los trabajadores*. Mexico City: El Colegio de México, 1979.

Underhill, Ruth. *Papago Woman*. Prospect Heights, Ill.: Waveland Press, 1985 [Copyright: Holt, Rinehart & Winston, 1979. First published as *The Autobiography of a Papago Woman*, Memoir 46 of the American Anthropological Association, 1936].

Urban, Greg, and Joel Sherzer. "Introduction." In Urban and Sherzer, eds., *Nation-States and Indians in Latin America*. Austin: University of Texas Press, 1991.

Van Young, Eric. "Agrarian Rebellion and Defense of Community: Meaning and Collective Violence in Late Colonial and Independence-Era Mexico." *Journal of Social History* 27, 2, 1993: 245–70.

———. "Conflict and Solidarity in Indian Village Life. The Guadalajara Region in the Late Colonial Period." *Hispanic American Historical Review* 64, 1, 1984: 55–79.

———. "The Cuautla Lazarus: Double Subjectives in Reading Texts on Popular Collective Action." *Colonial Latin American Review* 2, 1–2, 1993: 3–26.

———. "Dreamscape with Figures and Fences: Cultural Contention and Discourse in the Late Colonial Mexican Countryside." *Le Nouveau Monde—Mondes Nouveaux*. Paris: CERMACA, Ecole des Hautes Etudes en Sciences Sociales, 1992.

———. *Hacienda and Market in Eighteenth-Century Mexico. The Rural Economy of the Guadalajara Region, 1675–1820*. Berkeley: University of California Press, 1981.

———. "Man, Land, and Water in Mexico and the Hispanic Southwest." *Mexican Studies/Estudios Mexicanos* 1, 2, 1985: 396–412.

———. "Mexican Rural History since Chevalier: The Historiography of the Colonial Hacienda." *Latin American Research Review* 18, 3, 1983: 5–61.

———, ed. *Mexico's Regions. Comparative History and Development*. San Diego: Center for U.S.-Mexican Studies, University of California, 1992.

———. "To See Someone Not Seeing: Historical Studies of Peasants and Politics in Mexico." *Mexican Studies/Estudios Mexicanos* 6, 1, 1990: 133–59.

Vara, Armida de la. *La creciente*. Mexico City, 1979.

Vidal, Hernán. "The Concept of Colonial and Postcolonial Discourse: A Perspective from Literary Criticism." *Latin American Research Review* 28, 3, 1993: 113–19.

Vidargas del Moral, Juan Domingo. "Elecciones constitucionales en la Sonora de 1814: "Diputación en Alamos, cabildo en Ures." In *Memoria. XVII Simposio de Historia y Antropología de Sonora.* Hermosillo: Universidad de Sonora, 1992: 333–47.

———. "La intendencia de Arizpe en la independencia de Nueva España: 1810–1821." *Historia General de Sonora.* Vol. 2: *De la conquista al estado libre y soberano de Sonora.* Mexico City: Gobierno del Estado de Sonora, 1985: 299–320.

———. "Sonora y Sinaloa como provincias independientes y como estado interno de Occidente." In *Historia General de Sonora.* Vol. 2: *De la conquista al estado libre y soberano de Sonora.* Mexico City: Gobierno del Estado de Sonora, 1985: 321–57.

Villalpando Canchola, Elisa. "Algunas consideraciones demográficas sobre la Pimería Alta a fines del siglo XVIII." In *Memoria del XV Simposio de Historia y Antropología de la Universidad de Sonora.* Hermosillo: Universidad de Sonora, 1991: 1–44.

Villalpando Canchola, María Elisa. *Los que viven en las montañas. Correlación arqueológico-etnográfica en Isla San Esteban, Sonora, México.* Hermosillo: Instituto Nacional de Antropología e Historia, Noroeste de México 8, 1989: 9–94.

———. ";Significaba para ellos prestigio? El uso de la concha en Sonora." In *Memoria del XI Simposio de Historia y Antropología de Sonora.* Hermosillo: Universidad de Sonora, 1987: 21–33.

Voss, Stuart. *On the Periphery of Nineteenth-Century Mexico. Sonora and Sinaloa, 1810–1877.* Tucson: University of Arizona Press, 1982.

Warman, Arturo. *"We Come to Object." The Peasants of Morelos and the National State.* Baltimore: Johns Hopkins University Press, 1980.

Wasserstrom, Robert. "Spaniards and Indians in Colonial Chiapas, 1528–1790." In Murdo J. MacLeod and Robert Wasserstrom, eds., *Spaniards and Indians in Southeastern Mesoamerica. Essays on the History of Ethnic Relations.* Lincoln: University of Nebraska Press, 1983: 92–126.

Weber, David J. *The Mexican Frontier, 1821–1846. The American Southwest under Mexico.* Albuquerque, University of New Mexico Press, 1982.

———. *Myth and History of the Hispanic Southwest: Essays by David J. Weber.* Albuquerque: University of New Mexico Press, 1990.

———. *The Spanish Frontier in North America.* New Haven: Yale University Press, 1992.

Weber, Max. *Economía y sociedad.* Mexico City: Fondo de Cultura Económica, 1987 [1944].

West, Robert. *The Mining Community of Northern New Spain: The Parral Mining District.* Berkeley: University of California Press, Ibero-Americana 30, 1949.

———. *Sonora. Its Geographical Personality.* Austin: University of Texas Press, 1993.

Whigham, Thomas. "Cattle Raising in the Argentine Northeast: Corrientes, c. 1750–1870." *Journal of Latin American Studies* 20, 1988: 313–35.

———. *The Politics of River Trade. Tradition and Development in the Upper Plata, 1780–1870.* Albuquerque: University of New Mexico Press, 1991.

White, Leslie A. *Ethnological Essays.* Ed. Beth Dillingham and Robert L. Carneiro. Albuquerque: University of New Mexico Press, 1987.

White, Richard. *The Roots of Dependency. Subsistence, Environment, and Social Change among the Choctaws, Pawnees, and Navajos.* Lincoln: University of Nebraska Press, 1983.

Wightman, Ann M. *Indigenous Migration and Social Change: The Forasteros of Cuzco, 1570–1720.* Durham: Duke University Press, 1990.

Wilcox, David R. "A Historical Analysis of the Problem of Southwestern-Mesoamerican Connections." In David R. Wilcox and W. Bruce Masse, eds., *The Protohistoric Period in the North American Southwest*, A.D. 1450–1700. Tempe, Ariz.: Arizona State University, Anthropological Research Papers 24, 1981: 34–35.

Wolf, Eric R. *Europe and the People without History.* Berkeley: University of California Press, 1982.

———. *Peasant Wars of the Twentieth Century.* New York: Harper & Row, 1969.

———. *Peasants.* Englewood Cliffs: Prentice-Hall, 1966.

Worcester, Donald. *Nature's Economy. The Roots of Ecology.* San Francisco: Sierra Club Books, 1977.

Wright, Erik Olin. *Classes.* London: Verso, 1985.

Index

Galindo Navarro, Pedro, 180

Gálvez Gallardo, José Bernardo, 43–44, 96, 179–80, 192, 266, 276, 327 (n. 29)

García Conde, Alejo, Intendente de Sonora, 97, 217, 234

Garrido y Durán, Pedro, Intendente de Sonora, 289

Gavilán, mining camp in the mission district of Ures, 145

Gerónimo, Opata governor of Bacerác, 152

Gila Valley, 22, 59, 96, 252, 261. See also Tohono o'odham, migration patterns

Gileños, 277–78. See also Athapaskan

Gil Samaniego, Francisco Ignacio, 191

Gil Samaniego, Juan Ignacio, juez comisario, 288–90

Gray Robes. See Franciscan administration of Sonoran missions

Grijalba, Juan Joseph de, 187

Grimarest, Enrique, Intendant, 187, 289

Gu Achi (Santa Rosa, Arizona), 58

Guachinera, 189, 258, 280, 288, 293

Guachuca, Pima ranchería, 153

Guadalajara, 2, 205–6, 227, 244; Audiencia de, 36, 172; commerce in, 327 (n. 14); merchant guild of, 43

Guadalupe (mining real of Ostimuri), 103

Guadiana, 31

Guanajuato: as mining frontier, 2, 205–6; suppression of popular protests in, 43

Guásabas, 38, 75, 144, 191, 259, 293

Guatemala, and Seri deportations to, 156

Guaymas, 26, 45, 86, 227, 229, 273–74

Guebavi, Santos Angeles Gabriel y

Rafael, 154–55, 202, 269; Dolores de, 253

Guépaca, 21. See also Huépac

Guepaverachi, 183

Guzmán, Beltran Nuño de, 30

Guzmán, Diego de, 30–31

Hacienda of Santa Barbara, 155

Halchidomas, 25

Hegemony, 280, 307–10; as Gramscian concept, xvii, 14

Hermosillo, 21, 45. See also Pitic

Heves, 24. See Opatas; Tegüimas

Hiach-eD [S-ohmakam], 22; agriculture and consumption, 49, 298; gift exchange and barter, 59. See also Tohono o'odham

Hobas. See Jobas

Hohokam, pre-Hispanic urban tradition, 28–29

Hokan languages, 25, 252

Holvez, Wenceslao, Jesuit priest of Satevó, Chihuahua, 151

Horcasitas. See San Miguel de Horcasitas

Huatabampo, 26–27

Huépaca, mission of the Sonora Valley, 182

Huidobro, Manuel de, governor of Sonora, 267, 304

Hymeris, 253. See also Pimas; Akimel

Ibarra, Francisco de, governor of Nueva Vizcaya, 31, 320 (n. 28)

Indé, mining real, 32

Indians: distinguished from vecinos, 195–96, 290–91, 294–97; "old" and "new" enemies, 270–71

Intendencias. See also Bourbon administration, 44

Cynthia Radding is Assistant Professor of History at the University of Illinois, Urbana-Champaign.

Library of Congress Cataloging-in-Publication Data

Radding, Cynthia.
Wandering peoples : colonialism, ethnic spaces, and ecological frontiers in northwestern Mexico, 1700–1850 / Cynthia Radding.
p.   cm. — (Latin America otherwise)
Includes bibliographical references and index.
ISBN 0-8223-1907-1 (cloth : alk. paper). —
ISBN 0-8223-1899-7 (pbk. : alk. paper)
1. Ethnicity—Mexico—Sonora (State)   2. Social ecology—Mexico—Sonora
(State)   3. Social change—Mexico—Sonora (State)   4. Social classes—
Mexico—Sonora (State)   5. Indians of Mexico—Mexico—Sonora (State)—
History.   6. Indians of Mexico—Mexico—Sonora (State)—Social conditions.
7. Sonora (Mexico : State)—History.   8. Sonora (Mexico : State)—Social
conditions.   9. Sonora (Mexico : State)—Ethnic relations.   I. Title.
II. Series.
GN560.M6R33   1997
305.8'0097217—dc20
96-35147
CIP